Collisions at the Crossroads

AMERICAN CROSSROADS

*Edited by Earl Lewis, George Lipsitz, George Sánchez,
Dana Takagi, Laura Briggs, and Nikhil Pal Singh*

Collisions at
the Crossroads

HOW PLACE AND MOBILITY MAKE RACE

Genevieve Carpio

UNIVERSITY OF CALIFORNIA PRESS

University of California Press, one of the most distinguished university presses in the United States, enriches lives around the world by advancing scholarship in the humanities, social sciences, and natural sciences. Its activities are supported by the UC Press Foundation and by philanthropic contributions from individuals and institutions. For more information, visit www.ucpress.edu.

University of California Press
Oakland, California

Library of Congress Cataloging-in-Publication Data

Names: Carpio, Genevieve, author.
Title: Collisions at the crossroads : how place and mobility make race / Genevieve Carpio.
Description: Oakland, California : University of California Press, [2019] | Includes bibliographical references and index. |
Identifiers: LCCN 2018042647 (print) | LCCN 2018050925 (ebook) | ISBN 9780520970823 (ebook and ePDF) | ISBN 9780520298828 (cloth : alk. paper) | ISBN 9780520298835 (pbk. : alk. paper)
Subjects: LCSH: Migration, Internal—California—Inland Empire. | Inland Empire (Calif.)—Race relations. | Inland Empire (Calif.)—Emigration and immigration—Government policy.
Classification: LCC HB1985.C2 (ebook) | LCC HB1985.C2 C37 2019 (print) | DDC 305.868/0794950904—dc23
LC record available at https://lccn.loc.gov/2018042647

Manufactured in the United States of America

26 25 24 23 22 21 20 19
10 9 8 7 6 5 4 3 2 1

For my parents, who gave me a past worth remembering

And for Eric and Elliot, who give me a future worth anticipating

CONTENTS

ILLUSTRATIONS

MAPS

FIGURES

ACKNOWLEDGMENTS

I feel fortunate to join the authors of American Crossroads, whose work has enriched my understanding of race and ethnicity in the United States. I received insightful reviews from series editor George Lipsitz, who helped me to think deeply about the ways inequality and injustice in inland Southern California manifest far beyond it. I am grateful to have also received comments from Natalia Molina, whose relational approach to race formation provided important pathways for this book. Matt Delmont's comments further pushed me to develop my analytic concepts. I am thankful to executive editor Niels Hooper, assistant editor Bradley Depew, and senior editor Kate Hoffman who have generously guided my manuscript from start to finish with expertise and enthusiasm.

The research for this project was made possible by generous fellowship support from the UCLA Equity, Diversity, and Inclusion Faculty Career Development Award, the Warren and Chris Hellman Fellows Program, the USC Office of the Provost, the Ford Foundation Dissertation Fellowship, and the Ford Foundation Predoctoral Fellowship. I also received support from the Mellon Foundation Summer Institute for Teaching and Professional Advancement (SITPA) at Duke University, where it was my great fortune to be paired with Deirdre Royster at NYU. This book is stronger for her honest criticism, unwavering enthusiasm, and brilliant feedback.

This project began under the guidance of George Sánchez. As my graduate chair at the University of Southern California, he taught me the complicated task of working beyond disciplinary boundaries and of rupturing binary racial frameworks. He also read the penultimate draft of this book. His rich knowledge of history, ethnic studies, Chicanx/Latinx studies, and the public humanities served as inspiration when the aims of interdisciplinary study felt overwhelming.

I was fortunate to have trained with a dynamic committee as a graduate student in USC's Department of American Studies and Ethnicity. I'm indebted to Laura Pulido's foundational work, bringing together geography, ethnic studies, and Chicanx/Latinx studies. Through seminars and reenergizing lunches at the Huntington, Greg Hise taught me to think deeply about regions, metropolitan space, and historical methods. Bill Deverell provided great insight into questions of memory and urban development in the American West. And, Kevin Breisch's passion for architectural history helped me question what stories might be uncovered through the built environment. I am likewise grateful to the faculty of UCLA's Department of Urban Planning, especially Anastasia Loukaitou-Sideris, Louis Takahashi, and Edward Soja, whose coursework and mentorship during my time as a master's student shape my understanding of urban history and analysis in Greater Los Angeles.

Every scholar should have the opportunity to develop their ideas in a postdoctoral environment as generative as the Cassius Marcellus Clay Postdoctoral Fellowship in the Department of History at Yale University. Steve Pitti mentored me in long conversations over lunch and asked me what I was reading with real interest in the answer. Moreover, he chaired a fantastic manuscript workshop with Matthew Frye Jacobson, Kelly Lytle Hernández, Tim Cresswell, and Laura Barraclough. I'm thankful to Matt for pushing me to wholly embrace my cultural studies training, for Kelly who encouraged me to call settler colonialism by its name and to consider whether there was a place for incarceration in this work, to Tim for his expertise in mobility studies. Laura Barraclough is the glue that helped bridge this interdisciplinary conversation, and the model of a doctor mom I needed in this work's final stages.

This work gained strength from Yale's Latinx Studies faculty, especially Alicia Schmidt Camacho, Dixa Ramirez, and Albert Laguna. Conversations with Mary Lui, Ned Blackhawk, Laura Wexler, Holly Guise, Dael Norwood, Rachel Purvis, Christofer Rodelo, Stephen Vider, the Asian American Studies Working Group, the Latin American Studies Working Group, the History Department, and the Program in Ethnicity, Race, and Migration provided key insights over lunch, in working groups, and through departmental talks.

I am grateful to the Bancroft Seminar on Latina/o History at the University of California Berkeley, where I had the privilege of presenting my entire manuscript. Perceptive comments from organizer Raúl Coronado, commentator Grace Delgado, and seminar participants, especially Margaret Chowning, Lisbeth Haas, David Montejano, and Christian Paiz, prompted me to think more about the role of the federal in shaping immigrants' regional experiences and the role of empire in the Inland Empire.

Chapter drafts were presented at academic conferences, including meetings of the American Studies Association, American Association of Geographers, American Historical Association, Urban Historians Association, California Preservation Foundation, National Association for Chicana and Chicano Studies, Latina/o Studies Conference, Columbia University Latin Lab, Huntington Library's Los Angeles and Metropolitan Studies Group, Autry Westerners, the Clinton Institute at University College Dublin, and the National Center for Suburban Studies at Hofstra University. I received helpful comments and had inspiring conversations with Emma Amador, Steve Aron, José Alamillo, Matthew Countryman, Vanessa Díaz, Lilia Fernández, Erualdo González, Juan Herrera, Clara Irazábal, Liam Kennedy, Phoebe Kropp, Jorge Leal, David Levitus, Laura Liu, Scott Lucas, Becky Nicolaides, Annemarie Pérez, Sandy Placido, Laura Pulido, Isabela Quintana, Sherene Razack, Alyssa Ribeiro, Mérida Rúa, Stevie Ruiz, Denise Sandoval, Andrew K. Sandoval-Strausz, Virginia Scharff, Mario Sifuentez, and Carmen Whalen. I'm grateful for their feedback at key moments in the development of this project.

I received help from numerous archivists and librarians. I am especially appreciative for the aid of the Boy's Republic, UCLA's Chicano Studies Research Center, Japanese American National Museum, National Archives and Records Administration at Riverside, Riverside Metropolitan Museum, Riverside Public Library, San Bernardino County Museum, Sherman Indian Museum, and Yale University Map Room, whose staff went out of their way to help me access important resources. A special thanks is owed to Xaviera Flores, Kevin Hallaran, Ruth McCormick, Jennifer Osorio, and Andrzej Rutkowski for their vast knowledge and immeasurable helpfulness. To Al Castro, Cande Mendoza, Cathy Gudis, Anthea Hartig, and Morrison Wong, I am grateful for your contributions to the history of this incredible region. Thank you also to the Historical Society of Pomona Valley, especially Mickey and Jim Gallivan, who exemplify a commendable commitment to public history.

Antonio Vasquez González, you saw the importance of preserving and sharing our community stories at a critical moment. You created an archive when there was none. It is through your labor, your commitment to our elders, and your dedication to a purposeful public history that this book exists. I am grateful to you and to all of the allies who support Inland Mexican Heritage and Casa de Culturas.

This project was strengthened by three talented research assistants at UCLA, Maria Nava Gutierrez, Yazmin González, and José Cardona. They made sense of census data spanning a century, located books and archives across Los Angeles, and helped generate maps of historic data for analysis. I can't wait to see how they will change the world. Anitra Grisales, Cate Hodorowicz, Pauline Lewis, Kathleen MacDougall, and Tamie Parker Song helped me find my voice and to write with honesty and purpose. Camille Pannu generously helped me make sense of legal sources, databases, and citations. Luis Camas and Omar Ureta contributed stunning photographs and an innovative mapping project.

I have the great fortune of working at UCLA, where I am surrounded by colleagues whose scholarship is foundational to the ways I understand race and ethnicity, twentieth century history, and space. My colleagues in Chicana/o Studies have been inspirational. Thank you to Leisy Abrego, Maylei Blackwell, and Gaye Theresa Johnson for their mentorship while writing. Much gratitude to Robert Chao Romero, Otto Santa Ana, and Charlene Villaseñor Black, who offered feedback on conference papers, abstracts, and the role of images in the text. I am humbled and thankful for Karina Oliva Alvarado, Judy Baca, Matt Barreto, Jessica Cattelino, Alicia Gaspar de Alba, Raúl Hinojos-Ojeda, Alma López, Reynaldo Macías, Susan Plann, María Cristina Pons, as well as colleagues across campus, who took time to welcome me to campus and to learn about my research, offering encouragement and conversations that enrich this project. I am fortunate to have a mentor like Laura E. Gómez, who has supported me in more ways than I can count. May we all be so lucky to have the guidance of such a bold, brilliant, and purposeful scholar. I am grateful for Robin D. G. Kelley, who has supported this project by offering critical guidance in a graduate seminar at USC, providing feedback on my book proposal, and sharing enthusiasm along the way. I am very fortunate to have had the support of my current Department Chair Eric Avila and former Chair Abel Valenzuela, whose collegiality, feedback, and wisdom have made my experience at UCLA a joy.

I appreciate the expertise and kindness of our departmental staff members, Sandy Garcia, Eleuteria (Ellie) Hernández, Chris Palomo, and Brenda Trujillo. It has been my great privilege to learn from our bright and bold undergraduate students in classes like Barrio Suburbanism and Space, Place, and Race. And, I've gained much from my graduate students, particularly in conversations during our Racial Geographies seminar. Their insights and innovation excite me about the shape of the field ahead.

In many ways, this book is rooted in my experiences as an undergraduate at Pomona College. Gilda Ochoa continues to be my model for a scholar, teacher, and activist. Matt Garcia met with me while I was working on a senior thesis about racial segregation in Pomona, my hometown, connected me with Inland Mexican Heritage, and introduced me to the field of American Studies. Frances Carreon, Toni Clark, Ana Cuevas, Corinne Dearborn, Carla María Guerrero, Juan Matute, Ricardo Ramirez, Linda Reinin, Ric Townes, Ann Quinley, the Draper Center for Community Partnerships, and the Chicana/o-Latina/o Studies Department each offered meaningful guidance and encouragement.

I thank alumni from the USC Department of American Studies and Ethnicity and Department of History for their invaluable mentorship, especially Deborah Alkamano, Adam Bush, Wendy Cheng, Rob Eap, Jerry González, Emily Hobson, Chrisshonna Grant, Dan HoSang, Hillary Jenks, Sharon Luk, Celeste Menchaca, Julia Ornelas-Higdon, Mark Padoongpatt, Ana Rosas, Abigail Rosas, and Margaret Salazar-Porzio.

My dear friends—Alexis Carrillo, Mimi Chau, Melissa (Beene) Clinton, Andrae (Rivas) Gill, Catherine John, Candice Knighten, Merina (Esparza) Myklak, Yumi Oda, Rachel Perez, and Jazmine Sunico—you have kept me grounded from elementary school to the tenure track. Thank you for your love, support, and humor.

Anything valuable in this book can be attributed to the brilliance of Sara Fingal, Jessica Kim, and Priscilla Leiva, who read the roughest drafts and by the sheer will of their spirit, wisdom, and expertise helped me develop them into chapters. Sara, you are wonderful, and thoughtful, and the queen of the meme. Jessica, you are generous, kind, and a fierce champion for justice. Presci, you have been a model of true interdisciplinarity, an expert consult when working through tough concepts, and a rock when I needed one.

I'm most indebted to my family. To my father, Vince Carpio, who taught me the value of the past and fighting for a just present. To my mother, Grace Carpio, who held my hand in the tough times and celebrated my joys in the good. My incredible siblings, Terri, Vinnie, Desiree, and Natalie, who are my champions and motivation. To my uncles, aunts, cousins, and my godparents, Bob and Tañia, for your unwavering love and support. To my grandparents, whose stories inspire this book.

To Eric, my husband, my partner, my friend. The GD. You have been to every car show, brought me lunch on the long days, listened to every conference paper, and demonstrated unwavering faith when I needed it most. I love you. And, to my precious Elliot. Oh, Elliot. You are my sunshine.

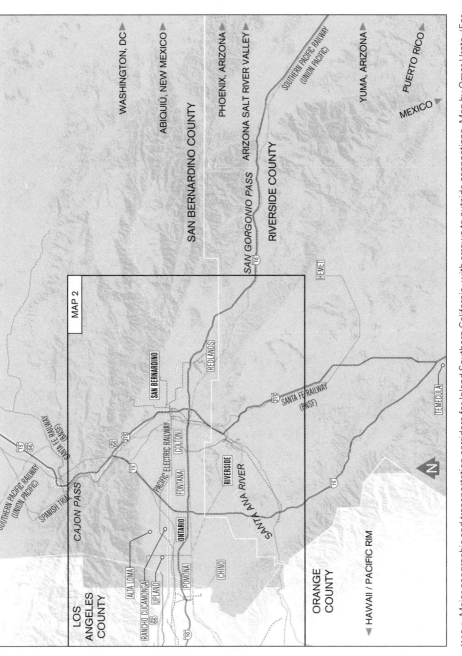

MAP 1. Major geographic and transportation corridors for Inland Southern California, with arrows to outside connections. Map by Omar Ureta. (For map sources, see Notes.)

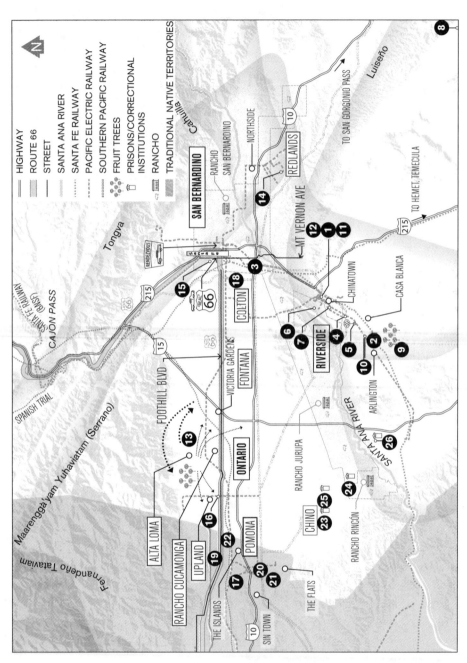

MAP 2. Inland Southern California, with key to sites. Map by Omar Ureta. (For map sources, see Notes.)

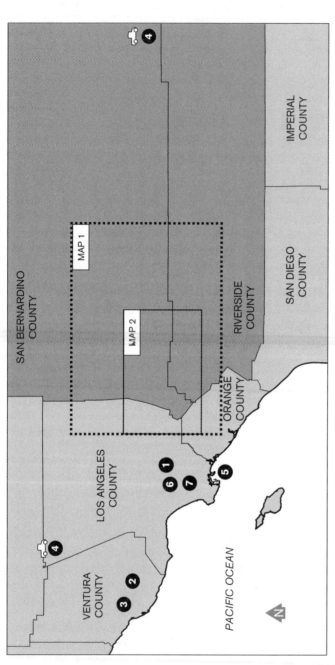

MAP 3. Regional Southern California, with key to sites in Ventura, Los Angeles, and San Bernardino Counties. Map by Omar Ureta. (For map sources, see Notes.)

CHAPTER 1
1 MISSION SAN GABRIEL

CHAPTER 3
2 SESPE RANCH
3 LIMONEIRA RANCH

CHAPTER 4
4 FAUL S. TAYLOR MIGRATION STATISTICS COLLECTION SITES
5 TERMINAL ISLAND / PORTS

CHAPTER 5
6 CENTRAL AVE
7 SHORT FAMILY'S L.A. RESIDENCE

Introduction

In the summer of 1993, Danny Flores parked his lowrider, a 1952 Chevrolet Fleetline adorned with painted roses and a chrome steering wheel, alongside four friends and their cars at Plaza Park. That afternoon the San Bernardino Convention and Visitor's Bureau was sponsoring the Rendezvous, a yearly celebration of Route 66 cruising heritage held in the city's downtown. The iconic highway, famously recalled in Nat King Cole's rendition of "(Get Your Kicks on) Route 66," acts as a gateway to numerous U.S. transportation corridors and serves as a central destination in Southern California. Embracing San Bernardino's place on the Mother Road, the Rendezvous festival draws close to 100,000 participants from across the Southwest each year. In a single weekend, the downtown district transforms from a restrained landscape of modernist county buildings and commercial storefronts into a dynamic display of automotive culture as families convene to celebrate the iconic symbol of western mobility. Local rock bands play nostalgic tunes from the 1950s, the expansive street show features custom cars, and participants share in a slow cruise through downtown. But Flores and other Mexican American lowriders had gathered away from the site of the Rendezvous, which lowriders had participated in since the festival's founding in 1990, to protest the festival's newly enacted lowrider ban.[1] Festival officials described the exclusion of lowriders as protecting the event's authenticity. Flores, however, attributed it to discrimination. To draw attention to the festival's fabricated placement in downtown San Bernardino, a mile away from the iconic highway, he chose the city's historically Mexican Westside for the lowriders' gathering, on what Flores has called "the real Route 66."[2] It was here that Route 66 carried travelers through California and that Mexican cruising culture had thrived for decades. Mexicans are among the many diverse groups discussed in this book that experienced their racialization through permissions and prohibitions on their mobility, but never without contest.

As Southern California experienced significant economic and demographic changes during the second half of the twentieth century, competing claims to Route 66 became powerful contests over the region's past, present, and future—and San Bernardino held a central place in these efforts. While the National Civic League had once selected San Bernardino for the prestigious All-America City award, by the 1990s the town faced stark challenges to its economic and social identity. The closing of both the Kaiser steel plant (1984) in nearby Fontana and the Norton Air Force Base (1994), as well as their supportive industries, led to sudden and devastating economic losses. Poverty, crime, and shrinking social services followed. Dovetailing with its deindustrialization, the city had recently become majority-minority. The white, non-Hispanic population continued to hold the single demographic majority, but barely so. Indeed, San Bernardino has become a national symbol for some of the most pressing challenges in (sub)urban America, where the seeming divisions of suburban and urban life bleed into one another.[3]

Like the city of San Bernardino, the tri-county region of inland Southern California faced major demographic shifts in the second half of the twentieth century. For instance, between 1970 and 1990 each county in the area experienced a rise in its Hispanic population, from 17 to 26 percent in Riverside County, 16 to 27 percent in San Bernardino County, and 18 to 38 percent in Los Angeles County. In Riverside and San Bernardino Counties, marginal growth occurred in the African American and Asian/Pacific Islander populations as well.[4] Further, at the metropolitan level, increasing racial tensions marked Greater Los Angeles following the Los Angeles Uprising (1992), which sharpened local racial divides and fears as the entire nation consumed violent images first of white police officers beating African American motorist Rodney King, and later of the urban riots that followed the officers' acquittal. In the following years, Californians would combine a fixation on crime and immigration enforcement at the ballot box in a resurgence of nativist hysteria. For example, a series of controversial racial propositions amplified tensions surrounding the state's growing Latina/o population,[5] from Proposition 187 (1994), which aimed to deny public education, health services, and benefits to undocumented immigrants, to Proposition 227 (1998), which nearly ended bilingual education in public schools.[6] In a large sense, social tensions in California responded to global economic restructuring as the financial gap between the rich and the poor widened, free trade agreements restructured large economic sectors, and neoliberal multiculturalism cast acts of international force as humanitarianism.[7]

As towns throughout inland Southern California attempted to respond to their new socioeconomic realities and increasing racial diversity, Route 66 heritage became a racially charged backdrop deployed by boosters to place lowrider cars and their Mexican American drivers on the opposite side of regional development. The Rendezvous festival in particular held a central role in urban revitalization efforts played out in Southern California. The festival tapped into a popular Route 66 nostalgia that recast San Bernardino from a place of danger and blight to an idealized post–World War II America where visions of hot rods and cruising on the Mother Road signified small-town America, upward mobility, and racial homogeneity. San Bernardino is also geographically close to Hollywood—land of James Dean's iconic Mercury in *Rebel Without a Cause* (1955), the daring racing feats of Steve McQueen in *The Great Escape* (1963) and *Le Mans* (1971), and the southern escapades of Bo and Luke Duke in a customized Dodge Charger adorned with a Confederate flag (1979–1985)—which lent powerful symbolism to Southern California cruising events. The potency of these alluring narratives is further revealed by their popularity among the populations written out of the scripts, such as people of color and women. Ultimately, the festival and the lowrider ban harkened back to a nostalgic past of postwar prosperity that both sanitized history and denied the complexity of a multiracial present. Like the perfectly restored classic hot rods and vintage cars around which the Rendezvous was organized, the festival suggested that San Bernardino too could return to its former glory as a white, middle class city. This vision negated the long historical presence of Mexicans on Route 66, an erasure made all the more possible with the formal removal of Mexican American lowriders from the festival. Furthermore, this image distanced the city from its working class, multiracial present.[8]

The conflicting claims to Route 66 made by Danny Flores and San Bernardino's Convention and Visitor's Bureau illustrate a larger set of twentieth-century tensions related to race, place, and mobility that form the subject of this book. Sitting uneasily alongside the nostalgic Americana of the 1990s redevelopment campaigns was the rise of regional policies regulating the flows and stoppages of Latina/o residents, or their "mobility"—a geographic concept referring to the ways we experience, manage, and give meaning to movement.[9] Throughout this book, the concept of mobility particularly applies to the everyday channels of movement in a community, especially for

Indigenous people and people of color.[10] By "everyday," I refer to the ordinary and extraordinary experiences embedded in the lived mobilities of a society.[11] For instance, in the years following the lowrider ban, police traffic checkpoints increased sharply in Latina/o majority communities throughout inland Southern California, a region encompassing parts of San Bernardino, Riverside, and Los Angeles Counties. With increasing frequency, blue and red lights trapped long lines of residents as they waited for police officers to confirm their sobriety, proof of insurance, and identity. While a 1990 Supreme Court decision had upheld the constitutionality of traffic checkpoints for the purpose of identifying drunk drivers, the line between sobriety checkpoints and immigrant checkpoints became porous when this practice was combined with a 1993 law (since nulled) prohibiting undocumented immigrants from receiving a California driver's license. That is, regional sobriety stops functioned as unofficial, wide-reaching immigration checkpoints. Regionally, citizenship status was used to impose heavy fees on undocumented drivers, to impound vehicles at towing companies' profit, and to foster a state of fear among all drivers when navigating their everyday movements between home, work, and school in Latina/o majority communities.[12] That is, Latinas/os experienced racialization through their everyday mobility and its management by state forces. Indeed, as this book demonstrates, throughout the twentieth century mobility functioned as a modality through which race was lived through forces as diverse as historical societies, Indian boarding schools, bicycle ordinances, immigration policy, incarceration, traffic checkpoints, and Route 66 heritage.[13]

Traffic checkpoints became a pressing site of contestation as they spread throughout inland Southern California. Operating under the guise of public safety, they were most commonly positioned in communities with large immigrant populations where municipal police departments disproportionately identified, criminalized, and penalized Latina/o drivers, documented and undocumented alike. That is, where Latinas/os of varying citizenship statuses shared space, they also were caught in a shared net, one that focused traffic enforcement efforts on majority Latina/o pathways through the region. Community groups formed in protest against the discriminating impounds, not to mention the heavy fees levied on residents by municipal governments and private towing agencies. These groups held demonstrations, testified at city halls, and filed legal action against municipal leaders.[14]

Local authorities met activists' efforts with staunch resistance. In one particularly volatile episode, an off-duty police officer belligerently disrupted a community forum addressing the checkpoints' municipal impact. Interrupting the meeting, he accused organizers of spreading false information and called one Mexican American audience member "a killer." In doing so, the officer hurled the common trope of immigrant drivers as imminent dangers. That the man accused was in fact a U.S. citizen highlights how policies targeting one group (i.e., undocumented immigrants) can be used to narrate and manage the movement of a broader cross-section of racialized people (i.e., Latinas/os).[15]

Both the Rendezvous festival's ban of lowriders and traffic checkpoints were local responses to the changing face of California and attempts to reinforce prevailing racial hierarchies by targeting the everyday mobilities of nonwhite drivers. These practices, as well as the ideologies supporting them, represent a continuation of the regulated ways racialized people have moved throughout the twentieth century. That is, the Rendezvous and the traffic checkpoints were two aspects of the same form of racialization: where the Rendezvous promoted nostalgia for a white American car culture, which erased Mexican American lowriders from the region's collective past, the traffic checkpoints actively turned public roads into volatile landscapes on which Latina/o drivers of various residency statuses were stripped of their ability to move in everyday ways. Ultimately, racial struggles over driving in inland Southern California demonstrate the ways mobility and place making have been central to constructing uneven power relations in the United States, particularly in practices that protect unequal access to land, labor, and claims to citizenship, as well as those that generate complex negotiations, contests, and even accommodation of hierarchical race relations.

I argue that mobility has been an active force in racialization over the twentieth century, one that has operated alongside "place" to shape regional memory and belonging in multiracial communities. As is examined in this book, tensions between police officers and Latina/o motorists have a long history in which racialized permissions and prohibitions on movement have been normalized in the region's social and spatial development, from bicycling ordinances targeting Japanese immigrants in the early 1900s to vigilante violence against African Americans who threatened suburban racial boundaries in the 1940s. This perspective underscores the shared ways that both the lowrider ban and traffic checkpoints stripped their drivers of mobility, and it prompts connections to how such practices position Latina/o residents as outsiders whose movements should be viewed with suspicion. With this recognition, one can move far beyond these particular cases to ask, how has the criminalization of certain forms of mobility provided some groups grounds for making spatial claims while prohibiting others? Or, how have certain bodies become conflated with particular types of movement at specific points in time? Along these lines, we can also ask how vagrancy laws, slave codes, immigration enforcement, sobriety checkpoints, joyriding ordinances, and other means of policing movement share continuities or ruptures with one another. Focusing on racial formation over the course of the twentieth century, I demonstrate how contests over movement have shaped racial hierarchies and regional attitudes towards a diverse set of migrant and resident groups.

INLAND CROSSROADS, THEORETICAL PATHWAYS

There are few places where mobility has shaped identity as widely as the American West and, more specifically, California. The state has been considered the "Land of Golden Dreams" for those seeking wealth in its mines, a port of entry for immigrants from the Pacific Rim and Western Hemisphere, and the definitive destination for Route 66 cruisers. But some locations and populations more than others sit at the state's major crossroads. Such is the case for inland Southern California, known at different times as the Citrus Belt, Orange Empire, Inland Empire, and Inland Valley. All roads lead here, where numerous trail, rail, auto, and air transportation corridors intersect, and where the Santa Ana Mountains, San Gorgonio Pass, San Jose Hills, and Mojave Desert form a physical passageway. These geographic corridors have since been expanded by fixed capital, including roads, boardinghouses, service stations, and warehouses to facilitate particular forms of movement. Distant points of influence stretch the region's borders into a complex web of economic, political, and social relations both national and international in scope. Moreover, the area has been home to numerous waves of migrant and immigrant groups, each dependent on exercising effective mobility to traverse an expansive territory that encompasses farms, factories, prisons, and suburbs. The range of mobilities generated here is complex and has distributed economic and cultural privilege in unequal ways, but never without contest.

Today, inland Southern California is most commonly known as the Inland Empire. The area includes the eastern suburbs of Los Angeles County, divided by the Interstate 10 freeway and State Route 57, and western portions of Riverside and San Bernardino Counties. Its western edges, bounded by the mountains to the north and desert to the east, extend south from San

Bernardino to Temecula and stretch westward from Redlands to Pomona. But it has not always been so. Rather than forming around static political or even geographic boundaries, regional borders have stretched and twisted with the contours of equally supple cultural and economic identities. As regions without strict governmental boundaries, places such as the Inland Empire, the Sunbelt, and the Gunbelt reflect how regions are actively constructed around their topography, economy, memory, and race.[16] This book, rather than approaching the region as a material truth, takes a regional formation approach historically grounded in critical race and ethnic studies in order to uncover how the region is constituted, reproduced, and challenged. In emphasizing the study of race at the regional level, I draw upon the work of geographer Clyde Woods, who asserts that it is through examining how racial dominance operates within regional power structures that we can uncover how practices of ethnic supremacy frame power's operation at multiple scales.[17] Through these approaches, I demonstrate that practices and representations of mobility produce racial hierarchies with close ties to regional economies and their larger capital chains.[18]

In inland Southern California, citrus established the regional economy and its related networks. Beginning in the 1870s, citrus became synonymous with inland development; promoters popularized the name "Citrus Belt" and organized dense networks through which fruits grown in local soil traveled across the globe. Capitalism mapped space in its own image as groves, packinghouses, banks, and transit hubs transformed the geography of inland Southern California into the center of an "Orange Empire," a global collection of regions dedicated to citrus production and connected through commercial exchange.[19] A detailed review of the shipping records for lemons, one of inland Southern California's principal crops, provides a telling snapshot of the dense pathways emanating from this region. As early as 1908, only about 0.1 percent of lemons processed by the cooperative Cucamonga Citrus Fruit Growers Association were shipped locally. Instead, the vast majority of deliveries were destined for far-off places, ranging from Arkansas City to Wichita.[20] The commercial popularity of lemons, oranges, and grapefruits from California's Citrus Belt also extended far beyond the nation. In particular, its famed navel orange reorganized landscapes across the world, including Australia, Japan, and South Africa, each of which invested heavily in the fruit. By the beginning of the twentieth century, inland Southern California was well established as the citrus capital: the federal Department of Agriculture chose the region as home to the U.S. Citrus Experiment

Station, the "Sunkist" brand of the California Fruit Growers Exchange was a household name, and the local navel orange was the nation's chief specialty fruit crop, an enterprise valued at $20 million in California alone. Most centrally, the movement of people and products through a gateway with dense national and transnational commercial linkages, including but not limited to citrus, has consistently held a fundamental place in inland Southern California's economic, political, and cultural life.[21]

The citrus industry also had close ties with Los Angeles, where association offices and wholesale markets comprised citrus's financial centers. Capitalist relationships between rural production and urban distribution formed regional connections across this 60-mile-wide territory. It was through Los Angeles's integration with inland Southern California that it came of age as a national metropolis. As William Cronon notes in *Nature's Metropolis,* his influential text on Chicago and its hinterland, new transportation technologies, including the diesel truck and automobile, positioned Los Angeles to become the nation's major twentieth century gateway. Just as Chicago's rise in the capitalist orbit was linked to revolutions in the flows of meat, grain, and lumber from the countryside to the city, Los Angeles's repositioning was contingent on the ecology and economy of its eastern hinterland. Likewise, as Los Angeles became increasingly central to capitalist development, inland Southern California became a crucial gateway through which commodities, people, and information moved. That is, Los Angeles and inland Southern California synergistically thrust each other into economic and population circulations that were both intimate and long distance in nature.[22]

My timeline is drawn around the region's entry into the international citrus economy at the beginning of the twentieth century and concludes with its decline at the start of the twenty-first century. Over the long twentieth century, tensions between mobility and settlement were the topic of intense regional debate, particularly as migrants traveled long distances to acquire land and to labor in the fields.

In recent years, the Inland Empire's population growth and warehousing industry has further tied the U.S. economy to an international trade system that stretches from Los Angeles across the Pacific Ocean. If, as economic geographers argue, gateways are fundamental to the maintenance of global capitalism, sites such as inland Southern California are "chokepoints" where transnational flows are locally experienced. By the 1970s, the connection between U.S. consumers and Pacific Rim products intensified with the advent of containerization, or intermodal freight transport, by which shipping containers move from boats to trucks to warehouses, beginning at the ports of Los Angeles.[23] As one journalist explained, "If you own stuff made in China—the phone in your pocket, the shoes on your feet—chances are good that some of it passed through an Inland Empire warehouse."[24]

In addition to its position in a dynamic capitalist network that ties regional development to scales both distant and intimate in reach, inland Southern California has been home to a significant multiracial and global population since the mid-1800s, thereby offering many compelling reasons why ethnic studies scholars should be interested in how racial formation and mobility unfolded in this particular region. Agriculturalists actively recruited workers from across the globe to pick, prune, and pack golden fruits, tend to growing households, and construct transportation networks linking Los Angeles to the rest of the United States. In the post–World War II era, the children and grandchildren of these workers settled in new residential communities while African American commuters found affordable housing with fewer restrictions in inland Southern California than those encountered in suburbs closer to Los Angeles. As a result, the contemporary national trend of immigrants and people of color increasingly choosing to settle in non-urban communities is an old story here. Notably, when compared to Los Angeles, which is often recognized for its population diversity, key areas of inland Southern California have held larger concentrations of Japanese, Mexican, and African American people at pivotal moments of social contention: in the era of the Yellow Peril prior to the beginning of the twentieth century, following passage of the 1924 Immigration and Nationality Act, and during the 1965 Watts Rebellion. Moreover, although the story of federal actions and global capitalism is alluring, their effects were experienced most frequently in their regional context. Specifically, efforts to manage workers' movements, challenges to prevailing racial hierarchies, and efforts to construct interethnic spaces in places like inland Southern California have been key forces in race making. Struggles over national and cultural belonging materialize in palpable ways at the regional level, where the policies, social relations, and economic flows of other scales—from the body to the global—come together.[25]

Also of interest to ethnic studies scholars is the way marked waves of settler colonialism and migration shaped the Citrus Belt. What differentiates settler colonialism from other forms of colonization is its function as an ongoing process of Indigenous dispossession and elimination in which settlers seek to remap and remain permanently in a territory. The emphasis of this book is on white (particularly Anglo American—that is, non-Hispanic descent) settler colonialism, but California experienced multiple waves of settlement on Indigenous territories, including the Spanish conquest (1769–1821) and Mexican secularization of mission lands (1821–1848). Part of possessing land has been transforming it into commodities through the exploitation of slave and nonwhite immigrant labor. In inland Southern California, the process of white settler colonialism included Native containment and the management of racialized labor towards the end of building agricultural communities in which whites dominated nonwhite groups.[26]

By "white" and "nonwhite," I refer to historically and geographically situated categories that shift over time. It is well established that racial construction is a process rather than a biological truth. We can think of "whiteness," for instance, as a set of hierarchically ordered groupings produced by the political and cultural circumstances of a society. White status has been a prerequisite for most forms of U.S. national belonging, and its stability as a category is contingent upon the exclusion of those considered nonwhite. For example, at different times Irish, Jewish, and Mexican people have slid in and out of the category of whiteness, depending on the given political context, individual class markers, and collective acts of violence against those with more tenuous racial statuses. As this book shows, one of the ways whiteness operates has been through exercising control over one's own mobility and managing the mobility of others. Produced in relation to whiteness, we can think of "nonwhite" as a broad group including those who have undergone processes of racial othering, as well as those with an emergent nonwhite identity shaped by a multiracial context, often across multiple generations.[27] For nonwhites, racialization is experienced as the multiple ways their mobility and immobility is coerced through systems of power. Although usually thought of as fixed categories, what is white and what is not white is ever shifting. Class, gender, and citizenship are each implicated in these processes, through the criminalization of impoverished white "tramps," immigration polices directed at preventing the entry of Chinese women and the formation of Asian American families, and staunch protest to the recruitment of Puerto Rican laborers with rights to U.S. settlement.[28]

Adopting a relational lens, this project breaks from binary oppositions between individual groups and a white center to uncover affinities and tensions manifested among and between aggrieved groups across the twentieth century.[29] As I discuss throughout this book, white American and European settlers arriving in inland Southern California in the 1870s established colonies in a multiracial region already occupied by Indigenous bands of Cahuilla,

Maarenga'yam and Yuhaviatam (Serrano), and Tongva-Gabrielino people, as well as resident Mexican Americans and the nearby Payómkawichum-Luiseño Indians. These white settlers were accompanied by Chinese laborers migrating southward from San Francisco where they worked in early rail and agricultural industries. Following the Chinese Exclusion Act of 1882, agriculturalists turned to new labor sources, fostering the regional growth of the Japanese, Korean, South Asian, Mexican, and African American populations. Asian workers, comprising the majority of these nonwhite migrants, settled in farming camps and semirural neighborhoods at the outskirts of towns. Later, as a result of intensifying immigration restrictions on Asia and parts of Europe in the first decades of the twentieth century, a growing Mexican population came to fill the primary labor needs of industrial agriculture. Contests between Mexicans and whites occupied the center stage of regional racial relations until midcentury, but not exclusively so. Rather, concerns with Puerto Rican, Filipino, and white Dust Bowl migrants each threatened to unsettle regional racial hierarchies. Following World War II, inland Southern California diversified at rates much faster than that for suburbs located closer to Los Angeles, becoming a significant destination for African Americans in particular. In each of these cases, it was the continual struggle to remap settler colonial space and the region's position as a multiracial gateway that would position mobility as a central catalyst in racial formation.

In inland Southern California, mobility was a central means through which settler colonists centered whiteness in the region's "moral geography." Coined by political scientist Michael Shapiro, moral geographies are implicit assertions that shape political and cultural understandings of space. When considering mobility, moral geographies include where and how certain racialized bodies are expected to move, as well as the stories that are told about those movements. But they have not been exhaustive in their reach. Rather, alternative mobility practices disrupted regional claims invented by state powers and its constituents to suggest new forms of belonging that embraced heterogeneity. As described by American Studies scholar Melanie McAlister, "different moral geographies can coexist and even compete; each represents a different type of imaginative affiliation linked to certain ideas about significant spaces."[30] A crucial first step to unsettling the domination of white settler society and its dominant moral geographies is to return to the original encounters between Indigenous and non-Indigenous societies, and to recognize the ways racialized labor has been used to advance or resist white settler control of the region.

Clearly, multiscalar tensions among global capitalism, regional identity, and American race relations originating here have manifested starkly not only in inland Southern California but throughout the United States—from the emergence of national networks exercising vigilante immigration enforcement, like the Minuteman Project and Save Our State, to the Warehouse Workers United campaign drawing attention to Walmart's domestic supply chain and its negative impacts on workers' health. With ramifications that stretch far beyond its physical geography, inland Southern California offers an exceptional site to study regional mobilities and racial formations that forge a central part of global capitalism's operations.[31]

THE INTERDISCIPLINARITY OF RACE, PLACE, AND MOBILITY

The present study builds upon a foundation of interdisciplinary scholarship concerned with the production of space and place to demonstrate that we cannot fully understand racial formation without also considering the role of mobility. As a starting point, I draw upon the influential scholarship of theorist Henri Lefebvre, who argued in *The Production of Space* (1991) that space is not a product, but a process linked to our social contexts and reproduced through the political economy.[32] In other words, when we recognize space as an active force in and of social relations, we are better able to recognize the ways spatial production and race making work synergistically. For instance, Kay Anderson's seminal study of British settler society unpacked the process by which the idea of Chinatown defined racial difference in turn-of-the-century Vancouver, British Columbia. Her work demonstrates that government constructions of Chinatown as an unsanitary and morally corrupt district served to produce a group of Chinese outsiders. Racial ideas of "Chinese" were given meaning through spatial designations, which served as a foil to white insiders.[33] From Chinatown to Wall Street, the study of space has pushed scholars to consider the intertwined relationships between racial meaning, the built environment, and the active remaking of ethnospatial borders.[34]

While "place" has been widely adopted by social scientists and humanists as an analytic concept since the 1990s, a new "mobility turn" has only become evident in recent years. Its growth is indicated by the rise of international centers dedicated to mobility studies, thematic panels at professional conferences, and special journal issues examining the field, most notably in the flagship journal of the American Association of Geographers.[35] But, with some notable exceptions, race and ethnicity have not yet emerged as major themes within these "mobility studies."[36] In contrast, cultural theorists and ethnic studies scholars have been talking about mobility and immobility for several decades. However, they have used a different language to describe its effects. Examples of this work include historical studies on Indigenous travel and removal in Creek Indian lands, debates over slavery and African American migration in Louisville, travel restrictions on migrant workers in San Francisco, and the historical rise of incarceration in Los Angeles.[37]

This work also draws on the theorizations of migration scholars who have long been interested in immigration, labor, and transnational families.[38] Whereas the field of migration studies is primarily concerned with global flows of human movement, however, mobility studies open up questions about how channels of everyday movement and stasis are constructed and how they are governed at different moments in time.[39] Weaving these scholarships, I demonstrate tensions between the ways immigration policy and local industries shaped regional attitudes towards migrant groups and the ways settler communities sought to maintain racial hierarchies through contests over policy and law, public memory, and the built environment. Migration helped define mobility in settler communities shaped by agriculture, in which the management of migrant labor was central to maximizing regional economic flows.

This book takes as a primary concern critical race and ethnic studies, which have looked to racial formation to understand how bodies and societies are organized through structural and cultural forces. These efforts have more often than not led to uneven power structures defined by a "possessive investment in whiteness," in which privilege is distributed along lines of whiteness and racial others compete against one another for those advantages.[40] These relationships are consistently and actively contested in "racial projects" that give race meaning in ways that allocate resources to the benefit of some groups and to the cost of others.[41] *Collisions at the Crossroads* focuses on policies and practices seeking to manage and give meaning to the ways people have moved, ways that in effect have shaped everyday experiences of race—from the arrival of white migrants to the Riverside colony and disavowal of Indigenous and Mexican American communities, to continued efforts aimed at populating the region with a global workforce from Asia and Latin America, predominantly Mexico, to the suburbanization of African American and Latina/o communities following World War II. In multiracial places like inland Southern California where colonialism and empire collided through agricultural capitalism, these formations occurred in relational ways. That is, the meanings of race attached to one group formed alongside those of its neighboring groups.[42]

A mobility perspective brings to the cultural and ethnic studies table a focus on the ways actors move through space and how such acts potentially disrupt racial and place-based meanings through their bodies and the technologies that enable those movements. While the result has often been a possessive investment in whiteness, this is not always the case. This book aims to unpack the conditions under which this investment is made at some times and negated in others. Specifically, I examine the ways mobility has been an active force in racialization, operating alongside "place" to shape regional narratives, access to property, immigration policy, and claims to cultural belonging from 1870 to the present. Bridging relational race studies and mobility studies, this book advances our knowledge of how mobility shapes racial formation, from the regionally specific politics of mobility that shape racial meaning, such as who is included in bicycle races, to uneven access to systems enabling movement, such as drivers' licenses. The ways in which different actors were able to access these systems, or not, were reflective and constitutive of racial hierarchies and were key battlegrounds through which power was shaped, experienced, and contested.

MAPPING THE CROSSROADS

The archives that drive *Collisions at the Crossroads* are engaged as both a practice of reinterpretation and a recovery of history. Elite agriculturalists, writers, and politicians have been setting the terms of debates on mobility for centuries, contributing to what historian Michel-Rolph Trouillot describes as a silence at "the moment of fact creation."[43] For this reason, the records generated by the dominant public sphere can only offer hints about how a multiracial workforce interpreted the values of migration, settlement, and place making. Nevertheless, from the sources available, scholars can draw inferences as to how laborers sought to mitigate the negative impacts of restrictions and regulations on their mobility.

I underscore these efforts in the coming chapters. For instance, Korean residents who migrated after the Chinese Exclusion Act (1882) sought financial stability by building communal kitchens and bathhouses catering to the needs of migrant citrus workers. Japanese residents subject to property restrictions after passage of the Alien Land Law (1913) called upon white allies to act as intermediaries in state courts. Mexican American youth living at the margins of metropolitan car culture in Depression-era California manipulated registration records to retain anonymity in response to new forms of police surveillance. It is difficult to assess the full cultural and social dimensions of how people targeted by mobility systems responded to these discourses and policies, but photographic records, the built environment, and reading between the lines of traditional sources offer clues as to how individuals and communities engaged mobility for personal, if not progressive, purposes.

From the 1930s to the present, the records of response become fuller. Family photographic records chronicle the significance of automobiles in workers' day-to-day lives, radio programs allow for alternative readings of popular culture, and the rise of oral history projects in the 1990s provide a repository of testimony by those who came of age in the mid-twentieth century. Their accounts uncover strategic efforts to navigate the push and pull of the citrus economy. At the same time, they reveal the limits of such efforts in a political economy stacked against them. Field visits and analyses of the material culture left behind further contextualize the dominant culture's vast efforts to re-narrativize the racial meanings infused in mobility. This work of historical recovery is a necessary first step to uncovering patterns of change and continuity over time. Where public memory is shaped by hegemonic structures that naturalize unequal race relations under the guise of neutrality, interdisciplinary scholars must produce a historical geography in which marginalized people are afforded recognition of their resistance, accommodation, entrepreneurship, compromises, joy, and movement.[44]

Despite the local and global significance of inland Southern California, its history has not been treated with the same reverence as other trade and migration centers. There is no dedicated archive to Inland Empire history. Likewise, mobility can be elusive, with records as fluid as the people it seeks to track. Reconstructing this story has been an interdisciplinary endeavor, both deep and wide in its scope. It has meant searching through the multinodal records of this region, from the halls of local libraries, to the filing cabinets of historical societies, to the basements of museums, to the planning records of city halls, to the dedicated research of local community historians, in order to thread together a cohesive, if not comprehensive, history of a region that even today defies stark borders. It has also meant scouring national records kept by the Department of the Interior, Department of

Commerce and Labor, and Department of Agriculture, reviewing individual Census entries and reading thousands of pages of the Congressional Record to uncover the details of racial contests both overt and covert, as well as regional and national in intention. At times, it has required searching for transnational evidence, such as citrus records originating in Brazil, international immigration agreements, and social science research by Mexican scholars, in order to unpack the multiscalar effects of a site where economic and social relations were far-reaching in origin and effect. And, it has meant encountering stunning gaps, where rich community histories deemed insignificant have been lost to scholars. These erasures are often betrayed by what historian Kelly Lytle Hernández calls the "rebel archive," where those who would be eliminated created their own records and defied their own erasure.[45] Novels, songs, photo albums, popular media, and gated lots with modest traces of buildings constructed long ago each offer insight into the relationship of race, place, and mobility.

This book also represents over a decade's worth of recovery efforts. It is the first academic use of the Inland Mexican Heritage (IMH) archives, an oral history and photography project concerned with the lives of Mexican-descent families in the Inland Empire. As a frequent partner of IMH in its oral history and documentary projects, I have witnessed the challenges of collecting community histories in a political environment often hostile to the humanities, particularly those that rupture staunch mythologies protecting the status quo.[46] Consider that in a place where the Rendezvous festival's ban on lowriders erased the long-standing presence of people of color from a celebrated national landscape and painted them as outsiders, traffic checkpoints could more easily occur as natural extensions of that same fictive past. This book seeks to uncover how these selective traditions operate as active agents in the ways we view our past, thereby revealing the intertwined histories of race making and mobility at this contentious crossroads.

As part of my methodology, I also examine maps as discursive texts that reveal racial and spatial relationships in the region. Often employed as tools of empire, maps have been used to lay new meaning on Indigenous lands and to assert racial boundaries in space. As discussed by critical cartographers, in mapmakers' efforts to delineate boundaries between people and places, space is created as much as it is reflected, largely in the service of uneven power relations. Maps can also challenge the status quo and raise public consciousness in support of interventionist agendas.[47] Brought together, inland Southern California's rebel archive reveals countermappings of the region that challenge traditional cartographies. Drawing on this tradition, the maps on pp. xvii–xx foreground the intersectional histories of this book. Map 1 highlights the major geographic corridors moving through this region, with arrows pointing outside the region towards national and international sites of connection and influence discussed in the book. Maps 2 and 3 remap the region with contested histories of place-making and movement, with keys to sites discussed in the chapters that follow. Native territories, Mexican ranch lands, and county lines cross one another. This is inland Southern California, where the past is ever present in the landscapes, stories, and bodies that occupy this space.

Chapter 1 provides a foundation for understanding the shifting social and spatial relationships of the region, from the establishment of the fledgling Riverside colony to its emergence as the center of a burgeoning Citrus Belt region. Culminating in President Theodore Roosevelt's 1903 visit and his symbolic commemoration of the first navel orange tree, the chapter examines the ways white migrants promoting the citrus industry laid new meaning on this multiracial colony. Regional heritage was combined with city planning and immigration policy to position white agriculturalists as singular "pioneers," Indigenous and Mexican residents as outsiders, and Chinese immigrants as illegal residents. Underscoring the divergent ways mobility shapes processes of social differentiation, I examine the emergence of what I call an "Anglo Fantasy Past" in Southern California—a selective tradition asserting that white migration catalyzed regional development through commercial agriculture.[48] In this analysis, I investigate Roosevelt's visit and settler colonial mythology alongside the erasure of Indigenous and Mexican dispossession and the regional effects of the Geary Act (1892), which in practice criminalized Chinese residents' pursuit of farming—the economic and symbolic backbone of the region. From a relational perspective, practices and representations of mobility were a key battleground for determining social constructions of race and economic participation as the citrus economy took hold, thus laying the foundation for contests over exclusion and inclusion in the decades to come.

As the nineteenth century closed, multiple federal and state policies further restricted Asian immigration and land use. Targeting Japanese immigrants, these policy changes manifested in hardening regional racial hierarchies concerned with managing the local travel and residential patterns of all Asian residents. Focusing on these conflicts, Chapter 2 considers the ways in which Japanese mobility was restricted as white residents grappled with the tension between their need for nonwhite agricultural labor and their desire for a white society complete with strict racial lines. Where Japanese residents, alongside other nonwhite workers, found their residential mobility limited to a few segregated sections of the town and its environs, bicycling became an important platform through which they claimed cultural citizenship. Where the bicycle was a national symbol of modernity and a popular regional sport, analysis of Japanese cyclists reveals how workers leveraged mobility to advance their social and economic positions across an expansive territory where advancement depended on effective movement. However, while Japanese men's widening regional mobility upon bicycles disrupted the social boundaries of public space and increased their work opportunities, the mainstream press claimed bicycling as a white sport and police officers targeted Japanese riders. Regional efforts to immobilize Japanese residents by enforcing rampant residential segregation and criminalizing bicycling were two sides of the same coin, each ensuring that mobile workers stayed in their proper place. Examining where these lines were successfully crossed, this chapter illustrates the ways one middle class Japanese American family, faced with the mortal consequences of restricted living, secured housing in a segregated neighborhood by embracing assimilation and policing potential residential incursions by other nonwhites, including working class Japanese, Mexican, and African American residents. This chapter suggests that policies targeting mobile Asian residents, whether they sought to move through the streets or to a new neighborhood, revolved around a perception of whiteness as fixed and denied communities of color the opportunity to move by conditions of their own choosing.

Where Chapter 2 is concerned with the question of how migrant groups were immobilized, Chapter 3 focuses on the conditions by which migrant groups were hyper-mobilized. It focuses on the ties between regional forms of racialization shaped by the citrus economy of inland Southern California and national debates over Mexican immigration policy. The efforts of regional agriculturalists to maintain an unhindered flow of immigrant labor produced sharp contradictions in their claims about ethnic Mexicans, including both the proposition that they were ideal permanent settlers with a commitment to home and that they were inherently "birds of passage" who naturally returned to Mexico at the end of the harvest without seeking permanent settlement in the United States. In each case, narratives of racial immobility and mobility provided a flexible "racial script" that eased the tension between oscillating local labor needs and federal concerns with immigrant settlement.[49] I focus specifically on the regional impact of World

War I citrus housing campaigns and a series of congressional hearings over Mexican immigration, known as the Box Bill (1926–1930). In the first hearing, ranchers argued Mexican immigrants were rooted familial workers in contrast to Japanese bachelors and impoverished white itinerant workers, whom they positioned as habitually mobile and undependable in times of labor shortage. Conversely, in the second hearing, agricultural elites claimed Mexican workers had a racial propensity towards mobility that ensured their voluntary return to Mexico. As ranchers called for Mexican immigration, they denigrated Puerto Rican and Filipino migrants. Exacerbating American racial anxieties towards Puerto Rico and the Philippines, territories that granted residents the right to free travel within the continental United States, Box Bill opponents successfully argued that circular migrants from Mexico posed much less of a threat to the racial integrity of the nation than "negro" colonial subjects. Examining the construction of a global racial hierarchy organized by each groups' ability to move or stay in place, this chapter uncovers how Box Bill opponents used regional constructions of Mexican people to place immigrant workers in a favorable position vis-à-vis other racialized workers that ensured Mexican immigrants' further vulnerability in the fields.

Chapter 4 follows the racial construction of Mexican "birds of passage" to its reverberating consequences in the Depression years. Agricultural production in the Citrus Belt required a choreographed movement through rotating harvest sites that made automobiles a necessity in Mexican households, thereby contributing to the appearance of cars in their songs, poetry, and photography. However, as car ownership became common across the nation in the late 1920s, Mexicans were actively erased from American ideologies of driving. For instance, social science reports denigrated Mexican drivers, and automotive showrooms routinely denied space to nonwhite consumers. This chapter examines the role of Mexican immigrants and Mexican Americans in early automotive practices, from when they outpaced Anglo Americans as motorists in the 1920s to the perception of driving as a white, middle class pastime that rendered Mexicans behind the wheel as suspicious by the 1930s. Specifically, this chapter employs cultural studies and social history to examine the increased policing of Latina/o drivers, particularly Mexicans, in the Depression era—emergent in the real-crime radio detective program "Calling All Cars," popular novels, and juvenile arrest records in metropolitan Los Angeles. The backdrop of migration from the Midwest to metropolitan Los Angeles is telling here. Where Latina/o youth's efforts to carve a space for themselves in the modern automotive culture were met by racial profiling, progressive labor advocates successfully advanced publicity campaigns that recast white migrants as western pioneers and jalopies as modern-day covered wagons that legitimized claims to settlement aid. In both cases, depictions of automobiles, driving, and the road had expressly racial dimensions that fostered white mobility while constraining the mobility of Mexicans.

World War II and the postwar boom led to profound regional transformations with significant reverberations for spatial and racial relationships. Chapter 5 examines the transition of the Citrus Belt into the Inland Empire, an emerging regional identity that signaled the decline of the flagship citrus industry and investment in multiracial suburban development between 1945 and 1970. Focusing on Pomona, an important geographic crossroad bridging Los Angeles and the Inland Empire, this chapter examines an exemplary majority-minority community that broke from the patterns of racial segregation chronic to Los Angeles and its inner-ring suburbs. African American and Latina/o suburbanization proliferated here as Angelenos looked east for affordable housing and new residential developments enveloped this former citrus town. Looking to the Pomona Valley's emergence as a gateway for inland living, this chapter unpacks the means by which communities of color attempted to achieve social mobility through residential mobility, as well as the reigning ambivalence suburbanization would hold for African American and Latina/o communities. Moreover, it takes seriously the mobility and immobility of those who entered suburban communities by force. Specifically, the growth of the Inland Empire cannot be separated from the rise of carceral development. Stucco walls and steel bars rose with one another on former rural lands. The chapter turns on a paradox: suburban development at L.A.'s far edges helped support the residential mobility of African Americans and Latinas/os while prison expansion made the region synonymous with the forced immobility of the region's racialized surplus workforce. Together, these cases examine suburbanization as a process with profound impact on the most and the least mobile populations of color in metropolitan Los Angeles.

The concluding chapter returns to Route 66 heritage as a racial project shaping the cultural and physical contours of regional movement. As inland Southern California experienced white population decline in the 1990s, city officials and boosters adopted a nascent nostalgia for agricultural heritage along the popular highway with very different resonance for white and non-white residents. Redevelopment campaigns drew upon Route 66 iconography in an institutional celebration of Depression-era and postwar white migration that firmly erased the multiracial past and present of the region. Specifically, this chapter focuses on the spatial and cultural effects of development around the Foothill Boulevard/Route 66 corridor and a regional lifestyle center called Victoria Gardens, an open-air mall designed to evoke the community's evolution from a rural citrus town to a modern main street. Of central importance is the reemergence of Route 66 nostalgia as the region shifted from a minority to a majority Latina/o region. With the historical context provided in earlier chapters, the Conclusion demonstrates the continuing need for social justice strategies that place the right to mobility at the core of their mission.

Across the broad stretch of inland Southern California history, the value placed on the mobility of racialized populations fluctuated. In each instance, the discourses, practices, and technologies of mobility were produced alongside racially uneven economic development, white property accumulation, and power over the movements of a racialized workforce. The legacy of these practices persists as an organizing principle of race with broad consequences. These are part of a larger, global manifestation of practices delineating lines of citizenship through movement, which are evident in the passbook system of apartheid South Africa, Israeli checkpoints along the Palestinian West Bank, and the erection of special administrative regions requiring mainland Chinese nationals to bear permit when traveling or working in wealthier regions. As *Collisions at the Crossroads* demonstrates, though uniquely expressed in response to each locality and time, mobility and place making consistently serve as agents delineating citizenship through the production of difference.

ONE

The Rise of the Anglo Fantasy Past

MOBILITY, MEMORY, AND RACIAL HIERARCHIES
IN INLAND SOUTHERN CALIFORNIA, 1870–1900

In May of 1903, a large crowd congregated at the Pachappa train station in Riverside, California, to welcome President Theodore Roosevelt. Residents closely followed news of his western tour and eagerly anticipated his visit during a presidential journey spanning the American West. Alongside planned stopping points at major monuments like Yellowstone and the Louisiana Purchase Expedition, the City of Riverside was an ideal site to commemorate the frontier dream fulfilled. Located sixty miles inland of Los Angeles and the site for the introduction of the navel orange thirty years earlier, Riverside had become the center of a burgeoning citrus industry rivaling those in Florida, Louisiana, Portugal, Italy, and Brazil. When Roosevelt arrived, he praised the community for its abundant orange groves, saying, "Here I am in the pioneer community of irrigated fruit growing in California. . . . You have made of this city and its surroundings a veritable paradise."[1]

After a night's rest at the renowned Mission Inn, Roosevelt joined residents in the resort's courtyard to celebrate the ceremonial replanting of Riverside's first navel orange tree, an imported "parent tree" from which the region's groves were budded. John North Jr. of the Riverside Historical Society offered the president the shovel. Accepting the honor, he declared to the crowd, "I am glad to see, Mr. North, that this tree shows no signs of race suicide."[2] (For more on race suicide, see chapter 2.) Roosevelt departed shortly afterwards, leaving behind an enduring symbol of regional and racial identity. His visit highlights the key dimensions of this chapter: the ways mobility was racially differentiated through national mythologies; the growth of citrus capitalism and the establishment of its legitimacy over other forms of regional development; and the construction of racial hierarchies through an Anglo Fantasy Past that elevated white settlers as pioneers, erased Indigenous and Mexican dispossession, and located Chinese residents as perpetual foreigners.

Their positioning of citrus as emblematic of the region reflects the ways Riverside's residents sought to transform inland Southern California from a peripheral Mexican ranch economy to a center of capital-intensive U.S. agriculture. Riverside was founded three decades before President Roosevelt's visit, as one of several colonies in Southern California. Led by John W. North and James P. Greves of New York, the town was established in a valley already settled by longtime residents, including a local Indigenous population, Mexican ranch communities, Hispanos who had migrated from New Mexico, and whites, including European immigrants and U.S.-born immigrants who had arrived when the valley was still Mexico. The pageantry surrounding the replanting of the navel orange tree, a fruit foreign to the region and representative of U.S. commercial agriculture's growth, reveals the production of what cultural-materialist Raymond Williams has called a "selective tradition" to refer to the ways some versions of a society's past are emphasized as "tradition" and others are negated. These traditions privilege the dominant class, legitimize the present order, and point towards a future that maintains the social and economic status quo. Yet, they are also vulnerable to historical recovery and opposing positions, particularly by marginalized groups.[3]

The selective tradition of the parent navel orange tree was foundational in regional mythologies of mobility and settlement at the beginning of the twentieth century. In a celebration of U.S. progress, the town's residents commemorated the westward migration of white settlers as the starting point of *meaningful* development in an idealized narrative that claimed and glorified the colonization of a multiracial desert through Anglo American fruit. By doing so, they not only claimed the past but also validated the uneven ways privilege in the realms of property and cultural belonging were accorded to white migrants while constraining claims to place by Indigenous people and communities of color.

This chapter examines the emergence of this Anglo Fantasy Past in order to understand two aspects of the relationship between racial formation and mobility. Mobility is an analytic comprised of physical movement, the social meanings attached to that movement, and the policies facilitating or hindering it. The first aspect of the relationship between racial formation and mobility this chapter examines is internal migration by Anglo Americans from the eastern United States to inland Southern California. It investigates how long-distance migrants who traveled west were differentiated from those with generational ties, including the local Indigenous and Mexican-descent populations, and how colonialism was erased, despite continual claims to place by the dispossessed. Notably, it was through western movement that white migrants positioned themselves as racially superior to the longtime residents and claimed themselves to be the rightful occupants of the region, largely through the development of the citrus industry.

The second aspect of the relationship between racial formation and mobility concerns regional movement. This movement encompasses the travel comprising daily life and the regional spatial formations shaping local mobilities and immobilities—that is, how people were permitted to move or prohibited from moving. In contrast to practices celebrating white settlers were policies and laws regulating the everyday movements of Chinese immigrant workers also living in the region at this time.[4] Rather than excluding Asian people altogether, regional power brokers' primary goal was to control migration and settlement in a fluid response to changing regional labor demands. Examined together, racial projects attaching meaning to long-distance internal migration and regional movements reveal the ways selective tradition permeated ideas, policies, and practices of racial mobility.

This story begins in Riverside, a center of inland Southern California's agricultural economy built on white settler colonialism, which in this context we can understand as an ongoing process of Indigenous dispossession driven by citrus's profitability.[5] Inhabited by Indigenous Cahuilla, Maarenga'yam and Yuhaviatam (Serrano), and Tongva-Gabrielino people for thousands of years (estimates for the arrival of the earliest California populations are dated between 12,000 and 13,000 years ago), the Spanish incorporated present-day Riverside into Mission San Gabriel in 1771. The mission church was about 10 miles east of the Los Angeles Plaza.[6] After an independent Mexico secularized the Spanish missions in 1831, socialite Juan Bandini established Rancho Jurupa (1838) and Rancho Rincón (1839) from the mission's former eastern holdings. Over the next fifty years, land moved through many hands. Flood, drought, and hostile attacks proved insurmountable challenges to the Mexican ranch economy. When American migrants settled here in the 1870s, they would permeate the region with commercial agriculture.[7]

After experimenting with various crops, the newly arrived residents found that citrus fruits yielded impressive profits. In a short time, the sweet and colorful Riverside navel orange became iconic of a region that would come to be known as the "Citrus Belt," a fertile valley populated by Anglo American farmers. At the same time, Chinese residents operated cooperative farms where they grew and delivered vegetables throughout the region. However, the criminalization of Chinese settlement prevented their successful entry into the more lucrative citrus industry. For instance, municipal ordinances and regional enforcement of the 1892 Geary Act instituted a pass system for Chinese laborers that policed Chinese citrus farmers' everyday mobility. The celebration of white migrants—culminating in President Roosevelt's replanting of the navel orange tree—combined with the selective criminality of Chinese migrants within the region prompts further consideration of how mobility inherits disparate racial meanings and how those meanings have affected the distribution of power in multiracial places throughout the long twentieth century.

Prior to the arrival of President Roosevelt, citrus growing increasingly shaped the economy, geography, and people of inland Southern California. The mythology of the navel orange—manufactured by the Riverside Historical Society, promoted by the U.S. Department of Agriculture, and adopted by President Roosevelt—erased core components of local history that, if acknowledged, would have undermined the exclusivity of white American migrants' claims to the region. When celebrating horticultural expansion by white settler colonists, brokers of cultural production justified a racially segmented landscape that paralleled the distinctions they described between inferior and superior fruits. Nevertheless, despite the dominance of the white settler colonial narrative, counternarrative-based claims to place persisted, in the Sherman Institute's record of American Indian child runaways, in the San Salvador parishioners' efforts to reify the meaning of the Catholic Church, and in Chinese immigrants' efforts to establish lucrative farms. Despite these counternarratives, both longtime inhabitants' resistance and continued multiracial settlement were buried under a selective tradition subjugating all nonwhites to a system of colonial rule custom-made for each racial group according to the specific challenges they posed to citrus capitalism.[8] Tracing the place of mobility in the selective tradition of the planting of the parent navel orange tree reveals the intersecting mechanisms through which regional identity became synonymous with whiteness and, in the process, uncovers the symbols, institutions, and policies that were drawn upon as racial hierarchies unfolded in the emerging capitalist landscape of California.[9]

A COLONY FOR CALIFORNIA: DISPOSSESSION AND
WHITE SETTLER COLONIALISM

In 1870, John W. North and James P. Greves recruited eastern families to establish a communal colony in Southern California. Both abolitionists from upstate New York who had traveled to the West during the Civil War, North and Greves had attempted similar efforts before in Michigan, Minnesota, Tennessee, and Wisconsin. In this newest endeavor, they hoped to build an agricultural community near the projected line of the Southern Pacific Railroad. In a leaflet promoting the endeavor North wrote, "We wish to form a colony of intelligent, industrious and enterprising people, so that one's industry will help to promote his neighbor's interests as well as his own."[10] Early on, they envisioned a colony of quality schools, public libraries, churches, fertile farmland, and irrigated lots in the healthful environment of Southern California. North and Greves followed on the heels of earlier California colonists, including those who established a Mormon outpost in San Bernardino (1852), Stockton migrants seeking an alternative to depleted Northern California gold mines in Compton (1867), and the children of German immigrants who relocated from San Francisco to establish Anaheim (1869).[11] Each fed into the larger imperial impulse of the westward expansion of a U.S. empire. While resident American Indians and former Mexican citizens sought to defend their claims to Southern California in the aftermath of the Mexican-American War, internal migrants were busy remapping the region for Anglo American settlement.[12]

In March of 1870, North and Greves began recruiting settlers to their Southern California colony. They printed leaflets with bold headlines proclaiming "A Colony for California." Recruitment agents in Iowa, Michigan, New York, and Massachusetts were tasked with attracting prospective migrants to invest in the agricultural endeavor, which they did with some success. About a hundred people signed on as prospective colonists. After four months of scouting potential properties, representatives of the Southern California Colony Association (SCCA) purchased a site nestled in the inland valley, about sixty miles east of Los Angeles. Although North originally intended to settle closer to Los Angeles, and nearly did so in present-day Pasadena at $10 an acre, the association chose the inland location at less than half the price. Built on the site of the failed California Silk Center Association near the Santa Ana River, the SCCA adopted the name Riverside for its new town.[13]

As the colonists arrived in Riverside, the presence of large Indigenous and Mexican populations in the valley surprised them. Long predating the colonists' arrival, Cahuilla, Maarenga'yam and Yuhaviatam (Serrano), and Tongva-Gabrielino people were settled in the basin. Not far beyond these groups lived the Payómkawichum-Luiseños. California's diverse Indigenous population included about 300,000 people and 78 distinct language families. Although the Spanish had forcibly relocated Indigenous communities to mission land, some successfully evaded removal. But avoiding geographic displacement did not preclude economic dislocation; at the time of California's annexation by the United States, many who remained on Native land were pushed into manual labor, such as digging irrigation ditches, tending crops, and serving local households.[14] Others were forced into the service of new settlers due to the California vagrancy law, by which the labor of American Indians and later Mexicans were sold to white contractors and agriculturalists if they were found to have "no visible means of living, who in ten days do not seek employment, nor labor when employment is offered to them."[15] In the years to follow, California Natives were ever present as laborers in public spaces, domestic workers in private households, and wards of the state in Indian boarding schools.[16]

When the Mexican government secularized the Spanish missions (1834–1846), Mexican elites most successfully laid claim to the California countryside. These were the large land grants of a Californio elite, including Europeans and Americans who became naturalized Mexican citizens, converted to Catholicism, and married Mexican women. Elite Mexican women also acquired property, largely through inheritance or kinship ties. Conversely, the vast majority of Indigenous people were dispossessed of communal lands. However, some did successfully petition for land grants, including Serefino de Jesús, Emilio Joaquin, and I. Ramón Rosauaro Valueria, all of whom were affiliated with Mission San Gabriel. Petitioning for land based on women's labor to the mission, at times non-Indigenous husbands of Indigenous women also successfully claimed land titles. Yet, most Indigenous women remained landless.[17]

Later, when the United States annexed Alta California, American law upheld Mexican property rights according to the articles of the Treaty of Guadalupe Hidalgo (1848), and extended U.S. citizenship to former Mexicans living on the annexed land; however, it offered no such recognition to Indigenous people. Shortly after California statehood (1850), an expatriate of the mission system, Antonio Garra, attempted to unite inland tribes in a revolt that would extend property rights to Indigenous people. However, the plan was thwarted when Garra tried to collaborate with Juan Antonio, chief of the Cahuillas, who later submitted Garra to the custody of U.S. authorities.[18] The divergent responses to U.S. encroachment on American Indian lands by Garra and Antonio are a poignant reminder that Indigenous communities have been differently positioned alongside one another in the colonial process. One tribe's relative acceptance by new colonial authorities has often been achieved at the expense of another.[19]

In addition to long-standing Indigenous communities, the newly arrived Riverside colonists encountered Californio ranchers such as the Alvarado, Lugo, Palomares, Rubidoux, and Vejar families. One traveler wrote, "Handsome bands of sixty to eighty horses passed here Sunday, Monday, and Tuesday, and yesterday—There is a much larger Spanish population in this country than I had supposed."[20] The dispossession of California Indians contributed to frequent raids on these Mexican ranches, as Native people procured livestock and vital supplies consolidated by ranchers in a landscape where they had few economic options. Perhaps unexpectedly, these conflicts contributed to the multiracial tapestry of inland Southern California. After Garra's arrest, theft was largely attributed to distant tribes originating from across the Southwest, including the Ute, Mojave, and Paiute people. Horse robberies were so common that traders were required to undergo inspection before entering Cajon Pass, a popular trade route.[21] Indigenous people's dissident economic possibilities accompanied their conflicting claims to land as Anglo American conquest transformed it to property. As described by historian Angela Hudson in her study of travel in Creek Indian lands, "it is difficult and perhaps counterproductive to try to disaggregate acts of theft from acts of resistance."[22] Robberies and even violence could exist simultaneously as acts of necessity, profit, and aggression along the conduits of commerce that cut through inland Southern California.

In an effort to protect their property holdings, Californios recruited Hispano families from New Mexico. Hispano culture thrived in the Southwest, where Spanish American identity emerged as a form of ethnic agency and resistance to racial marginalization following the Mexican-American War. By claiming a European heritage, Hispanics of various backgrounds aimed to distance themselves from the denigration levied at Mexicans, an ethnoracial category prescribing an inferior Indian racial identity.[23] Contributing to the complex demographics of inland Southern California, rancher Antonio Lugo recruited New Mexican Hispanos to settle along the Santa Ana riverbank of his property, covering portions of present-day San Bernardino County.

In exchange for the 1842 formation of Politana, a protective settlement separating the Lugos' holdings from Indigenous attack, Antonio Lugo conferred 2,200 acres of land to the first wave of Hispano emigrants. They hailed from Abiquiú, New Mexico, a main meeting point on the Spanish Trail, which linked Santa Fe to Los Angeles. In recruiting from this trading gateway, Lugo drew from a population of Indigenous and Hispanic settlers long tasked with deterring raids through forming a colonial buffer zone, an exercise they had engaged in throughout the eighteenth century in New Mexico. Soon after establishing Politana, Lugo's southern neighbor, Juan Bandini, also recruited New Mexican settlers in exchange for protection from frequent raids.[24]

In total, about 250 people were recruited from Abiquiú to the Lugo and Bandini ranches between 1840 and 1850. Upon this land, the Belarde, Moya, Peter, and Garcia families, along with many others, established the neighboring communities of La Placita de los Trujillos (1844) and Agua Mansa (1845). Before North set his sights on inland Southern California, the New Mexican migrants had already cultivated individually owned subsistence farms along the riverfront, spotted the countryside with grazing cattle, organized a community school, opened a dance hall, built a cemetery, and erected a church that duplicated the layout of their Abiquiú home.[25]

Contests over land ownership as well as natural disasters hastened regional transformations favoring the Anglo American settlers in the second half of the nineteenth century, when California quickly gained statehood following the discovery of gold at Sutter's Mill. Faced with continual raids on his property by both American Indians and the new Anglo settlers, including a collective attack by a band of 200 Southwest Indians and a robbery by Texan John Irving's renegade gang, Lugo sold 40,000 acres of his ranch after U.S. statehood to a Mormon colony from Salt Lake City. This included the future site of San Bernardino, a major rail and trading community located a dozen miles north of Riverside. The following year, La Placita, Agua Mansa, and the neighboring community of Jurupa were consolidated into the township of San Salvador, named so after the local Catholic Church.[26]

Although San Salvador persisted into the mid-1850s, a flood destroyed much of the community in 1862. Many New Mexicans remained in the area to preserve familial relationships and religious ties to the San Salvador Parish, but the town never truly recovered from the flood's devastation. Additional pressures, such as the cattle industry's decline, drought, and state land policies strengthening white squatter rights proved insurmountable to most of Southern California's Mexican population. The California Land Act (1851), which placed the burden to prove land title on property holders, and the Homestead Act (1860), which extended the right to homestead in the public domain, were particularly effective in legitimizing white settlers' claims. By 1860, the majority of California property holdings had been transferred to white migrants, an experience of land loss that varied little by race, class, or gender for Californians of Indigenous and Mexican backgrounds.[27] Where the racial reconstruction of property in other parts of the Southwest took several decades to accomplish, resulting in a diversity of Mexican-Anglo relations that varied widely by county and class, land dispossession occurred quite swiftly under the U.S. expansionist system in California.[28]

The process of Indigenous and Mexican dispossession by European settlers was well underway by the time of the Riverside colony's arrival, but it was by no means complete. Cattle ranches and farm society temporarily existed in a state of competition, where changing land uses were accompanied by conflicting racial and regional categories. Considerable stress existed between the New Mexican colonies and the Riverside colony, the latter of whose unfenced alfalfa fields were enjoyed by San Salvador's grazing livestock. Where livestock were once free to roam across the valley, a new "no-fence" law (1872) favored farms over cattle. The law transferred the burden of fencing from agriculturalists, who had been responsible for erecting fences, to those who raised livestock, who were now required to prevent their animals from foraging on private property. As the former Mexican citizens were prohibited from grazing cattle, they were pushed into a racially stratified capitalist structure that limited their economic opportunities.[29] In the subsequent decades, many became section hands for the rail lines of the Southern Pacific, field hands on Riverside citrus farms, and manual labor for the Southern California Cement Company.

Through promotional materials, colonists were lured to California by visions of a New England colony, but Riverside developed within a multiracial landscape of contiguous, if contentiously related, communities. Contests among diverse bands of Indigenous people, the rearrangement of people and land through the Spanish mission system, and Mexican land grant distribution each produced layers of privilege and hardship among inland residents predating Anglo American occupation. It was during the period of transition for settler communities, from Mexican to American California, that North arrived with a small group of scouts to a valley already well populated with

Indigenous, Southwest American Indian, Californio, and New Mexican Hispano people.

North and other Anglo American colonists marked a new wave of dispossession and settler colonialism, one that claimed land by operationalizing whiteness as the center of national belonging and property ownership. Even though these privileges were unevenly drawn in previous regimes, they did not compare to the ways racialization reproduced and reaffirmed the United States as a white nation steeped in Native disavowal. Drawing attention beyond the formal state mechanisms that govern Indigenous dispossession, these examples show what Aileen Moreton-Robinson names "white possessive logics," or the "commonsense knowledge, decision making, and socially produced conventions" that circulate whiteness as inevitably linked to a nation-state's "ownership, control, and domination."[30] The ensuing years would be marked by Anglo American efforts to produce white possessive logics laying claim to this contested territory through an agricultural mythology of golden fruit. At the same time, these efforts compelled alternative place-making practices, including resistive acts rejecting white settler colonialism in inland Southern California.

CREATING AND CONTESTING REGIONAL HERITAGE

Ownership of the valley and expansion into new western frontiers meant not only making legal claim to the land, but also overlaying it with new cultural meanings. That is, the arrival of white eastern migrants to inland Southern California was accompanied by efforts to define and differentiate their place in a multiracial territory. Mapping was one way new meanings were laid down. Through mapping—a process that naturalizes and fixes space—the colonists used an old tool of empire to lay new meanings upon the landscape, meanings that signified Anglo American possession. And it was through the mythology of the navel orange that Riverside colonists situated themselves as the rightful and most important occupants of inland Southern California.

This mythology simultaneously positioned longtime residents and Chinese migrants as undeserving, while erasing the roles of violence, exploitation, and force in restructuring regional racial hierarchies to the advantage of white settlers. It was in this context that a federal Indian boarding school called the Sherman Institute, as well as the San Salvador Church, emerged as sites where counternarratives destabilized the logic of white settler mythologies. They did not, however, successfully decenter popular Anglo American heritage campaigns that actively recoded inland Southern California according to the hegemonic ideals of the new colony and the western imperialism of the Roosevelt administration. Although the Spanish-American War (1898) is often considered the primary turning point in the U.S. history of empire, for its expansionist overseas agenda, the imperialist impulse was already well underway in places like Riverside, founded more than a quarter century earlier.[31]

Maps

In 1875, North and Greves merged the SCCA with the New England Colony founded by Samuel Cary Evans and William Sayward to form the Riverside Land and Irrigating Company. The developers immediately began the task of remapping the landscape. Rather than objective truths, maps are active producers of space that require deconstruction. Geographer John Brian Harley notes that "cartographic facts are only facts within a specific cultural perspective."[32]

Distancing the landscape from its first occupants and multiracial legacy, the primary boulevards of Riverside's downtown Mile Square were a storyboard of lead developer Samuel Evan's westward migration. To the east was Indiana Ave., named after Evan's birth state, and to the west was California Ave., named after his new home. The third boulevard, located between Indiana and California, was Magnolia Avenue. Described by one colonist as "the pride and glory of Riverside, and the pioneer of many beautiful avenues in Southern California," Magnolia Avenue showcased Riverside's irrigated landscape with specimens from across the world, including magnolias, pepper trees, blue gum trees, and grevilleas. Smaller streets intersected these boulevards, each named after a U.S. president: Washington, Madison, Jefferson, and so on.[33] These labels both placed the young western colony squarely within American geography and forced the city's topography into a hierarchical ordering that naturalized U.S. sovereignty. In a span of less than ten years, the Riverside colonists overlaid a nationalist landscape on a space that had recently been called Jurupa, a name given by Indigenous inhabitants, which is believed to refer to the local sagebrush that dots the valley.[34] Operating well beyond grids on paper, spatial markers in cartography were accompanied by institutionalized efforts to create a founding narrative tied to western pioneer mythologies and the celebration of agricultural capitalism. Moreover, they were met with countermaps, as bodies in motion rein-scribed an alternative moral geography in the region.[35]

Historical Societies

Cartographic mapping was only a first step in the larger remapping process undertaken by white migrants when they arrived at Riverside. Among the most impactful organizations establishing a white possessive logic in inland Southern California were the local historical societies. The primary criterion for member-ship in Riverside's first Pioneer Society was having arrived to the colony within two years of Riverside's founding, between 1870 and 1872. In effect, the label of "pioneer" was tied to a narrow chronology of migration that included the colo-nists following North and Greves and excluded those who had already estab-lished homes in the region, primarily in the Indigenous and Mexican commu-nities. Membership was later extended to settlers who had joined the colony by 1873—but without the possibility for new membership, natural attrition led to the society's early demise. It was when word of President Roosevelt's western tour reached Riverside that local heritage once again became a significant factor in regional identity. Anticipating Roosevelt's May visit to Riverside, the Pioneer Society re-emerged in January 1903 as the Riverside Historical Society.[36]

The Riverside Historical Society adopted protection of the region's first navel orange trees as a primary cause and, in doing so, cultivated a powerful selective tradition around the origin of the navel orange. The discovery of the navel orange in its homeland of Brazil and rebirth in Riverside began in some accounts as the romantic tale of a traveling American woman, and in others as an adept observation by a U.S. consul. In either case, the sweet fruit and bold color of the seedless laranja de umbigo (or, navel orange), set it apart from other varieties.[37] Recognizing the fruit's quality and value, a consular officer wrote of the exceptional breed to Dr. William Saunders, the superin-tendent of experimental gardens and grounds at the propagating gardens of the U.S. Department of Agriculture (USDA) in Washington, DC. Through joint efforts that spanned two continents, Saunders secured twelve samples of the navel tree. Hopeful of the fruit's commercial value in the hands of U.S. ranchers, he tested samples. At the urging of Eliza and Luther Tibbets, former neighbors of Saunders who had recently moved near Riverside, he sent the last two trees to California.[38]

The Tibbets were unconventional protagonists. Luther had a reputation for filing frivolous lawsuits; Eliza moonlighted as a spiritualist medium; and each had divorced multiple times before marrying one another. When Luther ventured west in 1870 to join the small colony of Riverside migrants, he settled on the outskirts of the town to avoid the collective irrigation costs paid by the rest of the colony. Like other colonists, the Tibbets experimented with various agricultural endeavors in their early years of settlement. They searched without success until the two orange saplings arrived. In popular retellings of the navel's origin story, Eliza planted the trees by her doorway. Without access to the colony canals, she used her dishwater to irrigate them. In these accounts of the navel's origin, it was Eliza's insightful dedication and the fruits' inherent suitability to the inland climate and soil that caused the young plants to grow.[39]

From all of the possible versions of the region's past, the arrival of the navel orange and its development by white migrants was chosen as its benchmark. The exclusivity surrounding membership in the Riverside Historical Society reflects the seriousness with which colony residents viewed the preservation/construction of the past, and it shows the restrictive environment in which the meaningful past was envisioned. Its stated mission was encouraging friendly relations among members, perpetuating the memory of local heroes, and preserving the city's historical resources. As stated by honorary vice-president Mary F. Darling at the society's inaugural meeting, "Riverside is our adopted home, let us worthily cherish it."[40] Darling's suggestion that members had passively "adopted" Riverside, as if it were orphaned, circumvents the erasure of competing claims to the territory. These sentiments were echoed by society members: Lydia Twogood recalled the determination of the early settlers and their efforts to irrigate the "desert" and beautify the "barren" colony, and Elmer Holmes encouraged careful preservation of the early settlers' history with an eye towards future development.[41] As noted through members' testimonies and other local accounts, it was from the struggles, successes, and superiority of these early pioneers that the modern citrus rancher was born.

Although the society carefully protected regional heritage with restrictive membership regulations, such as requiring sponsorship by two current members, nowhere in the bylaws did it expressly prohibit Indigenous and Mexican people from applying. Yet, where direct references to race were missing in membership requirements, the line between local residents and migrant settlers served as an effective tool for racial exclusion. As outlined in Article 1 of its constitution, "Persons born in this State are not eligible to membership."[42] What I call the "migration requirement" inherently prevented Indigenous,

Mexican-descent, and other longtime residents from taking an active role in determining which regional histories were significant and which were not. The stark absence of Spanish surnames among officers and committee members reflects the effectiveness with which the constitution erased competing historical visions of inland Southern California, as well as ideas of what the region would become.

In this sense, Riverside's historical society was unique. As described by scholars of public memory in the Southwest, other California historical societies often incorporated Mexican American women who traced their ancestry to Spain. However, in a space where the presence of longtime resident Californians posed a threat to the burgeoning agricultural economy of the Riverside colonists, such inclusion was rendered a fundamental violation of the society's constitution. Instead, lines of inclusion and exclusion were drawn on the fault lines of nativity versus in-migration, with Indigenous and Mexican-descent people on one side and Anglo Americans on the other.[43]

Indian Schools

Efforts to link meaningful community history with the arrival of Riverside colonists existed dialectically with the erasure of Indigenous communities. Just before the historical society's founding, Riverside became home to the Sherman Institute, an off-reservation boarding school for American Indian children operated by the federal government.[44] The purpose of the school, as described at its dedication by A. C. Tonner, assistant commissioner of Indian Affairs, "[was] to enable the Indian, who can no longer exist in a wild state, to meet the requirements of modern progress and to appreciate and secure for himself the best there is in our civilization."[45] Through the use of "our," Tonner effectively laid claim to California and cast the students as outsiders on Indigenous land.

Early promotional materials echoed this sentiment. Evading the reality that white settlers' sense of belonging was dependent on the active and ongoing dispossession of Indigenous people, developers described a natural landmark in the shape of an Indian arrowhead on the foothills of the San Bernardino Mountains as an "emblem of a fading race," and beckoned tourists with views of the "ruins of an ancient civic race."[46] Described by historian Jean O'Brien, local narratives of the "vanishing Indian" have denied Native people a place in modernity and assigned primacy to non-Indians, who are credited with "first" developing the region.[47] Tasked with the systematic

Four students in military-style uniforms at the Sherman Institute boarding school, 1900: (left to right) Atkin Lomasse, Jimmie KeYazzie, Hosteen Quez, and Lora Tan Gy. Shades of Los Angeles Collection, Courtesy of Los Angeles Public Library.

elimination of incongruous Indigenous cultural practices, the Sherman Institute operated with strict schedules, line drills, grooming parameters, and military-like uniforms that stripped children of their diverse Indigenous bands' individual signifiers. Where mapping placed new meanings on the region's topography and the Riverside Historical Society narrowed local history to a period of migration largely excluding nonwhite people, the Sherman Institute actively targeted American Indian cultural practices and replaced them with a militarized assimilation campaign. In doing so, it followed the logic of federal Indian policy, which demanded the placement of Indigenous children in boarding schools, separated from their families, who were confined on distant reservations.[48]

Rupturing the myth of betterment that was integral to the boarding school's legitimacy, many students at the Sherman Institute resisted federal efforts to eradicate their cultural ties. According to registration records kept by the Department of the Interior, students reported profound homesickness for their communities located across the Southwest, including the Pueblo,

Navajo, Pima, Hopi, and Paiute nations, among others. In the most extreme cases, students protested their dislocation through mobility— that is, by running away. In an attempt to protest cultural loss, American Indian children retraced their steps through the physical act of movement and, in the process, created countermaps etched with bodies in motion. But a successful homecoming was rare and accompanied by risk. When students attempted multiple escapes, their efforts resulted in further immobilization. Among the most threating consequences for running away was "discharge," a term echoing the militaristic tone of the school: it meant transfer to the Preston School of Industry, a state-ran juvenile reform institute near Sacramento.[49] In contrast to Sherman, which offered educational courses and job training with the aim of assimilation, Preston was punitive in nature, with a history of student abuse and a prison-like environment. In the years to follow, deviant mobility would often be addressed through extreme forms of enforced immobility, including binding bodies in place through incarceration.[50]

Where the historical society celebrated Riverside migrants as pioneers, the Sherman Institute removed from sight the challenge posed by American Indians to Anglo American settlers' exclusive claims to the region. In doing so, the institute obscured the histories of Anglo American settlers by displacing, isolating, and incarcerating American Indian youth, whose very bodies countered the idea that the colonists had occupied empty land and gained its rightful title through development. The graves of Sherman students at the school cemetery today provide physical evidence that colonists' claims to this nation were neither absolute nor uncontested. Rather, settler colonialism was only possible through active elimination. Nevertheless, students challenged their confinement through their mobility, such as when running away, but also at other times in work, classes, and play.[51]

The Riverside Historical Society's campaign to link the region's meaningful past solely to white migration and the Sherman Institute's efforts to eradicate Indigenous societies, were two sides of a similar campaign to ratify the contemporary social order. These populations' relationships to mobility were starkly divergent. For white pioneers, western migration was a voluntary act imbued with honor and credited with developing the region's flagship citrus industry. For Indigenous populations, their Native status thrust them outside of these mythologies, and immobilized them within state institutions. Where American Indian youth could not be integrated into roles that supported the new regional hegemony, they were forcibly removed.

While runaway Indigenous children undermined the Anglo American's efforts to sever the physical link to their home communities, the San Salvador Church served as an important repository of memory for Mexican American Catholics—Californio, New Mexican, and elsewhere in origin—as a place of pilgrimage. Each summer, residents celebrated the feast of Saint John, patron saint of a Mexican land grant that had formerly covered much of inland Southern California. The festival included practices of charrería, or Mexican rodeo, in which ethnic Mexican men and women wore embroidered outfits, draped their horses in saddles ornamented with silver, and showcased their roping, riding, and racing skills. As described by one observer, "A cock would be buried in the ground with only its bobbing head above, then a rider on a keen gallop would sweep down to catch that head . . . [which] often was carried off as a prize."[52] Held annually, the festival linked together Catholic communities, who literally retraced their place in the region through movement. At the center of this alternative mapping for parishioners of San Salvador was the church, largely abandoned at this time but still the symbolic epicenter for the community's history. The vigil of Saint John was announced each year with the ringing of the parish bell, giving notice to those in attendance that mass would be offered the next morning in celebration of the feast day.[53]

The importance of the San Salvador church for inland Southern California's Mexican American community is highlighted by parishioners' continual efforts to maintain the parish bell from the 1860s through the 1910s. The bell held an important symbolic significance in the community, where it hung in front of the church and was rung to announce mass, marriages and deaths of community members, and annual celebrations. The bell was cracked during the flood of 1862, but the parish priest quickly organized a fund to replace the damaged community symbol. Monies and metals for its casting were collected from parishioners, largely Hispanos who were now spread throughout the region as a result of natural disaster and land dispossession. Transplanted but still tied to the church, families donated their jewelry, spoons, and brass pieces to be melted and used in the casting.[54]

Its completion in 1866 was cause for celebration. As recalled by Pastor Peter Verdaguer, when the bell was finished, "Hundreds of people were present when the Mexican broke the mould, and when the bell was seen there was a shouting which resounded from hill to hill."[55] Although newly cast, the bell held within it the galvanized heirlooms of a now regionally diasporic

Catholic community and its casting forged individual possessions into a living icon of collective memory. Through the act of return and tithing, congregants retraced their history in a region that actively tried to place Mexican people in the past and instead strengthened their networks that now radiated outwards.

The new parish bell embodied San Salvador itself, and the community was resilient in its efforts to retain this important symbol of ethnic Mexicans in the valley. Weighing near 1,000 pounds, the bell was hung from a tower at the time of its casting in 1866, laid down in front of the church and then suspended from a tree when the tower collapsed in 1881, and moved to a new parish serving the descendants of the community when the San Salvador parish church was closed in 1893. In an effort to raise funds for a new church, the congregation sold several liturgical artifacts from the original building in 1912, including a Spanish missal dating to 1791 and a copper aspergillum used to sprinkle holy water. By this time, Hispanophilia had spread throughout much of Anglo California, making such relics cherished memorabilia. Despite continued economic hardship and demographic dispersion, the congregation refused a hefty offer to purchase the bell by a local curio collector and hotelier, Frank Miller. When the new San Salvador church burned in 1916, the bell was one of few relics to survive the blaze.[56]

San Salvador's efforts to restore and retain the parish bell despite flood, financial strain, and fire is a compelling foil to President Roosevelt's replanting of the parent navel orange tree. The bell was a powerful signifier of community history that foregrounded Mexican history over that of Anglo American settlement. Notably, both symbols claiming regional heritage reflect European empires that colonized Indigenous territories. However, by this time, ethnic Mexicans and Indigenous people were positioned much closer to one another on the regional hierarchy than either was to Anglo Americans. The ultimate fate of the bell is a telling reflection of the ways Mexican claims to the region, despite their zealous efforts, were disavowed by circulation of white possessive logics. Unable to recover from the cost of the fire, the San Salvador parishioners reluctantly sold the bell to Miller in 1918.[57] Rather than continuing to be used by a living Mexican population, the bell hung in Miller's faux-mission resort hotel for observation by white tourists and Protestant newcomers seeking a nostalgic taste of a bygone Mexican California.[58] This is the same Mission Inn where Roosevelt had stayed during his 1903 visit to Riverside.

San Salvador parish bell at Agua Mansa, near Colton, ca. 1881–1893, negative 1911. History Collection, Courtesy of San Bernardino County Museum.

The racial exclusivity through which the region's history was narrated reflects an active process of erasure. Alternative histories persisted, but none were recognized as significant traditions by cultural institutions with the means to support, repeat, and transform them into regional heritage. These examples underscore the systematic suppression and elimination of women, the working class, and ethnic minorities from the cultural landscape, or what urbanist Dolores Hayden has described as "historicidal."[59] Historicide as enacted here betrays white migrants' urgent desire to reify their exclusive claims to regional development, belonging, and possession. Through restrictive membership policies, participation in the Riverside Historical Society became a racial marker of whiteness that bestowed the honorific title of pioneer on some residents and denigrated others as wistful reminders of a precolony past. An effective and persistent selective tradition was founded in the society's first call to action: designating the protection and commemoration of the region's first navel orange trees.

CREATING THE ANGLO FANTASY PAST AND
THE MYTHOLOGY OF THE NAVEL ORANGE

Spanish mission priests were the first to introduce oranges to California. Since at least the beginning of the nineteenth century, oranges were cultivated alongside grapes, figs, and pears for local consumption. It was from the saplings at Mission San Gabriel that the Californio ranchers Antonio Lugo and Jean-Louis Vignes began producing the area's first commercial groves.[60] The mission variety of orange was popularly integrated into the imagery of the "Spanish Fantasy Past." As described by scholars of public memory, the "mission myth"—a term coined by author Carey McWilliams to describe white nostalgia for a romantic Spanish era in California—replaced tales of violent conquest with the myth of inevitable progression towards Anglo American civilization. This Spanish Fantasy Past and mission myth are evident in popular state iconography, and include pious priests, sultry señoritas, rustic mission bells, and picturesque red tile roofs.[61]

Even before there was a Spanish Fantasy Past, the arrival of the navel variety of orange signified its own mythology, what I call the "Anglo Fantasy Past." This selective tradition erased the effects of racial capitalism—whereby capital accumulation accentuates difference, thereby producing race, to exploit the devaluing of nonwhite people and their labor—on regional development and replaced it with the celebration of white ranchers' endeavors with semitropical fruits.[62] That is, the Anglo Fantasy Past evaded the impacts of new property regimes and the citrus market on a multiracial region, and replaced those impacts with images of resourceful white ranchers, bucolic women, irrigated landscapes, and lush navel-orange groves. A companion to the Spanish Fantasy Past's mission myth, the Anglo Fantasy Past's navel myth provided a narrative of early California invoking the entrepreneurial spirit of Anglo American farmers as they transformed a Mexican desert into a capitalist cornucopia. Often operating alongside one another, the Anglo Fantasy Past and Spanish Fantasy Past both positioned whites as the superior race, placed Indigenous and Mexican residents in a precapitalist past, and naturalized Anglo American hegemony in economic, political, and cultural life.

The navel myth may be embodied by Eliza Tibbets, a steadfast migrant woman who nurtured golden fruit that would define a region for generations to come. For her efforts, Eliza has been credited as the "mother" of the citrus industry, a metaphor alluding to her nursing of the young saplings near her kitchen door, and also reflective of the anthropomorphized qualities extended to the fruit, the exceptional progeny of white migrants. The specifics regarding the navel's arrival to Riverside vary across accounts and have caused much debate in local newspapers, USDA articles, and publications by public historians, ranging from argument about the quantity of trees received to whether it was Eliza who requested them. In each reiteration of the navel orange's introduction to Riverside, though, one outcome is consistent. The trees gave birth to an industry that redefined the region.[63]

The selective tradition of the navel orange lent legitimacy to citrus production and deliberately connected the region's history to white migration and American capitalism while sweeping away alternative modes of production, as well as the people who exercised them. The navel orange celebrated by the Riverside Historical Society was different from the mission variety cultivated by Spanish missionaries and Mexican ranchers. Introduced to inland Southern California by the USDA, the navel orange represented the stretching arm of the United States into California following the Mexican-American War. Neither a local crop nor a mission fruit, the navel orange was a highly specialized, capital-intensive, labor-demanding, imported commercial commodity. The navel was noted for its sweet taste, bold color, and seedless fruit, but its expansion into a national market was predicated on both the migration of white settlers and the movement of goods. Accordingly, the Riverside Historical Society's plan to replant the parent navel orange tree was a fitting symbol of the region's replacement of Native communities for eastern colonists, northern Mexico for American California, and the Californio ranch economy for capitalist agriculture.

The navel orange first gained national recognition when awarded first prize at the World's Industrial and Cotton Centennial Exposition in 1884. Held in New Orleans, the fair included international exhibit halls featuring industrial innovations in factories and mills, livestock, and agriculture. The Horticultural Hall was dedicated to fruit exhibits and included displays from Russia, France, England, Mexico, and Central America. Beating out international competitors, the Riverside navel orange attracted a global market eager to try the sweet and seedless fruit. Recognized in a world venue, but credited to the unique climate and soil of inland Southern California, news of the navel's superior quality spread. Farmers from across the region populated the landscape with trees springing forth from clippings of the colony's original navel orange trees. Local citrus growers soon began organizing into large cooperative organizations, to collectively pack, ship, and market their fruit for national and international markets. By 1897, the largest of these organizations managed 11 district exchanges, 37 associations, and 70 sales representatives throughout the Midwest and East Coast.[64] The small agricultural colony of Riverside would experience rapid growth, speculation, and capital investment in the years to follow, as it became the center of an Orange Empire.[65]

National recognition of the navel orange intersected with the integration of Riverside into a larger capitalist economy. In 1875, the Southern Pacific Railroad finished its line from Los Angeles to Colton. Located only seven miles from Riverside, the new station closed the link between the inland agricultural colony and the seaside ports, which were accessible by connector rail in Los Angeles. By 1881, the Southern Pacific connected Riverside to both the East Coast and the San Joaquin Valley, providing direct rail access to San Francisco. The Santa Fe Railroad arrived in San Bernardino soon afterwards. Its loop line linked citrus-growing towns in a belt, while the Pacific Electric Railway provided local service to communities between Los Angeles and San Bernardino. Stretching transportation lines, combined with technological advances like ventilated freight cars (1887) and ice-bunker cars (1889), which extended the fruit's shelf life, expanded the market and created a regional citrus boom.[66] The navel orange emerged at the precise moment Riverside began to be connected to a larger set of economic circuits, enabling it to become the region's flagship export in an international market.

Inland Southern California became a citrus region not because it was naturally destined to become so or because it was in the primary interest of the area's residents, but because it was integrated into the global marketplace at great profit. As described by economic geographers and environmental historians, capitalism produces nature in its own image, in this case to facilitate the growth of commercial fruits. As Neil Smith notes, "Predictably, the production of nature has followed a path guided less by extreme unthinkability of the physical event, more by the profitability of the economic event."[67] That is, the potential for economic gain has often reshaped nature even where the extreme efforts required to alter the physical landscape would seem inconceivable, such as building a tropical oasis in the South Pole or irrigating a desert to grow citrus fruits. The expansion of capitalism to Southern

California created new economic circuits, wage-labor relations, and landscapes to facilitate the growth of specialized agriculture.

As the circulation of citrus emanated out from inland Southern California, the navel became iconic of a region now promoted internationally as the Citrus Belt. Citrus labels—colorful paper advertisements placed at the ends of citrus crates and shipped across the world—reveal the ways citrus cooperatives produced an image of inland Southern California that reinforced regional mythologies. Orange magnates artfully created a picture of Southern California that concealed the dark side of the sunshine state, privileging natural landscapes, individual fruits, and agricultural fields. In addition to hiding the stark effects of industrial agriculture on Southern California's semidesert environment, images produced by the citrus industry effectively erased the racialized labor in the groves and packinghouses, at this time largely provided by Indigenous and Chinese workers. In a review of nearly three thousand archival crate images produced by area citrus growers, about 40 percent represent the fruit standing alone or within a natural landscape seemingly divorced from human interaction.[68] Although Southern California's oranges became a symbol of pristine nature, in practice, "The fruits of Eden became signs of empire in the making," one whose fictions were further circulated in regional festivals, literature, and art celebrating the achievements of white growers.[69] The economic circuits of the Citrus Belt were aided by a selective tradition that tied together frontier mobility, whiteness, and the navel orange. It romanticized the migration of easterners and welcomed the integration of the American West into the nation, a Mexican desert transformed into the American fruit basket.

The Citrus Belt was not alone during this period in its blending of a selective regional heritage and development of an agricultural monopoly by a small agricultural elite. For instance, in the Mississippi Delta between 1880 and 1920 the dominant cotton plantation economic system was augmented by expansion of the plantation tradition, consisting of Confederate monuments, traveling minstrel shows, nostalgic literature, and the film *Birth of a Nation*. Consider also the myth of tri-cultural harmony in New Mexico, a myth predicated on the clear separation of Indigenous, Spanish, and Anglo identities in order to foster a distinct regional identity beneficial to the tourist economy. Likewise, remembrance of the Alamo in Texas falsely proposed that Mexicans and Anglos occupied distinctly separate sides of the statehood debate, as Texans continued to fight over the relative economic dominance of cattle ranching relative to farming.[70] In each case, regional development, selective traditions, and economic monopolies walked hand in hand.

The mythology of the navel orange reached maturity during Roosevelt's western tour. Throughout the American West, towns along the president's travel route invited him to commemorate sites of national and local significance. He laid the cornerstone to Yellowstone's gateway in Montana, dedicated a Young Men's Christian Association (YMCA) building in Iowa, marked the opening of the Louisiana Purchase Exposition in Missouri, and broke ground for a monument to the late president William McKinley in Northern California. Each event was celebrated by local news media and officially archived within Roosevelt's presidential speeches. As preeminently representative of inland Southern California, the Riverside Historical Society chose the replanting of the Tibbets' orange tree for the president's participation. Through this symbolic act, Roosevelt would imbue white migration and commercial citrus expansion with national legitimacy and regional dominance.[71]

When the historical society successfully acquired one of the two parent navel trees for the ceremony, its placement became a question of symbolic importance. Previously obtained by the city, the first tree had been replanted on a donated lot at the corner of Magnolia and Arlington Avenues. Placed to face the late family homestead of Luther and Eliza Tibbets, the tree's planting at this busy intersection served as a physical link between the city's humble beginnings as a colony and its emergence as a modern center of commerce.[72] Symbolic of Riverside's origin, the replanting of the second tree would likewise reflect the citrus industry's prominent role in regional development. Following much deliberation, the historical society agreed to plant the second parent tree in the courtyard of the Mission Inn.

Owned by Frank Miller, the same man who would later acquire the San Salvador parish bell and a respected member of the historical society's executive committee, the Mission Inn was celebrated as emblematic of the city. It had recently undergone reconstruction from a modest adobe cottage to a building in the mission revival style. Although architect Arthur Benton drew on multiple influences to execute Miller's eclectic vision, the resort hotel was largely designed as a grandiose facsimile of the premiere symbol of Spanish California. Arcades, patios, repeating arches, clay tile roofs, plaster covered exteriors, and bell tower each evoked a romantic portrait of mission life.[73] Historians have attributed the allure of the mission myth to the belief in a linear trajectory from Spanish conquest of the Americas to the U.S. invasion of Mexico; the myth also quelled anxieties surrounding racial, class, and national identities at the onset of California modernity; and the myth bolstered attempts to replace tales of violent conquest with the story of an inevitable progression to Anglo American civilization.[74] Ultimately deemed underutilized in the hands of Spain and Mexico, pre-Anglo California was portrayed as an open territory ripe for the productive hands of Anglo American farmers. As described in *Southern California* (1877), an early promotion publication of the Riverside Land and Irrigation Company:

> It is a matter of surprise to many that visit us, that more has not been accomplished; but it must be borne in mind that the aborigines and their successors, the Mexican and Spanish races, were so long isolated from the "rest of mankind" that there was no stimulus to exertion other than to get sufficient to eat and keep them[selves] comfortable.[75]

By placing the navel orange tree in the courtyard of the Mission Inn, the historical society recognized citrus growers as the rightful inheritors of California in a narrative celebrating Anglo American migrants' ability to turn a Mexican desert into an American garden. The parent navel orange tree was emblematic of this transition. Akin to placing an American flag in conquered soil, the strategic placement of the navel tree in the central courtyard of a mission-facsimile resort hotel definitively decentralized Indigenous, Spanish, and Mexican claims to the region, and relegated them to a conquered past.

These mythologies about mobility became a key battleground through which claims to inland Southern California were contested. The celebration of the navel orange's origin—a symbol of regional development introduced through white migration—served as an "imperial transition narrative" for the citrus communities of inland Southern California. As explained by postcolonial and feminist scholars, these mythologies turn populated lands into empty spaces, credit modernization to white settlers, and assume an inevitable progression towards capitalism. Urbanist Laura Barraclough explains that narratives of rural land organized around frontier ideology have actively constructed racial and spatial categories in the American West. Myths and symbols of rural land are created, and in turn shape material inequality and national belonging.[76] In this respect, seemingly mundane efforts to monumentalize an orange tree do not merely reflect the ways Riverside colonists understood their regional identity. Their efforts expose the ways recent settlers attempted to shape the world around them within an ongoing process of U.S. conquest that imbued white migration with regional dominance. Yet, Indigenous and Mexican-descent people were not complicit in their own erasure, as evidenced by the Sherman Institute runaways and the San Salvador parish bell diaspora. Looking to these multiracial landscapes, we are better able to see how diverse groups who occupied distinct racial and economic positions simultaneously confronted white settler agendas that reduced each of them to racial outsiders of a bygone era.

Notably, the navel orange origin myth leaves out two central characters: the Tibbets's live-in domestic, Ah Lan, and a young African American girl, Nicey Robinson. Lan was among the first Chinese immigrants to settle in Riverside and, like many Chinese domestic workers, he would have performed essential tasks for the family, such as cleaning, laundry, and cooking.[77] His responsibilities likely extended outside the household as well, for instance to general gardening. If the Brazilian navel orange trees credited with the birth of the citrus industry were sustained by the Tibbets's family dishwater, as the origin tale suggests, then Lan may have been the one to water them. Or, perhaps it was the young Nicey Robinson, who had accompanied Luther when he traveled from Virginia to California. Robinson was among the earliest African American settlers to travel to Riverside from the American South, most of whom worked as farm laborers and road builders, but also as grocers, electricians, and pastors.[78] Chinese immigrants, such as Lan, and African American migrants, such as Robinson, went without the honorific title of "pioneer" bestowed upon the white migrants of the Riverside colony. They were left out of official historical accounts in which the mere presence of Chinese, African, Indigenous, and Mexican-descent people challenged the hegemony of white claims to regional development. Rather, the erasure of some migrants was considered necessary so that others could become pioneers.

CONTROLLING CHINESE MOBILITY IN THE WHITE CITRISCAPE

The Riverside colonists were not the only migrants arriving in the region during this period; white settlement occurred alongside a significant Chinese migration. Applying a mobility paradigm to policies directed at these Chinese immigrants underscores the ways race shaped the experiences of nonwhite migrants. Although American Indians provided much of the region's labor upon the colony's founding, demand quickly rose beyond what they could meet. In response, the Chinese Consolidated Benevolent Association and labor firms like Griffin and Skelley recruited and coordinated the migration of Chinese workers into the Southwest's seasonal mining, rail, and agricultural industries.[79] Riverside's earliest promotional materials note Chinese labor with reticence: "At present the people are forced to rely upon Chinese help in the house, for cooking, etc., but from necessity, not choice."[80] Yet, some Chinese residents became important labor intermediaries as merchants while others operated cooperative vegetable farms with considerable success. But they were blocked from sizable participation in the region's flagship industries. Although Chinese immigrants were recruited for their labor, white migrants actively worked to manage Chinese mobility and immobility in the emerging colony by constructing racial hierarchies that facilitated the flow of the citrus industry to the privilege of white settlers.

The Chinese Quarter, Chinatown, and the Citriscape

The Anglo Fantasy Past remained entrenched in an idealized racial geography that separated white space and Chinese space. Although Census records note a growing Chinese population throughout the tri-county area in the years leading up to President Roosevelt's visit, despite the long Chinese presence in the region, city directories covering central Riverside list no Asian surnames and businesses until 1905.[81] Insurance maps from this period locate Chinese rooming houses at the far edges of the Mile Square (in the Chinese Quarter) and on the outskirts of the Tesquesquite Arroyo several miles away. The Chinese Quarter included a mix of wooden boardinghouses, laundries, and general stores, each of which catered to Chinese residents and migrant workers.[82] One-room dormitories provided bleak dwellings for traveling laborers who slept on wooden planks or dirt floors. Those unable to afford a boardinghouse gathered in camps throughout the streets. Within these spaces, tents clustered together and laborers shared open fires, meals, and company.[83] These were largely bachelor spaces, as the 1875 Page Act—which prohibited the immigration of Chinese prostitutes by requiring women to provide additional documentation at their own expense—led to broad hostilities and exclusion levied at all Chinese women. Such laws generated a gender imbalance that prevented females from immigrating in large numbers—between 1870 and 1880, only 4.6 percent of the Chinese immigration population were women—and discouraged long-term familial settlement.[84]

The Chinese Quarter existed in a dialectic relationship with the "citriscape." As explained by historian Matt Garcia, citrus growers took great pride in exhibiting their ability to harness nature not only in the groves they cultivated, but also in the uniformly and rationally designed towns of the citrus region. Creating a virtual citriscape, or a carefully manicured and designed citrus landscape, the neat grid system of streets and boulevards echoed the regimented rows of citrus groves that financed urban development.[85] For instance, planners designed Victoria Avenue as both a direct physical and symbolic connection between citrus production and the American households it supported. As the main transportation artery linking the citrus grove district of Arlington Heights to the residences of downtown Riverside, the boulevard was lined in an imperialist display of ornamental plants from across the globe. These landscapes were reproduced and circulated in orange crate art, spreading well beyond inland Southern California the illusion of a white citriscape.[86] The Romanesque Loring Opera House, French Beaux-Arts Riverside County Courthouse, and grand estates of individual growers further stood as monuments to the economic accomplishments of white growers, their dominance over nature, and the inherent superiority of Anglo American California.[87] The Riverside Chamber of Commerce described the scene in 1933:

> When one stops to think of the thousands of attractive homes in the navel orange districts that have been established and are being maintained through the successful culture of this variety, it becomes apparent that the financial returns for the crops, large as they may be, have not been the most important outcome of this outstanding development.[88]

The citriscape projected citrus growers' social aspirations onto the built environment through both flora and architecture, enterprises that required constant nonwhite labor to maintain.[89]

Where the citriscape showcased the advances of capitalist agriculture, Riverside's Chinese Quarter became a local referent for the racial and moral divisions between white settlers and Chinese migrants. It was a common topic of complaint among Riverside's city leaders and *Riverside Press* editor Luther Holt, whose office was located near the quarter. The popular newsman focused his tirades on Chinese washhouses, encouraging Riverside residents to patronize non-Chinese businesses. Drawing on policies criminalizing

Chinese launderers in San Francisco, Holt characterized laundries as a sign of unsanitary living in a city otherwise celebrated as the salubrious home of citrus fruit. Chinese laundries remained utilized by a multiethnic clientele, but in October of 1885 a thinly veiled segregationist ordinance was passed that targeted laundering, ironing, and nuisance within a square mile of downtown. Where laundry ordinances selectively targeted Chinese business owners in Los Angeles, the Riverside law was reportedly directed at single Chinese men washing their own clothing outdoors. By criminalizing daily life and communal uses of public spaces, the municipal code pushed Chinese residents out of the downtown business district, claiming it as a white space.[90]

Public policy actively reorganized the city to reaffirm racial lines as Riverside's (primarily white) downtown expanded into areas that had formerly been marginal to the city and largely occupied by Chinese residents. Between 1885 and 1887, fire insurance maps show that Chinese-occupied buildings were replaced with wagon and carriage services. Responding to population growth, the district swelled with buildings and a new thoroughfare was added between Main and Orange Streets.[91] Despite anti-Chinese sentiment, Chinese workers were essential to regional development as commercial citrus agriculture spread. Instead of eliminating the Chinese presence in Riverside, Chinese workers were erased from the new downtown center and displaced to the town's increasingly distant margins, where a new "Chinatown" formed about five miles away from the Chinese Quarter, in a seven-acre district north of the Santa Ana River. Bisected by a new "Mongol Avenue," the reinforced link between race and space was firmly announced in the city's official geography.[92]

Despite municipal efforts to set Chinatown as a site apart from the city, its relationship to Riverside was mitochondrial. Chinatown was the site through which the citrus industry and Riverside itself were powered as bodies moved back and forth across its borders to supply labor to the whole. Symbolic boundaries were resilient, but physical boundaries were porous membranes through which growers, contractors, and workers traveled to keep the citrus industry running. From Chinatown, citrus growers were supplied the manpower for their groves' cultivation. Moreover, Chinese workers provided expertise in citrus cultivation, stemming from the orange's earlier presence in China's Pearl River Delta. Among their many contributions, Chinese immigrants taught growers to individually handwash citrus leaves, a remedy for the cottony cushion scale that threatened the harvest in the 1880s, and introduced the "Chinese pack," a packing method enabling long-distance shipments.[93] Because of their interdependencies on Chinese labor, inland communities held ambivalent attitudes towards Chinese workers, simultaneously exhibiting xenophobia typical of Californians in this period and recognizing Chinese workers' important role as laborers in the flagship citrus industry.[94] Chinatown was more than a space of racialization. It was a circuitous landscape in which the traffic of labor and Chinese expertise was mediated between white and nonwhite space.

The spatial relationship between Chinatown and the rest of Riverside underscores that place and mobility operate dialectically. Preserving the perception of Chinese fixity was critical to municipal authorities' and developers' efforts to maintain the illusion of a white citriscape, free of racial ambiguity. That is, efforts to police the spatial boundaries of Chinatown were integral to maintaining the perceived impermeability of racial borders.[95] In municipal promotional materials, newspapers, and maps, Chinatown existed in clear juxtaposition to the regimented groves and white neighborhoods of the central city. Yet, the regional agricultural economy was largely dependent on Chinese immigration and labor. Thus it was the management, rather than the elimination, of Chinese mobility that was of central concern to boosters and city planners, evident in policies criminalizing everyday practices, such as laundry, and the relocation of the Chinese Quarter to a shifting municipal edge.

The Geary Act

A series of restrictive immigration acts enacted by the federal government provided a new set of tools for regulating Chinese mobility that played out at the regional level. Where the 1875 Page Act banned virtually all Chinese women, as well as contract workers, and where the 1882 Chinese Exclusion Act prohibited almost all immigration by Chinese laborers, an 1892 amendment known as the Geary Act tightened restrictions on Chinese immigrants already living in the United States.[96] Notably, the law added a provision requiring all Chinese laborers to register and carry a certificate of residence verifying their right to be in the country. Aptly described by one scholar as "America's first internal passport system," laborers found without a certificate were to be immediately arrested.[97] Many Chinese residents challenged the integrity of the Geary Act, even refusing to register in the face of harsh penalties. However, the Supreme Court upheld the federal government's right to exclude Chinese immigrants as a matter of national sovereignty.

Prior to the Geary Act, immigration screening was applied only at the crossing of a national boundary. After the passage of the Geary Act, federal agents had the authority to monitor, detain, and question the validity of all Chinese movements *within* U.S. borders. In effect, the Geary Act justified an elaborate system that regulated Chinese mobility far from official ports of entry. And, it divided residency into categories of authorized and unauthorized for the first time. Under a law that marked all Chinese bodies as potentially criminal, even exempt groups—including students, teachers, merchants, and diplomats—were subject to living in the "shadows of exclusion."[98] As illegal residency became a federal crime for the first time, residents who did not register became criminals. In contrast to historian Mae Ngai's "illegal alien," for whom unauthorized entry at national borders made one vulnerable to deportation, the legality of national entrance was inconsequential for what might be called the "illegal resident."[99] Rather, it was the refusal to register within the boundaries of the nation—or suspicion of this refusal—that marked one as criminal.

The United States has often coded mobility in law as a means to criminalize the movements of laborers, which has proved essential to maintaining capitalist-intensive regional economies. For instance, in a number of ways the impact of the Geary Act in the American West can be likened to the Fugitive Slave Act in the American South. This 1850 federal act initiated a policy in which all runaway slaves were to be captured and returned to their southern slaveholders. The parallel points towards the use of law to enact spatial strategies that circumvented subversive mobile practices. In both instances, federal law placed a racial limitation on the right to mobility, marked all members of particular groups as potentially criminal, including exempt Chinese merchants and free African Americans, and subjected residents to imprisonment and forced labor. Runaway slaves deemed property were returned to their captors; Chinese residents (who were foreign nationals) determined to be in violation of the Geary Act were subject to compulsory deportation. The comparison ends in the degree of dehumanization and bondage experienced by its targets.[100] Operating below the federal level, state legislation too has enacted migration restrictions on convicted criminals, vagrants, and the ill, categories often veiling race.[101]

The Geary Act's internal pass system set the foundation for subsequent restrictions placed on several other groups' mobility, extending its significance well beyond the initial target of managing Chinese immigrants. For instance, laws restricting Chinese immigration enacted at the beginning of the twentieth century reappeared as supporting evidence for Arizona's 2010 Senate Bill 1070, which proposed state-level immigration requirements in addition to those already enacted at the federal level. AB1070 is a close echo of the Geary Act in its shared mandate that immigrants carry a series of required documents and its stipulation that officers determine a person's immigration status "where reasonable suspicion exists that the person is an alien who is unlawfully present in the United States."[102] Such blanket expansions of immigration surveillance granted to local law enforcement have promoted increased racial profiling of Latina/o residents. The oppression of one group has quite frequently been the precedent for the oppression of other groups, from that of runaway slaves in the South, to unregistered Chinese laborers in the West, to Latina/o immigrants in the Southwest.[103]

Whereas in the aftermath of the Mexican-American War, slave patrols surfaced to police African American bodies in the South, Chinese inspectors emerged to monitor, threaten, and criminalize mobile Chinese residents in the American West.[104] Employed by the Chinese Bureau of the Customs Service and the Chinese Division of the Office of the Superintendent of Immigration, these inspectors functioned as the regional arm of federal enforcement. The duties of Chinese inspectors—who are predecessors to the Immigration and Naturalization Service (INS) and Immigration and Customs Enforcement (ICE)—drew them well beyond the ports and border checkpoints of national boundaries and into inland communities like Riverside. The Geary Act had expanded immigration enforcement from the U.S. border to the U.S. interior. Although the inspectors' jurisdiction was restricted to surreptitious border crossings, a 1916 federal ruling would later determine that the act of transit could be defined as up to two hundred miles north of the border. This act codified in law what inspectors were already adopting in practice: the broad criminalization of Chinese mobility through federal allowances practiced at the regional level.[105]

Of particular importance to understanding the criminalization of Chinese residents in California is the work of Inspector John Putnam, "the most thorough, as well as most daring officer of their peculiar service in ferreting out and deporting Chinese unlawfully within the United States."[106] A Connecticut-born transplant who held political office in Wisconsin, Putnam moved to California after he was appointed to the position in 1898. His jurisdiction included the 12,000 Chinese immigrants living from San Luis Obispo to Fresno, and covered all of Southern California with the exception of San Diego. He would hold this position until his death in 1904.[107] Distant from the port of San Francisco, where the majority of Chinese nationals were processed, seditious inland immigration originating from the U.S.-Mexico border crossing at San Diego was Putnam's primary concern. He boasted: "Chinamen now and then come into the country from Mexico, walking across the border without hindrance. As soon as they reach Los Angeles they are picked up and deported, for their characteristics quickly betray that they are newcomers."[108] Chinese immigrants increasingly entered California by way of Mexico, where Mexican authorities encouraged the growth of Chinese laborers.[109] Putman prioritized immigration enforcement along these migrant circuits, which took him into the long-standing Chinese communities of the Southern California interior, over a hundred miles north of the border. Maintaining the line between citizen and alien was no longer reserved for national borders. Immigration enforcement was increasingly a regional matter and it was on the regional scale that technologies policing Chinese mobility manifested.

Transformed by immigration law, the circuitous nature of Chinatown now offered a means for federal agents to criminalize Chinese residents and their movements at the regional level. Legally, the Chinese Exclusion Act exempted middle class and elite professionals, including merchants. The Customs Department defined a merchant as a person involved in buying and selling goods, at a "fixed place of business," conducted in one's name, and at no time engaging in manual labor. Although Chinese businesses were concentrated in the segregated spaces of Chinatowns, what might be called the "fixity requirement" did not account for business activities between and beyond Chinese migrants' accepted racial geography. By linking exemptions to fixed space, merchant status became a grey area open to interpretation by the court. That is, if a Chinese inspector found a Chinese merchant while he was in an act of movement, the inspector could initiate the merchant's deportation. The travel necessary for everyday transactions in Chinese-dominated employment, such as laundry delivery, vegetable peddling, and migrant fieldwork, potentially placed Chinese people in the unprotected category of laborer, regardless of their class status. Since few occupations were clearly fixed or unfixed, the Geary Act created an opening by which inspectors such as Putnam could use broad discretion to initiate deportation proceedings against virtually any Chinese resident, even those exempt from the law. In the Citrus Belt, federal immigration law and regional racialization combined to criminalize Chinese merchants who engaged in farming.

Channeling the natural irrigation of the Santa Ana River, Chinese residents had carved a regional niche in growing and delivering fresh vegetables. Federal records of Chinese residents seeking return certificates, granting them federal permission to return to the United States after visiting China, provide an archive of these endeavors. For example, less than two miles from San Bernardino, Sam Gong worked as a foreman at the Quong Chong Yuen ranch. The farm consisted of fifty acres and employed eleven men who cultivated the vegetables. Hom Oie, another farmer, worked as a vegetable gardener for ten years on a plot in Colton. His sixty-acre plot, Get Sing Gardens, cost him and his two partners $11 a month in rent. In Redlands, Lee Quong managed an eighty-acre vegetable lot with nine partners. Having grown the vegetables from seed, he valued the land between $3,000 and $4,000 dollars.[110] Unlike the citrus endeavors of eastern migrants that required high start-up costs ($3,500) and several years of financing (three to five years) before producing mature fruit, Chinese farmers could grow vegetables like lettuce and celery within months.[111]

The selective tradition of the navel orange claimed that white migrants better utilized land than the nonwhite people who had previously occupied it. However, the exclusivity of these claims was vulnerable to competing endeavors by Chinese growers, whose agricultural success proved they too could transform the landscape into fertile farmland. Rather than include Chinese farmers within agricultural visions of the citriscape, symbolic divisions separated Asian and white farmers. Court transcripts of immigration officials' interviews with Chinese cultivators show they commonly referred to Chinese-operated vegetable plots as "gardens."[112] Conversely, officials invariably referred to orange orchards managed by white operators as "ranches." In the early years of citrus cultivation, the stratification between vegetable "gardeners" and citrus "ranchers" served as a racial boundary between Asian and white.[113] In inland Southern California, the discursive divisions between vegetable gardening and citrus ranching would double as a legal distinction between exempt residents and deportable aliens.

United States of America vs. Wong Fong

The Geary Act institutionalized a system that dispossessed Chinese farmers of long-term agricultural investments and served as a warning to those pursuing a similar path. The case of Wong Fong, a Riverside merchant who co-managed Chow Kee and Company, is illustrative of how the Geary Act deterred Chinese merchants from becoming farmers. Like other Chinatown merchants, Fong was exempt from the otherwise expansive and harsh immigration laws excluding Chinese laborers from the United States. Following the reconstruction of his Chinatown store, which had burned down, Fong temporarily visited China. Although the Geary Act had passed by the time of his November 9, 1893 departure, there was not yet a state office where Chinese residents subject to the act could register. Moreover, the question of the act's constitutionality still remained open. Regardless, by maintaining his interest in Chow Kee and Company, Fong should have retained his exempt status as a merchant. Building on his investment in the store, Fong returned to Riverside, where he signed a lease and agreed to co-manage a 120-acre farm below Chinatown near the Santa Ana River in August of 1895. However, soon afterwards, he was accused by Inspector Putnam of being a laborer subject to deportation for living without a certificate of residence.[114]

Although a merchant, Fong's exemption from the Geary Act was reversible when he embarked on agricultural pursuits reserved for Anglo Americans in the Citrus Belt. On his farm, Fong operated in a management position that echoed the responsibilities of many citrus ranchers. He employed Chinese laborers to plant, plow, and harvest his crops. Assuming his business was at least as busy as neighboring gardens, Fong's plot would have needed four wagon teams to deliver his vegetable yield each day.[115] As manager, Fong handled the bills, supplied provisions for his workers, and supervised sales. However, it was during his general operations as a manager that he was arrested: Inspector Putnam stopped Fong while attaining a vegetable wagon license and placed him under arrest as a laborer without a certificate of residence. His targeting by Putnam as a wagon driver was not unique. That Chinese immigrants could not be both merchants and mobile underscores the broad jurisdiction under which Chinese inspectors could evoke arrest under the Geary Act.[116]

Chinese farmers facing trial as a result of the Geary Act found themselves reliant on white allies to differentiate themselves from manual laborers subject to mandatory registration. In accordance with the law, burden of proof no longer lay with the immigration officials, but with Chinese residents. Fong could not rely on his own testimony for his defense. Chinese testimony was viewed as incompetent and subject to enhanced burden of proof when bearing witness under federal law. Since he was under trial for a residence card violation, Fong was required to provide testimony by non-Chinese witnesses.[117]

Fong called upon his landlord, Pliny Evans of the Riverside Land and Irrigating Company. Evans benefited heavily from Chinese payments and it was in his interest to protect Fong's lease. Speaking in Fong's defense, Evans explained:

I wouldn't consider a man that rents 120 acres a farmer, I would consider him a rancher. Rancher and farmer are two different things. He was a rancher, we are all ranchers in that section. I am a rancher. . . . When I speak of [the] defendant being a rancher I mean that he rents some land, [he is the] overseer of the ranch. Undoubtedly the defendant does work about his ranch, the same as we all do up there.[118]

Implicit in Evan's testimony is an attempt to defend Fong by distancing him from Chinese "farmers" and instead emphasizing his "rancher" status, a term imbued with racial and class signifiers. For the court, the line became a legal one. The decision to include or exclude Chinese merchants within the definition of "rancher" meant the difference between giving elite Chinese immigrants access to capitalist agriculture or deporting those who tried to cultivate crops as violators of the Geary Act.

The court defended the latter option. Despite the mountain of evidence in Fong's defense, federal district judge Olin Wellborn found Fong guilty and subject to deportation.[119] An appeal was filed challenging the judge's decision. It asserted that Fong had not lost his status as a merchant and that his status was unaffected by his farming endeavors. After more than a year in detention, Fong was released following the reversal of Wellborn's decision.[120] Nevertheless, Putnam had grown emboldened. With the court's early support, he did not hesitate to continue arresting Chinese residents allowed legal entry to the United States.[121] As noted by historian Grace Delgado, deportation decisions driven by anti-Chinese politics marked admission into the United States as conditional, temporary, and easily withdrawn.[122] In inland Southern California, threats of forced deportation reaffirmed a difference between white and Chinese agriculturalists in ways that delineated property and regional forms of movement along racial lines. For white colonists, agricultural pursuits affirmed their claims to the region. For Chinese residents, to pursue agricultural development, to own a farm, to encroach on a pursuit defined solely as white, was to risk expulsion from the country.

FRUITS OF OUR LABOR: ROOSEVELT, RACE SUICIDE, AND THE NAVEL ORANGE

It was a spring morning in May of 1903 when the long-anticipated president arrived in California. The *Riverside Daily Press* followed the president's journey closely. The primary newspaper of the "home of the navel orange" reported frequently on his schedule, speeches, and the latest plans of the president's welcoming committee.[123] The members had spent months organizing a welcome worthy of a war hero-turned-politician, including a parade featuring marching bands, state politicians, and members of the infamous Rough Riders. Though it was his first visit to California, Roosevelt had built his public identity on his image as a rugged frontiersman. Famously marching up Kettle Hill in the Battle of San Juan, Roosevelt was celebrated for his indomitable courage. Like the frontiersmen who expanded the American nation in the *Winning of the West,* a four-volume history of western expansion, "Colonel" Roosevelt relived the frontier saga he had long admired by asserting U.S. dominance in the battlefields of the Caribbean. For Roosevelt, and for indeed many of his contemporaries, the journey across the western frontier represented the origin of a distinctly American race.[124] Tracing the steps of early European American migrants in a thoroughly modern fashion, Roosevelt traveled across the American West by train as he visited towns, met with local residents, and commemorated monuments during his western tour.[125]

Combining Frederick Jackson Turner's frontier ideology with evolutionary science, Roosevelt believed the American race was forged through racial conflict in the West, and that in each successful battle it progressed towards a more advanced state of being. But he feared that the higher racial class of U.S.-born citizens descending from Anglo-Saxons was at risk of extinction in a process known as "race suicide." The ease of industrial capitalism and immigrant population growth, he warned, led down a road ending in degeneration. In other words, life was now too easy in the East, making once-hardy white immigrants on eastern shores soft and weak. Where the heroes of the frontier era once guarded the hereditary key to success, their descendants now risked an uncertain future of racial decline. The burgeoning fields of the American West offered a source of relief. If eastern industry promoted the survival of unfit immigrants and decorous gentlemen, western agricultural capitalism might preserve the fertility and virility of white Americans.[126]

For Roosevelt, the residents of Southern California were the descendants of the hardy western pioneer. Throughout his speeches he praised average Californians for their role in developing the nation. In the first of these addresses, held in Barstow, Roosevelt congratulated residents for continuing the early westerners' efforts by building new cities and preserving the state's natural beauty. In Redlands, he addressed the crowd as model Americans, proclaiming, "You the men of the West, the men pre-eminently American, the men and women who illustrate in their lives exactly those characteristics which we are proudest to consider as typical of our country, I greet you because I am at home with you."[127] By introducing industry, cities, orchards, ranches, and a white citizenry, Roosevelt declared, agricultural communities were "preeminently American."

Upon arriving in Riverside, Roosevelt was guided through a full schedule of events. In a single afternoon, he toured the citrus district, dedicated a palm at the head of Victoria Avenue, and rode downtown in a carriage bedecked with roses. The president's procession culminated at a decorated platform where he addressed the crowd. He praised the beauty of Riverside and its surroundings as a "veritable little paradise."[128] The material prosperity of the city's abundant citrus groves was a striking example of the conservation and irrigation principles he advocated throughout his western visit. For Roosevelt, Riverside was a model of the success possible when the natural resources of the West combined with white American settlers' industry and national investment.

Roosevelt linked the success of the orange-bearing district to the proliferation of the white household. Just as fruit had multiplied in an arid desert, so had American families. Demonstrating their dedication to the fight against race suicide, the Riverside welcoming committee placed white schoolchildren holding flowers and American flags along Roosevelt's parade route. Demonstrations like these, where a chorus of 1,000 students sang "The Star-Spangled Banner" along Main Street, reaffirmed the sexual power of U.S. manhood and the potency of the American nation.[129] It was through fruit that Roosevelt recognized this exchange. During his formal address Roosevelt stated, "I am mighty glad, my fellow citizens, that you do so well with fruits and crops and all that. But . . . I am even more pleased that you are doing well with children."[130] He turned to the schoolchildren and stated, "there is no race suicide here."[131] For Roosevelt, the schoolchildren were the physical embodiment of U.S. development, better breeding practices, and the American nation's stretching hand into the western frontier. That is, white children were the fruit of U.S. empire. Met with applause, the president's statement reflected the link between agriculture and the white household actively seeded by Riverside boosters.

Just a block away from the white schoolchildren, the students from the Sherman Institute were living with the brutal consequences of western expansionism. In truth, avoiding race suicide meant more than better breeding. It required exercising power over "lesser" races and forcing assimilation

President Roosevelt transplanting navel orange tree in courtyard of Mission Inn, 1903. Archibald D. Shamel Papers, Courtesy of Special Collections and University Archives, Tomás Rivera Library, University of California Riverside.

into Anglo American society, practices embodied in the Sherman Institute. As Roosevelt declared in a speech held two days later in Ventura, California:

> [The pioneers] could come here, our people could come here, and conquer this continent only because of the individual worth of the average citizen, because the average pioneer had in him the quality which made him fit to do battle with, and to overcome, wild man and wild nature.[132]

Whether Mexican, African, or Chinese descent residents participated in these events goes unstated. Although several photos document the president's visit, the dense crowds make it hard to discern who attended. What is clear is that they were not included in the official program nor recognized as part of those congratulated for their citizenship.

That evening, Roosevelt attended a banquet held in his honor and stayed at the finest room at the Mission Inn resort. Before departing the following morning, the Riverside Historical Society asked him to participate in the replanting of Riverside's original navel orange tree, the "parent" of the industry that had come to define the region. According to a commemorative issue of the *Citrograph,* a widely read citrus trade publication later published as the *California Citrograph,* this replanting endeared the president to residents more than any other act. Historical Society president John North Jr., son of the Riverside founder, explained, "It is the progenitor of that great industry which has done most to make Southern California famous.... The fruit of this tree is so perfect, its descendants so numerous, its prosperity so great . . . that we believe it merits your unqualified approval."[133] Referring to Roosevelt's work against race suicide, North's comment drew a smile from the president and laughter from the crowd.

The Brazilian trees, like the colonists of Riverside, were simultaneously migrants and pioneers. Although imported, both the navel orange and the citrus ranchers had become synonymous with the region in both local and distant markets. Alternative histories persisted in these communities, but none were recognized as significant traditions by cultural institutions with the means to transform them into regional heritage. Instead, brown bodies became subservient to the pageantry surrounding the navel. By placing the tree in the courtyard of the Mission Inn, the historical society recognized citrus ranchers as the rightful inheritors of California in a narrative celebrating Anglo American migrants' ability to turn a Spanish desert into an American cornucopia. The morning that Roosevelt replanted the tree, several young American Indian boys from the Sherman Institute were called to "wait" upon him. Although their presence has been left out of subsequent accounts, their names—John Ward, Willie Pollard, Stephen Alimos, Camille Ardillo, Clemente Subish, Frank Isle, and Randolph Marservey—serve as a reminder that the pioneer status of Riverside settlers depended on claims to occupied land reorganized through conquest.[134]

As Roosevelt accepted the shovel from the president of the Riverside Historical Society, he stated, "I am glad to see, Mr. North, that *this tree shows no signs of race suicide.*"[135] It is no accident that this statement paralleled the one made the day before by the president in his address. Just as the white children at Roosevelt's parade represented the growth of the American nation into the West, the blooming tree served as a fitting anthropomorphic symbol of Roosevelt's ideal national body. Through Roosevelt's words, "there is no race suicide here," the parent navel tree was transformed from an emblem of Riverside's citrus industry into a model for the superior American race emerging from the combination of frontier mobility, capital expansion, and power over races deemed inferior.[136] The commemoration of the navel orange tree, like the procession the morning before, rewrote regional history and celebrated racial stratification in a drama of imperialism, in this case christened by Colonel Roosevelt himself.

In 1893, historian Fredrick Jackson Turner placed internal migration west-ward at the center of American identity in his infamous essay, "The Significance of the Frontier in American History." By Turnerian logic, west-ern movement across the open continent had transformed a diverse group of European immigrants into American settlers. However, the closure of the frontier and the end of western expansion fundamentally changed the mean-ing of mobility.[137] As nonwhites sought a place within the agricultural economy that dominated inland Southern California, migration and settle-ment would be reimagined from fundamentally American to a racial threat. Selective memory over regional mobility became a battleground through which claims to inland Southern California were contested by Indigenous communities, longtime Mexican residents, white migrants, and Asian immi-grants, among others, who comprised the diverse tapestry of the region.

A decade after Turner presented his frontier thesis, Riverside elites gath-ered in the courtyard of the Mission Inn to celebrate the modern rise of a citrus region and its pioneering founders. Alongside the Spanish Fantasy Past, an Anglo Fantasy Past naturalized bifurcations between migrants and natives, citizens and foreigners, farm laborers and ranch owners. Celebrating the westward migration of Anglo American farmers, regional heritage circu-lated a celebratory narrative of regional development—a white possessive logic—centered on the brave efforts of pioneering farmers to settle on and transform an underutilized desert into a cornucopia. In the hands of Riverside residents, the mission myth transitioned into the myth of the navel orange, emblematic of the rising citrus industry. Accompanying these eco-nomic transformations, selective tradition helped fashion a region based on its primary export. Described as "the beautiful land of sunshine, fruit and flowers," "the garden spot of the continent," and "paradise on earth," the inland valley region of Southern California was so popularly affiliated with oranges, lemons, and grapefruit that it was called the Citrus Belt.[138] The Anglo Fantasy Past gave cultural reference to a process of dominating alter-native subsistence systems in a unilateral tale of progress that attached regional possession to white migrants and disowned those of its earlier occupants.

In the Riverside Colony, migration was imbued with social significance. It was through westward movement that pioneers were separated from Natives and settlers were separated from "late arrivals," most notably in this instance Chinese immigrants.[139] In each case, mobility and settlement inherited starkly divergent racial meanings that reified the hegemony of white settler colonialism. This selective tradition—from state fencing laws to the federal Geary Act—obscured policies of dispossession and repossession privileging internal U.S. migrants. Nevertheless, communities written out of the Anglo Fantasy Past were not complicit in their own erasure. Rather, Indigenous and Mexican-descent people remapped regional history with their bodies, by acts of escape and pilgrimage. Their perseverance stood as an alternative archive to celebratory mythologies of white migration. When their presence proved too threatening, American Indian bodies where pushed out of place, contained, or imprisoned in boarding schools. Concurrently, the regional movements that comprised Chinese residents' daily lives were regulated by municipal planning decisions and federal immigration policy. They too resisted, through refusing to comply with new restrictions, defending in the courts their right to residency, and drawing on white allies. Examined together, internal migration and regional movements reveal the ways selective tradition permeated ideas, policies, and practices of mobility to shape racial formation, as well as the tactics undertaken to oppose this control. The following chapter unpacks the ways subsequent waves of Asian migrants were integrated into a citriscape imagined as white, even as tightening immigration laws heightened citrus ranchers' reliance on increasingly diverse labor migrations.

TWO

On the Move and Fixed in Place

JAPANESE IMMIGRANTS IN THE MULTIRACIAL
CITRUS BELT, 1882–1920

During her stay at Riverside's Mission Inn, popular novelist Gene Stratton-Porter wrote *Her Father's Daughter* (1921), a morality tale centering on the racial tensions between a promising white student, Donald Whiting, and a rising Japanese student, Oka Sayye. As their high school graduation nears, Sayye has surpassed his classmates as the top candidate for valedictorian, leading to a series of conflicts with Whiting. The novel's protagonist, a younger student named Linda Strong, scorns Whiting for allowing Sayye to outperform him: "You and every [white] boy in your class ought to [be] thoroughly ashamed of yourselves. Before I would let a Jap, either boy or girl, lead in my class, I would give up going to school and go out and see if I could beat him at growing lettuce and spinach."[1] With Strong pushing him forward, Whiting is compelled to vie for the honorific title of valedictorian, a competition that inherits significance as a racial and national contest for dominance between Anglo Americans and Japanese nationals.

The stakes embodied in the battle between Sayye and Whiting reflect the insecurity surrounding white racial supremacy in the first decades of the twentieth century. Military victory in the 1905 Russo-Japanese War had secured Japan's role as an imperial power in the eyes of most Americans. Forceful occupation and annexation of Korea, soon afterward, further affirmed Japan's potential as either a helpful ally or a dangerous rival along the Pacific Rim. As potential allies, Japanese immigrants were recognized as members of an advanced nation and celebrated for adopting western standards of dress, English, and Christianity. For instance, when the first Japanese American student was scheduled to graduate from Riverside High School in 1905, he made local headlines that celebrated his accomplishment. Born in Japan, and later becoming a U.S. citizen, Arthur Kaneko was a popular student and an avid athlete, who played on the track and lacrosse teams and held the position of football quarterback. On the day of his graduation, Kaneko was invited to sit on the stage and selected to give a speech on the Japanese nation.[2]

But where the first years of the twentieth century pointed towards the potential for cooperation, the promise of friendship quickly gave way to division from 1906 forward, marked in California by the segregation of Japanese children in public schools, exclusionary property laws, and federal immigration restrictions. It was in this tense climate that Stratton-Porter learned of Kaneko's graduation, fifteen years after the fact. Reflecting growing racial insecurity towards Japan, she would loosely base *Her Father's Daughter* on these events. Stratton-Porter wrote, "When Japan sends college professors to work in our kitchens and relatives of her greatest statesmen to serve our tables, you can depend on it she is not doing it for the money that is paid them."[3] As portrayed in the novel, Japanese immigrants were deemed a surreptitious national menace who should be approached with suspicion.

The passage of the 1882 Chinese Exclusion Act and subsequent rise in Japanese immigration to the United States catalyzed a significant shift in the racial geography and hierarchies of inland Southern California. Although an Anglo Fantasy Past had remapped this multiracial region as white before the end of the nineteenth century, federal immigration policy and the continuing need for labor contributed to the regional labor force's rapid diversification in the first decades of the twentieth. These long-distance global movements to the heart of citrus production created a "contact zone," where people previously separated by geography were now reconstituted alongside one other by the labor demands of commercial citrus.[4] The racial binary of Chinese workers and Anglo managers was destabilized as Japanese, Korean, South Asian, African, and Mexican-descent people moved to the California Citrus Belt. As recent arrivals formed working class multiracial neighborhoods, regional authorities addressed population change by developing new strategies to keep racial minorities in their place.

This chapter is primarily concerned with the racialization of inland Southern California's Japanese population, towards whom the state of California held the most "acute" concern and for whom intersecting scales of criminalization—from the bodily to the federal—starkly shaped experiences of movement and fixity within the region.[5] As the symbolic heart of the Citrus Belt, as well as Southern California's epicenter of Japanese migration, Riverside became the focus of statewide debates over race, place, and mobility.

Examining authorities' hostile attitudes towards Japanese residents reveals the unsettled contradictions of mobility within capitalism at the beginning of the twentieth century. Although global immigration and regional labor migration were essential elements of commercial agriculture, inland communities pathologized Asian mobility in everyday life. Workers were supposed to move in particular ways, at specific times, in and to predetermined spaces. For example, when the navel orange harvest had been completed, Asian workers were expected to rotate to the next crop. This movement represents a "spatio-temporal fix" to the labor surplus created by agriculture's seesaw economy, as the potential for profit making shifted from one crop to another across the seasons.[6]

Within the citrus economy, one's freedom to control one's own mobility presupposed economic autonomy, status as a modern subject, and cultural belonging. As an extension of these presumptions, mobility was infused with racial meaning—with whiteness conferring the right to self-directed movements and the mobility of nonwhites tied to the demands of the crops.[7] When nonwhite workers pursued agency over their own movements, or when they pursued long-term settlement, officials went to great lengths to maintain spatial divisions, utilizing everything from police harassment to the state courts. The most extreme forms of protest were reserved for bodies "out of place," those occupying spaces or exhibiting behaviors that ruptured the myth of racial fixity, which presumed that whites and nonwhites occupied separate spheres. Indeed, settler colonialism has relied on organizing bodies in space in order to maintain the perceived legitimacy of racial distinctions.[8] Whether in times of lean or plenty, multiscalar policies reinforced power hierarchies in everyday life by regulating nonwhite mobility.

This chapter examines the changing relationship between racialization and mobility in the Citrus Belt following President Roosevelt's 1903 visit to Southern California. It is framed by debates over mobility and spatial fixity between two stringent policies targeting Asian residents: the Chinese Exclusion Act (1882), which restricted laborers' immigration, and the California Alien Land Law (1913), which denied Asian immigrants the right to own property. Specifically, it examines dominant attitudes towards Asian migration in white settler communities, particularly Japanese migration, as well as the range of strategies Asian immigrants developed as they struggled to control their own movements. I investigate the development of multiracial neighborhoods as the citrus labor force diversified in response to the Chinese Exclusion Act, the oscillating celebration and criminalization by local authorities of Japanese bicycling practices, and the movement of a middle class Japanese family into a previously white neighborhood. Focusing on debates over Japanese mobility, these investigations also bring to light variations in whiteness, from the racial insecurities of recent European immigrants and their descendants, to the racial allowances extended to elite Mexican descendants of Californios, to the broad criminalization levied at impoverished white itinerant workers.[9] Viewed together, the three cases explored in this chapter uncover how white elites aimed to manage mobility as a means to maintain a regional racial hierarchy and maintain the prevailing racial contours of the agricultural economy.

FROM CHINATOWN TO MULTIRACIAL CONTACT ZONES

Where the second half of the nineteenth century saw the rise of a regional economic system in which agricultural profit was largely dependent on Chinese immigrants' labor, the end of the century witnessed significant demographic changes that restructured regional race relations. Most notably, a decline in the regional Chinese population resulting from the Chinese Exclusion Act (1882), Geary Act (1892), and a destructive Chinatown fire (1893), shifted racial concerns to other nonwhite groups. In the decade following the Chinese Exclusion Act, inland Southern California's Chinese population dropped by nearly half. This number further declined by a third between 1900 and 1910.[10] Yet, even this stark dip fails to account for the policies' full effect since it does not count migratory Chinese workers, which prior to the act increased one citrus town's total Chinese population from 500 to upward of 2,000 people during the peaks of seasonal labor.[11]

A massive fire in Riverside's Chinatown in 1893 exacerbated the effects of exclusion on the Chinese population. Despite residents' desperate efforts to quench the blaze, the fire caused severe human injuries, $50,000 worth of property damage, and burned 75 percent of Chinatown's commercial and residential buildings. Municipal officials deemed the fire an accident, the unfortunate consequence of an exploded lamp; however, the more accurate cause was the active spatial marginalization of Chinatown, and municipal disinvestment in Chinatown's built environment. When the Chinese population had been pushed from downtown Riverside to the city's periphery about a decade earlier, municipal services had not followed. The nearest hydrant would have required a 1,650-foot hose to reach the community, now located at the city's edge.[12]

Chinese residents adopted various strategies to the hardships they faced in the wake of federal restrictive immigration measures and the Chinatown fire exacerbated by municipal neglect. Some chose to leave the United States altogether, returning to China with whatever savings they had mustered. Others moved to urban centers, particularly Los Angeles, where they invested in alternative ventures, including laundries, grocery stores, and meat markets. In the State of California between 1890 and 1910, the Chinese population fell precipitously in rural areas, from 33,718 to 11,986 residents. This solidified what in 1890 had only been a *slight* urban settlement bias. Merchants who remained inland carved a niche as intermediaries between ranchers and newly recruited Japanese, Korean, South Asian, African, and Mexican-descent populations.[13]

Responding to U.S. immigration restrictions on China as well as the termination of the Hawaiian contract labor system, ranchers reimagined the transnational circuits of the Pacific Rim as conduits for inland citrus labor. Hawaii became the most important of these nodes. Japanese workers were heavily recruited to the islands in the 1880s. Hawaii's workforce further diversified as Korean, Portuguese, Filipino, and Puerto Rican workers entered the agricultural market, most frequently in sugar cane production. California ranchers drew heavily from these migrant flows. Hawaii became a central node in a larger imperial system funneling labor from U.S. colonies to expanding West Coast industries.[14] Beckoned by the Orange Empire—a collection of regions throughout the world dedicated to orange production and connected through commercial exchange—transnational circuits formed between East Asia and Hawaii stretched to Southern California.[15]

As growers eagerly sought new circuits of labor, the tri-county area as a whole—Los Angeles, Riverside, and San Bernardino—diversified. According to Census records, the Japanese, Korean, South Asian, Mexican, and African American populations grew throughout the region at this time. But their proportions grew unevenly. In Los Angeles County, for instance, the combined Asian population (2.2 percent) closely matched the concentration of foreign-born Mexicans (2.3 percent) and slightly exceeded that of African Americans (1.9 percent). Conversely, Asian residents comprised a notably larger share of the population in San Bernardino and Riverside Counties than in Los Angeles County. For instance, in San Bernardino County, the combined

Asian population comprised 3.4 percent of the populace, while foreign-born Mexicans were the nonwhite majority at 8 percent. In Riverside County, it was the Asian population that comprised the nonwhite majority, at 7.4 percent, followed distantly by the foreign-born Mexican population, who still held a notable population proportion at 4.8 percent, outpacing that of Los Angeles. The differences in immigration patterns between the Mexican and Asian population can be attributed to the relative importance of rail versus agricultural industries in each county, in which laborers were recruited to San Bernardino County from northern Mexico and migrant currents were drawn to Riverside County from the Pacific Rim. Paralleling African American population trends in Los Angeles County, where they comprised a small proportion of the nonwhite population, African Americans held a slightly smaller share of the county populations in both Riverside (1.5 percent) and San Bernardino (1.1 percent). Yet, Riverside County (4.6 percent) and San Bernardino County (1 percent) held a higher Indigenous population than Los Angeles County (0.01 percent).[16] Taken together, it is evident that compared to Los Angeles County, Riverside and San Bernardino Counties held far larger nonwhite populations, each with variations in demographic composition. The fruits of a Los Angeles metropolis envisioned as a "white spot" depended upon a hinterland of nonwhite workers.[17]

As the citriscape's racial borders were disrupted by diverse migrants' fluidity, maps reasserted spatial and racial fixity. This is most evident in the City of Riverside, where 75 percent of the county's Japanese population resided.[18] Prior to the tightening of the Chinese Exclusion Act through the Geary Act (1892), informal place designations had delineated Asian spaces from the rest of Riverside, such as "Chinese Quarter" and "Chinatown." Yet, these earlier "geographies of difference" were not officially designated in the city's formal geography.[19] In Riverside, for instance, Sanborn maps—detailed block-by-block town maps prepared for insurance companies—identified individual buildings by race, with designations such as Chinese, Chinese boardinghouse, or Chinese dwelling written on top of built structures. However, they did not apply racial categorizations to neighborhoods *as a whole* prior to 1892.[20] It was only as the workforce diversified that racial-spatial designations emerged in Sanborn maps, thus reifying the racial meanings attributed to particular places.

Critical cartographers have used the term "posting" to refer to a spatial proposition expressed in the sign plane of a map. For instance, the demarcation of a mountain range on a map does not reflect an uncontested truth about the existence of such a site. That is, where a range begins or ends or the very distinction of a range as a separate entity from its surroundings is not a passive geographic truth. In the same way, when a set of water systems with forks and bends are mapped/signed as comprising a single river, they are not in and of themselves coherent. Rather, the cartographer proposes to the viewer the existence of such a place in the physical topography of the world. By recognizing postings as propositions about not only space, but also race, we can recognize how the circulation of signs on maps promote particular power relations.[21]

The first significant instance of what I call a "racial posting"—or a spatial proposition of race expressed in a map—occurred in the aftermath of the Chinatown fire, when city planners designated Chinatown's main thoroughfare as "Mongol" Avenue. Sanborn maps further revised its representation of the district by designating the neighborhood as a singular "Chinatown" (on the map published in 1895). The change was accompanied by growth in residential areas throughout the city that were defined by the ethnicity of their occupants, including "Japanese shacks," "Japanese shanties," and "Korean settlement" (as signed in 1908).[22] That no such spaces existed for Mexican and African American populations at this time can only be partly attributed to the lower population figures of these groups. Much more to the point is the white preoccupation with Asian populations in West Coast communities at this time.[23] Mapmaking is always a process that creates meaning, most frequently in accordance with dominant interests. Where racial residential boundaries were in flux, maps emerged as a way to actively construct factuality. By naming sites through racial postings, the city's racial geography was not only known, but propositioned.

It was when racial lines in physical space were the most fluid that official demarcations of racial difference were the most necessary for maintaining cultural hegemony. By 1895, racial postings proliferated, reaffirming racial boundaries and the perception of fixity at points of multiracial rupture. Where official maps suggest minoritized groups occupied distinct spaces, city directories detailing the addresses of households and businesses provide contradictory evidence, suggesting instead that these populations were spread throughout the city. In the years between the Geary Act and the Gentlemen's Agreement (1907), in which Japanese and Korean labor migration was restricted in a bilateral agreement with the United States, city directories grew to include dozens of sites rented, owned, and occupied by Asian- and Spanish-surnamed people.[24] This aligns with the work of Asian American Studies scholars who have asserted "Chinatowns" were never homogenously Chinese, but rather places of multiracial congregation. As demonstrated in the case of

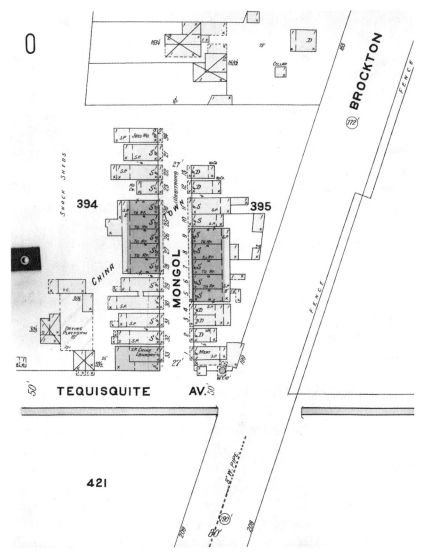

Insurance map of "China Town," Riverside, 1908. Courtesy of the Sanborn Map Collection, Riverside Metropolitan Museum, Riverside, California.

Riverside, Chinatown was an ideological designation aiming to reify race through the myth of spatial fixity, or the falsehood that nonwhite bodies occupied distinct places and that white spaces were wholly homogeneous.[25]

Flattening the multiracial contours of the city, cartographic representations of racial sameness obscure the shared structural conditions that concentrated nonwhites in particular places. Japanese and Korean immigrants arriving in Southern California after 1892 now encountered a dense city rather than the small colony of earlier years, and they founded small settlements throughout the town. Yet, Asian, Mexican, and African American migrants' residential choices were still shaped by economic limitations and racial discrimination.[26] Cost, city ordinances, and preexisting networks pushed people of color along particular circuits of settlement. Riverside's central downtown, the northern agricultural fields, the Eastside district, and the Casa Blanca neighborhood each served as fertile areas for these recent arrivals.[27] As remembered by Alice Kanda, a Japanese woman whose family resided and owned a store in Casa Blanca, "My mother learned to speak Spanish before she even learned to speak English."[28] Resultant of what historian Kornel Chang has called "double movements," or border crossings that integrate formerly disparate regions and populations into American empire, acculturation in multiracial spaces required a different set of demands than that of the city as a whole.[29] Japanese in origin and American in residence, the Kanda family established a home in a multiracial area of diverse interactions characterized by clashes, collaborations, and new complexities produced by empire.

Riverside's racialized geographies reconstituted formerly discrete groups into new contact zones that aggregated previously separated populations alongside one another. Foremost, contentious national identities remained strong between Japanese and Korean immigrants. This strain reflected Japan's imperial hold on Korea shortly following the Russo-Japanese War, when Japan occupied Korea under a colonial regime (1910–1945).[30] Nevertheless, at the federal and state levels, U.S. government officials did little to differentiate them. Census figures separated Chinese, Japanese, and "Indian" populations originating from Asia in its state composition datasets, but made no such demarcation for Korean people. Likewise, a major statewide study of Asian-descent residents by the governor's office, *California and the Oriental: Japanese, Chinese, and Hindus* (1922), made little effort to discuss Korean immigrants as a group distinct from Japanese immigrants. The aggregation of Japanese and Korean populations by U.S. government officials makes it hard to determine if or how Korean residents were racialized differently from Japanese residents. Both the Japanese and Korean populations were limited in where they could live, economically segmented to manual labor, and denied the opportunity to naturalize. Nonetheless, local mappings, oral accounts of early Riverside, and newspaper records suggest that white racism did not fully overshadow internal tensions among Southern California's Asian population.

Tense colonial relationships exacerbated Japanese and Korean interactions, which materialized as rifts ranging from avoiding eye contact in the streets to public assertions of nationalism. Further, Korean residents formed their own labor bureau separate from that of Japanese contractors. Boldly printed in the local paper, an ad by the Korean labor bureau proclaimed, "Give us a trial and we will convince you that we are not afraid to work."[31] In another example, Korean workers publicly rejected aid from the local Japanese consulate and the Riverside Japanese Association. In a high-profile case of vigilante action, Korean workers recruited for farm work in nearby Hemet were violently confronted at the train depot by a hundred white laborers, who protested their arrival, since they were offered lower wages than those earned by white workers previously employed in the fields. Where the Riverside Japanese Association moved to become the public voice and source of restitution for the event, implicitly asserting Japan's authority over Korea, the victims of the assault strongly rejected Japanese jurisdiction over Koreans living in the United States.[32] If Anglo America lumped Asian migrants under the singular racial category of "yellow peril," Asian inhabitants themselves rearticulated distinct national identities that suggest the ongoing impact of colonialism originating in the Pacific world. Yet, the social identities Asian migrants brought with them would face new pressures when encountering ubiquitous trials of racialization levied at them in inland Southern California.[33]

Regardless of struggles within migrant populations, these conflicts paled in comparison to the systematic oppression levied at newly settled Asian, Mexican, and African American populations as a whole. Upon arriving in Riverside, residents deemed nonwhite encountered strict expectations about where they were allowed to move and where they were allowed to stay. These boundaries were reinforced by police harassment, state policies, and daily conflicts with other local residents. That is, the fluidity of global migration was met by policies and practices enforcing local immobilities. In their everyday lives, nonwhite migrants navigated a complex mental map of routes to be taken and avoided. Routes were shaped by the accumulated knowledge of where criminalization or harassment were most likely to occur, from fines for bicycling downtown to the risk of deportation for vending vegetables on public roads. Racial hierarchies were enforced and developed in the multiple ways residents were told how they could or could not move, whether in daily travel or when creating a home.[34] Concerted efforts were made by municipal forces to ensure nonwhites remained strategically immobile.

Although nonwhite residents lived throughout the city, they were concentrated in districts with little municipal investment and located at far distances from county resources. Mary Paik Lee's autobiographical description of her family's Riverside sojourn is a rare window into the experience of Asian migrants entering the Citrus Belt at the beginning of the twentieth century. Her parents emigrated from Korea, labored on a Hawaiian sugar plantation, and relocated to Riverside where they opened a kitchen catering to Korean workers. Lee recalled her first impression of the community's spatial outlines following her arrival: "The Japanese, Chinese, and Mexicans each had their own little settlement outside of town. My first glimpse of what was to be our camp was rows of one-room shacks, with a few water pumps here and there and little sheds for outhouses."[35] Even as a child, the racial contours of Riverside were vividly apparent to Lee. Like other Korean migrants who arrived in California, Lee's family lived in housing originally constructed for Chinese rail workers in the 1880s.[36] The residents' countries of origin may have changed, but racial lines and unequal access to quality housing were stubbornly persistent.

Often located on the outskirts of town, residents of multiracial neighborhoods had little access to public transportation. Poor roads further inhibited personal movement between the margins of the city and its center. For instance, in October 1905, residents of Casa Blanca—located about two miles south of downtown—held a neighborhood meeting in an effort to draw attention to the "long-suffering quarter" and the "deplorable conditions" faced by its residents.[37] In a letter reprinted in the *Riverside Daily Press,* resident Sam Hayward protested the lack of educational, postal, transportation, police, and fire services accessible to the roughly 300 residents. Among his grievances, distance from municipal resources was foremost. Hayward wrote,

Our children have to walk—rain or shine—two miles to school. If you want to receive or post a letter you have to walk from one-half to three-quarters of a mile. . . . If you should be waylaid or assaulted, you don't have to cry for help because Eighth and Main is too far away. If you should be belated and forgot your lantern, you must take your chances as to chuck-holes, hitching posts, brush, etc.[38]

The racialization of spaces like Casa Blanca, as well as Arlington, Chinatown, and the Eastside, held deep material costs for all of their residents, including white residents such as Hayward. But they were unevenly distributed by race, which shaped residents' housing options, where they could work, and how they were received outside of the district. The multiracial workforce living in these districts were immobilized by lack of transportation and physical separation from municipal resources. Although the nonwhite population had grown and housing opportunities increased, legacies of disinvestment first levied at Chinese laborers were newly reproduced in Riverside's multiracial geography.

Central to the challenges faced by residents like those in Casa Blanca was the dialectic of spatial marginalization and mobility. As an agricultural community, movement was an absolute necessity for employment. Farmworkers living within Riverside were required to migrate to nearby farms and orchards, but the primary sites of residence for nonwhite laborers were frequently located notable distances from areas of employment. Further, since field work and harvests occur on rotation, with certain crops requiring attention at different times of the year, workers' transportation needs shifted frequently. Complicating regional mobility, public transportation options were limited. For instance, the Pacific Electric Railway, or Red Car, traveled between cities, but reaching areas of employment outside of towns required moving from public railways to other means of transport.[39] That is, workers were largely dependent on private transportation, from walking to riding a bicycle.

But each mode of travel offered divergent opportunities and costs. Wages were not standardized across fields, and workers with the highest personal mobility were the best situated to identify where maximum pay was being offered and to shift location as prices climbed. Conversely, those with low personal mobility became a captive labor force, whose options were limited to employment opportunities within their local spatial network. For instance, many residents of Casa Blanca worked at the nearby rock quarry, and residents of Mount Vernon in San Bernardino were frequently employed at the adjacent facilities of the Santa Fe Railroad. Mobility had material benefits that could expand the circumference of industries in which a worker could participate. Immobility was accompanied by limited employment opportunities, reinforced by governmental patterns of spatial disinvestment.

RACING RIVERSIDE WHEELMEN AND JAPANESE BICYCLISTS

Cycling was a celebrated way of life in Riverside, where clubs from throughout Southern California met in highly attended spectacles of athletic prowess. By the 1890s, the city was a heralded center of the sport. Ideal for long-distance riding, Riverside's city roads were described by the *Land of Sunshine* magazine "as the finest thoroughfares" in the region.[40] The Riverside Wheelmen—the city's principal cycling club—claimed a membership twice as large as any other in the southern counties. As described in an issue of the *Overland Monthly* (1896), "All the early racing men in Southern California outside of the few at Los Angeles were Riversiders and wore the orange and black [team uniform]."[41] Each September beginning in 1892, clubs from throughout Southern California arrived by train to participate in Riverside's annual invitational meet, whose route stretched from the city center, south to Temecula, and west to Los Angeles. Races were preceded by decorative parades in the downtown Mile Square, where participants were greeted with fanfare. For those seeking a thrill, speed races were held in the newly constructed Athletic Park, which had replaced Southern California's first cycling track, also in Riverside. It was equipped with the most modern advances in racing and spectatorship, including a specially prepared surface, spectator stands, training quarters, dressing rooms, showers, and a ladies' parlor.[42]

From the rise of breakfast cereal and nutritional science to the founding of the Boy Scouts, the decades spanning the beginning of the twentieth century were marked by a popular interest in fitness and health. Athletic skill was a primary means through which white men expressed racial supremacy and male dominance, particularly as prevailing ideals of manhood faced new challenges, such as narrowing middle class career opportunities, the Women's Suffrage Movement, and immigrant workers' electoral advances. In response, displays of male and racial dominance in sporting and fitness competitions—from bodybuilding to fasting—surged during the Progressive Era (1890–1920). Like other health debates at the time, bicycle advocates promoted ideologies of white racial supremacy that assumed a sharp contrast between Caucasians' physical prowess and that of primitive outsiders deemed unable to exhibit control over their own bodies. In Riverside, a cycling epicenter, the tensions between white supremacy and racial insecurity would clash on the track.[43]

In 1893, the League of American Wheelmen (LAW), which oversaw the national rules and regulations of bicycle racing, drew a color line explicitly denying membership to African American cyclists. This led to the creation of separate leagues, a pattern of segregation that fit other sports at the time, most prominently baseball, with its National League.[44] National racial exclusions targeting African American riders found further articulation in the Southwest, where bicycling was so thoroughly internalized as a white sport that this racial principle did not need to be articulated in formal guidelines.

Members of the Riverside Wheelmen cycling club, 1896. Courtesy of the Photograph Collection, Riverside Metropolitan Museum, Riverside, California.

Even after California's withdrawal from LAW, neither race ledgers nor press reports detailing the roster of Riverside Wheelmen activities included Asian or Spanish-surnamed people. This reflected a more stringent practice than other leagues in the region, a minority of which included Spanish-surnamed men. However, where minimal allowances were made for Latinos, none were made for Asian cyclists.[45]

This exclusion was heightened by the location of the Athletic Park track, a stone's throw east of Chinatown. Although a minority of independent groups supported a color-blind model of ridership and nonwhite cyclists formed their own leagues, racing was a racially exclusive activity associated with white sportsmen and legitimized by admiring spectators, celebratory press accounts, and commercial sponsorships.[46] Nevertheless, nonwhite men actively engaged these racial-gender constructs in order to position themselves within the realm of power, authority, and civilization imbued in turn-of-the-century ideals of manhood. And when they did, they often evoked strong responses from the white public, ranging from inclusion to incarceration.

Bicycling remained popular in Riverside from 1891 to 1900, but quickly declined among elite circles as the automobile was adopted for touring and as beloved local cyclists retired from the sport.[47] Where bicycles had previously embodied the pinnacle of modernity and progress for their novelty, speed, and symbolic forward motion, their accessibility across social strata in subsequent years enmeshed the bicycle in working class and nonwhite mobilities. It was when cycling lost its cache to motor racing in the first decade of the twentieth century that competitive cycling among Japanese residents reached a climax. Its rise paralleled the bicycle's popularity in Asia, where manufacturers had begun producing bicycles for domestic markets. Japan was at the forefront of Asian production, later followed by India and China. Japan eagerly adopted the bicycle: consuming foreign imports, establishing sporting goods and repair shops, developing Japanese-branded bicycles, and equipping the national army with the western technology. Popular among the middle class, bicycles remained an aspirational item for the rural poor.[48]

Japanese bicycling athletics were particularly significant for Japanese-American relations in a period when the United States linked sports to national strength.[49] The *Riverside Wheel* had earlier underscored the link between cycling, nationhood, and modernity when it reported that Chinese diplomats and the Japanese Minister of Mails had adopted cycling in 1895, noting, "Now who says the Chinese are behind the times?" and "The Japs are up-to-date."[50] This narrative placed Asians at the margins of bicycling culture at the same time it drew attention to their participation. Nevertheless, bicycling became an important practice in demonstrating Japanese sportsmen's equal footing with U.S. athletes, as Meiji Japan (1868–1912) adopted western markers of culture in an assertion of modernity, masculinity, and nationalism.[51]

With funding from the Riverside Japanese Association, which promoted community relations and commerce, Japanese cyclists completed a new track on Adams Street between Magnolia and California Avenues in November of 1905. The track itself was three-eighths of a mile in circumference and banked on the curves to increase riding speeds. Like the Wheelman's now-retired Athletic Park, a grandstand and clubhouse were built beside the raceway. Located four miles south of Athletic Park, the Adams Track's proximity to the Japanese camp of the Arlington Heights Fruit Company suggests both a spatial and a symbolic claim to the sport by Japanese residents.[52]

Where cycling had once served as a stage for praising white male athleticism, the decline in its popularity created an opening for Japanese immigrants already socialized in the sport's merits when living in Japan. That is, the exclusionary practices of white wheelmen and their fans in previous years now dissipated as motorsports fulfilled the early role of the bicycle as a symbol of white modernity and manhood. Rather than resistance, the local media announced the Adams Track's inaugural race with zeal. As described by the *Riverside Daily Press,* "The Japanese are enthusiastic sportsmen, and particularly enthusiastic bicycle riders, and as they promise a revival of the old sport which one time was so popular in Riverside their first race meet will undoubtedly be attended by an interested crowd of spectators."[53]

The event represented a high point in Japanese-Anglo relations, a moment when Riverside's Japanese population successfully recruited white support by capitalizing on residents' fondness for bicycling. For instance, the press predicted exciting races and local merchants supported the event by donating generous prizes, including cash, clothing, and bicycle supplies. The track's opening further interested a broad cross section of regional residents, who anticipated colorful Japanese customs and American fanfare. Riverside socialites held a well-documented fascination with Japanese arts and culture that was reflected in their enthusiasm for the event.[54]

The nationalist contours of the track's dedication were quite explicit. The inaugural race was planned as the closing event in a gala honoring the birthday of the Meiji emperor, a celebrated leader who advanced capitalist industrialization and Japanese expansion in the Pacific. Although Asian immigrants shared racialization, western nations uniquely recognized Japan as advanced in military prowess, education, and commerce. The gala embraced the potential for a friendly alliance between the two nations, celebrating Japan-U.S. relations with music by the Sherman Institute's military band, including both the U.S. and Japanese national anthems, and hailing three cheers for the U.S. president and Japanese emperor. Even Riverside's mayor presented an address praising the emperor. The formal speakers' program was followed by a display of Japanese arts and technology, including an opera celebrating international relations and daytime fireworks. The festivities themselves were held in the downtown Loring Theater, a popular venue for regional events located at the heart of the city. Although the mayor, county officials, and their "American friends" were all in attendance, the event's stakes were highest for Japanese residents, who simultaneously represented the Japanese nation-state and sought recognition as peers by middle class white Americans.[55]

Reinforcing the focus on Japanese-American relations inscribed in the birthday gala, the cycling meet was a tool for renegotiating Japanese residents' place in the city and reaffirming the position of Japan as a global power alongside the United States. At a time when Asian immigrants were broadly denied U.S. citizenship by federal law, riding a bicycle was a practice in "cultural citizenship," in which groups could claim community belonging and self-definition.[56] It is no accident that five out of the six races planned for the inaugural celebration were restricted to Japanese participants. Only the last competition was open to all riders, "Japanese, Americans, Indians, and even Russians."[57] This race too, as all the races had been, was officiated by popular Japanese athlete Jimmy Osaki and judged by prominent Japanese residents, including H. Fujii, S. Meto, and Ulysses Kaneko. Newspaper reports confirm that the three top finishers on the multiracial roster were Japanese riders. Races created a forum in which white spectators could witness Japanese sportsmen's skill, and where Japanese men determined the grounds of success.[58]

There is a discernible element of autonomy to moving through public space that is common when racialized bodies ride upon mobile technologies—from African American motorists driving undetected through the racialized geography of wartime Los Angeles to the spectacle of Mexican American lowriders cruising slow and low in contemporary Texas.[59] At times, access to the most cutting-edge forms of travel could literally position Japanese men alongside Anglo men, as happened in the case of a Japanese man named Horabi. Riding a motorbike in a period when even the largest manufacturers produced only a few hundred units a year, Horabi participated in the first motorcycle run out of Riverside in 1907. Positioned in a group photograph alongside white participants, rather than at the margins, Horabi (third from the left in photograph) stands close to the other riders. He is leaning on his bike in full gear, including leather boots, gloves, cap, and goggles. He has a discernable smirk on his face as he gazes directly at the camera. Horabi's fashioning and bodily comportment reflect an intentional styling that embraces signifiers of the modern male subject and accentuate his own agency.[60] Riding a bicycle or motorbike was a cultural tool used by Japanese men to claim athletic equity with white sportsmen, but it was also freeing and exciting for its rider. Choosing the perfect cycle, adorning oneself in the latest gear, and speeding around a curve was a source of pleasure, which could be progressive in its own right.[61]

Participants before first motorcycle run, Riverside, 1907: (left to right) Will Warren, Lynn Watkins, Horabi, Horace Yeakle, Southerd, Harry Kreighbaum, Dee Woodward. Courtesy of the Roy L. Haglund Collection, Riverside Metropolitan Museum, Riverside, California (detail).

Japanese efforts to claim a place in cycling were tied to symbolic systems linking the bicycle to modernity, athleticism, and national belonging. In this regard, the bicycle's associations with western manhood were particularly important to challenging the feminization levied at Asian males, especially in the Pacific Northwest. As described by historian Nayan Shah, the "queer domestic" strategies of Asian immigrants—including shared male housing and feminized occupations like laundry—were habitually denigrated for the ways they defied white domestic norms.[62] On the racing track, Japanese men defied their feminization and were instead celebrated for their power and speed. They rode and were judged alongside white male cyclists, their victories were awarded monetarily, and their successes used to laud Japanese athletic ability. As described by scholars of sports history, activities associated with American identity could become venues for symbolic confrontations that were both social and political in nature. Reaffirming normative masculinity, Japanese cyclists asserted their cultural citizenship as athletic peers to white American men, and as nonsubordinates.[63]

The absence of female riders further suggests the intentional affiliation of Japanese cycling with manhood. This is a departure from bicycling practices in Japan, where bourgeois women rode bicycles in public spaces in claims to modern womanhood. Japan was exceptional among Asian countries in its adoption of cycling among women. For instance, cycling women in Vietnam would not become a common sight until the 1930s and cycling would remain largely an urban male activity in India and China until the 1950s, with the exception of female students.[64] Reflective of the Japanese nation's larger enthusiasm around western products and relations, women's engagement with biking conjures images similar to that of the U.S. "new woman." At both the national and local level, where they had formed their own cycling clubs by the 1890s, white women lobbied to expand the social conventions of respectability into public space through their bicycles. Whereas cycling by elite Japanese women in Japan gestured towards certain forms of political inclusion, a Japanese nation-building project seeking U.S. recognition, in part through immigrants' practice of western domestic norms, continued to hinge on bolstering male superiority through the marginalization of Japanese women in the United States.[65]

Despite initial support, the tension between Japanese nationalist agendas promoting acceptance as a modern nation and Anglo American efforts to maintain regional hegemony would conflict as dominant forces attempted to shape the meaning of Japanese bicyclists' mobility. Inclusion does not necessarily imply equality. Although the press recognized Japanese men's physical abilities, media accounts continued to draw racial lines between Asian men and white men through subtle denigration. News articles diminished Japanese masculinity by referring to cyclists as "boys" and reinforcing their nonwhite racial status as "little brown men." Conversely, the white cyclists of the Riverside Wheelmen had been referred to as "men," "clubmen," and, in some cases, "gentlemen."[66]

In a similar vein, the press now positioned cycling as an "old sport," divorcing it from prior associations with modernity, progress, and technological advancement. Japanese assertions of equity tied to the bicycle were further undermined by press depictions of Japanese men as unable to harness bicycles effectively. Instead, media accounts critiqued Japanese comportment and drew attention to points of chaos, such as a crash that occurred during the inaugural event.[67] Collisions were common in racing, but the uneven focus this one received presupposed Japanese racers' inability to master cycling and suggested they were poor imitators of white riders. Where manliness was equated with a man's ability to control his own body, Japanese men were deemed not only illegitimate as men, but a risk to other cyclists. In the context of global relations between the United States and Japan, the diminutive treatment of Japanese cyclists further reified claims of Anglo American racial superiority.

White Americans and Japanese immigrants leveraged bicycles unequally in the production of racial meaning and cultural citizenship. The limits of Japanese immigrants' ability to claim regional belonging was starkly underscored during World War I, when cycling was aligned with nationalist agendas that promoted health, pleasure, and gas conservation. Experiencing a renewed resurgence among white riders, bicycling events were embraced as a "revival," a return to "the good old days," and as "restoring her [Riverside's] lost cycle glory." Photographs of white cyclists once again adorned the pages of local newspapers, particularly in the patriotic displays of the 1917 and 1918 Bicycle Day parades, a national event hosted regionally in Riverside. After the war, the city held a Victory Parade, in which crowds lined the streets to observe decorated bicycles, military marches, and patriotic floats. Accompanied by cyclists, the floats bore colorful flag displays, members of the American Red Cross, and Lady Liberty escorted by the Boy Scouts of America. These symbolic acts of white participation in cycling as a national exercise overshadowed the continued popularity of bicycles among Japanese residents, whose races never received the popularity of media accounts featuring white cyclists in the 1890s through 1910s. Although active in cycling culture, even receiving awards in Bicycle Day events, recognition of Japanese participation was a whisper compared to the celebration of white participants.[68] The habitual erasure of Japanese cyclists during wartime once again placed the sport squarely within the realm of Anglo America. That it shifted so starkly underlines that the value of bicycling oscillated not with ridership, but according to the rider.

POLICING SUBVERSIVE MOBILITY

If in leisure spaces bicycles enabled athletic and patriotic displays by riders, bicycles served a utilitarian purpose in everyday life. At the turn of the century, bicycling had been an elite activity embraced by an urban middle class who exercised influential lobbying campaigns and conspicuous spending.[69] As the bicycle became more accessible to working class populations, with the development of the more affordable "safety bicycle," agricultural laborers

Japanese bicyclist at Arlington Heights Fruit Co., Riverside, ca. 1880–1920. Courtesy of Riverside Public Library.

increasingly adopted it for daily commuting. Bicycles proved a particularly important resource where multiracial housing was concentrated at the city's edges and commuting was requisite for agricultural employment. Chinese laborers had adopted bicycles for everyday transportation in the Citrus Belt in the 1890s.[70] The bicycle's importance to daily work flows persisted throughout the early twentieth century. Described in 1918 by John R. Gabbert, president of the Riverside Chamber of Commerce, the bicycle was "essential" for "the man who works in the packing houses or citrus groves away from the residence district."[71] At the same time, bicycles threatened to curb the local labor supply in times of greatest need. A person on a bicycle exerted less energy and covered more ground than a person on foot, enabling the rider to identify a larger range of job opportunities and to seek competitive wages in the groves. Bicycling increased what mobility scholars have called the motility—or access to and potential for geographic and social mobility—of agricultural workers. But their motility also created a new set of problems for the citriscape.[72] Even though ranchers and workers shared a means for travel in the bicycle, they often conflicted in the end goal of that movement.

Where workers' control over their own mobility was potentially subversive, institutional structures diligently criminalized Japanese cyclists. This policing was atypical for the Citrus Belt. In the early twentieth century, local media accounts described the Japanese population as exceptionally law-abiding. A review of individual offenses logged in Riverside County Criminal

Dockets from 1897 to 1913—which record criminal proceedings from complaint to judgment—confirms that Japanese residents were rarely prosecuted for violent crimes. Moreover, the actions for which they were arrested yield no discernable pattern.[73] As described by District Attorney Evans in 1912, "Those little brown men steer clear of courts and are not often mixed up in criminal proceedings."[74]

And yet, despite the potential for cooperation displayed at the Japanese emperor's birthday gala and Adams Track's opening races, the following years were marked by distinct backlash directed at the Japanese resident community. At the municipal level, Japanese men riding bicycles were habitually approached by police. Between 1907 and 1913—the years between a binational "Gentlemen's Agreement" banning the immigration of Japanese laborers to the United States and the California Alien Land Law prohibiting Asian immigrants from owning land—over half of all Japanese arrests in Riverside were for bicycle violations (58 percent).[75] If bicycles provided workers some control over their mobility, then bicycle laws allowed local officials the authority to transform that power into a criminal act.

Rendering certain bicycling practices unlawful, practices that were themselves a response to the circular movement of crops, public policy stripped Japanese riders of their full motility power. An important turning point in cycling enforcement came in 1910, when the city council passed a highly publicized ordinance regulating all traffic and travel. The events leading up to the new twenty-page ordinance were closely followed in the press. When passed that May, the ordinance was formally announced in the city's leading paper; hundreds of notices were sent by the mayor to livery stables, garages, and registered vehicle owners; and posters were erected at all major city entrances. Discourses of public safety and police enforcement were underscored. The local press reported that "steps are being taken to see the joy rider and careless motorist are brought to time" and "traffic ordinance violators may not expect to escape arrest and prosecution in Riverside."[76] Although media attention focused on speeding motorists, the ordinance itself, as well as subsequent amendments, heavily regulated commonly held cycling behaviors, such as speeding, racing, riding on sidewalks, and evening cycling without a light. Moreover, the ordinance signaled a new era of police enforcement. Enabled by cutting-edge technologies, the city heightened the police's surveillance capabilities by equipping police with motorcycles "for use in running down" traffic violators, and by extending special privileges to officers, such as requiring all privately owned vehicles (a category inclusive of bicycles) to surrender the right of way.[77] If bicycles and automobiles offered the public new means to navigate the city, they were also met with new forms of governance outlining and managing proper patterns of movement.[78]

Cyclists in multiracial neighborhoods were more vulnerable to traffic restrictions than their cycling counterparts elsewhere. For instance, the same benign neglect that led to the spread of the Chinatown fire contributed to negligent care for roads in multiracial neighborhoods. Places that lacked public lighting or had streets that were unpaved, muddy, uneven, or wet proved particularly dangerous. Thus, cyclists faced with the choice of walking their bicycle along poorly maintained boulevards or riding upon sidewalks had more incentive to choose the latter option, a prohibited practice. Essentially serving as a tax on Japanese cyclists, bicycle penalties placed the burden of uneven infrastructure on riders themselves. If found violating bicycle restrictions, residents were guilty of a misdemeanor and subject to fines ranging from $5 to $100. Adding to the severity of this penalty was imprisonment from ten to thirty days for a first offense. Three or more offenses could levy fines of $100 to $500 and a jail sentence of fifty days to six months.[79] For workers dependent on daily wages, such fines could result in even deeper poverty. Those unable to pay the charges for their deviant movements were subject to imprisonment, one of the most extreme forms of immobility.

When on bicycles, Japanese men became targets for police harassment. Although the original records of these arrests are no longer available, their frequency points towards the systematic targeting of Japanese riders.[80] In his 1977 dissertation on Riverside's Japanese community, sociologist Morrison Wong carefully recorded these arrests. He found that Japanese people were cited for cycling infractions at a rate ranging as high as 22 percent of their share of the population.[81] Research on police enforcement of motor vehicle infractions in later decades show similar disparities in arrest records. For instance, aggressive racial profiling in the 1930s and 1940s resulted in high arrests of Mexican American youth for joyriding, an infraction most commonly enforced when they drove outside of Los Angeles barrios. And, research on post–World War II Washington, DC, found that young African American cyclists routinely faced racially oriented policing, especially when moving from poor African American neighborhoods to affluent white communities. Because the frequency and public nature of such violations placed arrests at police discretion, laws regulating cyclists in Riverside could, likewise, be used to initiate arbitrary harassment, particularly at sites where nonwhites were deemed out of place.[82] Given the racial contours of the citriscape, for instance, Japanese riders may have been most vulnerable to discriminatory enforcement in the downtown business district, where speed limits were the lowest and riding conventions the most staunchly outlined. Threat of abuse, fear of detention, and heavy fines could each help ensure that Japanese workers moved in prescribed ways through distinct places.

The heavy penalties placed on Japanese bicyclists are one manifestation of officials' larger focus on managing residents' movements. Of all criminal offenses, vagrancy was by far the most commonly enforced. In a review of countywide criminal cases initiated from January 1897 to December 1906, over half involved vagrancy. These infractions were commonly supplemented with additional criminal charges of begging, intoxication, and lodging in a car. By and large, vagrancy charges—a misdemeanor accompanied by fines or jail time—were levied at white offenders. This is also true of neighboring Los Angeles County, where poor white men comprised the majority of prisoners (90 percent) at the turn of the century, as law enforcement focused their efforts on public decency crimes. Where whiteness conferred certain privileges, not all white mobilities were treated the same. Instead, they were bifurcated along class and ethnic lines. The tramp panic of 1870–1930, for instance, was most commonly levied at poor, homeless, and mobile men of U.S.-born and Irish origin. While western travel for resettlement and elite sport were celebrated, displaced workers' movements were criminalized as threatening forms of rootlessness.[83]

The type of mobile infractions levied against a particular group paralleled the specific threat that group posed to the hegemonic order, in this case a white settler society organized around the racial hierarchies of capitalist agriculture. For instance, stealing a bicycle was another serious county offense. Bicycle theft was categorized as grand larceny, a felony, and persons charged with bicycle theft were subject to trial with bail set as high as $1,000. But, no criminal cases of this type were charged against Japanese residents.[84] This was because the threat Japanese riders posed to white hegemony was not to individuals' possessions, but to the white desire for racial containment and control of workers' movements, a desire authorities worked hard to meet in the production of spaces ranging from Chinatown to the citriscape to multiracial neighborhoods. On a bicycle, Japanese laborers moved faster and with less risk than when upon foot. Speed and facility of movement expanded the range of sites they could occupy, including those where they were typically unwelcome. Where the normative white person was marked by their ability to move—as in western migration, tourism, and sports upon new technologies of transportation—the nonwhite body has often been marked as immobilized, except when in the service of the racial social order.[85]

Despite attempts to direct workers' migration solely towards the accumulation of capital, mobility was never wholly controllable. Workers regularly engaged in bicycling for their own purposes, from expanding their economic opportunities to self-fashioning an athletic identity to riding for the pure joy of it. When viewed from this perspective, the tension between bicycle laws and cycling practices embody what geographer Don Mitchell has called the struggle of "finding ways to control the movement of labor, and . . . of finding the means to make that mobility subversive."[86] Whether racing on a professional track or riding through the city center, Japanese cyclists had the potential to leverage their mobility's economic and social value, but their efforts were limited by the changing meaning of these movements when exercised by nonwhite bodies.[87] With the rise of the automobile, Japanese immigrants carved a space for themselves in the cycling world. The opening of Adams Track marked a day of cooperation and buy-in from Riverside elites, including the press, socialites, and the mayor. However, the success of these events further underscores the vast distance between that special day and the everyday, particularly as federal and state policies targeted Japanese immigrants. Ultimately, Japanese men's ability to harness the bicycle for their own purposes was accompanied by risk, and their gains were tempered by the resilience of racial divisions.

Bicycle laws help explain how regional officials responded to the threat of Japanese mobility through public policy, practices whose very possibility can be linked to the long history of state efforts to control the movements of people of color. Names changed and boundaries moved, but racial space consistently served to reproduce labor relationships central to the functioning of capitalism in agricultural communities.[88] The proliferation of multiracial neighborhoods and Asian bicyclists at the beginning of the twentieth century undermined a myth of containment buttressed by a legacy of restrictionist racialization. The following section examines the ways Japanese residents were racialized as hyper-mobile and the ways public policy both normalized this discourse and regulated the perceived threat to white domesticity.

MIGRANT HOUSING AND THE *HARADA* CASE
IN THE ERA OF THE ALIEN LAND LAW

In the California Citrus Belt, Asian residents were drawn into a contentious struggle over fixity and flow, one emerging from the contradiction between the region's need for migrant labor and a settler colonial impulse for racially exclusive residential spaces. Where picturesque homes and orange groves formed the heart of the citriscape, multiracial dormitories were vilified for their association with migrant workers. On the national level, social scientists proposed that frequent migration was a physical condition caused by psychological or physical shortcomings. For instance, during the late nineteenth century's "tramp panic," the phenomenon wherein social scientists and public officials became preoccupied with studying and criminalizing white itinerant men, mobility was deemed a psychological deviance from the norm.[89] Conversely, for nonwhite populations in the early twentieth century American West, mobility was a category that came to define their racial nature, rather than being the abnormality it was considered for white people. Overlooking legal systems that promoted routine displacement, Japanese mobility was instead pathologized as an innate inability to assimilate to Anglo American norms. This section analyzes two tools of routine displacement aimed at preventing the permanent settlement of nonwhite workers: policies criminalizing migrant dormitories and state policies preventing Asian home ownership. It does so through an analysis of the first test of California's Alien Land Law, *State of California v. Jukichi Harada,* concerning a Japanese American family who attempted to move from a multiracial boardinghouse to a single-family home in a previously white neighborhood. As advanced by settler colonial theory, Indigenous displacement and the possession of land by white settlers were accompanied by efforts to undermine the permanent settlement of a nonwhite, immigrant workforce.[90]

Boardinghouses provided spaces where migrant workers from across the globe formed intimate, multifamily, homosocial households that challenged the conventions of normative white domestic life. Building on these arrangements was the opportunity to manage restaurants, bathhouses, and dormitories, which provided some residents middle class status within the Asian American community. As a case in point, Mary Paik Lee's family opened a kitchen and bathhouse catering to Korean workers soon after arriving in Riverside. In order to start the business, her father took advantage of credit extended to him by Chinese merchants. With the additional help of their Korean neighbors, the family constructed a mess hall and bathhouse using wood and tin found in a nearby junkyard.[91] From shared experiences of Japanese imperialism in Asia and U.S. segregation, the family found alternatives to ranch labor, formed affinities with established Chinese residents, and fostered a sense of community among Korean immigrants.

While boardinghouses offered migrants relative economic autonomy, municipal authorities approached these spaces with hostility.[92] For instance, in 1913, Police Chief Frank Corrington led a "clean-up crusade" targeting downtown boardinghouses serving migrant workers. As reported by Chief Corrington, "This is the first move on the part of the department to clean these places up, and I propose to see that they are kept clean."[93] The idea of cleanliness is one we return to later. True to Corrington's word, three years later the city would increase migrant surveillance through an ordinance that required lodging houses to keep a public ledger of all occupants.[94]

The 1913 clean-up crusade began with an investigation into a lodging house run by Jukichi and Ken Harada, Issei (first-generation Japanese) settlers with strong ties to the Riverside community and managers of the popular Washington Restaurant and its boardinghouse. Although the Haradas largely catered to migrant workers, the police discovered two escaped Native students from the Sherman Institute lodging together in the building. While young boys and girls were strictly segregated into male and female dormitories on the institute's grounds, police found the runaway boy and girl occupying the same room in the privacy of the Harada boarding house. The raid reveals the ways that practices targeting migrant workers intersected with forced American Indian relocation to create a double criminalization, that of Native mobility and nonwhite settlement. For the unnamed Sherman students, the raid undermined their attempt to run away and resulted in their return to the Sherman Institute for reprimand. For the Haradas, it meant a formal charge against Jukichi for "renting a place for immoral purposes." Jukichi was ultimately released with a mandate to deny housing to "questionable lodgers," in this case Native youth.[95] In the multiracial citriscape, white settler colonialism was simultaneously complicit in the elimination of Indigenous youth and the criminalization of multiracial worker housing.[96]

The clean-up crusade was not the last challenge the Haradas would face in attempting to establish a place for themselves in Riverside. The Haradas' lives were further shaken when Jukichi and Ken unexpectedly lost their five-year-old son, Tadao. That winter, the young boy suddenly and violently choked in his father's arms. When investigators discovered the child was suffering from diphtheria, an upper respiratory illness associated with poor housing and ventilation, Jukichi attributed Tadao's death to the family's cramped quarters and prolonged exposure to the migrant workers who rented rooms in the house. Motivated to find a healthier environment, the family purchased a single-family home at 3356 Lemon Street near downtown Riverside.

The same year that the Haradas were cited in the clean-up crusade and lost their son Tadao, the State of California passed the Alien Land Law (1913). The law prohibited all Asian immigrants, or "aliens ineligible for citizenship," from owning property.[97] Extending to Japanese, Chinese, Korean, Polynesian, Filipino, and other Asian-descent groups well into the 1940s, California's anti-Asian land law was one of the first in the United States, spanning from the Pacific Northwest to the Southeast. Although they filed the new house under the names of their three American-born citizen children, the Haradas' effort to move from the boardinghouse to Lemon Street was quickly challenged by their neighbors.

That Jukichi and Ken Harada were denied the right to naturalize and that their American-born children were granted national citizenship at birth was law. However, the question of their residential integration was a matter of debate. What had begun as a conflict among neighbors acquired legal significance when the State of California initiated a lawsuit, *State of California v. Jukichi Harada*. Proponents of the case argued that the home purchase violated the racial integrity of the neighborhood and the intention of the California Alien Land Law. Opponents asserted that the family had assimilated to U.S. standards and that they had the right to occupy a home for use by citizen children. Both debated who was expected to migrate, who had the right to settle, and who could claim cultural citizenship in inland Southern California. In a high-profile decision, the court ruled in favor of the defense. Legal scholars and historians, most notably Mark Rawitsch, have carefully documented the Harada trial.[98] Rather than reiterate their work here, I focus on the implications of the case for a multiracial constituency—including Mexican, African American, and working class Japanese families—as various stakeholders debated who was to be included in a citriscape Riverside's colonists had imagined as white.

When the Haradas' future neighbors heard the house had been sold to a Japanese family, they organized into the Lemon Street Committee and offered to purchase the home from the Haradas. It was perhaps the neighbors' tenuous claims to whiteness that catalyzed their staunch protests. Whiteness at the beginning of the twentieth century was not a monolithic racial identity, as it is imagined today, but a marker of suitability for citizenship.[99] Where fragmented racial identities on the East Coast differentiated Anglo-Saxons from Celts, "not-quite whites" could slide into a more secure racial position in the American West by participating in acts of discrimination and violence against those who were more clearly nonwhite.[100] As a neighborhood comprised of immigrants and the children of immigrants, including Adam Farr, Cora Fletcher, Georgina Porter, Edward Roberts, George Urquhart, and Sarah Wetz, the Lemon Street residents had more in common with the Haradas than they were willing to recognize.[101] Defending their claims to racial belonging meant participating in practices that reaffirmed the geographic boundaries of their whiteness, foremost the segregation of residential space. Eager to reinscribe the racial exclusivity of the neighborhood, the committee offered the Haradas an increase of $500 on their original buying price—the cost of white racism.[102]

Attorney Miguel Estudillo was the driving force behind the prosecution. His own ability to benefit from white privilege underscores the contingent nature of race in twentieth-century California.[103] As a matter of law, Mexican-descent people were extended white status when the Treaty of Guadalupe-Hidalgo was signed following the Mexican-American War in 1848. Legal status, however, did not necessarily include racial recognition. Instead, the incorporation of Mexican elites like Estudillo into whiteness required substantive claims to European ancestry and demonstrable assimilation into Euro-American society. Described as "a native son of California" by one of his contemporaries, Estudillo traced his lineage to the Spanish military, as well as to early Californio ranchers José Estudillo and Louis Rubidoux. Historian John Nieto-Phillips has argued that discourses around the label "hispanidad" in the Southwest originated in struggles against ethnic Mexicans' political marginalization and their efforts to collectively identify with whiteness, even if at the expense of others. Similarly here, Estudillo's claims to Spanish identity allowed him to evade discrimination and integrate into an elite class of white American professionals. That he served as a San Diego County clerk and that he was admitted by the California Supreme Court to practice law is evidence of racial passing's benefits. Upon moving to Riverside in 1899, Estudillo held various government offices, including positions within the State Assembly and Senate. His membership in the racially exclusive Jonathan Club in Los Angeles, and his marriage to a direct descendant of the Mayflower, Minerva Cook, further indicate his ability to cross white racial boundaries.[104] Even if an elite man of Mexican descent could access white privilege, as in the case of Estudillo, circumstances were yet uncertain for a middle class Japanese family.

The affront to Riverside residents was not that the Haradas had purchased property, but that they did so in a white neighborhood. Although the Alien Land Law originated in concerns over Asian access to agricultural land, the law was selectively enforced. As described by legal scholars, little more than a dozen escheat actions were taken between 1913 and 1942.[105] Oral histories with Japanese immigrants living in nearby Citrus Belt towns, such as Etiwanda, Upland, and Cucamonga, describe the law as having had little effect on their holdings. Rather, Japanese immigrants successfully circumvented the law by employing strategies such as purchase through a citizen spouse and white allies.[106] Likewise, several Japanese residents became homeowners in this period.

But in Riverside, their choices were limited to the multiracial Eastside, Arlington Heights, Chinatown, and Casa Blanca neighborhoods. Months earlier, the Haradas themselves had purchased an Eastside lot in the name of their American-born daughter, Mine Harada. Later, they bought a second home in the same neighborhood.[107] Located in a space where many Japanese, Mexican, and African American residents had settled, the addition of another Japanese-descent family raised no attention. Mine explained that "No one bothered or hollered because it was across the tracks."[108] Further, spokesperson Jacob Vandegrift testified, the Lemon Street Committee had offered to purchase a home for the Haradas on the Eastside, if they agreed to move.[109] That a Japanese American family could buy a home in a multiracial neighborhood without garnering attention—nonetheless, with the support of white residents—suggests that even where discriminatory legislation existed, day-to-day occurrences were required to catalyze legal action. At the local level, fear of racial rupture was a more powerful agent than concerns over violations of the Alien Land Law.

The Haradas could have lived peacefully in the Eastside neighborhood, but they never occupied the home they bought. Instead, they chose a potentially contentious path to reside on Lemon Street. Motivated by their son Tadao's early passing, Ken and Jukichi were seeking a healthier environment for their children. It is unlikely they could have found such a setting in the Eastside neighborhood. According to a survey conducted by Inspector Luther Mott of the California Commission on Immigration and Housing, 78 percent of homes in the Eastside, as well as the Casa Blanca and Arlington neighborhoods of Riverside, were "lacking sewers (in Casa Blanca) [and were] deplorably overcrowded, poorly ventilated, and breeding places for disease."[110] That the Eastside was largely home to a multiracial workforce was no coincidence, but its close spatial proximity to Lemon Street—separated by four blocks and a railroad track—marks these inequalities as shocking. Whiteness had material benefits denied to those of middle class status alone, and the only way the Haradas could access those benefits was by moving to a white neighborhood. The Haradas positioned themselves in an intermediary position between middle class whites and working class nonwhites that allowed them increased access to the advantages of whiteness.[111]

Jukichi's response in what would follow is both logical and jarring. He attempted to access white privilege by physically and discursively distancing his family from the working class African, Mexican, and Japanese American families who occupied multiracial districts. Where race and social geography were hopelessly intertwined, the Haradas exercised one of the only options available to them as a family seeking access to municipal resources otherwise denied to Asian residents: a "possessive investment in whiteness." As described by George Lipsitz, "The power of whiteness depended not only on white hegemony over separate racialized groups, but also on manipulating racial outsiders to fight against one another, to compete with each other for white approval, and to seek the rewards and privileges of whiteness for themselves at the expense of other racialized populations."[112]

The Haradas successfully used the aid of Japanese and white allies to protect their property rights in the U.S. courts, but they did not seek to disrupt broad practices of segregation aimed at nonwhites. Instead, they hoped for inclusion on the other side of the line by positioning themselves as different from those who were clearly behind it. The Haradas were not alone in this approach, but rather were early adopters of a strategy commonly used by legal activists and advocacy groups seeking access to the benefits of whiteness— such as the League of United Latin American Citizens' later efforts to challenge the segregation of Mexican American children from Anglo American children in 1930 by underscoring their shared legal status as white. The actions by LULAC and the Haradas both reflect avenues of redress taken by racially disadvantaged groups seeking to confront racial inequity by drawing themselves closer to whiteness and conforming to racial anxieties directed at other groups.[113]

The Harada case received wide interest, and the media attention that followed cast the family as exemplars of American acculturation. Despite controversy over the family's right to own property, by all accounts the Haradas attempted to assimilate into prevailing Anglo American values by practicing Christianity, learning English, raising citizen children, and establishing a single-family home. The local newspaper reported, "[Jukichi] and his family are members of the Methodist mission of this city and it is a matter of common repute that they are quiet, clean, respectable people."[114] Upon immigrat-

Harada family portrait: Jukichi, Masa Atsu, Ken (rear); Mine, Sumi, Tadao (front), ca. 1911. Courtesy of the Harada Family Collection, Riverside Metropolitan Museum, Riverside, California.

ing, Jukichi had even attempted to naturalize, but his application was denied. Although ineligible for national citizenship, as the result of a federal naturalization law targeting Asian immigrants, the family had consistently asserted their cultural citizenship through active participation in the dominant currents of Riverside's daily life. For instance, when assuming ownership of the Washington Restaurant, Jukichi and Ken decorated it with American flags and posters of U.S. presidents.[115] Whether such displays were a remnant of past management, an appeal to an Anglo American clientele, adherence to

Tokyo-based campaigns urging immigrants to conform to U.S. norms, or a personal manifestation of patriotism in their new home, is difficult to know. What is certain is that in public life they embraced an American identity.

The cost of the Haradas' investment in whiteness was the further marginalization of the Japanese, Mexican, and African American working class populations of Riverside and its environs. The local press printed Jukichi's denigration of other nonwhites:

> [Jukichi] Harada objects to living in that section of Riverside in which the Japanese, Mexicans and negro population are segregated. He says he does not want his children to be compelled to associate with negro and Mexican children. He is carefully educating his children, one of the boys being in high school and an exceptionally good student.[116]

This account's appeal to its audience lay in the racial triangulation of Asian Americans to whites, on the one hand, and to Mexicans and African Americans, on the other. By denigrating the presence of other nonwhites, middle class Japanese residents appear preferable by comparison. In this particular example, Jukichi's son Masa Atsu Harada is positioned as more intelligent than African American and Mexican youth living on the Eastside. However, even if deemed superior when compared to inferior "negro and Mexican children," the valorization of the Harada children still reinforced the inherent intellectual supremacy of white children.[117] Although seemingly sympathetic, press coverage of Jukichi seeking "the *right* sort of environment for his children" naturalized the superiority of white residents. That is, it reified the value of segregation by shifting the source of unequal housing conditions from economic and political disparity to the inherent inferiority of nonwhite people.[118]

Jukichi's claims to white space depended on distancing his family from the multiracial migrant workforce recruited to labor in the area's groves. Recall that when Tadao passed, Jukichi had blamed the workers that rented rooms in his boardinghouse for Tadao's illness. Interviewed years later, Jukichi noted, "We always lived ourselves in the lodging house. It was filled with Mexicans and others; *but* we tried to keep it nice and clean."[119] His language reflects the rhetoric of the clean-up crusade that had targeted his boardinghouse a few years earlier. Cleanliness, in this sense, had two different meanings. On one level, it implied keeping an orderly home. Seeking fresh air, a yard, and open space, Jukichi and Ken sought to protect their children from the health hazards they attributed to Tadao's death. Jukichi explained, "Perhaps it was the dust; perhaps it was living all the time in the house without a good place to play. But, anyhow, our children were sick much of the time."[120] His allusion to cleanliness also possessed a racial dimension. As recalled by Mine Harada, their boarders were "mostly laborers, usually people that couldn't find places to live, Mexicans and Japanese."[121] Allusions to dust, disease, and the restless pursuit of cleanliness each served as metaphors for the disorder of migratory spaces occupied by racial and ethnic others deemed "out of place."[122] Whether at the economic or racial level, the association between boardinghouses and dirt were tied to moral assumptions about these spaces' occupants.

At first look, Jukichi's critique of other Japanese families is confusing. It is notable that he does not protest "associating" with Japanese residents, as he does African American and Mexican residents, but he does "object" to living in the same section. His protest demonstrates the class divisions held between Japanese laborers and the Japanese middle class in California at the beginning of the twentieth century. These distinctions would have been instilled in families like the Haradas in Japan, prior to their emigration, where ideas of civilization were rooted in middle class norms that echoed westernization. As described by historian Eiichiro Azuma, white racism in the United States fostered class tensions within the Japanese American community, who were pressured to justify their U.S. presence through the adoption of white, Protestant, middle class norms. For instance, in the name of Japanese nationalism, immigrant women were taught gendered expectations around dress, hygiene, cooking, and daily manners.[123]

Class distinctions were partly expressed through heteronormative family structures. Although extracted from legal consideration and absent from press accounts, Ken's position as a middle class Japanese woman was a central mobilizer in the case. As an educated Christian, Ken was a model wife whose very presence distanced the family from critiques levied at the laboring bachelors who comprised the majority of California's Japanese immigrant workforce. More generally, a Japanese household that included a wife correlated with higher rates of home ownership during this era.[124] On the whole, both wage-earning and self-employed males had similar marriage rates, at 48 percent for the former and 52 percent the latter. However, married, self-employed men were more than twice as likely to occupy single-family households in the United States—at 69 percent for married, self-employed men compared to 31 percent for unmarried, self-employed men.[125] Moreover, after the first Alien Land Law was passed, Japanese wives became essential to property acquisition. Where "aliens ineligible for citizenship" were denied land, and marriage was impermissible with Anglo Americans as a result of miscegenation laws discouraging interracial relations, it was through bearing citizen children that Japanese nationals were able to secure the legal right to property.[126] That is, property laws gave Asian motherhood a significance that motherhood did not have for non-Asian women.

Relative to other nonwhite populations, the residential Japanese community was more easily accepted in Riverside. As later described by Sumi Harada, "On the whole they treated the Japanese with indifference and a few were even friendly."[127] Yet, Japan's efforts to equalize Japanese emigrants and Anglo Americans through facilitating the adoption of western middle class norms—taught in Japanese schools and through the circulation of manuals—were ineffective in fully combatting white racism in the United States. Even as the Haradas found stable employment and community recognition for their efforts to assimilate, their racial exclusion was a lingering reminder of Japan's subordinate status within a U.S. system that linked property with whiteness, regardless of one's class background or a family's gender composition. In this and many other senses, bootstrap narratives fall short when suggesting social mobility could be achieved through hard work and dedication; one racial trajectory is not synonymous with all racial trajectories. On the contrary, nonwhite immigrants have vastly different experiences of integration, experiences often marked by the legacy of white racism.[128] In the course of defending middle class Japanese American claims to property, Asian-descent people remained "indelible outsiders," and social damage was exerted on working class Asian, Mexican, and African American residents.[129] Although the Harada family chose what was best for their family under the threat of very real consequences, as attested by the untimely and tragic death of their son, recognition of the Haradas' ability to defend their claims to space should not exclude critique over the ways a possessive investment in whiteness reaffirmed the racial order.

The Harada case represented a victory for opponents of the Alien Land Law, but anxiety directed at Japanese residents did not dissipate. Although Judge Craig affirmed the Harada children's property rights as American-born citizens, his finding foreshadowed the tightening of the Alien Land Law.[130] Large excerpts from his opinion were reprinted by the local press:

> Doubtless many of the neighboring residents, as well as others, object to the presence of the defendants as neighbors, but that is not sufficient reason for

depriving these children of their property. The law is not sufficiently broad to deny the right to own land to the American born children of aliens ineligible to citizenship. The law must be enforced as it is written and its terms may not be enlarged by the courts to include others than those mentioned in the statute itself. If an embarrassing or unfortunate situation results by reason of the limitations of the statute, the remedy is not to be sought in the courts, for they cannot deny to American citizens the right to own or hold an interest in land under our laws as they now exist.[131]

The judge lamented the court's inability to enforce property restrictions that were not explicitly denied by the law. In doing so, he pointed to the specificity of the Alien Land Law, which only excluded Asian immigrants from the right to acquire property. The statute, he explained, cannot protect against "embarrassing or unfortunate situations," in this case the integration of a Japanese-descent family into a white neighborhood. Notably, the opinion concluded that "[the courts] cannot deny to [Japanese-descent] American citizens the right to own or hold an interest in land under our laws as they now exist."[132] His statement gestured towards—if not outright invited—the revision of the Alien Land Law that followed shortly after his decision.[133] Rather than representing a moment of transgressive victory, the outcome of the *State of California v. Jukichi Harada* reflects the high stakes of residential mobility and the currency of an investment in whiteness where minoritized people had limited opportunities to occupy spaces of their own choosing.

PEDALING FORWARD, PEDALING BACK

At the beginning of this chapter, Gene Stratton-Porter's novel, *Her Father's Daughter*, serves as a prelude to the passage of the more restrictive Alien Land Law in 1920. The competition for class valedictorian between Donald Whiting and Oka Sayye exemplified the contest between American exceptionalism and the perceived threat from Japan to the United States. In the novel's telling, Sayye was not only integrating into the American school system but also surpassing white students, undermining the superiority of the white American race. And yet the dispute was not one between recognized equals.

Throughout the novel, Sayye and his fellow countrymen are portrayed as both hard working and cunning. both intelligent and violent. In his attempts to outshine Whiting, Sayye is a formidable threat who unabashedly resorts to mimicry, violence, and deception. Whiting, on the other hand, ultimately overcomes Sayye by tapping into his own inherently superior capacity. And then—twist!—as *Her Father's Daughter* unfolds it is revealed that Sayye is not a teenager at all. He is an adult man posing as a youth—concealing his true identity by dying his hair black and wearing rouge—in order to unfairly advance in the U.S. school system.[134] Sayye is exposed as a villain willing to resort to murder to protect his advancement. In an attempt to kill Whiting, Sayye accidentally falls to his death at the bottom of a dark canyon. Aware of his surreptitious act, and thereby implicated in it, Sayye's fellow Japanese countrymen retrieve the body to bury his deception. Even on the cultural front, or perhaps especially so, white supremacist ideologies maintained that Japanese residents posed a mortal threat to Anglo Americans that could only be overcome by watchful vigilance of any potential advancement.

In the decade that Arthur Kaneko, on whom Stratton-Porter loosely based her character Oka Sayye, graduated from Riverside High School, Riverside's Japanese population had much reason to be hopeful about the potential for integration. Kaneko's graduation made headlines; cultural events such as the celebration of the Japanese emperor's birthday and bicycling races drew popular audiences; and families like the Haradas achieved many markers of cultural assimilation to Anglo Americans' approval, such as speaking English and practicing Christianity. These earlier signs that equitable relations might have occurred between Anglo Americans and Japanese residents mark white efforts to maintain racial dominance in the following years as all the more shattering. Whether policing Japanese cyclists on the move or Japanese American families seeking sites of permanent residence, officials at multiple levels of governance were galvanized in the defense of racial lines. Practices limiting mobility marked entire neighborhoods as racially apart from the central city, infantilized Japanese sportsmen claiming equal footing with white athletes, and denied nonwhite families the label of neighbor when seeking refuge from the most heartbreaking of circumstances, a child's death.

An approach grounded in relational racial formation, emphasizing the ways in which groups interconnect with one another, reveals the complex strategies adopted by Japanese people seeking to defend their right to mobility and its impact on the groups around them.[135] They adopted new mobile technologies such as using bicycles to seek better-paying jobs; they engaged in spectator sports to buttress their claims to modern manhood; and they petitioned the courts and the media as allies in their battle for recognition as neighbors. Yet, even where symbolic and material claims to citizenship were met with some success, whiteness was staunchly guarded. In the case of Japanese bicyclists, the local media and police force mobilized to undermine Japanese claims to racial equality, as well as to disincentivize the links between physical and economic mobility through hefty cycling fees and incarceration.

Likewise, individual gains did not always translate into collective advances or a dismantling of white supremacist ideologies. In the case of the Haradas, access to home ownership in a formerly white neighborhood did not widen the grounds of racial inclusion for other marginalized populations. Instead, a possessive investment in whiteness further reified the exclusion of working class Asian, Mexican, and African American populations from the citriscape. Moreover, modest gains by one nonwhite group could ignite white settlers' efforts to reify the existing racial order. Within a year of the *Harada* ruling, the California state legislature passed a second, more constricting Alien Land Law. Approved by ballot initiative in 1920, the law renewed and tightened the restrictions of the 1913 policy with overwhelming support from the California electorate (75 percent). Where many Japanese immigrants were able to circumvent the 1913 law, the 1920 expansion caused a precipitous decline in Japanese agricultural holdings.[136] Further hindering Japanese integration, the Immigration Act of 1924 attempted to halt immigration from Asia. Chapter 3 examines changing relationships between race making and mobility as the number of Mexican workers eclipsed that of Japanese laborers.

THREE

From Mexican Settlers to Mexican Birds of Passage

RELATIONAL RACIAL FORMATION, CITRUS LABOR, AND IMMIGRATION POLICY, 1914–1930

Imagine a young man named Regino traveling from Mexico to the United States. He has been displaced from Mexico by national policies calling for the privatization and mechanization of the countryside. Located far from centers of national governance, Regino begins his migration from the interior northward, stitching together seasonal work in the cotton and beet industries. Still struggling to make a sustaining income, he hears news of lucrative job opportunities in similar industries further north, in Arizona, California, and Texas. U.S. agriculturalists have helped pass a small but legal immigration loophole that ensures contract laborers can migrate from Mexico during shortages, such as those identified during World War I by the Secretary of Labor. Arriving to work for his new U.S. employers, Regino finds his wages and living conditions far inferior to those he hears of in neighboring agricultural fields and northern industries. But Regino's employer has him under close watch, incentivized by the bond he expects to receive upon his worker's return to Mexico at the contract's completion. Even if Regino were able to manage his way across the locked fences that enclose the ranch, he might be deterred by the risk of capture by police patrols surveilling the county to ensure Mexican immigrants remain within local boundaries, where labor is sorely needed. And, even if Regino could convince the patrolmen that he was an American citizen, his bare legs would be a dead giveaway that he was attempting to skip out on his employer, since the rancher confiscates his pants at the end of each workday, stripping Regino of his clothes and his mobility in the process.[1]

This story was precisely the experience of many Mexican immigrants at the beginning of the twentieth century—with variations on the details. As the twentieth century unfolded, agricultural communities went to great lengths to fix migrant workers in place. During World War I, when citrus demand spiked and simultaneously white laborers were recruited to battlefields abroad, ranchers heavily invested in filling orange groves with nonwhite immigrant workers. As they did so, they competed heavily with northern industries, and with each other. Through incentive and coercion, they aimed to bind workers to place, now envisioning successive generations of nonwhite workers where they had previously planned for rotating seasonal migrants.

Across the Southwest, white ranchers adopted a myriad of strategies to ensure that workers—particularly a Mexican immigrant workforce displaced by a national revolution—did not leave ranch properties for competing jobs in other regions. In order to fence in workers—literally and otherwise—the ranchers petitioned Congress for guest worker allowances; they created contracts, erected gates, and established curfews. They pathologized single male laborers with the highest rates of mobility, and, in some cases, took workers' pants away at night, ensuring that they could not leave without notice. The halls of Congress, national trade publications, regional Chamber of Commerce meetings, and local social service surveys were all forums for determining how to manage laborers' flows and stoppages.

Despite their renewed efforts to recruit an immigrant workforce, whites' claims to the exclusivity of their space within the Citrus Belt were steadfast. However, not all mobilities and immobilities were treated equally. At the same time the Alien Land Law (1913) was enacted throughout the Pacific Northwest, denying land ownership to Asian immigrants, and later also denying long-term leases (1920), the federal Department of Agriculture (USDA) advocated for the mass adoption of citrus worker housing. Trade publications, USDA photography, and research journals each hailed permanent housing—from bunkhouses to single family homes—as the solution to labor shortages caused by World War I (1914–1918). Targeting a recent wave of immigrants from central Mexico, southwestern agricultural interests promoted the long-term settlement of Mexican workers, even while the Alien Land Law actively denied it to Asian residents. Although seemingly contradictory, citrus ranch housing programs and the Alien Land Law were similar in purpose: they were both efforts to police the boundaries of whiteness and to control nonwhite mobility. Agricultural workers were caught in the unsettled contradictions of capitalism, where logically migrants should have been able to operate as free agents but in reality found their movements tied to the will of their employers. Under racial capitalism, whereby the dominant class exploits the social and economic devaluation of nonwhite people, the mobility of Mexican and Asian workers was carefully managed towards the end of reproducing the citrus economy and its racial hierarchies.[2]

Citrus ranchers' eager recruitment of permanent Mexican laborers was exacerbated by the Immigration Act of 1924, which shifted prevailing interpretations of Mexican immigrants from that of ideal settlers to that of circular migrants. Where the act largely banned Asian immigration and placed new restrictions on immigrants from Europe, it exempted Western Hemispheric immigrants from the national quota system, thus increasing ranchers' reliance on Mexican workers. However, in January of 1926, the House Committee on Immigration and Naturalization convened to revisit the exemption of Mexican workers at the bequest of Texas congressman John Box. News of the forthcoming hearing sent a panic wave through the California Citrus Belt, because it could potentially place Mexican immigrants on a restrictive quota. Agriculturalists sprang into action, gathering written protests and sending representatives to Washington to give testimony before the committee in order to support Mexican exemption. From 1926 to 1930, Congress echoed with a vibrant claim that starkly contradicted the logic of the earlier citrus housing campaigns: Mexicans were "birds of passage," temporary workers who arrived at the harvest, departed at its completion, and provided essential migrant labor unsuitable for white families.

Examination of World War I citrus housing campaigns alongside the immigration debates of the 1920s reveal the divergent ways nonwhite people experienced racialization through their mobility. As agriculturalists struggled to maintain the citrus industry's growth and safeguard their labor supply between World War I and the Box Bill debates, racial formation was tightly tied to workers' "motility," or their potential for movement as shaped by economic resources, social categorizations, and citizenship status.[3] During World War I, agriculturalists promoted citrus housing as a means to enlist and retain Mexican workers. In contrast to interpretations of Japanese and white itinerant workers as rootless, agriculturalists eagerly praised Mexican men's ties to their families and the ranch. Conversely, during the immigration debates of the 1920s, agricultural interests fended off potential immigration restrictions on the Mexican labor pool by suggesting Mexican workers were inherently circular migrants, who returned to Mexico at the end of each season. At times, Box Bill opponents levied both arguments concurrently, portraying Mexican immigrants as place-bound settlers with close ties to home, and as birds of passage who would labor to white agriculturalists' benefit without seeking permanent citizenship. Within these debates, workers' mobility was assigned divergent values, foremost for Mexican immigrants and Puerto Rican migrants, but also Native American and Filipino laborers, so much so that they were described as occupying different racial statuses.[4] Examining the World War I citrus housing campaign and the Box Bill debates together suggests that the conflicting agendas of agricultural expansion—which required nonwhite labor but heralded white nationhood—were resolved through how various migrant groups were racially positioned as either fluid or fixed in place.

It is a compelling irony that those who move the most often experience the greatest restraints on their mobility—from the shifts in capitalist forces that commonly initiate migration, to administrators' attempts to manage those movements through public policy. How power manifests in relation to the question of flows is reflective of what geographer Doreen Massey has called "differentiated mobility": "some people are more in charge of it than others; some initiate flows and movement, others don't; some are more on the receiving-end of it than others; some are effectively imprisoned by it."[5] Throughout this period, we see concerted efforts by racialized populations to navigate their differentiated mobility. The San Francisco-based Japanese Association of America issued memorials protesting the restrictions on their settlement created by the Alien Land Law; Mexican workers abandoned contracts to seek higher paying industrial opportunities in northern regions; Puerto Ricans moved across the ocean to secure employment and called upon their rights as citizens to protest poor worker housing conditions; and individuals brought together by long-distance migrant flows negotiated romantic relationships. This chapter looks to the ways national debates over the mobility of nonwhite subjects were informed by regional racial hierarchies, and how multiscalar contests over race and labor shaped workers' experiences of race, place, and mobility at the everyday level.

THE UNEVEN EFFECTS OF HOME OWNERSHIP FOR MEXICAN AND JAPANESE RACIAL FORMATION

Although a compilation of multiple accounts, the circumstances described at the opening to this chapter were not uncommon among Mexican immigrants who traveled vast distances to work in U.S. industries—and who then found themselves bound to space via a combination of policy, surveillance, and racial profiling. Competition from higher paying wartime industries for employees and increased international demand for citrus fruits led to a sudden farmworker shortage in the Citrus Belt. Sunkist advertising campaigns had increased the orange's popularity as Americans earned more disposable income. With wartime conditions halting competition from foreign producers, citrus had never been more profitable in Southern California.[6] Yet, ranchers eager to increase production found themselves in deep contests over labor. In an inversion of previous practices, in which citrus ranchers had drawn upon seasonal migrants, the USDA now pushed for the permanent settlement of a Mexican workforce—that is, settlement that was accompanied by increased controls and surveillance of workers' movements.

Ranchers' need for laborers was exacerbated by restrictive immigration policies that created new categories of inadmissible immigrants (1917) and that placed quota limits on national origin (1924). Notably, immigrants from the Western Hemisphere were exempted from these restrictions. For Mexican nationals, their status as "nonquota immigrants" combined with southwestern recruitment efforts to promote migration northward. Internal migration was a crucial survival strategy for dispossessed Mexican citizens in the first half of the twentieth century. The administration of Mexican president Porfirio Díaz (1876–1911) had facilitated the privatization and consolidation of land following the Mexican-American War (1848). The effect of the resulting mass displacement was an armed revolt, the Mexican Revolution (1910–1920). However, it was not until the administration of Lazaro Cárdenas (1935–1940) that the reform movement resulted in significant land redistribution. In the interim, migration between agricultural industries, such as sugar and tobacco, became an essential tactic for Mexican citizens seeking a sustaining income.[7] While Mexican farmers were displaced by Porfirian policies, U.S. reclamation and diversification efforts generated a booming agricultural industry that required thousands of new workers. Drawn by higher U.S. wages, Mexican workers entered a market artificially transformed by federal investment in agriculture and irrigation.[8]

In the Citrus Belt, the transportation networks used to ship fruits aided regional access for Mexican labor. For instance, in 1909, the manager of a boarding contractor operating along the Santa Fe rail line estimated that 25,000 Mexican laborers were carried by train from El Paso, Texas to San Bernardino, California in a single year.[9] Given the extent of Mexican immigration to Southern California, citrus producers across the country looked to the region as a model for Mexican recruitment. Unlike crops in adjacent regions that required migrant labor to maintain their rotating harvests, citrus required a nearly year-round workforce to prune, pick, and pack in the fields.

Standardization was fundamental to marketing agricultural products. Oranges, in particular, depended on maintaining the perception of "the most perfect products of nature."[10] Foremost in need of skilled handling was the navel orange, a regional specialty first cultivated in Riverside. As a result, citrus communities were in exceptional need of a stable workforce. In the context of a national labor shortage and rising international profits, a permanent Mexican labor force became particularly alluring.

Agriculturalists were active in the promotion of Mexican immigration. It was at their urging that the Department of Labor (DOL) reversed stipulations enacted by the Burnett-Smith Immigration Act of 1917—which mandated literacy tests, tightened contract labor provisions, and charged an eight-dollar head tax—in order to promote Mexican recruitment. While broadly limiting immigration elsewhere, the 1917 act enabled ranchers to secure farm labor and formalized the emerging bond between agricultural expansion and Mexican workers. Specifically, Section 3 of the act allowed employers to contract for immigrant laborers if the Secretary of Labor determined importation was a national necessity. Ensuring workers remained bound to the fields and their employer, those who immigrated under Section 3 risked incarceration and deportation if they abandoned farm labor or sought employment in nondesignated industries. Described by one historian as "the first Mexican farm labor program," over 80,000 Mexicans were recruited for labor under Section 3 of the 1917 act.[11]

By placing responsibility for Mexican return migration in employers' hands, the Section 3 exemption heightened their investment in controlling workers' movements. Agricultural laborers were permitted national entrance under bond, which was to be reimbursed upon their return. Since the employer often paid the bond, laborers had little incentive to stay on their contracted ranch, especially in a labor market with readily available and better paying industrial opportunities. Although workers risked deportation if they were found abandoning a contract for industries unapproved by the Secretary of Labor, it was the rancher who bore the immediate cost. When low wages, abuse, or general malcontent was met with "skipping," ranchers found themselves not only short of labor but also shouldering the cost of an unfulfilled bond. Yet, rather than improve conditions to increase worker retention, ranchers often adopted extreme measures to secure labor. As mentioned, some ranchers removed workers' shoes and pants overnight in order to prevent them from leaving.[12] Although extreme, ranchers' attempts to fix workers in place were quite predictable. Under work contracts approved by the federal government, ranchers' dependence on Mexican workers was formalized, and control over immigrant workers' movements was incentivized.

It was in the context of shifting wartime choreographies and with the support of immigration law that Mexican migrants were pursued as a permanent labor force throughout the citrus communities of Southern California. Where mainstream media coverage, in the throes of a world war, failed to acknowledge the growing wave of arriving Mexican workers, the citrus trade publication, *California Citrograph*, readily recognized ranchers' dependence on a Mexican workforce—and it circulated strategies for securing their labor.[13] In 1918, USDA scientist Archibald Shamel published a multipart series, "Housing the Employees of California's Citrus Ranches," focused on the recruitment and retention of Mexican workers. The widely circulated report detailed the housing practices of Southern California's largest citrus ranchers.[14] Foremost in these conversations was the management of Mexican mobility, or more accurately, their immobility.

Central to recruiting Mexican workers and reproducing racially bifurcated labor relations between management and multiracial laborers were housing practices. Using "spatial engineering" for the purposes of "social engineering," the absolute racial divisions perceived between white ranchers and nonwhite laborers were revealed in the series' descriptions of worker camps.[15] The program at Rancho Sespe in Ventura County is exemplar of how ranchers' preference for Mexican workers was codified in the built environment. Rancho Sespe was located about a hundred miles from Riverside, in Fillmore, and although all Rancho Sespe laborers were provided housing, white, Japanese, and Mexican workers were each housed in separate residences. White families paid about $6.50 a month to rent four-bedroom houses equipped with plumbing, painting, and repairs. These "California houses" cost the ranch approximately $1,000 to construct. Conversely, Japanese families paid $6 a month to rent smaller three-bedroom homes (with a shared communal bathhouse) that cost only $650 to construct.[16] Nearly equal rent did not ensure equal living conditions; housing conditions were bent to a racial logic that assumed white families required a higher standard of living—and more privacy—than Japanese families, thus situating white and Japanese families quite differently on the ranch.

Altogether different conditions applied for the housing of Mexican laborers, who were required to build and finance the construction of the homes that they would then own. For the cost of lumber, $10 a month was deducted from the worker's wage.[17] This policy uniquely indebted Mexican laborers to ranchers for the use of building materials. Moreover, it physically tied Mexican home ownership to the ranch-owned property it was built upon. That is, home and earth were divorced from one another.

As could be expected, these differences in racialized access to property created varying relationships to mobility and settlement among workers. California law, compounded by the economics of seasonal agriculture, consistently pushed Japanese residents into mobility, where their hopes of national belonging were perpetually destabilized. Claims to citizenship have long rested on a myth of western progression from migrant to settler to U.S. "native," replacing the Indigenous population; however, Asian residents were denied a place in this narrative.[18] And yet, this rejection was not without its contests. For instance, in a memorandum to President Woodrow Wilson, the Japanese Association of America addressed their struggle to set roots faced with the 1913 Alien Land Law, writing, "most of the Japanese in the state, with their families, are forced to wander about from one place to another without any definite aim of settling down."[19]

Sociologist Ralph Burnight similarly observed that the Alien Land Law served as a formidable obstacle to Japanese *and* Japanese American settlement. Very few immigrant families purchased land under the names of their American children after 1913, accounting for only 380 acres of land across the entire state. A study of Japanese farm holdings conducted by the Bureau of Agricultural Economics in 1944 further suggests that the law pushed American citizens of Japanese descent into only brief stints of land tenure, stemming from their fear of white violence and legal challenges to their property claims.[20] The Alien Land Law fostered land insecurities that undermined the ethnic Japanese community's ability to claim national belonging and to fulfill the norms of white domestic life on which cultural inclusion rested.

Shortly following the 1920 passage of further constrictions in the California Alien Land Law, Mexican citrus workers began to outnumber Japanese laborers. The transition accompanied a drop in the total proportion of Japanese residents between 1920 and 1930. Counting Mexican-descent people as a distinct race for the first time, 1930 census records reveal the Mexican population (6.5 percent) accounted for more than three times the combined Japanese population (1.7 percent) in California. Although the Japanese population remained largely concentrated in rural farm communities, demographic change helps account for the shift from Japanese to Mexican labor sources as industry needs continued to grow, immigration restrictions tightened, and the Mexican population increased.[21] Moreover, where state policies like the Alien Land Law denied Japanese immigrants the opportunity for long-term occupancy, thus pushing them into circular displacement, citrus ranch housing practices fixed Mexican workers in place, for instance by tying them to homes they constructed on employer-owned land. For Mexican workers, citrus companies created a cost-benefit paradox to mobility. Mexican housing provided an incentive for settlement and a disincentive for migration.

USDA accounts of citrus housing ignored the ways immigration policy and ranchers' housing initiatives impacted workers' varying patterns of migration. Instead, the accounts linked workers' propensity for movement to race. In Shamel's 1918 series, Mexican workers were consistently portrayed as innate settlers. For instance, in interview excerpts describing Mexican people's domestic lives within the self-constructed dwellings that predated company housing, ranch managers praised them as the "best type" of labor, emerging each Monday morning from their "impoverished sordid-looking camp."[22] James Culbertson, manager of Limoneira, an extensive lemon ranch in Santa Paula, described Mexican laborers as "men with clean washed clothing—jumpers and overalls, as well as shirts and bandanas—showing the wholesome effects of soap and water."[23] Shamel, likewise, lauded Mexican workers as unique from all others by their "frequent instances of unusual devotion to their work, solicitude for the mental and moral welfare of their children, and their striving for home surroundings made cheery with flowers and music."[24] Throughout the California citrus industry, labor shortage was accompanied by prevailing discourses that linked Mexican workers to homebuilding and family ties.

Shamel's five articles were accompanied by a photographic series highlighting the connection between Mexican people and settlement. One particularly striking image of a family posed in front of their company home illustrates the ways Mexican immigrants were racialized as inherently rooted. The people in the photograph appear as if caught in a candid moment. Unlike traditional portraiture—which is posed, planned, and focused on the subjects' expressions—the family are dressed casually, with children scattered throughout the yard as the father figure prepares to depart for work. In the

Home of Mexican family on Rancho Sespe, 1918. Archibald D. Shamel Papers, Courtesy of Special Collections and University Archives, University of California, Riverside.

photograph, the close attachment of the mother and her children to the home is emphasized by the family's placement behind a barbed wire fence. She is posed upon the doorstep with her hand resting upon the doorframe near a young boy. The physical connection of the woman to their home and the child emphasizes her dual role as household manager and mother. Conversely, the father stands beside an open gate in front of the yard dressed in his work overalls. Physically located at the intersection of his home's walkway and the road, the man links the Mexican household to his employer's citrus ranch. He is ideally located at the crossroads of labor and domesticity, an intersection that ranchers themselves were seeking to foster among workers during the World War I labor shortage when the photograph was taken.[25]

This photograph was one among many originally taken by the USDA as an ethnographic record of the Mexican household. Among these are images of the inland communities of Upland and Corona, which similarly show young children in front of their citrus ranch residences, including little boys standing in overalls and a little girl sitting among hanging laundry. Described by historian William Deverell, the logic of typicality functioned as a "cultural cryogenics" that rendered Mexicans knowable for both what they were and what they were not.[26] For instance, the image in this USDA photograph seems to capture an ethnographic truth about ethnic Mexicans' ties to home and family. Alternatively, when printed in the *California Citrograph*, the photograph was intentionally transformed from one of documentation to one of propaganda. This shift is highlighted by the photograph's caption, which was changed from its original USDA title, "House in Mexican Village," to the *Citrograph* caption, "Seven future employe[e]s in this family."[27] Although the image itself remains typical, the title's modification radically alters the function of the photograph from an USDA record to a tool of persuasion aimed at ranchers contemplating worker housing. "Seven future employe[e]s in this family" promises that worker housing is a wise investment in one's workforce.[28] Even if born in the United States, the children of Mexican immigrants were idealized as a permanent source of foreign workers tied to the ranch, but without claims to the land.

Although ranchers pursued company housing as a means to renew the citrus workforce, Mexican people themselves cultivated a sense of autonomy from homeownership. Mexican women commonly grew small gardens to supplement purchases from the company store and traded homegrown produce with their neighbors to supplement their diets. Children attended school year-round and, when out of the classroom, helped their parents in the groves. Families were guaranteed shelter during slow months, whereas in previous years they would have been expected to migrate to other industries in order to supplement the gap in citrus work.[29] Nevertheless, the gains from owning houses were tempered by workers' inability to purchase the land their homes were built upon. Instead, the benefits of long-term homeownership were as secure as a house built on sand. They were tied to workers' tenure on the ranch and vulnerable to their employers' whims.

Where ranchers now eagerly recruited Mexican immigrants, whom they heralded as ideal, rooted laborers, Japanese immigrants and their children were approached as racial competition and a domestic menace. This difference between the ranchers' attitude towards Mexican workers and Japanese workers is partly tied to Japanese residents' relationship to property. Just prior to the enactment of the 1913 Alien Land Law, the California Commission of Immigration and Housing estimated that about 6,000 Japanese-descent residents were employed as farmers, owning more than 210,000 acres of intensive crops in California, such as berries and vegetables. The growth of Japanese farms triggered white farmers' concerns that they would no longer have access to Japanese workers, who provided half of all labor in the peak citrus season. According to a congressional study (1911), Japanese farmers secured the best Japanese labor, while (white) American farmers struggled to recruit workers.[30] The Alien Land Law assuaged these fears. By preventing Asian residents from accumulating property, normative state functions helped ensure they remained a migrant workforce managed by white agriculturalists.

While long-term settlement was a normative expectation for white families, California law pushed an entire population of people into movement. The cost to Japanese immigrants and Japanese Americans across generations was twofold. The first was political. Japanese residents' living standards were considered evidence of their racial inferiority and outsider status. Among the most consistent critiques of Japanese families was the charge that women worked in the fields rather than occupying their proper place in the home. Social workers blamed Japanese women for impoverished living conditions, including unpainted shacks, substandard sanitation, and a lack of flush toilets. Their assessments did not account for the powerful role of public policy in shaping the domestic decisions of those impacted by the Alien Land Law. Without hope of retaining their property or long-term leases, the most logical economic investment for Japanese residents was the income they earned from raising crops, not from home improvements. Expenditures were better spent on goods that could be taken with them, such as tools, trucks, clothes, and other personal effects. Yet, these investments were viewed as wasteful spending by anti-Asian forces who critiqued dilapidated housing as evidence of Japanese residents' low standard of living.[31] By prohibiting long-term ownership and disincentivizing home investment, structures of white privilege produced the very behaviors that were then used to delegitimize Japanese people.

The second cost was economic. Japanese families were denied the chance to engage in forms of agricultural production requiring long-term capital investment, particularly those with the highest possibility for lucrative returns. Unlike vegetables, which can be cultivated in a matter of months, citrus groves require several years to bear fruit. If Japanese farmers accounted for 0.7 percent of all farm acreage in 1920 and we assume that an equal proportion of Japanese farmers would have entered citrus production were the Alien Land Law not passed, then we can roughly estimate half a million dollars as the loss of profit from exclusion in citrus enterprises in 1920 alone.[32]

Ranchers' preference for Mexican workers over Asian workers was organized along a racial hierarchy that equated immobile workers with passivity and mobile workers with subversive behavior. When compared to Asian migrant workers, Mexican immigrants were far more likely to travel as families. Moreover, they were not barred from purchasing property. The prevalence of families and ability to buy land set them apart from earlier waves of bachelor labor, now paralleling domestic norms associated with white families. Conversely, policies like the Alien Land Law ensured Asian immigrants remained in the migrant stream. By preventing Asian residents from accumulating property or settling into tenancy, normative state functions helped to ensure Asian residents remained a migrant workforce managed by white agriculturalists.

Although a counterpoint to Asian mobility, the celebratory rhetoric used by ranchers to depict Mexican families was not uniformly applied to all Mexican workers. Instead, ranchers described a stark contrast between Mexican families and Mexican bachelors. Where a tendency towards settlement was attributed to the former, a predisposition towards migrancy was attributed to the latter. According to rancher testimonies, married workers were more amicable, anxious to resolve disputes, and likely to reinvest profits into their homes. Where employers praised married men, they critiqued Mexican bachelors as "lawless, inefficient and unreliable."[33] Implicit in their critiques was Mexican bachelors' greater ability to leave their employer when better paying work opportunities emerged. Without the need for family housing or a cumulative investment in a home's equity, since they lodged in shared dormitories, Mexican bachelors could more easily leave one ranch for another. The racial logic used to suggest Mexican workers were ideally domesticized was quickly reversed when worker mobility was used subversively.

Ranchers positioned single Mexican men as an exception to the domesticity they celebrated in Mexican workers by drawing upon well-established tropes of the white fruit tramp. Shamel, the author of the housing series, explained: "These traveling vagabonds often slept under the open sky wrapped in their blankets, and gathered their meals from convenient gardens and hen roosts and cooked them in a tin can or pan over a campfire wherever they happened to be."[34] His critiques of poor homeless white migrants were consistent with those levied by social scientists, who criminalized migrants' mobility as vagrancy and their behavior as deviant.[35] Occupying parallel economic statuses and a similar intermediary racial position, as not-quite-white but seemingly superior to other racialized groups, the denigration of the fruit tramp provided a helpful comparison to Mexican bachelors, as ranchers grappled with the challenges of managing workers with high rates of mobility. Culbertson drew on familiar tropes previously used to describe white itinerant workers to castigate single Mexican workers in a report to the California Citrus Institute. As manager of Limoneira, he wrote, "Most of them worked well when they did work, but all too many of them made Sunday last an extra day or two, or stayed in our employ only long enough to earn a small pocketful of money."[36] Across accounts, single Mexican men were chastised for pursuing short-lived enjoyments such as gambling and drinking. Those tethered to the ranch, whether by familial or financial investment in a home, were uniformly preferred over those without dependents or property.

In actuality, the line between married and single workers was far from definitive. For instance, married men employed in the citrus groves of inland Southern California frequently migrated without their wives and children during the off-season. Traveling as "solos," a married man might appear to be a "bachelor" to a new employer. More accurately, the distinctions ranchers described between single and married men served as a substitute for the differences they viewed between mobile and immobile workers. For instance, when ranchers claimed to prefer Mexican laborers occupying family housing because they were dependable and loyal, in actuality that dependability and loyalty had a lot to do with workers' difficulty leaving a company home in which they were financially and emotionally invested. In the same way, those living in boardinghouses could more easily leave one job for another, regardless of whether or not they were married. Yet, in USDA accounts, the freedom of mobility was recast as slothfulness and criminal vagrancy, not because of workers' innate characteristics, but because of the threat it posed to ranchers' bottom line.

Logically, migrants operated as free agents in an open market, but racialized capitalism tied their movements to their employers. Although ranchers and farmworkers both struggled to leverage mobility for their own advantage, public policy helped channel workers' movements in ways that advanced white capitalist accumulation, thus favoring ranchers. As evidenced by the Alien Land Law, as well as the Geary Act before it, when Asian immigrants attempted to build permanent homes or embark on self-sustaining agricultural pursuits, their efforts were criminalized. Similarly, white itinerant workers were denigrated as an offense to white domesticity, a continuation of white workers' criminalization evident in the high rates of vagrancy arrests discussed in the previous chapter. Likewise, rancher support for company housing tethered Mexican immigrants to the land by celebrating their domesticity and denigrating its converse, movement. Examining these cases together shows that both the Alien Land Law and company housing denied workers opportunities for accumulating wealth through land ownership and helped reinforce ranchers' power over workers' mobility.

"BIRDS OF PASSAGE": MEXICAN WORKERS AND
THE 1920s IMMIGRATION HEARINGS

During World War I (1914–1918), citrus ranchers had eagerly recruited Mexican laborers. When wartime opportunities created a southwestern labor shortage by drawing U.S. workers to the urban north, agriculturalists proposed that Mexican immigrants were ideally prone to permanent settlement and long-term labor on citrus ranches. However, the 1920s proposal by Congressman John Box for a restrictive quota on Western Hemispheric immigration activated a stark shift in the ways Mexican workers were perceived during the following decade. Where scholars have richly investigated the immigration debates of the 1920s, a mobility discussion brings new insights, including how shifting cultural narrative constructions about movement shaped the structural conditions managing migrants' movements. It was in the context of these debates that ranchers recast Mexican workers as "birds of passage," who returned to Mexico at the end of the harvests, instead of as inherently rooted. Interrogating this shift suggests tropes of migrant and settler are best understood as two aspects of the same, long-running force of racialization—one whose most salient feature, whether as the basis for exclusion or inclusion, is a collective attempt to deny nonwhites property and defend white access to multiracial labor.

Immigration acts passed in the 1920s had a profound effect on U.S. ideals of citizenship, race, and nation building, with notable consequences for Mexican racial formation. The Immigration Act of 1921 was the first to place numerical quotas on immigration, limiting the number of admissible immigrants to 3 percent of residents of the same nationality recorded as living in the United States in the 1910 census. The second act reduced this calculation to 2 percent of foreign-born persons of each nationality recorded in the 1890 census and, further, banned from entry anyone ineligible for citizenship, including Asian-descent migrants previously allowed admission. Although the specific calculations used to determine admission numbers were subject to debate, quotas themselves were widely accepted as a means of reducing immigration with the aim of facilitating resident immigrants' integration and securing the dominance of white U.S. "native stock."[37]

Perhaps unexpectedly then, citizens of "contiguous countries" residing in the Western Hemisphere were exempt in both the 1921 and 1924 Immigration Acts.[38] As their numbers increased in the years to follow, Mexican immigrants would come under close scrutiny.[39] The series of hearings initiated by Congressman Box was a striking forum for these contests. Historians of the United States during this period have produced a wealth of scholarship concerning these debates, from their impact on Mexican racialization, to their role in placing Mexican immigration in the national limelight, to the links formed between Mexican labor and broader U.S. race relations.[40] My focus here is specifically on how opponents and proponents of the bill engaged in contests over the racial meaning of "Mexican" through debates over Mexican mobility, and the resulting impact of these positions on race making, for not only Mexican-descent people, but also for a variety of other racialized groups in the United States.

Mexican immigration figures in this period are notoriously unreliable due to illicit migration and misreported values. Nevertheless, all sources tell us that Mexican immigration spiked after 1910.[41] Congressman Box responded to this increase with a proposal to place Western Hemispheric immigration on a quota system. He argued that without numerical restrictions, the Southwest was vulnerable to economic degeneration. In addition to his concerns over labor, Congressman Box levied a series of critiques towards Mexican immigrants' racial character, suggesting that they deteriorated U.S. standards of living, burdened charitable organizations, and instigated political uprising. Additional quota proponents—including labor unions, social service providers, eugenicists, and small-scale farmers—used the metaphor of a "back door" to describe the threat posed by Mexican laborers, suggesting congressional negligence towards its household.[42] A series of hearings in 1926, titled "Seasonal Agricultural Workers from Mexico," were the first to propose quotas for the Western Hemisphere. Each promoted further restriction and each explicitly proposed that quotas be placed on Mexico.

The bills quickly encountered resistance from agricultural interests, who based their protests on economic grounds. The House Committee on Immigration and Naturalization argued that Mexican labor drove down the U.S. standard of living; agriculturalists argued Mexican workers received some of the highest wages in the country. The committee argued a labor surplus drove Mexican immigrants to cities in search of relief; agriculturalists argued there was a stark shortage of rural workers. The committee argued Mexican immigrants displaced white American workers; agriculturalists argued they filled positions unsuitable for white families.[43] In all cases, the racial distinctions between superior and inferior races were organized alongside categories of settled and migrant workers.

Opponents of the Box Bill argued agricultural labor was inherently seasonal and that the rotating nature of crops required a workforce that followed its peaks. White families, they argued, were unsuited for the migratory nature of this work, which required traveling vast distances, rooming in temporary quarters, and uprooting families. Instead, they argued, white men were better suited for managerial and higher-paying industrial work. Following this line of argument to its logical conclusion, quota opponents argued that Americans were forced to choose between two options. As stated by Dr. E. G. Peterson in an address before the Central Chamber of Commerce of the United States:

> Shall we force our own citizens to perform these largely physical labors, now performed in the areas under consideration by foreign labor or machinery, which are so distasteful to our own citizens and thereby encourage them to reduce their standard of living to the level suggested by such labor and remuneration or shall we import common labor sufficient to handle this phase of our industry and ask our own citizens to aspire to other more skilled employment?[44]

The only acceptable solution to the regional need for agricultural workers and the national desire to maintain a majority white population of skilled workers was to look south of the border. In Mexico, agricultural interests promised, there existed an ideal workforce of migratory unskilled laborers who would arrive to harvest crops and, of their own volition, return to Mexico at the season's conclusion.

Agriculturalists artfully concealed the ways capitalism pushed Mexicans into migration, even as they highlighted the industry's need for migrant laborers. According to agricultural interests, profitable production required a category of worker that was perpetually in motion. George Clements of the Los Angeles Chamber of Commerce, for instance, described two "castes" of farm laborers: the expert who engaged scientific methods, and the casual "roustabout" who moved from district to district to meet the labor demand in seasonal crops.[45] These accounts paternalistically placed responsibility for migrant workers on farm organizations. Clements explained,

> Casual labor, let me emphasize, must be fluid—must be mobile—and to be so must be fostered and cared for by some organization co-operative or corporate, that will not only be able to supply it to the farms as needed, but to undertake responsibility as to health, sanitation, advantages in education and character upbuilding, religious training and standards of living of the workers.[46]

The rancher assumed full power in this equation. Expanding U.S. agriculture meant not only maintaining exemptions for the Western Hemisphere, but also on Mexican noncitizens whose movements were micromanaged by agricultural interests. An extension of the Anglo Fantasy Past, ranchers described a vision of California in which Anglo Americans had laid the foundation for a cornucopia whose fruits were to be enjoyed by the descendants of white settlers, but would be picked by a workforce of nonwhite migrants.

In light of rising Mexican immigration to the United States, Congress faced many questions regarding the validity of the Western Hemisphere's quota exemptions. In response, ranchers credited congressional concerns with a fundamental misconception about Mexican people. The chairman of the Agricultural Committee of the Fresno Chamber of Commerce, S. Parker Frisselle, explained that "There is also in the minds of many the thought that the Mexican is an immigrant. My experience of the Mexican is that he is a 'homer.' Like the pigeon he goes back to roost."[47] In this account, Mexicans were not immigrants with the intention to settle as future citizens, as earlier European immigrants had done, but circular migrants residing in the United States only temporarily. They appeared for the harvest in flocks and, as quickly as they came, returned to Mexico to nest.

Earlier iterations of southern and eastern European immigrants as "birds of passage" offered a reference point by which to evoke the idea of seasonal nonimmigrant Mexican labor. Where immigrants originating from England, Ireland, Scotland, and Wales were commonly understood as old stock families intent on settling in the United States, the twentieth-century wave of immigrants from Italy, Greece, Austria-Hungary, and Russia were viewed as nonimmigrant laborers who would ultimately return to their home countries. According to Frank Warne, Special Expert of the Foreign Population for the U.S. Census, the majority of these sojourners remained in the United States for a period of eight to ten years. They then returned abroad.[48]

Enabled by mature migration chains facilitated by advances in transportation and communication technologies, these workers traveled between the United States and southeastern Europe with relative ease. In accounts preceding those about Mexican birds of passage, restrictionists had criticized white ethnics' circular migration. Like swallows followed the seasons, these accounts suggested that European birds of passage followed the rises and drops of the economy to the disadvantage of settled Americans. Described by the Committee on Immigration of the National Civic Federation, for instance, "[the European] 'bird-of-passage' class of workers ... think mainly of their own immediate economic needs with no permanent interest in the welfare of this country."[49] Critics argued that southeastern Europeans returned to their families abroad without setting roots and without contributing to the nation's welfare, and hence were unfairly benefitting from the higher wages offered in U.S. industries. They were accused of disloyalty to employers, plundering the United States of its wealth through remittances, and displacing American workers.

When considering critiques of southeastern European birds of passage, who were depicted as birds of prey, agriculturalists' praise of circular migration by Mexican immigrants in the post–World War I period seems counterintuitive. The discrepancy between white ethnic birds of passage and Mexican birds of passage can be explained by the divergent values placed on migration within the economic sectors they occupied. That is, it was inherently structured by capital. Although migrant labor was devalued as a loss in northern industry, it was considered essential to amassing profit in southwestern U.S. agriculture. Perceptions of various immigrant groups as birds of passage, and the cultural value ascribed to this identity in the early twentieth century, were not fixed. Instead, they oscillated according to the potential for profit attached to different migratory patterns. The aim here is to understand the ways racial formation impacted the perceived origins, coherence, and characteristics of this migration.[50]

In succession, agriculturalists reaffirmed the idea of Mexican birds of passage before the Committee on Immigration and Naturalization. T. A. Sullivan, representing the beet growers of Arizona's Salt River Valley, described Mexican workers as entering fields when needed, and then disappearing south each winter. S. Maston Nixon argued it was these same workers who returned north for the harvest. Howard Ottinger, representing a farm bureau in Minnesota, suggested most Mexican workers refused to stay the entire year, even if offered free permanent housing. In testimony after testimony, agriculturalists suggested Mexican workers arrived with their families in secondhand Fords to work the fields, and in the winter returned to Mexico with their pockets full of U.S. dollars.[51] There were only a few exceptions to ranchers' accounts of Mexican return migration—but these testimonies were in the minority. Rather, Box Bill opponents overwhelmingly claimed that only in the form of Mexican migrants would Congress find laborers whose inherent nature compelled them to follow the seasonal harvests and return abroad year after year.

The Immigration Act of 1924 catalyzed a series of debates over immigration from the Western Hemisphere to the United States. Reflective of the multiscalar nature of regional and racial economics, southwestern interests met in the halls of Congress to argue that seasonal migration was essential to the success of U.S. agriculture. In a stark shift from the housing campaigns of the World War I period, ranchers argued Mexican workers were circular migrants uniquely suited to fill this need. Their arguments drew on a preexisting discourse of birds of passage that was earlier applied to southeastern Europeans. Occupying similar economic and racial positions, the return migration of white ethnics offered an effective reference for Congressmen both unfamiliar with Mexican workers and concerned with increasing rates of immigration. Regional representatives from the Citrus Belt would play a central role in these debates, drawing on regional racial formations of Mexican workers and exacerbating concerns over racial change.

THE SOUTHWEST ADVANTAGE: LEVERAGING RACIAL CONFUSION OVER MEXICAN WORKERS

The first major congressional debates over immigration from the Western Hemisphere reveal much confusion over the frequency and nature of Mexican immigration. Although agriculturalists were well aware of the increased rates of Mexican permanency in the United States, they preached a regional gospel proclaiming that Mexican workers were inherently nomadic in nature and, therefore, ideally racially suited to agricultural labor. While Congressmen far removed from the Southwest struggled to understand the racial nature of Mexican people, agriculturalists from California and the Southwest more generally sought to maximize this confusion. In doing so, they hoped to position Mexican workers as ideally located between Native American and European races: obedient, manageable, and migratory.

At the time of the Box Bill debates, the majority of Mexican immigrants to the United States resided in Texas, Arizona, and California, with the largest concentration shifting from Texas to California throughout the 1920s. This change was particularly acute in the inland Southern California counties of San Bernardino and Riverside. By 1928 more than 40 percent of all inland births were of Mexican descent.[52] In 1929, the Central Chamber of

Commerce—an association of chambers across the United States—sought to determine the characteristics of the ethnic Mexican population and the extent to which agribusiness depended on their labor. Analyzing surveys collected in Redlands, a citrus community neighboring the county seat of San Bernardino with a Mexican population of about 1,000 people, we can see that most ethnic Mexicans had permanent ties to the region.[53] Supporting these accounts, ranchers' responses suggest Mexican-descent workers commonly owned or leased their own homes, worked in field labor for about ten months out of the year, and had established familial ties to the area. As succinctly stated by one grower, "Our [Mexican] laborers are mostly local."[54]

Oral histories collected by Inland Mexican Heritage, a grassroots effort to preserve the stories of Mexican-descent people in inland Southern California, reaffirm these accounts.[55] Like period sources, they suggest that Mexican migration to the Inland Empire expanded during the Mexican Revolution (1910–1920) and that, for many, this move was permanent. By the time of the Box Bill debate, Mexican families had established communities throughout inland Southern California, including sizable settlements in Claremont, Corona, Pomona, Redlands, San Bernardino, and Upland, as well as other area towns. These colonias were characterized by the presence of multigenerational families and dense social networks that spanned neighborhoods, and community institutions such as churches, schools, and mutual aid societies.[56] On-the-ground developments in citrus communities suggested a reality far from that of the birds of passage trope used to describe Mexican life in the halls of Congress. Although surveys and oral histories suggest that the Mexican-descent population was increasingly permanent in this period, agriculturalists sought to assuage concerns with population change by challenging the idea that Mexican workers settled long-term in the United States.

George Clements, manager for the Agricultural Committee of the Los Angeles Chamber of Commerce, was among the most adamant Box Bill challengers and his influence popularized the myth of Mexican return migration. For instance, in a Central Chamber of Commerce memo titled "Immigration Bill Big Economic Loss" (1927), Clements wrote, "The Mexican immigrant comes to the United States to sell his labor for United States dollars, without any idea of permanent residence, 85 percent of them return to Mexico at the completion of their employment, and the balance vacillate between the two countries."[57] Clements's assertion drew upon congressional testimony by Box Bill opponent John N. Garner of Texas. When asked what percentage of Mexican workers returned at the end of the harvest, he responded, "My observation is, living right here on the border, or within fifty miles of it, that 80 percent of the Mexicans that come over for temporary work go back."[58] Garner's anecdotal estimate was an overstatement. As reported by economists, only a small proportion of Mexican immigrants living in California returned to Mexico.[59] Through Clements's memo, however, Garner's casual observation became fact. It collapsed regional differences for the Texas border region, where migration was highest, and the national return migration. Yet, the figures of 80 and 85 percent quickly would become conventional wisdom.[60]

Claims equating Mexican immigrant workers with birds of passage were reaffirmed in the regional press, particularly the *Los Angeles Times,* whose publisher Harry Chandler appeared before Congress in opposition to quota restrictions.[61] Throughout the 1920s, the *Los Angeles Times* held to the line that agriculturalists faced an acute shortage, and seasonal Mexican migration was a dwindling resource that the region greatly need. For instance, in "California's Farm Labor Situation" (May 1926) the *Los Angeles Times* called for increased immigration to offset crop loss.[62] Further seeking to ease concerns with Mexican settlement, the paper ran a story under the headline "Mexico Has Her Own Ideas About 'Quotas'" on the cover of its weekly *Farm and Orchard Magazine* (April 1928), claiming that the Mexican Department of Labor urged nationals to remain at home.[63] A similar account, "Saviors of California" (December 1929), suggested Mexican settlement was dwindling: "It is known that thousands [of Mexican immigrants] return across the border after a season's work here, and if those returning under present conditions number as many as they did when passage was freer there is a net loss."[64] Another article, published in April 1930, dismissed restrictive immigration measures proposed by the Box Bill as "ill-considered" studies that were "framed on nothing but prejudice and theorist opinion."[65] Indeed, many Mexican nationals returned across the border, and the number of visas distributed to Mexican workers decreased in this period, exacerbated by economic depression—yet, population surveys and oral histories suggest Clements's and Chandler's insistence on consistent circular migration were largely wrong.

On both sides of the debate, stakeholders lacked access to reliable migration data. Unauthorized entry was difficult to estimate, local surveys collected only broad estimates, and immigration figures from the United States and Mexico conflicted.[66] Where authorities lacked statistical evidence, they instead turned to arguments about Mexicans' innate racial nature. Southwestern agriculturalists held a distinct advantage here, since Congress

exhibited much confusion over Mexican racial status. As described by sociologist Tomás Almaguer, ethnic Mexicans occupied an intermediate position
in California's racial hierarchy, where law granted Mexicans white status
under the Treaty of Guadalupe Hidalgo (1849), but cultural citizenship was
denied.[67] Review of the Box Bill debate suggests that questions about
Mexican racial status continued well into the twentieth century. One common assertion racially equated Mexicans with Indians, who were indigenous
to North America and early subjects to the rule of Spain. A second line of
reasoning suggested Mexican people were racially mixed mestizos of Indian
and Spanish origin. And, a third line claimed Mexican people were comprised of varying grades of mixed-race people, some better suited for settlement (white) and others prone to migration (nonwhite). Each proposed
Mexican people were ideally suited for hand labor and racially superior to
other foreign workers.

Box himself understood Mexicans to be largely of Indian descent.
Conflating Mexican Indians with American Indians, he asked why ranchers
could not recruit Native workers to complete tasks which they themselves suggested required a workforce predisposed to stoop labor and repressive heat? In
response, some agriculturalists testified American Indians would not do the
work.[68] Explaining the difference between U.S. and Mexican Indian populations, C. S. Brown testified that American Indians were nomads predisposed
to abandoning the fields in pursuit of hunting. Conversely, he explained,
Spaniards had conditioned Mexican Indians to be docile through generations
of supervision. For Brown, Mexican workers' passive acceptance of European
management uniquely suited them for agriculture.[69] C. V. Maddux drew further distinctions between American Indians and Mexicans, stating, "Those
Indians in Mexico were cultivating lands with their bronze hoes when Cortez
came here. . . . Those Indians up there in Montana are Crows, mostly, and they
are about just as good to a beet farm as a crow is to a corn farm."[70] Where Box
tried to collapse American Indians and Mexican immigrants into a single
racial category, Box Bill opponents sought to disarticulate the link. Rather,
they suggested Mexican Indians were distinctly prone to labor in the American
West under European American supervision.

Some Box Bill opponents distinguished between Native American and
Mexican laborers as two subsets of a singular Indian race, and others suggested Mexican immigrants comprised a distinct racial type of their own.
E. K. Cumming, representing the Nogales Chamber of Commerce,
explained, "There are several Indian tribes down there, but they are pure

Indian. The Yaquis are all pure Indian, and the Mayans and the Papagoes and the various tribes down there are pure Indian. The Mexican is part Spanish, with some Indian blood in him."[71] Cumming's observation drew from understandings of "mestizaje," a widely held racial ideology in the American West of blood mixture between Spanish colonizers and the Indigenous population of North America. Where eugenics suggested Indians were child-like outsiders, it also proposed European descendants could be assimilated. As mestizos, Mexicans occupied both worlds, at the same time both manage-able and racially superior to other nonwhites.[72]

The ideology of mestizaje enabled Box Bill opponents to distinguish among Mexican castes. Congressman Joseph Mansfield, for instance, dif-ferentiated between Mexican Americans and the Mexican "nomadic type" living in the Texas border region. He described the former as originating from the early Texas settlements, alluding to a landed Spanish elite, and the latter as living transborder lives, with half their time in Mexico and half in the United States.[73] Maddux further distinguished Mexican nomads from one another, describing on the one hand the "Godfearing, family-loving, law-abiding" Mexican common laborer, and on the other the illiterate "bor-der rat" who crossed unauthorized into the United States.[74] Congressman Claude Hudspeth of Texas described this distinction simply as that between "good Mexicans," those who follow and enforce the law, and "bad Mexicans," those who rob and terrorize U.S. citizens.[75] The racial ideology of mestizaje provided Box Bill opponents with a racial continuum along which they could assert that Mexican workers were inferior to whites, superior to American Indians, and undesirable only when coming from the lowest class unsuitable for labor.

Within the Box Bill debates, Mexicans existed as simultaneously Indigenous and foreign. They were cast as both Native to the region, uniquely suited to its hot climate and biologically adapted to hand labor, and as national outsiders, noncitizens uninterested in long-term settlement. Debates over Mexicans' racial position became forums for discussing whether they did or did not belong in the U.S. nation. Further, discussions of Mexican nativity underscore the marginalization of American Indians within an agri-cultural economy rooted in Indigenous lands. In both cases, the mobility of labor under capitalism was recast in racial terms. Mexicans and American Indians were each described as racial nomads, but only Mexicans were cred-ited as being manageable by white colonizers. They were birds of passage, swallows not "Crows," whose labor agriculturalists eagerly pursued. Box Bill opponents successfully argued their case in the 1926 debates. Soon after, a combination of continued immigration from Mexico and a natural disaster in the Caribbean would place the racialization of Mexican mobility alongside that of colonial subjects.

THE STORM: PUERTO RICAN MIGRANTS ENTER THE FIELD

The Box Bill debates continued throughout the remainder of the decade, but in 1930 the hearings exhibited a distinctive shift. The catalyst was a destructive hurricane striking over 1,500 miles away from Washington, DC. With highs of 150 miles per hour, the winds of Hurricane San Felipe (Okeechobee) traversed Puerto Rico in the summer of 1928. The hurricane left many on the verge of starvation, caused millions of dollars in property damage, destroyed the backbone of Puerto Rican agriculture, and pushed 250,000 rural people into homelessness.[76] The storm triggered a renegotiation of social relations between Puerto Rico and the continental United States. Questions regarding displaced Puerto Ricans combined with concerns over Filipino workers in the Pacific Northwest, who shared colonial status in the United States, to reshape the terms of the Box Bill debates. Where Puerto Ricans and Filipinos held rights to U.S. migration, and thus permanent settlement, agriculturalists positioned Mexican immigration as the nation's lone defense against the permanent settlement of colonial nonwhite people. That is, Mexicans were elevated as ideal workers and migrants through the denigration of Puerto Rican and Filipino settlers in an affirmation of southwestern racial hierarchies organized around laborers' mobility.

When Hurricane San Felipe hit Puerto Rico, residents' displacement became an area of growing national concern. Inland coffee crops and citrus groves in Puerto Rico experienced the highest losses, leaving rural people dependent on the Red Cross for relief. The *New York Times* reported aid organizations' chief concern was the "jíbaro," a term used to derogatively describe poor rural workers from the inland mountains where coffee was produced. Many migrated to urban coastal areas, where food and shelter were more easily accessed. This is also where sugar production was concentrated. The storm had cut the crop in half. Although recovery required many hands, the sugar industry could not absorb the bulk of displaced rural workers. The disparate losses of rural coffee versus urban sugar initiated a coastal migration whose limits were not yet clear. Federal relief was slow and insufficient when faced with an island consistently in economic peril.[77] Experiencing a yearlong depression, many Puerto Ricans turned to an alternative solution with continuing appeal in times when humanitarian crisis has been met with federal disinvestment. They left the island to seek employment on the mainland.

Throughout the twentieth century, Puerto Rico's political status facilitated continental migration. The United States took possession of Puerto Rico, the Philippines, and Guam from Spain when the Treaty of Paris ended the Spanish-American War in 1898. Unlike U.S. territorial possessions acquired from northern Mexico, including California, Spain's oversea holdings were never incorporated as states. Rather, in the first two years of occupation (1898–1900), Puerto Rico was held under military rule. By enactment of the Forsaker Act (1900), island residents became Puerto Rican citizens, a status subject to civilian rule with presidential appointments approved by the U.S. Senate. Soon after, the Insular cases (1901) created a new category called "unincorporated territory," which divorced territorial holdings from the eventual promise of statehood and initiated a new political status for Puerto Rican residents. As U.S. "nationals," Puerto Ricans had the right to travel, live, and work throughout the continental United States. National status did not, however, extend to rights of representation or trial by jury.[78] As described by immigration historian Mae Ngai, "nationals occupied a liminal status that was neither citizen nor alien."[79]

Occupying a new and unfamiliar category, national status facilitated migration to the continental United States, but it did not guarantee entrance. For instance, Puerto Rican national Isabel González was infamously detained at Ellis Island and refused admission to New York in 1902. It took trial in the U.S. Supreme Court to determine, definitively, that Puerto Ricans were not immigrants.[80] And, it was not until 1917 that the Jones-Shafroth Act granted Puerto Ricans U.S. citizenship. Yet, their citizenship conferred a secondary status lacking congressional representation and the right to vote in U.S. presidential elections. Despite the change in Puerto Rico's political status, continental Americans continued to perceive Puerto Ricans as foreigners, even where contract labor programs, social networks, and colonial relationships facilitated migration to the United States.[81]

Congress found it difficult to justify the continued immigration of Mexican labor in the aftermath of a natural disaster that had left its own citizens displaced and in need of relief. In similar conditions of economic and environmental hardship occurring in the past, government representatives had promoted Puerto Rican migration. Following Hurricane San Ciriaco

(1899), U.S.-owned sugar corporations recruited over 5,000 Puerto Rican people to Hawaii. After World War I, approximately 13,000 islanders were recruited to war industries. And, through publications in Puerto Rican newspapers, U.S. companies promoted migration to Latin American planta-tions.[82] Similarly here, Hurricane San Felipe was met with calls to redistrib-ute rural workers among western agriculture. But, in the context of ranchers' battles to secure Mexican immigrant labor in the congressional hearings, Puerto Rican migration faced unprecedented resistance.

Although Puerto Ricans were free to migrate to the U.S. mainland, the financial means to do so eluded most workers. For most people, the possibility of migration required contract programs and government-aided recruitment to resettle migrants throughout Hawaii, the Northeast, and the South between 1901 and World War I. Still, at the time of the first Box Bill hearing, in 1926, most southwestern ranchers were unfamiliar with Puerto Rican laborers. This would change soon afterward. At the cost of a reported $70,000, the U.S. Bureau of Insular Affairs aided in the resettlement of 1,500 Puerto Ricans impacted by the hurricane to the cotton region of Arizona's Salt River Valley in 1926.[83] Workers protested their labor conditions soon after arriving. Wary of Puerto Rican revolt, growers swiftly discontinued their recruitment activities.[84] In the eyes of ranchers, Puerto Ricans and Mexicans both appeared foreign, but they quickly learned that Puerto Ricans' U.S. citizen-ship carried with it protections that tempered rancher control.

As Puerto Ricans claimed their rights to free movement, local relief organizations, and government representation, they incurred the ire of ranchers through acts of protest not soon to be forgotten. In 1930, as the immigration debates continued, ranchers vehemently protested Congress's assertion that Mexican immigrants be replaced with Puerto Rican migrants. Their critiques permeated the Committee on Immigration and Naturalization when it assembled to discuss three bills (HR8523, HR8530, HR8702) per-taining to further restrictions on immigration from the Western Hemisphere. D. B. Wiley of Phoenix, Arizona testified, "We shipped in two boatloads of those Porto Ricans, and they were so entirely worthless as farm hands that we paid the fares of the third boatload which we contracted for, and let them stay home."[85] Kenneth B. McMicken, representing the Arizona Cotton Growers Association, echoed Wiley's dissatisfaction. He described Puerto Ricans as the "most unsatisfactory type" he had ever employed. According to McMicken, Puerto Ricans were unskilled workers who felt unduly entitled to public assistance: "They were not only unskilled but had absolutely no desire to even try to support themselves, their sole attitude being, 'You brought us here, now take care of us.'"[86] Ranchers adamantly claimed Puerto Rican migrants proved a poor substitute for Mexican immigrants.

The Arizona experiment taught ranchers that Puerto Ricans' status as U.S. citizens afforded them unexpected protections, leading to resistive efforts unavailable to Mexican immigrants. For instance, Puerto Ricans protested and abandoned their contracts when American companies failed to abide by their agreements. Although guaranteed comfortable houses and modern facilities, workers received tents, dilapidated adobes, and lumber shacks when they arrived—notably the same facilities that had housed Mexican workers.[87] In response, Puerto Ricans protested their living conditions to the Cotton Growers Association, state legislature, and governor of Arizona. And, they organized internally, through the Industrial Workers of the World rather than through the local Phoenix Labor Council, who alongside ranchers denigrated their members as anti-American "radicals."[88] Mexican workers would be equally exposed if mounting similar defenses. Without the state protections extended to Puerto Rican workers, they would have faced deportation for violating their work agreements.[89]

Puerto Ricans' ability to abandon unfair working conditions and to claim relief during restive actions underscores ranchers' advantage in hiring Mexican immigrants, whose noncitizen status kept them disempowered and denied them access to government assistance. This is not to suggest that ranchers did not try to keep Puerto Rican workers in place. To the contrary, they proposed loitering laws meant to silence organizers in the street and bind them to ranches. That is, they tried to immobilize them. As a unionist paper sarcastically noted, "Why not try putting a ball and chain on those pesky Porto Ricans, Mr. Walker?"[90] Yet, although Puerto Ricans' claims to citizenship were tenuous, even their secondary status provided better protections than those available to Mexican workers. It was by claiming those protections that Puerto Rican workers gained the ire of the Arizona Cotton Growers' Association.

Although continental Americans collapsed Puerto Ricans and Mexicans into the single category of foreigner, ranchers quickly learned citizenship status impacted the degree of control they could hold over labor. Foremost, citizenship (or lack thereof) determined ranchers' ability to bind workers to the ranch. The contract programs initiated by the Secretary of Labor during World War I had increased ranchers' investment in controlling the movement of Mexican workers into the post–World War I era. Without the right to migrate elsewhere, Mexican immigrants were left vulnerable to deportation if they were to refuse the work and living conditions set by local authorities. As overtly put by the Chamber of Commerce of the USA, "The American negro, the Porto Rican negro and the Filipinos cannot be deported if they prove later to be a crime menace. The Mexican can be."[91]

Puerto Ricans were also legally able to relocate to other industries. Whereas ranchers were bound to return workers to Mexico at the end of their government contracts, as U.S. citizens Puerto Ricans were held to no such conditions and many chose to withdraw from their contracts.[92] By claiming their rights to free movement, Puerto Rican workers both exercised their citizenship and gained the suspicion of California ranchers in a move that would have continuing resonance for the congressional hearings on Capitol Hill.

"BLACK DEVILS": THE DEBATE CONTINUES WITH NEW RACIAL THREATS

Where U.S. capitalists had previously turned to Puerto Rico in times of labor shortage, agriculturalists now attempted to shut the gate as the immigration debates of the 1920s continued into 1930. But they could not force Puerto Ricans, people with U.S. citizenship, to stay on the island, especially within the context of a natural disaster causing irreparable economic damage. Without immigration laws denying Puerto Ricans access to the continental United States, agriculturalists instead leveraged congressional confusion and national fears over colonial subjects to strengthen their claims for Mexican immigration. Specifically, they argued that as birds of passage Mexican immigrants posed significantly less racial threat than the migration of colonial subjects with rights to permanent residency. Ranchers' concerns with the unequal protections leveraged against them by citizen (Puerto Rican) and noncitizen (Mexican) workers were thinly veiled in Congress as an appeal to the unequal dangers posed by immobile (Puerto Rican) and mobile (Mexican) people. Miscegenation was at the core of how mobility and immobility played out in cultural constructions of Mexican and Puerto Rican workers in this period. Equated with homing pigeons, Mexicans were said to roam together as families across the national divide, thus preventing racial mixing. Conversely, migrant flows enabled by U.S. imperialism abroad were positioned as a threat to white women unaware of workers' colonial roots, marking Puerto Rican migration a question of both national and racial borders.

A statement by Fred Hart, managing editor of the California Farm Bureau Monthlies, is indicative of the ways Puerto Ricans were leveraged to promote Mexican exemption from immigration quotas. When reminded that Puerto Ricans held citizenship rights, Hart responded passionately:

> Let me ask you this question [Chairman]: Do you think that I should take this attitude from your statement, take back to my wife and family and my relatives that you are going to shut the Mexican out, so that if we are going to exist we must bring the Porto Rican in and put him alongside our families, the thin lipped Porto Rican, an agitator, a trouble-maker, and a man that I don't want my family to have to associate with continuously?[93]

Within his statement were three themes concerning Puerto Ricans that permeated the hearings. He suggested that without Mexican immigration, ranchers would be forced to recruit Puerto Rican labor. He alluded to the racial ambiguity of Puerto Rican residents, who could appear phenotypically white but harbored African lineage.[94] And, he suggested, associating with Puerto Ricans would taint the purity of white communities.

Box Bill opponents threatened that without Mexican immigration, ranchers would be forced to recruit colonial labor. Speaking of the Los Angeles region, Harry Chandler, president of the Los Angeles Times Corporation, warned Congress that ranchers would recruit Puerto Rican and Filipino workers if the Box Bill were passed. He described their recruitment as an act of "self-defense." Chandler drew upon congressional fears of increased demands for local relief, stating, "Well, when they are once here they will not go back home, as the Mexicans do—come and go to meet a seasonal demand—but they will be here and we will have to take good care of them when there is no work."[95]

His statement echoed claims made by Chambers of Commerce and their representatives since Hurricane San Felipe. George Clements wrote in 1928,

> [Mexican] labor excluded, we have but one place to turn—that is to the Porto Rican negro who as an American citizen in coming becomes a fixture. From a social service standpoint there is no comparison. The Mexican as an alien is returnable to his own country—the negro, just as indigents, once here must be taken care of.[96]

With the Mexican bird of passage as its opposite, the trope of Puerto Rican settlers seeking government relief was an early manifestation of the "welfare queen" and "culture of poverty" narrative, a popular trope positioning

African American women as dependent on state assistance and without a desire for financial independence.[97] Even in the immediate aftermath of a devastating hurricane, prolonged relief was likened to charity. "Work with food" was championed as a means to prevent the "unworthy" from attaining emergency relief and to avert a "permanent disaster"; that is, reliance on the U.S. government for recovery.[98] Similarly, when Puerto Ricans abandoned their contracts in Arizona, due to inferior treatment, acts of labor protest were recast as evidence of a poor work ethic. Where Mexicans were said to return to Mexico in the off-season, by racial predisposition or if needed by force, references to Puerto Ricans became synonymous with the permanent settlement of charity-seeking colonials.

Threats of Puerto Rican settlement reify the important role of California in these national debates. As a gateway to Hawaii, where large concentrations of colonial subjects were recruited to work in the sugar industry, California was cast as the last stand against racial outsiders' occupation of the continental United States. Increasing numbers of Filipino nationals, both in Hawaii and on the Pacific Coast, further exacerbated concerns about the nation's relationship to its territorial holdings. Congressmen warned that Hawaii's racial problem could quickly become California's.[99] Ranchers fanned the flames, claiming racialized colonials would quickly spread to the rest of the nation. In a cacophony of insults, California congressman Arthur M. Free described Puerto Rican and Filipino emigrants as the "scum of the earth," "the worst cancer," and "an ulcer."[100] Manipulating fears of Puerto Rican and Filipino settlement, California representatives championed Mexican labor as a safeguard against the permanent settlement of nonwhite workers in the continental United States.

Opposition to Puerto Rican migration—reframed as support for Mexican immigration—manifested most starkly in elaborate threats of a "negro" influx. Puerto Ricans were consistently described as dangerously ambiguous, appearing phenotypically white but harboring nonwhite lineage.[101] Drawn to higher-paying employment in the industrial North, African Americans were a relative minority in the Southwest. Although physically absent in significant numbers, interpolating racial blackness onto Puerto Rican workers, as well as those originating from the Philippines, proved an effective strategy for stirring fears of a nonwhite hoard.[102] Where Mexicans were, supposedly, easily racially identifiable by their skin color, Box Bill opponents claimed that as a multiracial people of mixed Portuguese, Spanish, Taíno, and African descent, Puerto Ricans posed an insidious threat to the racial composition of the nation. Following Mendelian rationale, a "red haired, blue eyed, freckle faced, thin nosed and thin lipped" Puerto Rican was suspected of harboring the primitive genes of an Indian or African, masked underneath genes of the Portuguese or Spanish colonizer.[103] Conversely, Mexican people were stripped of their African ancestry, erasing the consistent historical presence of Afromexicanos on the North American continent.[104]

Southwestern agricultural interests described Puerto Rican migrants as an insidious danger to the white race. Unlike other nonwhites, the "Portuguese nigger," as Clements openly referred to them, could easily blend with the general population, marry white women, and spread their inferior genes. Speaking before the Lemon Men's Club, he warned, "Biologically, they are a serious menace, particularly in California and the border states where we have so many dark skinned races and blends; since they are without the distinguishing features of the negro there is no protection."[105] Their mobility made them all the more threatening, since it shielded them further from racial detection by erasing their Caribbean origins. It is not coincidental that the fluidity of racialized bodies has often been described through racial metaphors of movement, foremost "passing." Now relocated to California, "where we have so many dark skinned races," Puerto Ricans proved an invisible, but insidious, threat to white racial purity.[106]

Ranchers portrayed Puerto Ricans and Filipinos as "black devils" who could easily blend with the general population. Charles Teague, Federal Farm Board commissioner and owner of the Limoneira, reported in the *Saturday Evening Post*:

> If, as some claim, there is some social problem connected with the immigration of Mexicans, those who are proposing the closing of the door to them will bring to the Southwestern states a much more serious one by forcing the agriculturalists to bring Puerto Rican Negroes or Filipinos.[107]

Teague's characterization of Puerto Ricans as "negroes" was far from exceptional. Epithets such as "the Portuguese nigger," "black rascals," and "black devils" were commonly placed upon colonial subjects following the Spanish-American War.[108] For instance, in the Philippines, U.S. control of overseas territories was justified by interpolating a black racial status that equated island residents with child-like people incapable of self-government. These narratives likened the United States to a benevolent parent guiding primitive societies towards civilization.[109] Likewise, in earlier debates over Puerto Rican independence, public opinion was tied to U.S. racial perceptions of its residents. Those who saw the island's inhabitants as African or Indigenous to the Caribbean continued to question their ability for self-governance. The opposite was also true. In cases when Puerto Ricans were whitened in the popular U.S. imagination, they were better positioned for cultural inclusion.[110] In both the continental United States and overseas territories, black racial status served to reinforce an unequal power structure that naturalized white American superiority.

Box Bill opponents narrated the danger of racial blackness to the American nation through the perceived sexual threat colonial migrants posed to white women. They warned of "social attentions," "intermarriage," and "crossbreeding" between American whites and the "negro" islanders who left to settle on the mainland.[111] As *there* became *here,* through human movement across territorial pathways previously envisioned as quite remote, colonial subjects were cast as sexual aggressors and white women were portrayed as passive recipients of their advances. Such attention elided the frequent sexual violence exercised by white men on women of color in the U.S. colonies. Concern over white women's susceptibility to nonwhite seduction both reaffirmed white males' power over women and reified the necessity for their protection by the state.[112] When exercised by those racialized as black, mobility with the potential to become settled was met by efforts to erect both geographical and sexual boundaries.

Similarly in the immigration debates, white agriculturalists employed tropes of white women's safety to protest the recruitment of Puerto Rican and Filipino migrants with citizenship and national status. As noted by Congressman Free of California, "We do not want those people that attack our women. We have the right to defend our homes."[113] The use of "our" marked both white women's sexuality and the U.S. nation as possessions owned by white men. Where interracial couplings undermined national assertions of white racial homogeneity, enforcing white men's exclusive access to white women's bodies was a means to uphold national and racial borders challenged by Caribbean and Pacific migrations. Notably absent from these debates was the impact of U.S. imperialism, a practice rooted in white migration and colonization in these very same territories.[114]

Where at the national level Mexican racialization was strongly tied to fears of Puerto Rican migrants by Citrus Belt representatives, at the regional level Filipino laborers posed the more imminent threat.[115] Public concern with interracial relationships in California was at an all-time high, where Filipino men were portrayed as a hypersexual threat to white purity in highly publicized racial altercations between white vigilantes and Filipino men across the state.[116] Opponents of Filipino migration drew on these fears to warn Congress of the impending spread of white-black relations across the nation.[117]

Concerns with Filipino migration were expressed quite viscerally in the Citrus Belt. When a Filipino citrus worker, Santiago Raynas, was accused of attacking Eunice Lawyer, an "attractive white girl" in Alta Loma in 1930, it sent ripples throughout San Bernardino County. Raynas met Lawyer at her family restaurant. When her father found a series of letters Raynas had written to his daughter, he forced the young man out of their restaurant. After Raynas's expulsion, he arrived at Lawyer's house, climbed in a window, and begged her to elope with him. Were she to refuse, news reports alleged, he threatened to murder her and to kill himself. Screaming for her parents, Lawyer was stabbed by Raynas three times in the arm and once in her leg with a pocketknife. During the confusion that followed, Raynas escaped through the family's front door. He was swiftly pursued by deputy sheriffs and caught ten miles away attempting to board the Etiwanda Pacific Electric freight train.[118]

The *Riverside Daily Press* and *Los Angeles Times* ran large headlines on the Raynas-Lawyer incident in a series of publications that read as a melodrama on the dangers of Filipino contact. The details of the case were highly sensationalized: a Filipino man "ripping" through a screen to get into a family home, "slipp[ing]" into the private quarters of a young girl's room in the midnight hours, "threatening" to murder the teenage daughter of a local businessman, or, perhaps worse, eloping with her consent.[119] Dating between Filipino men and white women was not uncommon, but interracial taboos were prevalent in Southern California. Exacerbating this particular ordeal, Raynas was a 25-year-old man, a full decade older than 15-year-old Lawyer. Upon capture by a deputy sheriff, Raynas begged that he not be taken to Alta Loma, the site of the attack, stating, "the white men will kill me."[120] His pleas foreshadowed his own persecution and a racialized discourse of Filipino sexual deviance that justified broad attacks on the larger Filipino community within inland Southern California.

The Raynas incident was one episode among many in a longstanding connection of Filipino sexuality with white women and white male vigilantism.[121] Although a single incident, the Raynas assault became a catalyst for widespread anti-Filipino sentiment and a rallying cry for an end to Filipino farm labor in the Citrus Belt. Similar cases in which white men assaulted white women were not generalized to white workers. Conversely, within two weeks, a committee of Alta Loma residents organized to exorcise all Filipino residents from the district. They visited area citrus groves, demanding that white workers replace Filipino workers, resulting in the firing of sixty Filipino men. Facing racial intolerance and economic stonewalling, many chose to leave the district altogether. Soon afterwards, the San Bernardino Central Labor Council, American Legion, and Native Sons of the Golden West joined forces to advocate for a full investigation into Filipino labor, a ban from public works projects, and restrictions against further migration into the county.[122] Whether from ignorance of Filipinos' protected status as "U.S. nationals" or blatant disregard, prominent organizations joined together to limit the Filipino presence in the region, both denying their rights to free movement across the United States and prompting some workers into preemptive mobility actions for their own protection, such as leaving the region.

In ranchers' portrayals of Puerto Ricans and Filipinos as a dangerous threat to white women, they positioned Mexicans as passive racial and sexual subjects. Drawing upon earlier discourses of Mexican people as Indians, Box Bill opponents reified ideas of hypodescent that claimed Indian blood was less harmful to the white racial stock than African or Asian blood. As described by Harry Chandler, "Every American knows, who is familiar with Indian character, Indian blood has never degraded our citizenship. An American who has a little Indian blood in his veins is generally proud of it, but if he has any negro blood or oriental blood he is not so proud of it."[123] When a letter submitted to Congress by the infamous eugenicist Charles Goethe claimed that "Indian" (Mexican) blood was a danger to white purity, opponents adamantly denied his conclusions. In a reply to Goethe, Congressman Garner warned that Mexicans were the only safeguard against Puerto Rican and Filipino population growth, stating, "are we willing to exclude the Mexican who has no such ambition or desire [to marry American whites] and as a result spread the negroes over the rest of our fair land and thus bring about the very situation of which Goethe complains."[124] Agriculturalists offered two possible futures: that of Anglo American agriculture aided by temporary Mexican immigrants or that of a racial melting pot where white women and "negro" men freely intermixed. Faced with the potential loss of an immigrant workforce vulnerable to deportation and its replacement by colonial workers with U.S. citizenship, ranchers argued that the Box Bill threatened to restrict the safest deterrent to permanent nonwhite settlement.

Unlike Filipino and Puerto Rican settlers, Mexican immigrants had been likened to "homers" since the 1926 hearings.[125] The relative benefit of homing pigeons—birds that travel vast distances to reunite with their mates—was heightened by the (perceived) danger of Puerto Rican and Filipino settlement and miscegenation. In a process of racial triangulation, whereby the valorization of one subordinated group occurs relative to the subordination of another group, Mexican immigrants were portrayed as sexually neutral in comparison to sexually aggressive "negro" colonials.[126] As described by agriculturalists, Mexican men only married Mexican women and were unlikely to pursue relations with white women. Mexican workers were credited with an inherent propensity for domestic cohesion. As described by one agriculturalist "[Mexicans] live together in their home and they are clean and they dress nice . . . and they take care of their families."[127] Describing Mexican workers' domestic lives as existing independently of physical settlement on U.S. ranches, as had been conflated in the earlier citrus housing campaigns, Mexican laborers were now said to either return to their partners over long distances or, alternatively, to roam together back and forth across the national divide as families.[128]

Historical accounts of Mexican households destabilize ranchers' claims that Mexican people rarely intermarried. Oral histories, for instance, provide evidence that relationships between Anglo and Mexican-descent people were not uncommon. Rita Radeleff recalled the relationship between her Mexican American mother, Tomasita Edith Velarde, and her Anglo American father, Palmer Leland Richardson. Living in Redlands and occupying a similar class position, the couple met while working for an affluent local family. Marrying in 1913, the couple faced resistance from Richardson's family on account of Velarde's previous marriage and Mexican background. As described by their daughter, "[His family] resented the fact I guess, that dad did not find a blond-haired, blue-eyed English-Scotsman or a Swede or something like that."[129] Despite laws and social taboos against interracial sexuality, race was never a fixed category. Geography, law, and sexual liaisons consistently undermined its boundaries.[130] Yet, in the halls of Congress, the risk of sexual relationships between white men and nonwhite women were described as a continuum from passive Mexican homers to sexually aggressive black settlers.

The question of Mexican immigration was not one of a good choice, but a better choice. When agriculturalists' support of Mexican immigration is viewed alongside congressional concerns with Puerto Rican migration, it becomes clear that, even if divergent, racial understandings of the two groups developed together. Although remaining geographically disparate well into the twentieth century, with Mexicans concentrated on the West Coast and Puerto Ricans on the East, racial formation occurred simultaneously on Capitol Hill. Ranchers manipulated congressional confusion over Mexican and Puerto Rican racial identities to suggest that Mexicans were Indian-like nomads who harvested seasonal crops and that Puerto Ricans were black colonials who relied on U.S. charity, despite their citizenship status. Existing fears of Filipino men's relationships with white women further heightened fears of migration from the colonies. Congressional ideas of what was Mexican and what was Puerto Rican developed through the prism of what the other was not: whether Indian or black, familial loyalist or sexual predator, migrant or settler.

The Committee on Immigration and Naturalization met again in May 1930 to discuss what the *Los Angeles Times* described as "one of the most surprising actions in years."[131] The meeting concerned the controversial Harris Bill (S51), a proposal introduced by Georgia senator William Harris to place immigrants from the Western Hemisphere under a quota restriction. Quickly following the passage of S51, Congressman Box proposed a nearly identical bill in the House of Representatives (HR12382).[132] The committee recommended the bill be passed with minor amendments. The report charged that Mexican immigrants were "not homogenous with the general population of the United States" and countered earlier testimony asserting that Mexicans only migrated for seasonal employment.[133] Although coming very close to enactment, oppositional forces postponed the bill. In 1930, the quota debates effectively concluded with the end of the 71st congressional session and Box's unsuccessful bid for renewed nomination.

MOBILE RACIAL HIERARCHIES

Between World War I and the long immigration debate of the 1920s, Mexican workers in Southern California experienced two very different forms of racialization tied to their mobility. In the first, they were positioned as ideal settlers who formed permanent homes and raised children who would provide a resident labor pool for the growing Citrus Belt. Migrating with the aid of immigration policy and recruited with the promise of citrus housing, the seeming rootedness of Mexican immigrants was positioned against the prevalent racialization of Asian workers and impoverished white workers as tramps with little desire to assimilate to white domestic norms.

However, as Mexican immigrants outnumbered Asian and European workers, the question of Mexican population growth was increasingly debated at the national level. Concerns from unions, eugenicists, and small farmers about the economic well-being of white workers and the racial integrity of the nation were met by assurances from southwestern agricultural interests that Mexican immigrants were no more than "birds of passage," a temporary racial other whose labor guaranteed the prosperity of U.S. agriculture. As critiques of Mexican immigration heightened at the end of the 1920s, the larger threat of aggressive black colonials heralded by Box Bill opponents minimized fears of these docile homers.

Drawing attention to Congress's confusion over Mexicans' and Puerto Ricans' racial status reifies the flexibility of race and the ways racial formation works itself out in immigration policy. The process of race making exists not only among seemingly disparate racial groups—the place of indigeneity and racial blackness being particularly relevant here—but also relationally for groups that we now understand as Latina/o. Although both Mexicans and Puerto Ricans were exempt from quotas under the Immigration Act of 1924, they were effectively placed on opposite sides of a racial hierarchy that ranked them by their ability to move or, conversely, to stay in place. In the process, Congressmen and ranchers far removed from both migrant communities extracted a diasporic African community from Mexico and placed it exclusively in the Caribbean. It was in a similar fashion that citrus ranchers had distanced Asian workers from Mexican workers in the World War I period. Race, in effect, was a signifier of the ways populations with varying degrees of mobility capital, or motility, were either allowed to move or not. Enabled by their own ease of movement across the continent to Congress, from distances quantifiably similar to those of the migrants they debated, it was white representatives of Southwestern Chambers of Commerce, agricultural cooperatives, and large ranchers who delineated the terms of the conversation.

The construction of Mexicans as racial homers had reverberating consequences in the Depression years that followed. Most starkly, "voluntary" campaigns managed by state and municipal governments in cooperation with the Mexican government compelled Mexican immigrants to return to Mexico, or to repatriate. Habitually coerced by social service agencies and public health institutions into leaving the United States, ethnic Mexicans were increasingly cast as scapegoats for worsening regional economic conditions. Simultaneously, the federal government increased its deportation efforts. In total, between 1929 and 1936 an estimated 400,000 to one million ethnic Mexicans left the United States for Mexico. Where in the era during and after World War I Mexican families were seen as an advantage since they rooted workers in place, making them a more reliable workforce, that asset became a liability in the Depression, when Mexican families were viewed as a national economic threat and far from temporary birds of passage.[134]

FOUR

"Del Fotingo Que Era Mio"*

MEXICAN AND DUST BOWL DRIVERS IN METROPOLITAN
LOS ANGELES, 1930–1945

In 1924, Blas Coyazo, 13 years old, attended his last day of school. His father needed him to drive the family car to Smiley Heights Park in Redlands, where he tended to the eucalyptus trees. Behind the wheel of their Durant, an economical touring car known for its rugged design, Coyazo traveled the winding road and passed the lush flora of Smiley Heights Drive to its scenic summit overlooking the valley. Young Coyazo joined his older brother, Sam, who managed orange-picking crews in nearby groves. Not yet strong enough to carry a ladder, Coyazo started at the bottom. He reached for the trees' lowest branches, picking the oranges that hung beside him. Standing beneath the tree, he placed the oranges into a homemade bag and transferred them into a large wooden box through the afternoon. Coyazo followed this pattern until the end of the harvest. When it concluded, he said his farewells to his mother and other family members, whom he would soon leave behind in Redlands's Northside. After loading their belongings into the car, he, his father, and brother piled in behind. The Coyazos' livelihood depended on their migration in pursuit of successive harvests across California.[1]

The combination of large-scale farming and seasonal harvests made mobility essential to agricultural communities across the Southwest. As discussed in chapter 3, the 1920s Box Bill debates had pushed the question of Mexican migrant farm labor and U.S. immigration into the national limelight. At first, Congress had been largely receptive to agriculturalists' assertions that Mexican nationals were "birds of passage" who provided essential labor when needed and returned to Mexico when the work was complete. But national concerns with Mexican immigration would heighten in the 1930s.

---

* "Of the Ford which was mine" or "My old Ford"

As the permanent Mexican American population grew and economic conditions deteriorated, Mexican-descent people were no longer described as circular migrants essential to agricultural industries, but rather became scapegoats for decreased agricultural wages and overburdened relief services. Consistent with earlier efforts to manage nonwhite workers' mobility and immobility—from the captivity of Indigenous children to the arrest of Japanese bicyclists—public concerns about the Mexican population manifested in the criminalization of motorists.

Racial formation and "automobility"—a term used by mobility scholars to describe the spatial and social relationships generated by the automobile—were inextricably tied together for Mexican people in metropolitan Los Angeles.[2] Before the Great Depression, social scientists viewed the Mexican population's access to automobiles as a regional economic necessity. After all, by the end of the 1920s, Mexican-descent people comprised 84 percent of California's nonwhite farm labor force. Their ability to move among groves was an integral part of that work.[3] Since seasonal employment was scattered throughout the region and public transportation was concentrated in cities, access to these jobs often required private automobiles. Whether headed to area ranches or construction sites, a caravan of Mexican workers on wheels would have been a familiar sight, one that signaled the flow of a lucrative economy.

During the Depression, however, the coupling of ethnic Mexicans with cars held new meaning for social workers, economists, and law enforcement officers. Exacerbated by the growth of Dust Bowl workers entering California, local officials viewed Mexican American and Mexican immigrant motorists as a surplus workforce seeking only relief checks.[4] The state responded forcefully. Most infamously, repatriation campaigns coerced and compelled Mexican immigrants to return to Mexico, often separating families and pulling U.S.-born children across the border in the process. Notable scholarship has recovered the sweeping effects of repatriation campaigns on Mexican communities in the United States, a vivid example of a government exercising mobility controls without residents' consent.[5] But we know less about those who stayed behind.

This chapter foregrounds regional mobility as an analytic framework for understanding Mexican racialization during the Depression era, from popular radio broadcasts to police surveillance on the roads. It focuses on the criminalization of the Mexican immigrants and mobile Mexican American youth who remained in the United States. Regardless of their citizenship status, these groups were denied services, policed, and incarcerated at uneven rates by government officials, who stripped them of their mobility in ways distinct from those applied to repatriates. At the same time, ethnic Mexicans found new meaning in the automobile. Mexican immigrants adopted the car as a lyrical device signaling life in the United States, Mexican American families adapted old economic strategies of regional migration as they adjusted to new economic conditions, and Mexican American youth self-fashioned their identities alongside this modern symbol of speed and freedom. In each case, mobility was a key battleground for accessing the state's resources and exercising cultural belonging in metropolitan Los Angeles.

When examining the contours of Mexican racial formation and mobility during the Depression, the automobile—as both a material tool for movement between points A and B, and a symbolic system through which personhood was given meaning—was key. As driving became synonymous with U.S. nationhood, Mexican motorists were increasingly excluded from an emerging form of national membership, one based on the shared social contract of driving. Their exclusion from this "republic of drivers" was exacerbated by statewide concerns with the internal migration of Dust Bowl migrants to California, whose own marginalization threatened to unravel existing racial hierarchies between white and nonwhite workers.[6]

Shifting narratives of Mexican motorists and their distancing from white migrants reveal the deep importance of mobility in constructing racial meaning in Southern California. When mobility was deemed central to the economic health of the state, such as in the years after World War I and during the Box Bill debates, it could function to reaffirm the cultural citizenship of the Mexican-descent population, often at the expense of other marginalized groups. But in the Depression era when mobility was deemed a social cost, it would fuel the increased criminalization of Mexican motorists. In each case, examining this shift uncovers the ways mobility was used to maintain the racial divide between ethnic Mexicans and American whites.

This chapter begins by investigating the myriad roles automobiles played for Mexican Americans and Mexican immigrants within the semirural communities of inland Southern California prior to the Depression. Because agricultural workers depended on small-scale migration among the local groves and, in the off-season, to urban centers, ethnic Mexicans owned automobiles at rates surpassing the general population. Cars and trucks figured prominently in labor relations and creative practice as the Mexican American and Mexican immigrant populations created socioeconomic lives responsive to the demands of regional travel. As public perceptions of mobility darkened in the Depression, automobility became fundamental to racial formation.

In this new economic context, the racial line between Mexican motorists and Dust Bowl migrants was vulnerable to collapse, but was ultimately reestablished. The writings and photography by agrarian progressives, such as Paul S. Taylor, Dorothea Lange, and John Steinbeck, alongside public efforts to reinterpret symbolic landscapes, like Route 66, literally placed white migrants, often lumped together as "Okies," on the same pathway as white pioneers. This investigation uncovers the ways narratives of mobility were recycled and, in effect, used to bleach Dust Bowl workers, mark ethnic Mexicans as foreign, and reestablish regional racial hierarchies. Further, it outlines the myriad of tactics ethnic Mexicans used when resisting their own marginalization, from leveraging their mobility as an economic asset to youth expressive cultures drawing on the automobile to construct their identity.

"AN ESSENTIAL PART OF THE HOUSEHOLD EQUIPMENT": THE AUTOMOBILE IN MEXICAN IMMIGRANT AND MEXICAN AMERICAN LIFE

By World War I, the automobile was already an integral part of life for Mexican agricultural workers in Southern California. For instance, prominent citrus ranchers provided laborers garages alongside bathrooms, running water, electricity, and other utilities they deemed absolutely fundamental to worker housing. As described by Archibald Shamel, a USDA scientist who wrote extensively on Mexican citrus workers, "[the automobile is] an essential part of the household equipment."[7] Local cooperative associations occasionally provided vehicles for their workers, but more often than not individual pickers and their families purchased their own. Like the Japanese bicyclists who preceded them, Mexican motorists used vehicles to maximize their work opportunities, and for self-fashioning themselves as modern citizens. Although at the national level cars were then largely owned by the white middle class, for use in leisure activities like tourism and cross-country travel, in the Mexican communities of Southern California automobiles were a working class item used to traverse uncertain economic and social landscapes.[8]

Disrupting national trends that linked whiteness and driving, period sources suggest that ethnic Mexicans owned automobiles at far higher rates than the Southern California population as a whole. A 1933 Heller

Committee cost of living study, by the University of California, sheds light on patterns of automotive proprietorship, expense, and usage. In a survey of a hundred Mexican-descent families living in San Diego, the Heller Committee found 26 percent of households owned and operated their own automobile. A similar survey taken in San Fernando, about thirty miles north of Los Angeles, found that nearly 40 percent of families residing in the "Mexican district" owned a vehicle. These figures are particularly significant when we consider that the automobile ownership rate in California as a whole was only 17 percent, about *half* of the rate for the Mexican communities of San Diego and San Fernando.[9]

Far from elite toys of the rich, automobiles were regularly a necessity for Mexican laborers. Only 2 percent of the vehicles counted in the Heller study had been purchased new. Rather, families typically bought their cars and trucks secondhand, often as an essential expense. Purchasing a vehicle was a financial hardship that required cutting back elsewhere, sometimes even on food. Nevertheless, for their drivers, automobiles' economic and cultural value exceeded their costs. Mexican respondents reported they used their vehicles for a variety of functions, including searching for work in surrounding towns, informal outings, and travel to family events.[10]

Car and truck ownership often translated into direct economic gains for Citrus Belt workers. Groves were spread throughout the region and laborers commonly lived in towns adjacent to large farms, moving among them as the crops matured. Families who owned automobiles could leverage this location gap between housing and the groves to earn extra income. Former citrus worker Howard Herrera remembered, "In those days you had to pay for your ride. Sometimes the house would pay it. If the house would hire a truck to take the crew to work they'd pay the driver for all the heads that would drive and arrive in the truck."[11] By transporting their neighbors to the fields, truck owners not only solved the problem of spatial dissonance, but also identified workers for the citrus cooperative in exchange for pay. In these roles, they served as recruiters, translators, and transporters. Women were often key in the relative success of these efforts. The son of one citrus foreman recalls that his mother provided warm lunches for riders as extra incentive to choose his father's crew over others.[12] For these services, Mexican families were financially rewarded, receiving a small payment for each rider or a portion of the profits from the harvest.

If Mexican motorists could increase their wages by providing a vital service to ranchers, their automobility could also be used to challenge employers' control over workers' livelihoods. Mobility enabled Mexican-descent workers to determine which employment opportunities—agricultural or otherwise—offered the most competitive wages. Those with access to private vehicles identified opportunities at a range much larger than previously possible, aided by a growing network of roads, their ability to carry multiple passengers, and the incentive of hauling cargo for additional payment. While vehicles widened the geographic scale and types of employment available to Mexican drivers, vehicles were also beneficial in times of collective action. Even if primarily used for daily transportation, a truck could moonlight as a mobile picket line, stage for mobile theater, or emergency shelter. During times of direct action, vehicles helped to galvanize workers and prolonged their ability to strike. In this sense, automobility could quite directly contribute to the collective's economic mobility.[13]

Automotive culture permeated not only the lives of those who moved, but also those in the communities that were passed. The largely Mexican Westside of San Bernardino is exemplary of this synergism. Later designated as Route 66, Mount Vernon Avenue provided residents entrepreneurial opportunities to offer services to long distance travelers, such as managing motels, bars, gas stations, and restaurants. Consider Mitla Café. In 1927, its owners, Lucia and Salvador Rodríguez, migrated to California, and soon after, Lucia opened a small taco stand. The side business grew into a local landmark where the Rodríguezes catered to Mount Vernon residents, including workers from the nearby Santa Fe railroad repair shop, and passing motorists looking for something warm and affordable to eat. A combination of its location on Highway 66, homey atmosphere, and foremost its Cal-Mex cuisine even earned Mitla Café a mention in the popular Duncan Hines travel culinary guide, *Adventures in Good Eating*.[14] Business leaders along the busy Highway 66 corridor often became community leaders and their businesses popular sites of community organization and place making.[15]

In addition to their economic value, vehicles held an important symbolic role for their drivers. Analysis of photographs collected by grassroots recovery efforts, such as Inland Mexican Heritage (IMH), further sheds light on the cultural significance of vehicles in Mexican agricultural communities. Looking to these personal family records adds a new perspective to those of the period's social worker reports, which erroneously equated Mexican automotive practice with those of white middle class families. In public events held by IMH throughout the 1990s and 2000s, residents of former citrus communities near San Bernardino were invited to contribute family photographs and oral histories as part of a recovery project focused on Mexican American communities. Among cherished images of weddings, returning veterans, and family gatherings, residents frequently submitted family portraits in which cars and trucks figured as prominent features of the image.[16]

Unlike government or professional photographs from this period, examining the function of automobiles within these self-selected compositions helps reveal the ways Mexican American people themselves positioned vehicles in their everyday lives. While members of the family and their friends occupy the focal point, they were often staged in the photographs sitting or standing on vehicles. On the one hand, this positioning points towards the frequent presence of automobiles in Mexican American life, which were conveniently present during both special family events and mundane daily passings. On the other, the frequent appearance of cars as a central part of the photographs' compositions underscores the subjects' desires to craft particular self-identities.[17] Automobiles represented more than vehicles for travel. Rather, they held distinct social significance for those involved at the moment of a photograph's creation. Where a group of youth dressed in their best outfits and standing in front of a car might represent the subjects' identity as a modern subject immersed in leisure culture, workers posing with a truck filled with boxes of oranges could emphasize a strong work ethic, upward mobility, or traditional links between masculinity and labor. Historian Phil Deloria has examined the ways images of both American Indians and automobiles have been used by non-Indians to signify important elements in American culture. When brought together, these signifiers have conjured a "palpable disconnection between the high-tech automotive world and the primitivism that so often clings to the figure of the Indian."[18] Where automobiles seemed anachronistic or unmerited when driven by nonwhites, photographs produced by Mexican American drivers were all the more powerful for the ways they disrupted normative expectations and bolstered self-representation in complex ways.

Where photographic records help to uncover symbolic systems attached to vehicles by multigenerational Mexican American populations, songs emerge as an archive of the meanings produced by Mexican immigrants. Corridos—poetry set to music—are cultural artifacts that archive artistic expressions of daily life.[19] In these songs, vehicles held an important symbolic role in conveying immigrants' experiences in the United States. As described by Mexican anthropologist Manuel Gamio, Mexican rates of vehicle ownership grew markedly among immigrants who had worked for a period in the

Joe Hernandez (third from left) and crew on work truck, 1938. Courtesy of Inland Mexican Heritage.

United States. A close reading of popular corridos collected by Gamio and reprinted by the Social Science Research Council in the 1920s uncovers an ambivalent attitude among Mexican immigrants towards cars—and by extension, an ambivalent attitude towards U.S. life in general.[20]

A consistent note among corridos was nostalgia for life in Mexico, and the internal tensions generated among immigrants when pursuing American economic mobility. The lyrics of "El Dónde Yo Nací," for example, use the car to signify dissatisfaction with U.S. consumer culture. The protagonist sings:

> No me gusta coche ni autómovil
> como al estilo de por aquí.
> A mi me gusta carreta de bueyes
> como en el rancho dónde yo nací.
>
> (I do not care for the cars or the automobiles
> like those found around here.
> I prefer the oxcart
> like on the ranch where I was born.)[21]

In this instance, the singer rejects the extravagant automobiles he views in the United States in favor of an old oxcart he owned in rural Mexico. At a literal level, his dissatisfaction indicates the singer's longing for the ranch where he was born, land owned by his family and free from the empty consumerism he observes in the United States. Seemingly nationalistic, the singer's nostalgia may also be read as a critique of political changes in Mexico, where privatization drastically transformed the countryside and large agricultural operations displaced many of the migrants. Dispossession pushed them to seek work in the United States.[22]

In a variation of this critique, another corrido titled "El Renegado" focused its criticism on Mexican immigrants seduced by U.S. markers of social status. The automobile in this corrido signals an immigrant who, upon gaining some profit, looks down upon his fellow countrymen who have not adopted a U.S. lifestyle. The ballad disapproves of the renegade's "dandy" attire and his conceit when driving a flashy car, "andas por hay luciendo gran autómovil."[23] Where the driver seeks attention by wielding control over the ultimate symbol of social mobility, the singer critiques this ostentatious display of wealth. The song discredits those immigrants who would negate their homeland and working class origins.[24] In both "El Dónde Yo Nací" and "El Renegado," the automobile represents a U.S. lifestyle that stands in opposition to a Mexico envisioned as rural, homeland, and anticapitalistic.

Looking to these creative expressions of Mexican immigrant life helps reveal illicit uses of automobiles unaccounted for in most oral histories. Further, they recast as autonomous subjects the drivers who might otherwise be considered deviant. For instance, the car is often described with fondness for the freedom it offers its driver. "El Fotingo," which can be loosely translated as "The Ford" or "The Jalopy," is one such example.[25] Although the jalopy is worn down and without seats, doors, or even lights, the song's lyrics recall moonlit nights when the driver's speeding Ford could be mistaken for a Willys-Overland. Where the old Ford represented economy and utility, the Overland had relatively more luxurious associations. By playing with the symbolic systems attached to the two models, the driver himself seems transformed in the moonlight from a worn-down laborer to a playboy bootlegger. The singer proudly describes flirting with women, smoking marijuana, and evading U.S. custom's officers while smuggling liquor across the border. The mobility enabled by his vehicle is a fitting metaphor for the intersections between Mexican and American life, particularly as the increasing ease of automobility blurred the boundaries between the two, just as migrating bodies and smuggled booze could disrupt the apparent solidity of national boundaries.

Rising automobile registration rates in Mexico rose with Mexican American and Mexican immigrant vehicle ownership in the United States.

Before 1910, there were no more than 3,000 vehicles registered across the Mexican nation. This quickly changed when Francisco Madero replaced Porfirio Díaz as president of Mexico in 1911. Fifteen years after abolishing a prohibitive tax on automobile ownership, registration increased from half a million to 17.5 million.[26] A continuing rise in vehicle registration was fostered by the arrival of the Ford Motor Company in Mexico City in 1925 and the construction of a vast new factory in 1932.[27]

Migration between the United States and Mexico further contributed to the growth of automotive ownership among ethnic Mexicans on both sides of the border. In December 1926, Mexico exempted repatriates from paying duty on U.S. items, including vehicles. Upon their return, 38 percent of all repatriates owned an automobile. The widespread resale economy in Mexican border towns may have further boosted Mexican Americans' ability to purchase low-cost Fords, creating a synergy between automotive manufacturing and policies in Mexico and Mexican Americans' automobility in the United States.[28]

Surveys, oral histories, photographs, and corridos each provide insight into the internal significance of automobiles for Mexican Americans and Mexican immigrants living in the United States. Vehicles were significant for increasing one's economic mobility, and served as important social symbols used in self-fashioning as well as lyrical devices used to describe immigrant life in Mexican America. Focusing on reports by social scientists in the next section reveals the external values placed on Mexican mobility at the economic crossroads of the 1920s and the Great Depression.

THE SOCIAL SCIENCE OF MEXICAN AUTOMOBILITY

The 1920s marked increased interest in the movements of Mexican-descent people. The Box Bill hearings had created over 1,000 pages of congressional records concerned with immigration from the Western Hemisphere and the growth of the Mexican American population. At the same time, the highly divisive debate cast the lack of reliable data on the topics of Mexican immigration and population growth into sharp focus. In response, government agencies and social scientists alike embarked on their systematic study. Among the most urgent aspect in need of research were U.S. patterns of internal migration by Mexican-descent people. Most notable among investigators was University of California Berkeley economist Paul S. Taylor and his migration statistics series, "Mexican Labor in the United States" (1927–1933). Funded by the newly created Social Science Council's Committee on Scientific Aspects of Human Migration, Taylor embarked on a multisite, multiyear study of Mexican migration within the United States.[29] Emerging as definitive on the topic, Taylor's widely cited study would both draw on racial logics of Mexican mobility and craft a typology for Mexican travelers that conflated racial character with transportation.

"Mexican Labor in the United States" focused on the internal migration of Mexican-descent people, a shared ethnoracial category comprised of both Mexican Americans and resident Mexican immigrants. For Taylor, "great seasonal mobility," "almost ceaseless movement," and "the basic fact of mobility" typified these Mexican laborers.[30] To the disruption of the bird of passage myth, Taylor found that even in the border region of California's Imperial Valley this movement was largely nation-bound.[31] Immigration figures during this period are often contradictory, but estimates consistently show that Mexican immigration had reached its height between 1927 and 1929 and steeply declined in 1930.[32] That is, in the period of Taylor's study, regional and not transnational migration defined Mexican mobility in the United States. Both widely cited by academics and discussed among government officials, Taylor's research became the definitive source on Mexican immigrant and Mexican American migration in the United States.[33]

Although seeking to tabulate Mexican migration patterns broadly, Taylor's investigations focused on the relationship between migration and regional industries. As such, his study of California was fundamentally concerned with determining the movement of Mexican agricultural laborers and the ways they responded to seasonal fluctuations through travel. In order to tabulate migration to, from, and through Southern California, Taylor strategically chose data collection sites located along major agricultural corridors. The first were the California State Department of Agriculture quarantine checkpoints near Arizona. Originally established to prevent the entry of diseases and pests hazardous to California produce, the quarantines now aided in quantifying the manual labor necessary for continued agricultural production. Located on the eastern crossroads of California at Blythe and Daggett, the checkpoints were instructed to record westbound vehicles driven by someone who was "obviously Mexican of the manual laboring class."[34] Another research site was a Standard Oil Company service station, off Highway 99 at Gorman. A central point between the Tehachapi and San Joaquin Mountains, Gorman represented a necessary crossroads for those traveling to sites of seasonal harvests. Similarly here, Taylor trained service station attendants to tabulate migrating farm workers.[35]

Taylor's site choices underscore the importance of roads to the agricultural economy and their varied promises to those who traveled along them. Routes were essential to agriculture, potentially beneficial to both workers and employers, but unequal in profit. For some, traveling led to fair wages and decent housing. For others, travel led to unemployment or destitution. Travel itself held high costs for agricultural migrants, including pay lost while in transit, unemployment in the off-season, homelessness, and increased vulnerability to exploitation. Although workers themselves had some agency over when and where they traveled, automobility was inextricably bound to the needs and desires of ranchers, whose potential for profit was tied to fluctuations in the crop.[36] Taylor leveraged the necessity of agricultural workers' seasonal migration to tabulate and extrapolate rates of Mexican migration through California.

Situating research sites along major agricultural arteries was a strategic choice, but assessors' ability to collect data based on racial categories was complicated by the subjects' speed. Even with mandatory stops, border station staff at the California quarantine checkpoints reported difficulty handling Taylor's data collection in addition to their day-to-day inspection activities.[37] Service station staff experienced even more complications. Without the ability to require drivers to stop, which was mandated at border checkpoints, gas station staff were heavily dependent on split-second assessments. Where intrinsic features of travel such as speed potentially undermined the integrity of Taylor's data, he adopted external racial markers to corroborate his findings. According to Taylor:

> The characteristic modes of travel and dress, the type and condition of car, and the physical types, etc., of the Mexican laborers in California were sufficiently distinct to make identification of the overwhelming majority relatively easy for those accustomed to look for them; and to render unlikely confusion with Negro, Asiatic, Filipino, or other non-white laborers.[38]

If bodies themselves could not be scrutinized to determine the race of travelers, Taylor proposed that the means of transport, vehicle maintenance, and automotive style could help determine racial differences.

What was "characteristic" of these laborers is unclear. The term's ambiguity begs the question of exactly how migrants were identified as "Mexican."

In Taylor's assessment, Mexican people were phenotypically distinct from whites, yet they could be mistaken for "Negro, Asiatic, Filipino, or other non-white laborers."[39] Where scholars of automobility have suggested driving offered African Americans the potential to "*pass* as the blank liberal subject," even if only temporarily screening their racial identity, Taylor sought to rupture the anonymity of Mexican travelers.[40] When phenotype was obscured, the means of travel itself served as proxy for the racial body.

Throughout Taylor's study, Mexican people were wholly and squarely associated with automotive travel to the exclusion of other forms of transportation. Rather than comprising their own categories, those riding by team and wagon were collapsed *within* the count of those entering by personal motor vehicle. Those carried by "autostage," or mechanized coaches transporting multiple riders, were excluded from the study altogether, although a sampling found that at least 16 percent of Mexican migrants chose this mode of travel. Those riding the train were also omitted. As explained by Taylor, few Mexicans would choose to pay the proportionally higher travel fees.[41] Rather, the train served as a class marker that separated Taylor's desired object, Mexican agricultural migrants, from middle class Mexican travelers.[42] Historian Kelly Lytle Hernández has described the policing activities of border patrol agents in the same period as one of profiling "Mexican Browns."[43] Similarly here, surveillance of Mexican mobility was a matter of identifying a specifically racialized set of classed bodies and reinforcing their subordinate position within the economy of the American West.

In attempting to quantify patterns of migration and vehicle ownership, Taylor created a coded set of suppositions about Mexican American and Mexican immigrant mobility. Specifically, he conflated certain forms of personal vehicle usage with Mexican racial identity and then used these racial assumptions to quantify Mexican migration patterns. By substituting material objects for physical bodies, he overgeneralized the prevalence of "Mexican" travel by car and limited his analysis to the travel of Mexican migrants engaged in agricultural labor. Doing so meant excluding whole segments of the ethnic Mexican population, including not only middle class travelers, but also those who did not fit neatly within phenotypic boxes or rode with racially ambiguous drivers.

In effect, Taylor's migration statistics functioned much like the tramp studies of the early twentieth century, which typified a distinct social subject characterized by its mobility. That is, Taylor brought "the basic fact of [Mexican] mobility" into being as a coded racial and class category of working class, "Mexican Brown," seasonal workers.[44] Although efforts were made to ensure the reliability of the data, the selection criterion itself was based upon popular perceptions of Mexican mobility to the exclusion of other types of movement—for instance, train travel by the Mexican middle class. As such, Taylor's study reaffirmed what the social scientist already assumed: that certain types of automobility were inseparable from race.

The automobile was an essential part of ethnic Mexicans' social, cultural, and economic experiences in Southern California, particularly for those engaged in seasonal agricultural labor. It connected them to far-off places and expanded the boundaries of daily life in Southern California. At any given time, a worker could be employed as a Redlands citrus picker, a San Joaquin cotton picker, or a Los Angeles bricklayer. At its peak, the equation between Mexican farmworkers and automobiles was so absolute that citrus ranchers provided garages to their employees, and Taylor could substitute certain forms of driving for Mexican migrants themselves. It is in this context that the shifting meanings of Mexican automobility in the 1930s can be seen as all the more shocking. As economic conditions worsened in the region, automobility was reserved exclusively for white residents and Mexican drivers appeared out of place.[45]

MEXICAN MOTORISTS IN METROPOLITAN LOS ANGELES

As the twentieth century progressed, the boundaries between Los Angeles and the Citrus Belt were increasingly muddied. Ease of travel, population growth, and residential sprawl made for increased crisscrossing of this metropolitan region. During the 1930s, old and familiar mobile practices intensified. For instance, displaced rural workers spent more time in urban centers searching for employment; municipal police officers surveilled state lines for incoming migrants; and the teenage children of agricultural workers drove across the region in pursuit of new leisure opportunities. In the midst of these changes, the movement of Mexican motorists from rural into urban spaces took on new meanings. This section examines how mobility was transformed from an economic asset to a social liability. Specifically, in the public eye, Mexican drivers would no longer be seen as agricultural workers following the crops, but were instead seen as public charges seeking relief, and dangerous juveniles looking for their next crime. In both cases, Mexican immigrant and Mexican American drivers were positioned as a direct liability to the social and economic well-being of the region.

Prior to the Depression, Mexican agricultural workers commonly employed metropolitan migration as an economic strategy. Already accustomed to seasonal shifts in the California harvests, as crops emptied in one region workers migrated to eastern and southern Los Angeles, where additional opportunities existed in construction, transportation, and manufacturing. For instance, Graciano Gomez, a longtime resident of Redlands, a citrus town, lived with his relatives in Los Angeles during the summers so that he could work in the city.[46] Likewise, when disproportionately impacted by Depression-era conditions, Mexican-descent people again turned to the long-tested strategy of regional mobility. From this position, it is not a coincidence that sociologist Emory Bogardus placed the beginning of the modern day-labor economy in 1930s Los Angeles. He recalled that "small groups of six, eight, or ten Mexican immigrant unskilled laborers would appear on street corners as far west as Western and Vermont Avenues and north to Washington Blvd, and wait for some unidentified employer to seek out their services for a few days, chiefly in rural areas."[47] The number dwindled as the day waned and men had either found employment or returned home. Workers in search of employment knit together opportunities as best they could across metropolitan Los Angeles.

Where the poor have been the most vulnerable and often the first to suffer in times of economic decline, mobility has been an essential asset. During the Depression, those unable to earn a subsistence income leveraged their automobility to access government relief. It was under these conditions that, as a child, Wally Sanchez carpooled twenty miles from Whittier to Los Angeles to collect public assistance. During the Depression years, Sanchez relied upon government-provided shoes and clothing. He recalled that "there were Mackinaw jackets, big heavy jackets, but they were red and green and they had corduroys. But, I mean, it was like a prison. Everybody in that goddamn school knew that you [laughter], you were getting all of this free stuff.... They pointed you out, you know?"[48] Relief was commonly accompanied by embarrassment. Six decades after the Depression, Angelina Sumaya Cosme remembered a purple dress issued by welfare, "If you had one of those dresses ... they were from the Welfare and everybody knew it. I'm not a proud person when it comes to saying to anybody whoever might be interested, that I'm poor, that I've always been poor. But I think I was a little hurt at that."[49] Unevenly impacted by declining economic conditions, during the Depression the Mexican-descent population on relief comprised close to twice their proportion of the Los Angeles County population.[50]

As Angelenos endured dire financial hardship, mobile Mexicans became a matter of growing concern among social workers. In 1928, Alice Evans Cruz published a popular short story in the professional social work journal, *The Survey,* that underscored the burden of Mexican immigrants on state employers.[51] In "The Romanzas Train Señora Nurse," automobiles served as a proxy for critiques levied at Mexican families and helped racialize them as public charges. Evans Cruz opened the tale by describing a social worker's first encounter with the Romanzas—a fictional family of Mexican immigrants—as they arrived on the highway:

> Curiosity getting the better of discretion, I went out into the dusty road and found, as I had expected, a prehistoric Ford in the last stages of decrepitude from which it appeared the entire population of Mexico, in assorted sizes, was tumbling furiously, at an imminent risk of life and limb.[52]

At the cost of only a hundred pesos, a dilapidated Ford had transported the family from Sonora, Mexico to California. Overwhelmed by the cost and attention required by the family, who suffered from a range of ailments and social maladaptations, the nurse concluded that the Romanza family would have to be returned to Mexico "as too much a responsibility altogether."[53] In the story, the Romanzas stand in for the range of social problems the writer attributes to Mexican immigrants, from teenage pregnancy to a backlog of medical procedures. Significantly for Evans Cruz, it is through their ease of travel from Mexico to Southern California by car that families like the Romanzas drained service systems at a cost to local social workers.

The writer's fictional account also highlights the ways automobiles were used to problematize the relationship between Mexican people and relief services. Before the Romanzas can be deported as public charges, they win a large lottery. Rather than settling their debts, the family spends their newly acquired money on luxury items, most conspicuously a new Dodge purchased on a partial payment plan, to replace the old Ford the Romanzas owned on arrival, which accurately reflected their poverty. Dodge had just introduced a new line of passenger cars that were markedly more expensive than not only Fords, but also their own previous models.[54] Learning of the Romanzas' extravagant purchase, the nurse scolded the family for spending their money on a vehicle that far exceeded their winnings. She chided:

> Why, Mrs. Romanza, this is terrible, to saddle yourselves with such a debt, and to be so foolish in the use of this money which, no matter how dishonestly won, should be used for your children's education, and food. I, with no family, have no overstuffed furniture, and certainly would not purchase all these useless things on a time payment.[55]

In response to the nurse's concern, Mrs. Romanza explains that the purchase was consistent with the nurse's own efforts to teach the family a U.S. standard of living. In their new Dodge car, Mrs. Romanza explained, the family "should ride about like [American] ladies and gentlemen."[56] The family's new possession distanced them from the "dirty Mexicans who had only a bed and a stove in their houses."[57] While shocking for the ways Mrs. Romanza implicates the nurse and American spending habits in the family's purchase, her explanation also indicates a discordant effort at U.S. integration. The family's automotive purchase signals an implicit critique of U.S. consumerism at the same time it proposes that Mexican immigrants were unable to control themselves when exposed to the breadth of consumer options available in the United States, as opposed to a Mexico envisioned as free of commercialism. Ultimately unable to pay off the debts they had accrued, the Romanzas trade the new Dodge car for an old Ford truck. Together, they leave in the same condition they arrived in, household goods hanging from the side of their vehicle and the family piled on top.

Questions of debt were foregrounded in car ownership, an expenditure second only to a house. Ford had placed the automobile within reach of middle class Americans by 1908 and nearly all cars were purchased with cash before 1919. This changed with the introduction of consumer financing by General Motors, when car sales became dependent on future rather than saved earnings. By the end of the 1920s, installment sales of automobiles rose from zero to 60 percent of total sales. Partial payment plans had become a staple of U.S. life, placing cars, washing machines, phonographs, and other high-priced items within households throughout the country. However, when the bubble burst, public faith in credit turned to blame.[58] Increasingly, the poor were impugned for their lack of foresight, and impoverished families who had relied on credit to acquire luxuries during more prosperous times were deemed culpable for their purchases. Paradoxically, if poor people's debt was to blame for Depression conditions, spending on high-ticket items was heralded as a potential path to recovery. Large manufacturers, economists, and government officials alike claimed aggregated consumer buying power could pull Americans out of the Depression. A "consumer citizenship" prevailed in which proper spending habits were equated with national unity, market egalitarianism, and the fulfillment of civic duty.[59]

Purchasing a vehicle was the ultimate form of "consumer citizenship," yet shopping for a vehicle further reaffirmed the social separation between whites and nonwhites. Showrooms were designed as large open spaces with high windows and flashy signage designed to attract the eyes of passing motorists. Inside, friendly salesmen greeted consumers, new cars were exhibited, and shoppers were welcomed as mobile citizens. The lavish experience of automotive shopping was dependent on dealers who systematically refused to assist shoppers of color. The practice of purchasing a car was one means by which residents experienced either their racial privilege or exclusion. Denied service in the showroom, racial minorities were forced to choose whether to hire a white go-between or buy used. As a key practice of consumer citizenship, showroom segregation denied nonwhites inclusion as mass consumers of high-ticket items and excluded them from practices of cultural citizenship affiliated with consumption.[60]

In the Depression years, many questions existed concerning who was a deserving citizen with the right to relief. Automobiles were a key battleground in this debate. While ethnic Mexicans turned to automobility as an economic relief strategy with roots in agriculture, the car itself became a symbol through which they were blamed for exacerbating Depression conditions, and simultaneously were excluded from practices of consumer citizenship credited with collective relief. Dust Bowl migrants added to the migrant panic as local residents struggled to make sense of these newcomers. This is, after all, the era of the "bum blockade," in which the Los Angeles Police Department (LAPD) set up roadblocks on highways far removed from Los Angeles in order to deter out-of-state migrants. But concern was not spread out equally. The next section interrogates the ways progressives battled to recast Okies (white Dust Bowl migrants) as modern-day frontiersmen arriving in a dystopic American West and deserving of both public sympathy and assistance.[61] However, in doing so, progressives left unchallenged the belief that Mexican motorists were foreigners taking advantage of U.S. relief.

"GYPSIES BY FORCE OF CIRCUMSTANCE": DUST BOWL
MIGRANTS AS MODERN DAY PIONEERS

> I drove from the San Louis Obispo county down to Pomona and
> the pea fields at Calipatrio and the Imperial Valley, and I had not
> gone far before I realized that something fundamental was hap-
> pening in our rural sections. I had seen, years before, a great
> number of Mexican agricultural laborers. I was astounded to find
> that within the course of 4 or 5 years the complexion of the labor
> supply was enormously changed. Here I saw pea pickers from Ver-
> mont, Oklahoma, Arkansas, and Texas, and on the cars gathered
> around the fields licenses [that is, license plates] from other states.[62]

Throughout the 1930s, the migrant worker population shifted considerably.
Mechanization of the U.S. heartland and the ecological disaster known
as the Dust Bowl contributed to mass displacements from the rural South
and Midwest to northern industry and western agribusiness. Large relocations of inland migrants to the West Coast combined with aggressive repatriation campaigns to alter the face of the California migrant labor force
from brown to white. But the lines between these categories became slippery
as the dire economic and social ostracism experienced by U.S. whites upon
arrival in California threatened to darken them. In a racial project attempting to foster sympathy and aid for Dust Bowl families, progressives would
work to reposition these migrants as white at a time when their racial status
was quite unstable. Entering a long debate over the deserving and undeserving poor, they reached back to pioneer mythologies to position white internal
migrants as inherently settlers, mobile only temporarily, and worthy of
relief.[63]

In total, an estimated 300,000 people entered California in search of work
during the Depression. The defense of state lines emerged as a strategic
response to out-of-state migrants' need for aid. As westward migration
increased, Los Angeles established more than a dozen border patrols throughout California. Far removed from the City of Los Angeles, the checkpoints
served as a blockade against migrant workers who, in previous years, agriculturalists had actively recruited.[64]

Stationed at points of entry from November 1935 to April 1936, a staff of
136 police officers sorted the employable from the unemployable, sending the
latter back across the state line. Described as a "flat disregard of constitutional provisions" by progressive lawyer and author Carey McWilliams, the

patrols at the California border denied U.S. citizens their constitutionally guaranteed right to sovereign movement across state lines.[65] Blockades were just one of many strategies used to stem the flow of relief away from interstate migrants. In other instances, local governments offered free gas to migrants headed across county lines, municipal police broadly enacted vagrancy laws, and, in the most extreme manipulation of migrant flows, Mexican and Filipino residents were offered one-way tickets to their countries of origin in a massive repatriation movement between 1929 and 1936.[66] Highlighting the tension between national and local cultural citizenship during economic panic, the defense of state lines reveals California residents' deep concern with internal migration and the distribution of scarce resources among residents.[67]

Local governments' exclusionary mobile technologies were broadly applied. As a result, their sweeping strategies realigned existing power arrangements that had upheld distinctions between white and nonwhite workers. As interstate migrants entered the California agricultural landscape in search of employment, racial lines were muddied and whites were "blackened."[68] As described by critical race and ethnic studies scholars, race is an unstable category within which various European-origin groups have been ordered, sometimes at the risk of racial othering. In Depression-era California, the racial status of white migrants was vulnerable. As one example, historian Charles Wollenberg describes a central California community in which white migrants were relegated to sitting in the segregated section of the theater alongside African Americans.[69] Migrant status was enough to disrupt their racial standing, resulting in their literal positioning alongside other, nonwhite races. In times of economic depression, the privileges of whiteness could be fickle and potentially revoked.

At the same time that migration unsettled the category of whiteness, it allowed for new forms of racial affiliation. Where solidarity had previously been drawn along racial lines, the broad exclusion of migrants of different backgrounds created the conditions for an expanded social consciousness based upon shared employment and propinquity. Eunice Romero Gonzales, the daughter of an orchardist, fondly described Fairbanks Ranch near Redlands as one such site—as a place where displaced white, resident Mexican, and African-descent workers formed close ties, and multiracial forms of socialization were commonplace. She remembered, "My dad used to like to have people over and sing and dance, play music. They were more like family gatherings than big parties."[70] Scholars of the Depression era have highlighted such moments of multiracial interaction, but their potential for social transformation was limited. Over time, whiteness and its affiliated privileges were reinscribed. As historian Devra Weber noted, white migrant workers struggled to develop a shared class-consciousness while their favored racial position reinforced their faith in upward mobility and American individualism.[71] In Depression-era Los Angeles and its Citrus Belt hinterland, the scale between multiracial class-consciousness and white privilege was tipped.

Where forms of racialization experienced by white migrants entering California were in flux, the reiteration of racial divisions was fostered by an unlikely source. The split was aided, to different degrees, by the writings and advocacy of leftist "agrarian partisans," well-known artists and intellectuals who drew attention to displaced workers victimized by capitalistic domination of the land, including economist Paul S. Taylor, photographer Dorothea Lange, and author John Steinbeck.[72] Where U.S. whites were at risk of becoming the next casualties in a long wave of racialized migratory workers, progressives overtly differentiated American-born whites from the Chinese, Japanese, Filipino, and Mexican workers who preceded them. In gripping academic reports, popular books, photographs, and newsprint, they successfully recast a multiracial agricultural landscape as virtually white.

Described in recent work, progressives' focus on the plight of white families was either a strategic tool adopted to foster public support or, more nefariously, was a reflection of their own beliefs that white families were exclusively capable of challenging a corrupt California agribusiness.[73] Here, I am less concerned with the internal/personal intentions of agrarian partisans than the ways they engaged narratives of mobility in order to produce racial subjects with different claims to public empathy and, by extension, access to government support.

Perhaps the most well-known authors of Depression-era public scholarship are Dorothea Lange and Paul S. Taylor. Works produced by the married pair foreground the ways progressives defended Dust Bowl workers' whiteness and worthiness for aid by reengaging narratives of frontier mobility. Consider *An American Exodus* (1939), a vivid portrayal of the Dust Bowl plight told through a curated selection of photographs and interviews with migrants. Compiled over the span of four years, the book was published shortly after John Steinbeck's *Grapes of Wrath* (1939) and Carey McWilliams's *Factories in the Field* (1939). Although without the same mass readership as Steinbeck and McWilliams, *An American Exodus* was read alongside these popular works as critiques of American agribusiness.[74] An integral and unique part of this larger canon, Lange and Taylor's visually rich book underscores the important role of automobility in the whitening of Dust Bowl migrants, a striking foil to the ways "The Romanzas Train Señora Nurse" placed Mexicans squarely in the role of foreign other.

An American Exodus features over a hundred photographs paired with interview excerpts that consistently conjure images of early western pioneers. This link is made explicit by the book's title image and cover line, "Covered Wagon—1939."[75] Like frontiersmen, migrant families are photographed piled into trucks looking forward to an uncertain but promising horizon. The book is organized in two parts. The first half establishes the toll of mechanization on farmers in the states of the South, Midwest, and Plains. Throughout these early chapters, the reader is consistently presented with images of packed cars. Rather than the single male travelers of earlier migrant chains, families overwhelmingly occupy these vehicles. Like the voyager in a covered wagon, they have filled their vehicles to capacity in preparation for the westward journey.

Lange photographed the travelers while immobile, often parked alongside interstate highways. Their vehicles frequently encase the facial profiles of the subjects nestled within. That is, the metallic border of the automobile frames the travelers. Underscoring the characteristic dignity of Lange's portraiture, the focus on facial expressions imbues the photographic subjects with the mythic heroism of frontier travel depicted in earlier western art. Consider, for instance, George Bingham's iconic 1851–1852 painting, *Daniel Boone Escorting Settlers through the Cumberland Gap,* which portrays a caravan of settlers upon horseback traveling into a shadowy landscape with light upon their faces, suggesting their heroism with religious overtones.[76] Likewise, as the tool of travel, the Dust Bowl migrant's car borrows from this pioneer iconography. Earlier reports published by Lange and Taylor served as precedent for this transmogrification of the car into the iconic covered wagon of frontier travelers, including a report they published aptly titled "Again the Covered Wagon."[77] In this modern-day coupling, the new frontiersmen travel by highway and covered wagons have evolved into automobiles, the now-mythic symbol of Dust Bowl exodus.

Providing a striking photographic archive of economic displacement and migration, *An American Exodus* presents an image of the Dust Bowl in black and white. The first half of the book establishes that capitalist mechanization indiscriminately harmed African American and white farmers alike. The book is progressive for the ways it evokes sympathy and underscores the failed promise of emancipation through the words and images of African American farmers themselves. However, in suggesting that the long-stretching arm of slavery was replaced with a shared form of economic disenfranchisement, albeit without attention to the uneven distribution of its costs by race, the book and its images portray U.S. citizenship in Anglo and African American terms only. Chinese, Japanese, Mexican, and other nonwhite workers appear nowhere in this first half of the book and, by extension, are written out of a powerful narrative intent on demonstrating the negative impact of the Dust Bowl on U.S. farmers. Through their absence, Asian and Mexican populations seem to exist only as foreigners to the land.

There is a singular exception to this black/white binary in the second half of Lange and Taylor's book, which turns its attention to the arrival of displaced white migrants to the American West. It is a single image portraying a crew of Filipino lettuce cutters with the caption "To perform its 'stoop labor' California agriculture has drawn upon a long succession of races: Chinese, Japanese, Hindustanis, Mexican, Filipinos, Negroes, and now American whites."[78] Rather than the sympathetic portraits of whites and African Americans that comprise earlier chapters, the image here serves only to emphasize the dehumanizing nature of farm labor formerly assigned to foreign, nonwhite workers. The Filipino crew is photographed as if a single unit, with their heads turned to the ground. Unlike Lange's iconic portraiture, which highlights her subjects' facial expressions and personal agency, the personifying effects of her work are lost here, which emphasizes instead an indiscriminate pack.

Notably absent from the second half of the book are African Americans. Though highlighted as victims of mechanization in earlier chapters, they are neither photographed in transit from their destitute inland positions nor upon arriving in the American West alongside white midwesterners. Instead, images of exodus in cars, trucks, and by foot are reserved exclusively for white families within Lange and Taylor's ethnographic chronicle. While historians have underscored the significance of the "great migration" for African American settlement in industrial centers, including Los Angeles, there is no place for them within this pioneer trope.[79] Instead, both African Americans and immigrant workers serve in their own ways to illustrate the denigration of U.S. farmers and to heighten a call for reform aimed at white families.

Dust Bowl migrant driver framed by car window. A67.137.38243.2 Dorothea Lange, *Midcontinent*, August 1938. © The Dorothea Lange Collection, the Oakland Museum of California. Gift of Paul S. Taylor.

An American Exodus was neither unique in its mythologizing of white migrant laborers as latter-day yeomen nor was it the only piece of progressive literature to do so at the expense of nonwhite workers. John Steinbeck, the Pulitzer Prize-winning author who immortalized the plight of California migrant families in *The Grapes of Wrath* (1939), played the greatest role in transforming white migrants from tramps into the Joads: displaced families pushed into migrancy by industrial agriculture and the pursuit of a permanent home in the American West. In his account, white mobility is part of a larger set of narrative tropes that construct Dust Bowl migrants as sympa-

Filipino lettuce cutters. A67.137.38263.1 Dorothea Lange, *Last West, Stoop Labor* (detail), 1936. © The Dorothea Lange Collection, the Oakland Museum of California. Gift of Paul S. Taylor.

thetic figures worthy of settlement assistance. An important and often overlooked precedent to his novel is a collection of his articles titled *Their Blood Is Strong* (1938). Notably, the booklet was accompanied by Lange's Farm Security Administration photography, including her iconic *Migrant Mother* (1936). Although Lange's portfolio included several portraits of mothers from diverse backgrounds with their children, the popularity of the portrait of Florence Thompson, a woman of mixed ancestry who passed for white, further suggests the importance of Lange's work in crafting this narrative.[80]

Throughout *Their Blood Is Strong*, the multiethnic landscape of western field labor is cast as monolithically white. Steinbeck writes:

They are small farmers who have lost their farms, or farm hands who lived with the family in the old American way. . . . They are resourceful and intelligent Americans who have gone through the hell of drouth [drought], have seen their lands wither and die and the top soil blown away; and this, to a man who has owned his land, is a curious and terrible pain.[81]

Here Steinbeck contrasts these deserving white American migrants with undeserving foreign immigrants. In succession, Chinese workers were described as accustomed to a low standard of living which white labor would not tolerate; Mexicans were depicted as ineffective organizers without rights; and Filipinos were characterized as a miscegenating threat.[82] As a whole, Asian and Mexican workers were depicted as the past of farm labor, each presenting a unique threat to Jeffersonian agrarianism. White migrants, by juxtaposition, were situated as the future of farm labor, a shift calling for industry reform.

More than mere propagandists relegated to the forum of popular literature, agrarian partisans were recognized as specialists on the migrant crisis. In particular, Taylor regularly spoke before Congress on the topics of interstate migrant labor and the agricultural economy. In his testimonies, the Berkeley economist consistently described Dust Bowl migrants as displaced farmers pushed out of rural life by the profit-driven mechanization of the countryside. Rather than linking migration solely to migrants' choice, his testimony credits their mobility to the shifting economics of agricultural production. Testifying before Congress, he described "tak[ing] to the highways heading west" as the last alternative of displaced farmers with few other options.[83] Workers, here, appear as victims of an inverted western promise embodied in frontier mythology. Whereas American exceptionalism suggested migrants would be met by the reward of upward mobility, the plight of Depression-era farmers in the American West demonstrated that the "ladder from laborer to owner . . . becomes increasingly a matter of inheritance."[84] If the western frontier had once signified opportunity and open land, it was now an irrigated landscape monopolized by insatiable capitalists.[85] Migrants from Oklahoma, Arkansas, Texas, and Missouri were consistently painted as a continuum of western-bound, modern-day yeomen in a vain search for the agrarian dream. California, "the last west," was a gilded landscape—one transformed by settlement, mechanization, and an endless stream of disposable farm labor. And the highway was its conduit.[86]

Like Taylor's earlier equation between ethnic Mexicans and cars in "Mexican Labor in the United States," for progressives the automobile had become synonymous with this renewed wave of white migrants. Lange and Taylor write, "To even the poorest of these an automobile is a vital necessity and the cost of its operation cuts a large figure in the family budget. The car must be fed gasoline and oil to make the next harvest, or to get to and from the fields, and its vehicles must be kept shod before the feet of the children."[87] Just as Fords stood in for Mexican Browns in Taylor's 1920s study, references to jalopies, flivvers, and tin lizzies were interchangeable with white migrant families in Taylor and Lange's 1930s collaborative work. Their writing ties a narrative of settlement exclusively to white migrants, whose images were paired with quotes that highlighted a desire to settle: "People has got to stop somewhere. Even a bird has got to nest" and "What bothers us travellin' people most is we can't get no place to stay still."[88] Looking to Steinbeck's writing underscores an important racial distinction between the 1920s "birds of passage" and 1930s "auto campers." He suggests that white migrants were "gypsies by force of circumstance."[89] Whereas migration in the Box Bill debates presupposes movement as the innate characteristic of Mexican workers, white migration is presented here as diametrically opposed to the inherent nature of white families. For one group, mobility is deemed a racialized norm, and for the other it is a consequence of capitalist agriculture's failure, whose victims are in need of quick remedy.

Under Depression-era conditions, the racial meaning of white motorists was up for debate. When progressives proposed white motorists were economic "refugees" or "victims of mechanization," they competed with alternate understandings of white migrants that ranged from earlier iterations of southeastern European ethnics, such as "fruit tramps" and "hoboes," to new ethnoclass iterations, such as "auto campers" and "gasoline gypsies." The difference between "victims of mechanization" and "gasoline gypsies" was more than a matter of word choice.[90] Behind Lange and Taylor's references to pioneer mythology was an attempt to undermine negative perceptions surrounding the questionable ethics of the tramp and to emphasize the morality of the nuclear migrant family. As described by historian Nayan Shah, the close living quarters, shared domestic responsibilities, and possibility for erotic encounters among migrant men in the first half of the twentieth century had cast the tramp as a symbol of masculine ambiguity.[91] The cultural reinscription of the westbound migrant family in the 1930s helped alleviate these fears. Agrarian partisans reasserted the heteronormativity of poor white workers and transposed a morality attached to white mobility reaching back to frontier mythology. If earlier iterations of the wandering white tramp invoked disdain, progressives' aim was to replace him with the migration of displaced white farmers desperate to find a means of subsistence, settlement, and an end to their status as a mobile proletariat.[92] At stake was whether migrant workers would be recognized as either temporarily or hopelessly permanent racial outsiders, and only the former was likely to be met with aid.

The process by which the white migrant was transformed from a tramp to a pioneer depended upon an erasure. Contrary to progressives' portrayals of white migrants as small farmers in search of the agrarian dream, these expatriates of the U.S. South and Midwest preferred oil fields to orange groves. Recent scholarship has also found that white southerners, as a subgroup, rented along the metropolitan fringe where housing was affordable and agricultural labor was replaced by industrial opportunities. Contrary to the portrayals of Dust Bowl migrants presented by agrarian partisans, homeownership, family farms, and the pull of an unknown frontier did not characterize these migrants. In fact, they actively demonstrated an inclination for semirural industrialism.[93] Nevertheless, where racial categories were in flux, reaffirming whiteness meant linking migrant laborers with frontier mythology and prompting government officials to reinvest in a western promise of social mobility from migrant to settler.

By recasting white migrants as settlers in the making, agrarian partisans provided a moralistic argument for extending social and economic aid to homeless white workers. As noted in the preface for *Their Blood Is Strong,* "This is the most important social and economic problem that faces the people of the State of California. . . . *Your help is needed.*"[94] Oriented to public audiences, Steinbeck's work as well as Lange and Taylor's were supported by New Deal agencies intent on garnering positive publicity for their migrant camps, fostering public action, and securing social security benefits to agricultural laborers widely dispersed throughout the state.[95] *An American Exodus,* Lange's photography, and Steinbeck's *Their Blood Is Strong,* alongside other iconic texts, emerged out of political agendas seeking to recast migrants as racially white in the popular imagination, farmworkers once again worthy of saving, and to advance support for resettlement through government assistance. No longer dangerous outsiders, Dust Bowl migrants were likened by government advocates to Gold Rush adventurers, a rough and tumble crew that would assimilate into California if given the opportunity. Consider the words of Harrison S. Robinson, chairman of the Committee on the Migrant Problem, a committee of the California State Chamber of Commerce, "The future will know them, not as transients, but as part of hundreds of communities and as citizens of the State. Their good and the good of the State must merge."[96] In progressive circles, the "Okie" had become the "yeoman."

By channeling the sacrosanct image of the pioneer family traveling west and emphasizing the loss of the agrarian dream, labor advocates placed the responsibility for white migrants in the hands of the public. The poverty of white migrants was portrayed by agrarian partisans as the product of a declining political economy, and undeserving of moral condemnation. Likewise, white migrants' mobility seemed to reaffirm their eagerness to reenter the market economy, if only offered the opportunity. Conversely, the question of who was entitled to relief could be answered to the exclusion of a resident Mexican workforce. Ethnic Mexicans' erasure from pioneer narratives, and the marginalization of foreigners without the right to long-term settlement, provided the foundation for exclusionist legislation.

The same year as the publication of *The Grapes of Wrath, Factories in the Field,* and *An American Exodus,* California senator Ralph Swing proposed a scathing bill that would deny "aliens" access to government relief.[97] As described to the readership of the *Los Angeles Times,* its role was to "relieve the taxpayers of the cost of caring for indigent aliens who have no moral or legal right to be a burden on California."[98] While the "moral or legal right" to relief was extended to newly arriving internal white migrants, there was no such sympathy for the long-term laborers who had planted the seed of agricultural wealth. Like the social workers who lamented the arrival of the Romanzas as too much a burden altogether, state relief officials suggested Mexicans migrated to California during the Depression solely to seek government assistance.[99] If the image of westbound whites could soften fears of overburdened social agencies and evoke national responsibility for fulfilling the frontier dream, the parallel image of migrant Mexican families held no such transformation.

PIONEER ROUTES AND THE MADONNA
OF THE TRAIL MONUMENT

The process by which Mexican mobility was denaturalized cannot be divorced from the celebratory histories of white migration crafted by agrarian partisans in the 1930s. The evolution of Route 66 from a highway to a symbolic pilgrimage completed the process by which depictions of automobility were distanced from popular perceptions of what was typically "Mexican." The highway covered close to 2,500 miles and served as an east-west artery from Chicago to Los Angeles. With precedent in El Camino Real and the National Old Trails Road, Route 66 integrated already established highways and rural main streets into a single pathway, thus earning it the nickname "Main Street of America."[100] Where Mexican migration along Route 99 in northern Los Angeles County had connected Mexican identity to the car in Taylor's study of Mexican migration, Route 66 was a racial line through which white American identity was constructed. That is, depictions of roads and travel each had expressive racial dimensions.

The distancing of Mexican Americans from the automobile in metropolitan Los Angeles was exacerbated by the popularity of the Spanish Fantasy Past. The opening of Olvera Street, or the Mexican marketplace, and El Camino Real, or the King's Mission Road, each rendered ethnic Mexicans as a nostalgic reminder of a primitive past. The popularity of these sites, particularly El Camino Real, corresponded with the increasing accessibility of middle class Americans to automobiles and the shift from international to domestic travel accelerated by the Great Depression.[101] El Camino Real linked California's Spanish missions along a single road. By traveling the route, tourists could follow the tracks of Franciscans, both celebrating conquest and creating a "commonsense" evolution of racial progress. The Spanish Fantasy Past served to render Mexican and Anglo California as quite distant, and deemed white tourists as distinctly modern. As described by historian Phoebe Kropp, "Automobiles provided a ready example of the superiority of modern life because drivers believed that their vehicles represented the pinnacle of progress."[102] An extension of the disconnecting symbolic systems highlighted by historian Phil Deloria, specifically in his analysis of Geronimo and the Cadillac, Mexicans were rendered as fading objects amidst the scenery rather than modern subjects behind the wheel.[103]

Just as much a racial project as El Camino Real, but to a very different effect, was the Madonna of the Trail monument. The Daughters of the American Revolution (DAR) were leaders in historic preservation and patriotic pageantry. One such cause was the outlining, commemorating, and publicizing of national pioneer trails. Between 1928 and 1929, the DAR erected twelve identical monuments along the path of the National Old Trails Road, linking Baltimore, Maryland to Los Angeles, California.[104] As described by the National Old Trails Road Committee:

[These pioneers] reduced the dense wilderness to broad fields for cultivation; they harnessed great rivers, subdued the Indian, making him a good neighbor, and on the great plains in the long night-watches as they communed with the Great Spirit they gathered inspiration for greater adventure until, at last, after enduring every possible hardship, they laid their lives upon the altar of patriotism.[105]

The statue series, like the road itself, was envisioned as a memorial to the enduring sacrifice of the western pioneer and the taming of both the frontier and its Indigenous occupants.

The timely appearance of the statue series and the DAR's concerted efforts to commemorate the migrant family are exemplary of the prevailing social currency of pioneer mythology in 1930s Southern California, a mythology that provided fodder for those seeking to legitimate white migrants' claims to relief. Dubbed the "Madonna of the Trail," the monument assumed a sacrosanct value. Each rendition loomed large at 18 feet high from base to top, and the title itself recalled the Virgin Mary. Designed by sculptor August Leimbach, the monument featured a woman cradling a baby in her left arm and gripping a rifle in her right. She walks in tall grass surrounded by cactus bushes, while a young boy clings to her apron. The visibility of a partially covered rattlesnake further signals the precariousness of the situation and the bravery of these early migrants. Leimbach, a German immigrant, traced his admiration for the frontier and inspiration for the sculpture to his childhood:

When I was a schoolboy in the old country, the American history of the pioneer days made a deep impression on me. I thought often of those who had left the old home and all that was dear to them and had come to this country to find a hold for their ambition.[106]

From its inception, the monument series represented an imagined history of the "Wild West" and the "pioneer type" who settled the American continent.[107] In this sense, frontier mythology is a powerful selective tradition with extreme chronological fluidity.

Each statue, while identical, adopted an inscription specific to the history of the state in which it was erected. In California, the narrative spoke to a racial and social progression evident in the much earlier planting of the parent navel orange tree at Riverside's Mission Inn. The eastward-facing inscription reflected the past of the community. The inscription noted, "This trail, trod by padres in Spanish days, became, under Mexican rule, the road

Madonna of the Trail monument erected in Ontario, 1929. Photograph by Luis Camas, 2018.

connecting San Bernardino and Los Angeles, later the American post road." The inscription to the west pointed towards the community's future: "Over this trail, Jedediah Smith, seeking a river flowing westward, led a band of sixteen trappers, the first Americans to enter California by land."[108] The statue was a physical monument to a larger pageantry quite typical of Southern California, one that depicted an evolutionary progression from Spanish to American California, and that left unnamed the displacement of Indigenous people.[109] The statue was unique, however, in its national serialization and its focus upon the white migrant family, rather than the more popular Spanish Fantasy Past.

The California Madonna of the Trail statue was erected in Ontario, in a section of present-day Upland, at the crossroads of San Bernardino and Los Angeles Counties. Tellingly, it was placed at the intersection of the picturesque Euclid Avenue and Foothill Boulevard. Euclid Avenue served as a landscaped showcase of technology, irrigation, and botanicals for the city. The 200-foot-wide boulevard extended from the Southern Pacific Railroad to the San Antonio Canyon and was bisected by the streetcar. At the center of the Chaffey brothers' "model colony," Euclid Avenue was a physical display of advanced transportation, exotic flora, and charming cottages.[110] Intersecting Euclid Avenue was Foothill Boulevard, better known by its national designation as Route 66. The physical placement of the Madonna of the Trail monument along Route 66 at this particular place foreshadows the symbolic link between the pioneer migrant of the western frontier and the modern-day migrant of the Depression.

Memory was a contested ground on which white migrants were transformed into pioneers and Mexican migrants were left in the dust. The Madonna of the Trail monument and its placement along the National Old Trails Road (Route 66) was a racial project inscribing white mobility with value. It served a similar purpose to the ceremonial replanting of the Riverside navel orange tree discussed in Chapter 1, and progressives' depictions of white migrant families: it was a selective tradition that cast both the past and present in racial terms. The DAR's national monument series signaled the unique celebratory value of white mobility in the American West, while rendering Mexican people vestiges of a preindustrial era. Pioneer mythology would have reverberating consequences for the Mexican population in the decades to follow.

THE JOY AND CRIME OF LATINO AND LATINA YOUTH BEHIND THE WHEEL

While agrarian partisans busily transformed Dust Bowl migrants into the next wave of pioneers deserving of sympathy, Mexican-descent motorists faced an unprecedented rate of criminalization aimed at their mobility. Despite repatriation programs and slowed rates of immigration, the resident Mexican immigrant and Mexican American population continued to grow across metropolitan Los Angeles and its Citrus Belt. By 1930, the City of Los Angeles held 30 percent of California's resident Mexican-descent population, as well as the most sizable ethnic Mexican population in the nation. And they faced unprecedented rates of imprisonment, with arrests in Los Angeles rising from 3,915 in 1929 to 8,729 in 1939.[111] It was in the context of a visible Mexican demographic that youth of color faced increased criminalization for their movement.

Police oversight of the ethnic Mexican population between 1900 and 1920 had been primarily concerned with labor activity, such as breaking strikes and quelling unionization. But by the 1930s, the LAPD came into increasing conflict with resident Mexicans over questions of criminality, reflecting popular alarm over population change, the certitudes of the typological school of psychiatrics that linked crime to race, and statistical evidence of racially discriminatory enforcement by police of nonviolent crimes, such as insobriety and vagrancy infractions.[112] Whereas Mexican adults were largely arrested on public order charges or were immigrants awaiting federal deportation, Mexican youth were most commonly arrested for joyriding. The 1930s and 1940s saw the rise of state institutions aimed at punishing youth of color, who were disproportionately identified as feeble-minded and sent to military-style penitentiaries where they were subject to harsh punishments and sterilization. This was one stop in a long line of institutions separating Latino boys from their families, who were credited with sowing the seeds of their children's delinquency. Among these establishments was the Sherman Institute in Riverside. Mechanisms originally designed to separate and discipline Native youth were now routinely applied to Mexican and Puerto Rican boys, who found themselves wards at this off-reservation boarding school.[113] This reorientation underscores that tools designed to manage the movements of one racialized group could easily be adapted to manage another.[114] Conversely, enrollment records for the Boy's Republic in Chino shows that Latino boys were rarely sent to reform schools, which sought rehabilitation through self-government and vocational training.[115] Widely circulated accounts of deviant drivers were met with municipal police efforts targeting young drivers to undercut nonwhite mobility.

Analysis of the popular 1930s radio docudrama *Calling All Cars* underscores changing perceptions of nonwhite motorists and growing concern with Mexican American youth, and Latinas/os at large, against a backdrop of economic decline, migrant surplus, and the public's awareness of a growing, permanent Mexican population. Based on cases encountered by the LAPD, the docudrama ran between 1933 and 1939. The series reflects larger efforts to glorify law enforcement advanced by J. Edgar Hoover's Federal Bureau of Investigation and the motion-picture industry, as glamorous portraits of high-profile bandits and mobsters competed for the public's attention. In thirty-minute episodes, *Calling All Cars* dramatized true crime, its realism heightened by the voice of an actual police dispatcher at the beginning of each broadcast. It was through episodes with colorful titles like "Cookie Vejar Killing," "Caliente Money Car Holdup," "Hammers in Honduras," and "Muerte en Buenaventura," that listeners across the West Coast learned of the lurid dangers posed by Latina/o drivers in the City of Angels.[116]

A broadcast titled "Missing Mexican Sheiks" (1934) is illustrative of how automobility was cast as suspect when engaged by nonwhite bodies. The episode begins with a crime committed against a Japanese woman, which initiates police pursuit of two unidentified suspects across the sprawled geography of metropolitan Los Angeles. The distraught woman explains to the police that two men in a sedan had pulled beside her and demanded her money. However, their duties are complicated by the woman's broken English and the racial ambiguity of the suspects. As described across police radio, all cruisers were to keep watch for "two bandits, number one dark complexion, Mexican or Filipino about 20 years of age wearing a dark suit and gray cap, number two is also dark, wearing a gray suit and gray cap."[117] Mexican and Filipino men occupied a similar racial position in California, both largely employed in agricultural labor and often sharing segregated neighborhoods. Without a clear description of the suspects or their vehicle, the situation underscored the tension between the freedom of white automobility and its threat to public safety when exercised by brown bodies in multiracial places.[118]

In the course of pursuing the two suspects, the LAPD detectives adopt multiple methods of police surveillance newly enabled by the automobile. They invoke the eyes of fellow police cruisers over the radio, track car owners through vehicle registration, and erect traffic checkpoints to distinguish criminals from the law-abiding mobile public. Suspicious that the robbers are heading towards a drawbridge connecting the Port of Los Angeles at Terminal Island to the City of San Pedro, the detectives order that the bridge be lifted. Delaying traffic in the pursuit of the suspects, the police collect the license plate numbers of each passing motorist. The detectives record names and addresses and search each vehicle for Mexican and Filipino drivers matching the victim's description, for immediate arrest. When the checkpoint fails to unearth the suspects, the sedan itself became the center of the search. Found abandoned at the pier with the radiator still warm, the detectives conclude the suspects are nearby.[119]

If the mechanisms enabling automotive travel could be used to assist police surveillance, they could also be used to subvert it. Anticipating that police would attempt to track their vehicle, the suspects likely avoided the checkpoint by boarding a local ferry, as the detectives later surmised. In doing so, the boys successfully subvert a predictable police tactic, while also directing police resources to a futile and time-consuming checkpoint. To further ensure their slipping away from authorities, the boys had preemptively manipulated the car's registration, a compulsory form of identification meant to link a vehicle to its driver. By fabricating a false name and address, the boys invert authorities' attempt to trace the car and, instead, lead the officers to an abandoned school. The suspects' ability to manipulate the car's paperwork for their own benefit points towards a temporary window in history in which the driving public could more easily subvert surveillance as authorities struggled to keep pace with the growth in car ownership and the rise in a new set of affiliated crimes.[120]

Despite the suspects' best attempt to avoid capture, the episode suggests that the suspects are ultimately ill-equipped to counter the LAPD's vigilant commitment to automotive investigation. A few days before the incident, a warehouse guard named Sebastian had observed two boys in Sheik's attire, a popular subculture drawing inspiration from film star Rudolph Valentino.[121] They were taking photographs with their girlfriends in front of their car. Vehicles were commonly used in self-fashioning, as we have seen in the prevalence of photographs taken with cars in the Inland Mexican Heritage archive. In these images, Mexican Americans are photographed while physically connected to their vehicles—for instance, draping themselves on top of cars and trucks. In the particular docudrama episode, the use of the car for nonincome-producing leisure might be considered an extension of the Sheik style itself. Like the zoot suit of the World War II era, the Sheik was an assertive aesthetic with sexual undertones that conveyed excess, expense, and flamboyance.[122] This cultural statement was particularly bold in the tight economic conditions of the Depression. However, in the broadcast of the "Missing Mexican Sheiks," the link between Mexican American youth and their cars was not a means for racial and gendered performances. Instead, the car was reinterpreted as an instrument for crime, and the photographs a precursor to mug shots.

It was while the Sheiks snapped photographs that the guard collected the license plate of the young couples in *anticipation* of criminal activity.

Jessie Ortiz and friend posing on fender of car near San Timoteo Canyon, 1928. Courtesy of Inland Mexican Heritage.

Sebastian explains, "They were innocent enough. Had a couple of girls with them and they were taking pictures. Here's how the hunch comes in. Somehow they didn't look on the up-and-up to me, so I took the license number of the coupe they were driving."[123] His hunch rested on the presumed guilt of juvenile men of color in 1930s Los Angeles. Although engaging in "innocent" behavior, the presumed criminality surrounding Mexican American youth led the guard to interpret their presence with suspicion. Their anonymity was betrayed by the license plate on the vehicle, which the guard collected with the expectation of future criminal activity. Their presumed guilt deemed legitimate, the detectives cross-reference the license plate number with information collected during the checkpoint earlier that afternoon. Using data on file with the Department of Motor Vehicles, the detectives track the young women to their apartment and, ultimately, apprehended their boyfriends, the two male suspects.[124] That the Latina women owned the car further underscores racial deviance via the rupture of gendered codes that would consign women to the private sphere.

In the case of the "Missing Mexican Sheiks," mobility was associated with a threat to the social and economic order, one requiring police intervention and deserving of the public's suspicion. In the cultural production of this incident as a radio broadcast, the audience was invited to imagine themselves as detectives in the hunt as they listened to the story unfold. Casting the LAPD as heroes, youth of color were relegated to the role of bandits. In the hands of Mexican American boys, the car became a vehicle for crime and racialized them as juvenile delinquents. In the hands of Latina girls, the car was a means for unchaperoned encounters with sexualized male criminals. And, in the context of the Great Depression, the use of the car for both illicit and leisure activities would have been viewed as particularly deviant, for the ways it indicated waste and fiscal irresponsibility, much like the Sheik style.[125] When in the wrong hands, the broadcast suggested, automobility could bring drivers to a halt and the economy to a stop.

Like the Mexican American boys', Latinas' associations with the car were similarly read as deviant. As drivers, the women in "Missing Mexican Sheiks" are, at best, implicated as morally questionable for the ways the car facilitates their unchaperoned encounters with male criminals. The women's ethnoracial background is unmistakable. Dolores González and Mona Martínez both speak with heavy Spanish accents and González is specifically identified as Puerto Rican. As not only young women riding with boys, but as drivers themselves, González and Martínez subvert both the gendered and racialized expectations of proper Latina behavior. Both pay the price for these transgressions and are ultimately arrested for suspicion of robbery. In fictionalized accounts, Latina drivers are consistently framed as "bad women," described by Chicana Studies scholar Alicia Gaspar de Alba as women who reject patriarchal structures and the limited social roles of virgin, mother, or whore. Whereas these transgressions are used to paint women as deviant, from a Chicana Studies perspective Latina drivers can be viewed as mobile agents whose lives defy the norms of both white domesticity and Latina womanhood.[126]

A poignant example of the complicated experience of Latina motorists within a republic of drivers can be found in John Fante's semiautobiographical novel, *Ask the Dust*. The Depression-era story centers on Arturo Bandini's struggle as a writer and his volatile relationship with a Mexican American waitress named Camilla Lopez. Their relationship is reflective of their racial and gendered positions in Southern California. Bandini, who painfully remembers the earlier rejection he has faced for his own marginal whiteness in Colorado, casts Lopez into the racial role of a "filthy little greaser," "brown princess," and "a cheap imitation of an American."[127] Lopez actively tries to claim an American identity, often without the same success as Bandini's, who as an Italian American experiences his own claims to whiteness once in Los Angeles through the racial marginalization of ethnic Mexicans like Lopez.

Bandini's sadistic efforts to highlight Lopez's marginality undermine Lopez's own attempts to claim an explicitly American identity, foremost through car ownership. In one attempt to distance herself from the racial slurs cast upon her by Bandini, Lopez leverages her Ford Roadster, which she has registered under the distinctly Anglo American pseudonym Camille Lombard, after the white Academy Award–winning actress Carole Lombard.[128] For Fante, car ownership serves as a poignant means to express Lopez's American identity while at the same time revealing its limits. In her car, Lopez aggressively moves through the glittering lights of Los Angeles, honking, yelling, and causing a spectacle with her masculinized behaviors that prevent the free movement of other drivers. Betraying her efforts to join a community of drivers who share an inherent social contract based on safety and precision, Lopez is neither able to demonstrate control over her vehicle nor over herself.[129] Despite these limitations, Lopez's ownership offers her a sense of agency in a city that would deny her the opportunity for self-definition. When Bandini seeks to caution her, she resists, exclaiming, "I'm driving this car."[130]

The trope of suspect Mexican American motorists and their cost to white American drivers was repeated across California. But it was not merely a product of popular culture. Racial disparities in arrest rates by the LAPD rose dramatically for Latina and Latino juveniles in this period, rising in parallel with incarceration rates for Latina/o adults. Between 1930 and 1940, arrest rates for Latina girls increased from 17 to 22 percent and for Latino boys from 17 to 32 percent. Whereas girls were primarily arrested for morality crimes, boys were most frequently brought into the juvenile justice system for violating the California Motor Vehicle Act. In particular, they were arrested for joyriding, or driving a stolen car for enjoyment without the intent of permanent theft. About 90 percent of all cars used for joyriding were found abandoned and recovered within a week.[131] Because the police could not definitively know whether a driver was a vehicle's legal owner or not, pursing a joyriding case was at police discretion, often colored by profiling. These cases were most commonly initiated when Latino boys were found driving outside of their designated barrios.[132] Thus police attention to joyriding suggests the real crime was the violation of white space by nonwhite youth, whose mobility became hypervisible in a period when the car was coded as white and Mexican American mobility was viewed with suspicion.

RACIAL DRIVERS

In the early decades of the twentieth century, depictions of Mexican American automobility underwent a series of profound transformations. Following the immigration debates of the 1920s, investigations of the resident Mexican-descent population squarely associated them with the automobile, at the time a promising symbol of economic integration. The onset of the Great Depression catalyzed a stark change in what had been generally positive attitudes towards Mexican motorists. As driving became ubiquitous in metropolitan Los Angeles, Mexican, and Latina/o drivers more broadly, were actively portrayed as outsiders unfairly seeking relief and a danger to the white public. Dust Bowl migrants too were at risk of this racial blackening due to their shared class position; however, agrarian partisans successfully recast the Okies as yeomen within progressive circles. Where Mexican residents, as well as a broad range of Latina/o and Asian-origin populations, were marked as perpetually migrant outsiders, New Deal resettlement programs presumed white migrants would eventually integrate into the general white population, moving past their marginalization and reintegrating into Anglo America. As explained by Ruth Tuck, an anthropology student at the University of Redlands, "[an] Okie with a good job, a nice car, and a decent suit of clothes could not be distinguished, superficially, from the grandson of a pioneer."[133] Once again, narratives of white western pioneers were powerfully operative in transforming white migrants into white "natives."

By examining changing perceptions of motorists across metropolitan space, we are better able to understand how racial associations with mobility impact the lives of Mexican-origin people. For Mexican drivers before the 1930s, owning a car was deemed essential, a means for economic and social mobility. However, for the resident Mexican population of the Depression era, driving was accompanied by high risks, such as incarceration. Ironically, it was by driving that Mexican American youth were so frequently stripped of their freedom of mobility. Mexican immigrants and Mexican Americans challenged racial hierarchies that cast them outside of U.S. cultural citizenship, through song and photography, but not without protest or with equal effect as those seeking to keep them in place. The fluidity of academic studies, popular culture, and surveillance directed at motorists reveals the deep importance of mobility in constructing racial meaning in Southern California, where driving could either function to reaffirm cultural citizenship or to fuel a discourse of deviance in a multiracial landscape.

FIVE

From Citrus Belt to Inland Empire

MOBILITY VS. RETRENCHMENT, 1945-1970

Shortly following the end of World War II, O'Day and Helen Short purchased a five-acre lot in Fontana. It was a vacant parcel located near the downtown with a view of the mountains, a blank slate on which to build a new house and life for their family. Although O'Day worked as a refrigeration engineer and had earned a high school diploma, no small feat for a Southern African American man in this period, the Shorts still needed to rent a house in a segregated section of South Los Angeles for several years before they could afford the purchase. It would have been a tough task for African American buyers to find a single-family home outside of this overcrowded district, but the Shorts persevered.[1]

With his eyes towards life in the suburbs, O'Day traveled the hundred-mile round trip between Los Angeles and Fontana to hammer, drill, and drywall a home from the dirt. O'Day and Helen likely imagined turning the lot into a home for their two young children, Barry and Carol Ann. One photograph of the family shows Helen's arms wrapped around her young ones—Barry standing tall in a button-down coat and Carol Ann with tight curls—as they smile at the camera on a tree-lined boulevard. Still under construction, the family moved to their Fontana residence in the winter of 1945. Soon after, they began receiving physical threats. This resistance was not unexpected in a town with a history of Klan activity and a racial line at Baseline Road, one traversed by the Shorts and increasingly concerning to white residents with each board of plywood that O'Day raised.[2]

The Shorts' stay in their new home was short-lived. Soon after the Shorts made Fontana their permanent residence, vigilantes threatened the family with overt violence and the sheriff's office warned the Shorts that they were "out of bounds."[3] Rather than back away, the Shorts called upon local police,

The Short family children: Carol Ann, 7, and Barry, 9, ca. 1945. Courtesy of *Los Angeles Sentinel*.

the FBI, and the Black press to defend their place in suburbia.[4] Familiar with southern hostilities, these two migrants from Mississippi and Georgia envisioned a future of residential and social mobility for their children in the outer suburbs of Los Angeles. Confident in their rights as homeowners, the family dug in their heels. Two weeks later, Helen and her two children were burned alive in their home when it erupted in a blaze. It would be a long five weeks before O'Day followed, suffering from first-degree burns and knowledge of his family's violent deaths. Despite cries for justice from their relatives, the Black press, and the Socialist Worker's Party, authorities deemed the fire an accident caused by O'Day himself.[5]

The massacre of the Short family in their Fontana home underscores the failure of the promise of home ownership for nonwhite families, especially the great risks they faced when encroaching on the citriscape's racial lines, and the vigilante efforts undertaken by regional residents and authorities when defending white racial privilege at the beginning of the second half of the twentieth century. At this time, the central towns and colonias of California's semitropical agricultural zone were transforming into the peripheral suburbs of Los Angeles. The end of World War II had sparked a mass migration to Southern California; returning soldiers, growing aerospace industries, and a housing boom were transforming the metropolitan fringe. From the 1940s forward, Southern California's agricultural industry steadily waned and in its place rose fields of stucco and steel.

Out of this declining Citrus Belt emerged visions for an Inland Empire, a regional landscape built on the preestablished hierarchies of industrialized agriculture that linked the Southern California suburban dream to the global movement of trade in the postwar period. As the overlapping and intersecting people of the region sought to keep pace with the transformations in this period, families like the Shorts, as well as fair housing developers and nonwhite real estate agents, confronted the entrenched racial hierarchies of white settler colonialism to take a stand against residential segregation. But they did so at great social, economic, and, at times, personal risk.

This chapter traces the suburbanization of the Citrus Belt as it became the Inland Empire—including the western portions of Riverside and San Bernardino Counties—from the rise of a multiracial suburbia to a dystopian picture of suburban decline. Specifically, it examines the relationship between mobility and racial formation in metropolitan Los Angeles as African Americans and Latinas/os, predominantly Mexican, found varying pathways to suburbanization following the war. Overall, they lived in the suburbs for many of the same reasons as white Angelenos, including access to jobs, opportunities for affordable home ownership, and pursuit of the suburban "good life." Yet, their pathways to suburbia were by no means equal to white Angelenos'. Where the suburbanization of rural and urban populations was quite typical of national migration patterns at the time, metropolitan migration held divergent costs and benefits for nonwhite suburbanites.[6]

If entry to the middle class allowed some minority populations to suburbanize, race shaped the material conditions and meanings of those movements in ways that were quite distinct from those for white homeowners. Most studies of postwar suburbia have focused on the restrictive residential development of inner-ring suburbs, those just outside the city core and located well within commuting distance. Revisionist scholarship has expanded this work to look at the ways communities of color have shaped suburban formation in these same spaces, illuminating nuanced stories of displacement, migration, conflict, and collaboration, particularly among Latina/o and Asian American homeowners.[7] Yet, with some notable exceptions, metropolitan scholarship has overlooked the complicated mosaic of developments just beyond the stucco curtain.[8] Due to entrenched racial barriers in housing, African American suburbanization often required movement from Los Angeles to its outermost suburbs, at and beyond the county's edges and exurbs. And for many Latinas/os, suburbanization meant staying put in communities they had formed much earlier, as early Mexican colonias transitioned into residential suburbs. A metropolitan perspective reveals the ambivalent outcomes of suburbanization for these minoritized communities.

The Pomona Valley encompasses a particularly dynamic geographic crossroads for this analysis. Located at the intersection of Los Angeles, San Bernardino, and Riverside Counties, the valley provides an ideal vantage point from which to view the birth of the Inland Empire. The former citrus town of Pomona was a harbinger for region wide change as the housing demands and economic aspirations of metropolitan Los Angeles stretched eastward with increasing fervor. Also, Pomona offers a compelling example of the ways white, Latina/o, and African American residents experienced suburbanization during the postwar era. It was an early site of fair housing development, had a sizable concentration of African Americans, and was a majority-minority suburb by the early 1970s. From this edge of the metropolitan region, we are better able to see both the possibilities for postwar racial integration and its continued limits well into the civil rights era.

Further, looking to the Pomona Valley reveals the ways the Citrus Belt's development into an Inland Empire depended on the imprisonment of those with the least mobility capital. Alongside the voluntary movement of suburbanites into the valley was the coerced mobility of prisoners sentenced to one of several state penal institutions. While inmates were increasingly immobilized by state forces, in particular following passage of the Uniform Determinate Sentencing Act (1976), increasingly hostile prison conditions catalyzed new mobility strategies among Chicana/o prisoners. Restricted from moving under conditions of their own choosing, they nonetheless used movement to reject state restrictions on their bodies, foster reciprocal networks between self-help groups and suburban educational opportunities, and shrink geographic divides among families.

As we turn to postwar housing developers, we see how the mobilities and racial formations discussed in the preceding chapters were adapted to the new economic and demographic realities emerging in the second half of the century.[9] The established regional selective traditions, social hierarchies, and agricultural economy were all changing. And they were doing so quickly. The transformation of the Citrus Belt into the Inland Empire follows a white settler logic earlier established in the development of the Riverside colony and now adapted for the postwar economy. The combination of a racialized geography, the rise of modern community planning, and investment in prisons facilitated regional transformations that remained wedded to mobility. Together, examination of these developments uncovers the ways postwar suburbanization impacted the most and the least mobile populations in metropolitan Los Angeles.

FROM CITRUS BELT TO SUBURBAN FRONTIER

Postwar population growth has received considerable attention from historians of Los Angeles and its environs, but population change across Greater Los Angeles did not occur evenly. Between 1940 and 1950, for instance, Los Angeles County experienced a 49 percent population growth. Yet, the surrounding counties of Riverside (61 percent), Orange (65 percent), Ventura (65 percent), and San Bernardino (75 percent) each experienced higher proportions of growth than the central county. Increased density was accompanied by major changes in industry, as inland agriculture gave way to militarization. The expansion of the March Air Force Base near Riverside, construction of Norton Air Force Base near San Bernardino, and Kaiser Steel in Fontana each contributed to an inland residential boom in the 1940s. Where the Los Angeles region achieved record rates of growth, it was its surrounding counties that experienced the most profound demographic and economic transformations.[10]

During wartime, the citrus industry boomed with the rising demand for fresh produce with each deployment of soldiers abroad. Likewise, in the postwar era, the Citrus Belt experienced unprecedented economic and residential development. However, as much as the postwar period is noted for growth, it is equally significant as a period of mass destruction. In the second half of the twentieth century, the flagship orange groves of the Citrus Belt were victim to a "culture of clearance" and that culture's primary tool of removal, the bulldozer.[11] As poetically described by one reporter, "The scent of orange blossoms that once wafted across the Valley from Sierra Madre to Etiwanda becomes fainter each spring as more of the scant remaining citrus acreage falls to the bulldozer's blade."[12] While groves were uprooted, so too were citrus packinghouses, and district exchanges rendered obsolete. As one industry collapsed, another would rise in its place.

With an eye on the changes initiated in the postwar period, inland agriculturalists sold their land at large profits to suburban developers who eagerly captured an expanding residential market, often paying from $7,000 to $10,000 for a single acre.[13] A farmer willing to relocate could make a considerable profit as federal irrigation projects opened new lands for agricultural development at prices as low as $2,000 an acre in central California. Simultaneously, the Arizona Yuma Project gifted returning veterans with farms of between 40 and 120 acres. In a fifteen-year period, these "homesteaders" transformed the mesa from a desert to alfalfa fields, cotton crops, and citrus groves. As described by one farmer, "The mesa was a flurry of activity with pickers and packers and trucks of loaded fruit roaring up and down the highways."[14] Reclaimed lands in Yuma attracted veterans from fifteen states, but the majority came from California. Replicating the racialized labor and management hierarchy of the Citrus Belt, Mexican immigrants were once again eagerly recruited as established California growers sought to transform the Arizona desert into an irrigated fruit basket. Aided by government programs, in the twenty-five years between 1945 and 1970, Yuma's citrus acreage increased fifteen times over, from 2,000 acres to 30,000 acres.[15]

As citrus production shifted into central California and southern Arizona, it rapidly declined in Southern California. Demand for housing, industrial shifts, and global agricultural competition each facilitated the industry's demise. In the first decade following World War II, Southern California lost nearly 25 percent of its citrus acreage. Packinghouses and district exchanges from across the region began closing their doors, while citrus byproduct plants fought vigorously, but unsuccessfully, for a central place in the frozen concentrate market. Although the byproducts market operated at significantly lower production costs than the fresh navel market, the shift to frozen juice placed California growers in direct competition with Texas, Florida, Argentina, Brazil, and South Africa.[16] As its agricultural profits declined, inland Southern California found itself at an important economic crossroads. From 1880 to 1940, the movement of citrus had facilitated the region's recognition as a Citrus Belt, a gateway of significant importance to flows of people and goods across the nation. But in the postwar era, the region's flagship crop was quickly being replaced by rows of stucco.

The Mississippi Delta's enclosure movement provides a compelling reference point for thinking through the California Citrus Belt's regional transformations. Described by geographer Clyde Woods, the Mississippi Delta received a plethora of federal investments following World War I that preserved planter power and profits by ensuring rising land values, principally due to federal flood control, subsidies, loans, and technical assistance to growers. Progress in this equation was linked to planters' land monopolization and the mass eviction of African American sharecroppers, prompting their outmigration from the region.[17] A repetition of method, but reversal in strategy, occurred in post–World War II California.

While in the Mississippi Delta less profitable farmlands were removed from production through government subsidies and depopulated via mechanization, in the California Citrus Belt citrus acreage was transformed into suburban housing for a burgeoning postwar population. In both cases, it was federal intervention that catalyzed regional economic and landscape transformations. Though unevenly distributed to white homeowners' advantage, the federal government's subsidized private home ownership was funded through the Federal Housing Authority's lending programs and the GI Bill's loans to veterans and by infrastructural investments, such as the Federal Highway Act and urban renewal campaigns in subsequent years. Simultaneously, federal reclamation projects restored profits to white farmers willing to relocate as citrus production spread further away from Greater L.A.'s core. Although the effect of regional transformations in the Mississippi Delta and California's Citrus Belt may seem divergent from one another—in the one case, "tractoring" led to mass evictions of African Americans, and the other, bulldozing ushered in a landscape of homebuilding and mass migration—their roots in federal intervention and the reinscription of white hegemony are parallel. Moreover, each strategy was accompanied by similar consequences: a diversification of regional economic activities, a failure to address staunch racial inequalities, and a rise in nonwhite imprisonment.[18]

Moving forward to the second half of the twentieth century, the towns that had formed the center of California's agriculture—the Citrus Belt—were now transforming into the peripheral suburbs of Los Angeles. The two regions had long shared economic, political, and social linkages. In particular, influential L.A. Chamber of Commerce representative George Clements had promoted a regional vision uniting inland Southern California and Los Angeles since the early twentieth century. Tasked with managing 200 agricultural producers within a hundred miles of the city, he championed a regionally oriented gospel that suggested downtown businessmen must be concerned with the welfare of the surrounding hinterland. He wrote, "Agriculture is the foundation upon which all other industry is built.... Agriculture represents 60 per cent of all commerce, 68 per cent of all national commerce and creates 50 per cent of all wealth, while all industry is dependent upon it for food."[19] Clements viewed Los Angeles and the Citrus Belt as a synergistic system of interweaving urban markets and agricultural products. The folding together of Southern California's urban and rural functions intensified in midcentury as increasingly aggressive processes of suburbanization enveloped each of them. Maximizing the region's location within a burgeoning metropolis, one increasingly knit together by freeway construction and the spread of multinodal industries, Citrus Belt developers would achieve what few other gateways have successfully accomplished. They reinvented the region as the California Inland Empire, the gateway between Los Angeles and the world.[20]

From the postwar period onward, Los Angeles and the Citrus Belt were increasingly imagined as a shared metropolitan area. Analysis of Los Angeles area maps reveals a growing popular imagination in which Los Angeles County and the Citrus Belt (inclusive of western San Bernardino and Riverside Counties) were spatially intertwined. For instance, road maps of "Los Angeles and Vicinity" published before World War II had portrayed freeway connections to San Bernardino and Riverside as the L.A. region's easternmost edges.[21] After World War II, however, maps of "Los Angeles and Vicinity" show a notable shift. Specifically, the borders stretch inland, with San Diego becoming the map's southern boundary and the Coachella Valley its eastern edge. In these shifting representations of metropolitan space, the county border between Los Angeles and San Bernardino/Riverside moves from the margins of these maps to their centers.[22] As a result, the Pomona Valley—including the cities of Pomona, Claremont, Upland, and Ontario—is positioned as the region's metropolitan crossroads. By the postwar era, the regional vision originally advocated by boosters such as Clements had fully matured.

Although continually distinct from one another in significant ways, from World War II onward Los Angeles and the Citrus Belt were increasingly imagined as a shared metropolitan area in which the Pomona Valley was both suburban fringe and suburban frontier. As suggested by changes in the cartographic imagination, L.A.'s postwar development cannot be separated from that of the Citrus Belt. This growth was not uniform, but instead marked by racial segmentation across metropolitan space. While demographic change in postwar Los Angeles County was characterized by simultaneous population diversity and segregation, when looking further east to San Bernardino and Riverside Counties, a different pattern emerges. As Los

Angeles's urban geography became increasingly racially stratified, the basin diversified.[23] In this expanding metropolitan context, developers would become key players in shaping regional mobility and its meanings.

HOME BUILDING AND FAIR HOUSING
AT THE SUBURBAN EDGE

Among the first to take advantage of inland Southern California's expanding housing market were private developers Ralph and Goldy Lewis, the founders of Lewis Homes and part of an unstudied inland Jewish migration. Ralph Lewis and Goldy Sarah Kimmel attended UCLA together and married in 1941 after graduating with matching degrees in accounting. When Ralph returned from war service abroad, the Lewises started an accounting firm, serving a roster of prominent real estate developers. Working from Los Angeles, they watched as their clients thrived in home building. Motivated by the GI Bill–fueled real estate boom, Ralph cut back on their accounting business to accept a position as the chief financial officer for John Lusk, a trail-blazing real estate mogul with 40,000 homes to his credit.[24]

Lusk inspired the Lewises to start a development venture of their own. As later recalled by Goldy, "We thought if they can do it, we can do it, too."[25] Embarking on a family business at the western edge of the former Citrus Belt, they established a home building company with spreading residential tracts as neat and extensive as the orange groves that preceded them. Among the leading and earliest developers in inland Southern California, the Lewises would become a model for multiracial exurban development. Staunch advocates of fair housing, they built an empire that both advanced racial integration and profited from the racial restrictions prevalent throughout the rest of the region. Exceptional, but not unique, the Lewises underscore the intertwined incentives of postwar segregation and diversity at the suburban edge.

Where Lusk concentrated his efforts on first-time homebuyers in Orange County, described by Mike Davis as "the home rush frontier of the 1950s" and noted for its prominent role in the conservative movement, the Lewises built their tracts on the declining agricultural lands of the Citrus Belt.[26] A semirural community of citrus towns already dotted the region, but the scale of suburbanization found closer to Los Angeles was not yet commonplace here, creating both risk and opportunity for developers willing to test the suburban hinterland. In 1956, Ralph Lewis and partner Robert Olin opened their first inland housing tract, Claremont Highlands. Located about forty miles east of Los Angeles and extensively advertised in the *Los Angeles Times,* the subdivision was easily accessible from the city by either traveling eastbound along Highway 66 or on the San Bernardino freeway. Transportation corridors were key forms of "mobile capital" that through investment in travel infrastructure facilitated connectivity between Los Angeles and inland Southern California.[27] Located in an emerging gateway, homes with multiple bedrooms, two bathrooms, and "futuramic" kitchens beckoned Angelenos to the crossroads of Los Angeles, San Bernardino, and Riverside Counties.[28]

The Claremont Highlands housing development was part of a larger "Move to Pomona Valley" campaign, which targeted veterans and nonveterans alike, encouraging them to purchase homes at one of six residential communities. Mortgages ranged from California's median home value to twice that amount, but they were offered with the incentive of low to no down-payment terms. That is, these homes cost more in the long-run, but less monthly—thus proving more affordable at entry. Developers underscored career opportunities in the valley's growing industrial plants, appealing to young families who sought proximity to employment and a suburban ideal of open space, safety, and shopping.[29] Within about a year of the campaign's kick-off, the media reported that hundreds of home seekers were drawn to the Pomona Valley on a daily basis. Ralph Lewis soon split from his partner Olin to launch a family business with Goldy and their sons, called Lewis Homes. Operating from the garage of their Claremont ranch house, the family embarked on a lifetime career of real estate development with a long-lasting influence on the shape of the region.[30]

The Lewises are significant players in the history of metropolitan development not only because of where they focused their building efforts, but also because of their commitment to fair housing prior to legislation in California and at a time when suburban development implied a white, middle class norm.[31] In this regard, their position as postwar Jewish developers—a minority with growing acceptance into the category of whiteness—is important to consider. The Lewises demonstrate the complicated positionality of American Jews in postwar Los Angeles. The link between race and property is well accounted for by historians and critical race scholars, who have underscored the ways private property has been subsidized and distributed according to lines of whiteness. As the racial category of "white" shifted to include previously excluded minorities in the postwar period, so too did residential patterns.[32] Gaining unprecedented access to areas of the city exclusively reserved for white homebuyers, Jewish residents moved and the real estate market shifted. In 1959, Jewish Angelenos accounted for nearly 40 percent of all homebuyers and Jewish homebuilders for nearly 20 percent of the profession. In a significant reorganization of the city's racial landscape, Jewish developers converted former oil fields and farms into single-family homes in Fairfax, Park La Brea, and the San Fernando Valley to meet the needs of upwardly mobile Jewish suburbanites entering the Southern California housing market.[33]

Even as the category of whiteness expanded to include American Jews, postwar developers did little to challenge the entrenched racial exclusion of those consigned to the other side of the color line. Two of the largest Jewish-owned housing developers, California City Builders and Julian Weinstock, refused to sell to African Americans.[34] When inclusion into whiteness was newfound (that is, vulnerable), marginal populations often defended their racial privilege by reaffirming the exclusion of others. From this perspective, the actions of Jewish homebuilders are by no means unique. For instance, there are ubiquitous, eerie echoes of the protests earlier levied by the Lemon Street coalition—of working class and immigrant whites—during the Harada case. Although there are notable exceptions, Jewish developers more frequently recognized their tenuous inclusion into whiteness and defended their privilege by guarding the already established racial geographies of Los Angeles.[35]

While postwar Jewish developers played an important role in reaffirming racial segregation in the historic neighborhoods of Los Angeles, a different story unfolded at the metropolitan fringe. Recall that instead of investing alongside other Jewish developers in the racially restricted tracts of western Los Angeles, Lewis Homes found its niche in the racially yet-to-be-determined cul-de-sacs of the Pomona Valley. The Lewis family represents a yet unexplored Jewish migration eastward into the inland valleys of Southern California that helped generate the region's multiracial tapestry, one that preceded the entry of mega-builders like Lennar Homes, D. R. Horton, and Kaufman & Broad.[36]

Contrary to the racial restrictions upheld by developers in Los Angeles, Lewis Homes had adopted a racially inclusive strategy of residential development. As recalled by his son Randall, "[Ralph] was a very strong advocate of fair housing and affordable housing at a time in California when those were not popular positions. . . . He was a visionary in that regard and very brave."[37] This is not an overstatement by a doting son. Ralph served as the chairman of the fair housing committee of the Home Builders Council of California, formally debated against his former partner Robert Olin—a staunch opponent of fair housing—at professional meetings, and spoke on the issue at public conferences alongside representatives of the NAACP.[38] Perhaps the Lewis family's faith provides some clues as to their unique position. Ralph and Goldy Lewis came from a Reform Jewish background, an explicitly progressive denomination that promotes a firm commitment to principles of inclusion. Active members of Temple Beth Israel in Pomona and frequent partners in intercultural initiatives in the city, the Lewis family may have brought an ethos of equal access that facilitated commitment to a multiracial clientele.[39] Their affiliations, actions, and the media surrounding the family certainly suggest they believed in fair housing.

Ralph Lewis was a principal member of the newly formed California Realtors for Fair Housing at a time when the California Real Estate Association (CREA) actively worked to repeal fair housing. It was the CREA that led the charge against the Rumford Fair Housing Act (1963) and sponsored Proposition 14 (1964), a ballot initiative passed by the California electorate to nullify the act and to ban future fair housing legislation. The CREA heavily petitioned and placed mandatory dues on its members to fund these campaigns, described by Lewis as "a futile expenditure of effort and funds which will hurt race relations in California."[40] At risk of personal legal injury and backlash from the CREA, he worked diligently on these issues.

His position reflects larger divisions among California realtors in relation to the CREA's anti–fair housing initiative, between those who viewed support of Prop 14 as unnecessarily costly and those who rejected CREA support as brandishing racial and religious discrimination. Lewis's objection to housing discrimination further reflects the protests of fair housing advocates, most notably the Congress of Racial Equality (CORE), which worked to uphold California's fair housing law and rallied in Pomona against the CREA's support of Proposition 14. And, his position reflects a more progressive stance on the proposition than some conservative Mexican American organizations, such as the Mexican Chamber of Commerce of Los Angeles, which first endorsed Proposition 14 but, in response to community pressure, later adopted a neutral position on the ballot measure.[41]

There was also an economic incentive for Lewis's position that suggests development at the suburban edge complicates any easy division between fair housing and segregation. The elite suburbs of North Los Angeles attained their value through restrictive land use and the pursuit of white homogeneity. However, recent scholarship on suburban development identifies a divergent trend in the Citrus Belt, where new cul-de-sacs offered a racial blank slate for home seekers and rapid low-density sprawl provided plentiful housing opportunities. As described by urbanist Deirdre Pfeiffer in her study of contemporary African American migration into these suburbs, "developers, eager to turn a quick profit in the unstable exurban market may value families' buying power over their race, ethnicity, or other characteristics, and lower down payment and other financial requirements to capture the broadest possible consumer base, indirectly enabling access among diverse groups."[42] Likewise, fifty years earlier, if developers sought a wide home-buying market in new exurban communities, restricting their clientele to white home seekers would prove counterproductive. Fair housing proved the most profitable model where aspiring African American and Latina/o suburbanites were denied lodging elsewhere and were willing to travel further distances as freeways connected Los Angeles to inland Southern California. As developers sought to turn a steady profit, the risk of new development in L.A. exurbs outweighed the risk of desegregation. That is, the Citrus Belt's dual position at the metropolitan fringe and its increasing travel connections to Los Angeles facilitated the neighborhood diversity evident in inland towns from the 1950s onward.

The Lewis brand of inclusive housing challenged earlier constructions of the citriscape that had bifurcated white and nonwhite households—including the production of selective traditions popularizing white settler colonial fantasies, police enforcement of racialized bodies out of place, and the circulation of public narratives delineating what constituted deviant from normative movement. Unprecedented racial and class diversity characterized these new land tracts, but they were accompanied by novel challenges. An earlier effort spearheaded by Claremont College professors to promote multiracial housing in the Pomona Valley is an important harbinger of the lingering limits to this endeavor. Described by historian Matt Garcia, in the late 1940s the Claremont Intercultural Council attempted to promote integrated housing by constructing a complex of homes sold at low prices to a multiracial community comprised of white and African American college students, as well as local Mexican American families. However, the council was unable to maintain a racially heterogeneous population. Where most Mexican American families stayed in the community for the long term, upon graduation students frequently moved on to new careers and sold their houses at a profit.[43] The Claremont Intercultural Council failed to recognize the temporality of class identities among upwardly mobile college youth.

Residential expansion quickly transformed a landscape of industrial agriculture to a sea of stucco. Although initially concentrating construction on single-family homes, by the 1960s Lewis Homes underwent a major transformation, expanding throughout California, Nevada, and Utah. As the company's reach extended, its office moved eastward from the Lewis family's Claremont garage, to a model home, to a satellite office in Pomona, to a consolidated office in Upland. Although located a short distance east of the Los Angeles County border, the move to Upland placed the company in San Bernardino County. Now physically and symbolically placed on the metropolitan fringe, the Lewises were increasingly recognized by professional organizations for their efforts to expand the Los Angeles residential market to the Inland Empire. Their achievements in this pursuit earned them recognition as Builder of the Year from *Professional Builder* magazine, the inaugural Entrepreneur of the Year Award from Ernst & Young, and the Arrowhead Distinguished Chief Executive Lecture at California State University, San Bernardino. By 1980, the company was consistently ranked within the top three private homebuilders in the country, serving as a national model for home design. With 50,000 homes to the company's credit, Lewis Homes has had a profound impact on the landscape of the former Citrus Belt and was among the first to validate the feasibility of inland housing development.[44] Although demonstrating the potential for profit making in inland communities through fair housing before it was codified in law, as the region matured into a suburban destination in later years, inland developers would once again reinvest in white settler colonial fantasies.

The inner-ring suburbs of Los Angeles are products of postwar incentives for homebuilding, built on a palimpsest of discriminatory home lending and racial restrictions. As real estate developers and industrialists moved inland, the former agricultural hinterland became a ripe site for eager developers seeking a place in the postwar boom. It was in an era of increased metropolitization and freeway development that the eastern edges of Los Angeles and western edges of the Citrus Belt were transformed into suburbia. Looking inland reveals yet unstudied trends in metropolitan development: the important role of Jewish developers in exurban Los Angeles, the dismantling of racial residential restrictions in new suburban developments prior to formal policies mandating fair housing practices, and the foundations for emergent links between race and mobility. Moving from homebuilders to home seekers, the next section examines what it meant to be home seekers of color in the age of fair housing and how the differential mobility of African Americans and Latinas/os shaped their pathways to suburbia.

RACIAL BROKERS AND BLACK/BROWN SUBURBANIZATION

As a waning Citrus Belt was knit tighter into postwar metropolitan Los Angeles, multiracial developers aided in its reemergence as a burgeoning Inland Empire, an affordable residential alternative to Los Angeles and Orange County. Where California's American Indian population was concentrated in urban centers and inland reservations and where middle class Latinas/os and Asian Americans carved space for themselves in L.A.'s inner-ring suburbs, African Americans and working class Latinas/os struggled to break through barriers to finding housing, from discriminatory home mortgaging to racial violence.[45] It was at the suburban periphery that African Americans and Latinas/os found new opportunities for housing denied to them through these formal and informal processes closer to the city. Yet, their pathways to suburbia were divergent from one another. For middle class African Americans, achieving the suburban dream often required commuting between fair employment opportunities in Los Angeles and integrated housing at the county's edge. For working class Latinas/os, suburban life was often thrust upon them, as historic colonias were enveloped by suburbanization. That is, African Americans and Latinas/os were each positioned differently along emerging residential development and metropolitan movement. In each case, African Americans and Latinas/os used their mobility to subvert metropolitan inequality and attempt to improve their material conditions.

The term "motility" has been used to describe mobility capital, or one's access to and potential for movement. Populations with high motility are generally perceived as privileged, conjuring images of the global businessman. Their mobility is shaped by access to resources, as well as their race, gender, and citizenship status, which enable free movement.[46] However, when looking to the migration experiences of nonwhite suburbanites between the crucial crossroads of postwar migration and fair housing legislation, motility as a form of power becomes complicated. Geographer Doreen Massey argues that social groups and individuals each experience a different "power geometry" in relationship to movement, meaning they are positioned differently from one another in regards to their power over movement and stasis.[47] Likewise, looking to multiracial suburbanization in the Inland Empire complicates the assumed equation between residential mobility and social mobility. Conversely, this analysis asserts the two should be disentangled from one another when considering African American and Latina/o residents of majority-minority suburbs.[48]

Notably, Greater Los Angeles was the only major metropolitan area in the nation to double its nonwhite suburban population following fair housing legislation.[49] As the meeting place between Los Angeles and San Bernardino Counties, the City of Pomona provides a critical crossroads for examining the meaning of these changes for African American and Latina/o suburbanites. Following World War II, Pomona was well poised for growth as a major economic center. However, as described by one *Los Angeles Times* reporter, "the growth they expected was middle-class white people very much like themselves."[50] Surprisingly for these residents, Pomona quickly shifted from having a nominal African American presence to a sizable conglomerate, one of only a dozen such cities in the region with this makeup. The already established Mexican American presence and growing Latina/o immigrant population further exacerbated white anxiety surrounding the city's demographic transformations, especially as self-identified Chicanas and Chicanos increasingly confronted police mistreatment and school inequality. Given these growing nonwhite suburban populations, projections by Los Angeles County predicted Pomona would shortly become majority-minority.

Latina/o and African American suburbanization was facilitated by the few real estate agents of color who had broken through the racialized exclusions of the board of realty, what I am calling "racial brokers." Exemplary of the important role of racial brokers in opening Pomona to nonwhite homeowners are the careers of prominent Chicano and African American realtors. As was common practice, young realtors needed sponsorship by an active real estate broker before they could become a realtor. As one of the first Mexican American agents in the Pomona Valley, Al Castro recalled the difficulty of locating a sponsor in 1964. A trained accountant, Castro would regularly meet his clients outside a Pomona restaurant, El Burrito. Owner John Riley was supportive of Castro, who set up his typewriter outside on the restaurant's picnic tables and completed his clients' income tax returns. Just as Lewis had watched Lusk excel in home building, Castro closely observed Riley. In addition to owning a restaurant, Riley worked as a real estate broker, one who benefited significantly from the postwar boom. However, when

Castro expressed his interest in becoming an agent himself, Riley discouraged him from pursuing the profession. Despite these initial barriers, Castro not only became a broker, but also helped hundreds of Latinas/os find homes, and many others to become agents themselves. It would take racial brokers like Castro breaking through the color line of the real estate profession to disrupt established red lines in the region's racial landscape.[51]

To dismantle the Board of Realtors' informal racial restrictions, realtors of color drew upon white allies already in the profession. Following a string of rejections from area brokers, Castro learned of a promising lead. A white broker named Oren Elliott—notable for advertising "unrestricted" properties in African American newspapers—was rumored to have sponsored the application of an African American realtor, Alex Marks.[52] With Elliott's sponsorship, Castro passed his realtor's exam in 1964 and received his broker's license in 1969, soon after the Civil Rights Act's passage. With his license in hand, Castro had the tools to open an office and hire agents of his own, many of whom were Mexican American.[53] Castro was among the first nonwhite brokers to receive their license in the Pomona Valley and to join the Board of Realtors, becoming an important liaison between Latina/o home seekers and the Pomona Valley's diversification.

Castro drew upon extensive regional networks in his work. He had grown up in southwest Pomona, the child of immigrants from Jalisco who came to the United States as farmworkers in order to escape unrest during the Mexican Revolution. Unusual for his generation, Castro graduated from high school, served in the military, and enrolled in community college as a full-time student under the GI Bill. When he received his real estate license, Castro began working as an agent for an all-white brokerage. Where his coworkers competed for floor time, seeking business from walk-in clients, Castro recalls spending his time backstage, making phone calls and knocking on doors.[54]

Castro describes his clients as almost exclusively Latina/o—Mexican and Central American in origin—over the course of his fifty-year career. Most were already renting in the city. He explained, "All of them were from Pomona, but most of them did not own a house. [Mexicans] were renting, other than the old people on 12th Street or Thomas or Grand. They owned houses. But then you have your children. . . . Where do you think they would go? They're renting."[55] Racial restrictions on housing and real estate agents with Klan memberships had earlier ensured Mexican workers remained concentrated in the southside barrios of this former citrus town.[56] Where the older generation (los viejitos) reveled in home ownership, their children and a growing immigrant population, which comprised 25 percent of Pomona's total Latina/o population, turned to multifamily housing with more affordable monthly payments. However, by comparing monthly rental rates to mortgage rates, appealing to female heads of the household, and holding free home buying workshops, Castro convinced his clients of the long-term advantages of home ownership.[57] Property is the primary means by which wealth is accumulated and parents pass on middle class status to their children.[58] Through racial brokers like Castro, Latinas/os shifted their status from those of renters in a dwindling Citrus Belt to suburbanites in an emerging Los Angeles exurb, the Inland Empire. And, many did so without ever leaving the municipality.

African American and Latina/o suburbanization were inextricably intertwined, but like a freeway interchange, their connections crisscrossed on separate planes. Tracing the story of Al Castro leads back to that of Alex Marks, as two major figures of Latina/o and African American suburbanization—never touching—passed one another in Pomona. Taken together, their efforts represent a "constellation of struggle," in which they each contributed to interethnic housing struggles that ruptured a historic citriscape.[59] Castro followed in the footsteps of Marks, who had earlier opened his own real estate office and hired four agents, several sharing a surname.[60] Marks was an important intermediary who facilitated African American migration into Pomona and surrounding areas on the eastern outskirts of Los Angeles County and western edges of the Inland Empire. Beginning in 1956, he marketed Pomona by championing its suburban qualities to Black Angelenos in the *Los Angeles Sentinel.* An African American–owned and operated newspaper, the *Sentinel* reached a sizable readership of middle class Black Angelenos who might be drawn to the Pomona Valley. Notably, both Marks and Castro used methods unusual for realtors at the time, adopting the strategy best suited to their clientele, such as circulating newspaper advertisements among the upwardly mobile African American population living in Los Angeles, and direct outreach to the Spanish-speaking population already living in the Pomona Valley.

Marks's earliest advertisements, appearing in the 1950s, promised modern one-bedroom homes for only $850 down and three-bedroom homes with hardwood floors and tile kitchens for $1,500 down. By 1960, similar homes cost as low as $185 down. Not only were these homes starkly more affordable than a few years earlier, but they were much cheaper than Los Angeles homes advertised in the same section, which ranged from $900-$5,000 down. For the *Sentinel* readership, the mantra of "Your Dollar Buys More in Pomona" rang true.[61] In addition to the falling down-payment rates, some homes were available on Federal Housing Administration (FHA) terms. Costing under $9,000, they were not only more affordable than those advertised in the earlier 1956 "Move to Pomona Valley" initiative promoted by developers like the Lewises, but they were also more affordable than those in California as a whole, where the median value ranged between $9,564 and $15,100 during the 1950–1960 decade.[62] If you were African American in 1960s Los Angeles, the suburban dream appeared to have a destination—and it was Pomona.

African American suburbanites used their mobility to pursue a form of inclusion habitually denied to them in Los Angeles. Given the history of residential apartheid and urban unrest in South Los Angeles, the promise of unsegregated living in spacious modern homes would have held special meaning for African American families.[63] In Black Los Angeles, even financial prosperity coexisted with intense housing restrictions. Where the segregated neighborhoods of South L.A. had notoriously dilapidated, overcrowded, and aging housing stock, inland homes were recently built modern residences with proximity to schools, shopping, and freeways. Marks emphasized this suburban lifestyle, boasting of "country living with all of the conveniences," including leisure amenities like swimming pools, patios, and spacious yards in "good areas."[64]

Space was a powerful draw. As another advertisement noted, "Invite the relatives. You won't be crowded when you have a Christmas dinner, in this air conditioned, spacious, 4 bedroom plus huge den home."[65] Instead of overcrowded and cramped quarters in the city, upwardly mobile African Americans were promised accommodations that could fit their extended families. Interestingly, here, the appeal made to potential clients was not distancing oneself from Black Los Angeles, but moving to an appealing annex.

African American Angelenos used their metropolitan mobility, or motility capital, to knit together geographically disparate economic, cultural, and housing opportunities across Greater Los Angeles. That is, relocation to the suburbs did not preclude continued ties to the City of Los Angeles and its centers of Black life. For instance, African American suburbanites heavily relied on urban employment opportunities, particularly government jobs with fair employment protections. According to the City of Pomona's community relations coordinator, the majority of African American residents (80 percent) commuted about fifty miles round trip per day to work. These long drives across the metropolis may have fostered sonic affinities among

African American Angelenos, as they tuned into L.A.-based stations and listened to music played by Black and Brown artists on their car radios, from WAR to Señor Frog. Churches, restaurants, and music venues catering to African American clients also remained heavily concentrated in the city, particularly around the Central Avenue corridor. Where economic and social life remained urban but middle class housing opportunities were restricted to the county edge, African Americans negotiated the resulting mismatch through physical movements. Freeways were simultaneously a scar and a suture that connected the Black middle class to housing opportunities in Pomona and back to employment and cultural opportunities in Los Angeles.[66]

The regional African American and Latina/o populations followed diverse pathways to suburbanization, as upwardly mobile individuals who commuted between cities, immigrants who had relocated from Mexico and Central America, and the children of citrus workers who watched their colonias transform into suburbs. Each set of experiences highlights the strategies people of color used to negotiate their mobility potential, both socially and spatially, within the specific context and possibilities of an expanding postwar metropolitan Los Angeles and its gateway.[67] Yet, despite the promise of integration based on shared class status, seemingly blank-slate post–fair housing suburbs soon reproduced disparities echoing those that had ignited Los Angeles in an urban rebellion, with long-term costs for African American and Latina/o residents.[68]

WHITE FLIGHT AND CHOCOLATE SUBURBS

Through the investment of fair housing developers, appeals of racial brokers, and uneven power geometries of African American Angelenos, Latina/o immigrants, and resident Mexican Americans, Pomona became a majority-minority suburb by the 1970s. One would expect such a site to be a model of fair housing and multicultural agendas given the platitude of racial tolerance following civil rights legislation. Instead, Pomona came to epitomize the limits of multiculturalism in the civil rights era. These chocolate suburbs, pockets where people of color pursued the suburban ideal, were ridden with the costs of metropolitan poverty, deindustrialization, and, yes, racism. Once described by writer Mike Davis as "the suburban nightmare," the City of Pomona was incarnate of the suburban dream unfulfilled.[69] As the region's racial geography shifted, racialized mobilities historically entrenched in the

Citrus Belt were powerfully operative in maintaining white privilege in the Inland Empire.

In earlier eras, racially restrictive housing covenants had prevented Mexican Americans from moving into middle class residential neighborhoods, such as Pomona's Ganesha Park, Lincoln Park, and Westmont, with a few exceptions being made for light skinned and middle class Mexican families.[70] Housing conditions were even more constricting for African American homebuyers. Where local courts had declared restrictions against ethnic Mexicans unconstitutional in *Doss v. Bernal* (1943), it was another five years before similar rulings were handed down concerning African American homeowners.[71] In 1948, the Supreme Court would declare judicial enforcement of racially restrictive housing covenants a violation of the Fourteenth Amendment, in *Shelley v. Kraemer*. Even then, it did nothing to prevent individuals from voluntarily entering into these discriminatory arrangements. The FHA itself continued to advocate for the practice of racial restrictions and covenants when nonwhite clients sought qualification for government-backed loans. Moreover, *Shelley v. Kraemer* would have fallen short of protecting nonwhite homeowners from violent retaliation, such as the reprehensible act of arson targeting the Short family.[72] Occurring only days before Christmas, the virulent violence against the Shorts underscores the great lengths to which both residents and authorities would go in order to maintain white racial privilege, as well as the great resilience and faith of families who took a stand against residential segregation.

The Pomona Valley was more diverse than other parts of metropolitan Los Angeles, but efforts to diversify the basin were not without consequence, nor were integrationist efforts met with open arms. Consider again Al Castro, a successful real estate broker with profits that allowed him to expand to a series of entrepreneurial endeavors, including a nightclub and bilingual newspaper, *La Voz*. Yet, in a career spanning fifty years, he recalls being the selling agent for only two white clients. The polemic nature of Castro's transactions underscores a period of intense white flight.

The Yorba neighborhood in northern Pomona, located adjacent to the Los Angeles County Fairground, exemplifies white resistance to demographic change. Once occupied by city officials and the mayor, in the winter of 1972 ten houses were placed for sale within only a few days of one another. The impetus was a single home sale to an African American family.[73] Further, those who advanced desegregationist agendas often did so at personal costs: in disapproval of such actions, Castro explains that the local board of realtors forcefully removed from the board Oren Elliott, the realtor who had sponsored both Castro and Marks. Far from an exceptional case, realtors who challenged the color line were routinely marginalized within the profession. Elliot passed away shortly afterwards, only about two months after employing Castro in his office.[74]

Resistance to desegregation did not stop the diversification of the region, as families of color continued to pursue new housing, open space, and proximity to war industries, even as a tightening economy and declining sales tax base further exacerbated regional racial tensions in the 1970s. Newer migrations of Black urbanites and Latina/o immigrants joined an already established community of African American, Mexican-descent, and, to a smaller degree, Asian and American Indian residents. Like Riverside, Pomona's agricultural economy had fostered the development of multiracial pockets at the city's edge.

Much of the growth in the Latina/o community originated from the children and grandchildren of barrio residents, whereas African American population growth largely originated outside of the city. African American newcomers were largely middle class commuters who settled outside of the historic barrio, at a distance from working class residents. These postwar African American suburbanites held relatively high rates of education. In census tracts with the largest concentrations of newer African American residents, rates of high school completion were above 75 percent, with college education nearing 25 percent. African American and Latina/o suburbanites shared certain forms of discrimination, but were separated by disparate socioeconomic positions.[75]

Despite African Americans' socioeconomic advantage, Latinas/os maintained relative racial privilege. As described by American Studies scholar Wendy Cheng, Asian American racial privilege manifests as model minority mythologies that collapse racial and class identities to cast Asians as exceptional.[76] Building on this theorization, Latinas/os experienced racialized privilege in a housing market that perceived them as either upwardly mobile marginal whites or docile "Mexican Browns." This privilege extended to the rental market. A 1971 study conducted by Claremont Graduate University PhD candidates found that African Americans were discriminated against at rates higher than both Mexican American and white renters. To varying degrees, African American (45 percent) and Mexican American (36 percent) couples were quoted higher fees and told units were unavailable at rates significantly higher than their white counterparts (4 percent) upon visiting the same advertised rental units.[77] Notably, if African Americans and Latinas/os faced varying degrees of class and racial disadvantages when seeking to access suburbia, their differences were overshadowed by the stark relative privileges enjoyed by white suburbanites.

Despite significant demographic restructuring inland, white suburbanization of the western edges of the Inland Empire did not lessen. Rather, nonwhite population growth redirected its flow. Where racial brokers helped open Pomona to Black suburbanites, as well as to Latina/o homeownership, racial steering and discriminatory banking practices served as formidable barriers to integration in neighboring communities.[78] Although Pomona's African American population grew from 4 percent in 1970 to 19 percent by 1980, the surrounding eastern cities of Claremont, Montclair, Ontario, and Upland maintained a relatively small Black population throughout this period. Likewise, Asian and American Indian populations remained relatively small and dispersed, never comprising a census tract majority. Although each of these sites experienced some degree of Latina/o growth, Pomona held the largest share at 31 percent of its total population.[79] By 1971, Pomona had become a majority-minority city.

Fast-paced population change was met by white suburbanites' efforts to navigate away from patterns of nonwhite suburbanization, both in terms of residence and everyday commerce. According to real estate agent John McGlothin, white home seekers entering his office openly stated they did not want to live in Pomona. Similarly, established residents had a difficult time with the city's changing demographics. As described by a Trinity Methodist Church pastor, "the oldtimers would like to see the Valley as a place of orange groves and gracious living."[80] Not coincidentally, their nostalgia referred to a time when the city was majority white and employment strictly racially segmented into white managers and Mexican laborers.

David Schmidt, assistant general manager of the Pomona Chamber of Commerce, expressed community leaders' concerns with white flight, noting that local businessmen increasingly moved their homes to the neighboring towns of Claremont and Upland. The marking of Pomona as a majority-minority suburb not only drove white suburbanization elsewhere, it also reordered regional patterns of commerce. The racial motivation of this shift was clear. As one resident noted, "How many white people shop in Watts?"[81] Exacerbating the costs of white flight, the opening of a mall in neighboring Montclair further siphoned the sales base away from Pomona. Once the center of local commerce, Pomona's abandonment by area shoppers was financially devastating following passage of California's Proposition 13 (1978), a tax reform that capped property tax increases at 2 percent per year until ownership changed hands. Property taxes decreased, but the quality of citywide public services—which were now serving a growing African American and Latina/o population—depended on these funds.[82]

Processes of suburban ghettoization at both the regional and municipal levels had undermined the promise of fair housing in L.A. exurbs. Latinas/os and African Americans were not only concentrated in Pomona, but also in definable areas of the city. The historically established Latina/o and African American populations largely lived in the city's multiracial neighborhoods in the southwest of the town. However, recent African American migrants entered completely new tracts without distinct racial characteristics. Nevertheless, they were quickly isolated in three neighborhoods, where African Americans comprised as high as 78 percent of the population.[83]

The majority of these subdivisions were developed in the 1950s, but sat largely empty as war industries declined. In the 1960s, the Veteran's Association and the FHA began repossessing the homes. Now reentering the market in an era of fair housing legislation, African American Angelenos increasingly purchased the properties. Tract homes with little to distinguish them were given names that emphasized their geography and social isolation from the city: the Islands, Sin Town, and the Flats. These residential blank slates, sites that had held the promise of racial integration, quickly had a "geography of difference" thrust upon them.[84]

The causes of Pomona's racial geographies were far from confined to the city. Rather, its pigments and contours, from white flight to adjacent suburbs and the ghettoization of Black suburbanites in exclusionary zones within the municipality, resulted from intertwined regional and global campaigns to reorder urban and suburban life. For one, the displacement of African Americans from the Los Angeles core to its periphery was part and parcel of a larger agenda to increase the city's potential for asset accumulation by privileged groups, including landlords, real estate developers, and municipal authorities. Elites unfairly benefited from housing discrimination directed at nonwhites, which pushed middle class African Americans and Latinas/os to the Inland Empire, and "dumped" the housing insecure in Central City East, which was known as Skid Row. Such forced relocation concentrated the human costs of privatization and the shrinking welfare state in places little travailed by the metropolitan middle class. These cases disrupt any simple equation between physical mobility and privilege. Where communities of color experienced a high degree of movement, they had little control over the racial hierarchies and spatial disruptions that gave rise to those movements.[85]

Not only was urban space differentiated in the interest of elevating property values, but so too was suburban space. Like the separation between gentrifying enclaves and homelessness in Los Angeles, the Islands, Sin Town, and the Flats produced poverty by concentrating African Americans into distinctly racialized spaces, even as Black Angelenos sought housing far from the central city. The retrenchment of these divisions in the Inland Empire reflects the far reach of public policies and deep cuts to social welfare passed in the 1970s and 1980s, which ensured nonwhite suburbanites would remain excluded from the benefits of suburbanization as their homes decreased in value and local services were underfunded. Racial and spatial inequity was shaped by regional elites' desire to attract federal and global capital via real estate, which in turn had radiating effects on asset distribution from the streets of Skid Row to the pockets of multinational developers. The messy moral geographies of "urban" and "suburban" reinforced the centrality of settler colonialism, whiteness, and private property in inland Southern California, even as it transitioned from the Citrus Belt to the Inland Empire.[86]

Although living in the suburbs, African American and Latina/o residents' experiences were far from the suburban ideal. For instance, by 1990, African American homeowners in the Yorba neighborhood would find their median home values at nearly *half* that of their neighbors.[87] Further, youth of color faced consistent violence from their white peers. In these newer exurbs, population distribution was such that neither African Americans nor Latinas/os comprised a majority at any one high school. A numerical minority, Black youth faced frequent harassment in schools where whites had the greatest enrollment, the most extreme occurrence of which led to the closing of Pomona High School for four days in January 1971. Tensions among students reflected larger school structures that stigmatized youth of color, such as measures that disproportionately sent African American students to "Thinking Chairs," siphoned them to continuation school, and failed to support school integration through busing.[88] Moreover, schools were slow to hire administrators of color, and counselors tracked students of color away from college-preparatory classes. As described by one Chicana mother, "They tell the children that because their parents are nongraduates, they themselves will never go to college. They expect nothing from the Chicano children, so they get nothing."[89]

The challenges encountered by students of color were met by new community organizations. For instance, African American parents organized Dropouts Anonymous and the Improvement Committee to address discriminatory disciplinary measures unevenly applied to Black youth.[90] In a parallel effort, a coalition of Chicana/o students staged a mass walkout in the fall of 1970. As reported by the *Los Angeles Times,* "students walked out of classes and picketed the district's administration building, demanding better representation in teachers and administrators and more curriculum on the Mexican-American culture."[91] The walkout—likely inspired by the 1968 Chicano Blowouts in Los Angeles—catalyzed formal complaints with state and federal departments. When progressive change failed to materialize by spring 1970, students threatened to take a more militant position. As described by one activist, "I am tired of living on my knees and am ready to shed blood or die for it, if necessary."[92] Paraphrasing Mexican revolutionary Emiliano Zapata, the student president of the local division of MEChA (Movimiento Estudiantil Chicano de Aztlán) signaled an affinity with Chicano nationalism and Indigenous control over local resources. Other activists denounced militant action, but pledged to take the battle to the ballots, threatening to replace the school board if necessary. The self-help strategies of Pomona's African American community and the movement-generating tactics of Chicana/o activists represent separate but consonant approaches to the shared problem of educational discrimination. Each approach was shaped by the unique manifestations of racism impacting their specific communities and reflected the divergent backgrounds of activists separated by class.[93]

The devaluation of property and siphoning of nonwhite children from suburban schools disrupted two major pathways for passing on wealth among generations. A major concern among sociologists is whether people of color can gain middle class status. More than a symbol of social mobility, home-ownership is the single asset in which middle class families hold the majority of their wealth. Moreover, relocating to a middle class neighborhood has often been a deliberate strategy used by parents seeking to provide new opportunities for their children. These neighborhoods tend to be white and suburban with benefits, including better-equipped schools, extended peer networks, professional role models, and socialization that allow youth to cross class boundaries.[94] Where communities of color have adopted spatial mobility to better their socioeconomic status, it has not always led to long-term social mobility. Rather, historic analysis of places like Pomona suggests that people of color pursue traditional pathways to suburbia against great odds, that middle class status is often a precursor to suburbanization, and that as people of color make inroads to suburban property ownership and schooling these gains may be quickly mitigated by white flight, fiscal abandonment, and exclusion from municipal resources. It also shows that people of color will take great pains to access the privileges of suburbia, including forming community organizations and taking collective action, particularly where it impacts their children.

On January 24, 1971, *Los Angeles Times* journalist Ted Sells highlighted Pomona's racial tensions in an article entitled "Pomona Gropes for Stability in Storm of Ethnic Change: Tight Economy Adds to City's Racial Problems," describing declining real estate values, sporadic violence, and discriminatory districting. The revealing report earned the ire of city officials and business interests alike. Pomona mayor Benjamin Lawing and banker Paul Walker published responses in the *Los Angeles Times* the following week. Both critiqued Sells, calling him an "outside agitator," and accused the article of "stir[ring] up the issue."[95] Lawing and Walker maintained that the city did not have a race problem. Pomona's elite carefully treaded potentially volatile waters as they navigated an era marked by both embedded white supremacy and nascent multiculturalism. Mayor Lawing, for one, pointed his finger back to Los Angeles and its surrounding cities. He wrote, "Are your readers not interested in the fact that the City of Pomona has for years opened wide its doors to people of all color and ethnic backgrounds, while many other cities have remained almost totally white by subtle means of discrimination?"[96] Although overstating the welcome received by people of color in Pomona, Lawing nonetheless charged the larger metropolitan area with discriminatory housing policies levied at African American and Latina/o communities. In this assessment, Lawing simultaneously evaded critiques directed at the city administration and relocated the "racial problem" from sites marked by ethnic change to suburbs beyond Pomona's boundaries. That Sells's article was published on the front page of the Metropolitan News section in the *Los Angeles Times* further underscores that ethnic change and interethnic conflict was a regional issue.

African American and Latina/o experiences of suburbia suggest that the assumed equation between residential mobility and social mobility should be disentangled when considering residents of majority-minority suburbs.[97] In the wake of the Watts Rebellion (1965), a racial and class uprising in Los Angeles provoked by underinvestment and police violence, the urban and suburban dichotomy seemed stronger than ever and those with the means to do so attempted to access the full benefits of postwar America by moving to the suburbs. For Black Angelenos, Pomona seemed to promise a suburban ideal of integration and proximity to regional resources. As African Americans moved in and whites moved elsewhere, leaving behind devalued homes and a declining tax base, homes were opened to working class Latinas/os denied access to proximate suburbs where land values remained steadier over the long term. The very same benefits that white residents had earlier enjoyed upon moving to suburbia—unrestricted access to neighborhoods, well-resourced schools, and a rich commercial area—were swiftly undermined as African Americans and Latinas/os occupied suburbs in greater numbers.

"PRISON VALLEY": FROM STUCCO WALLS TO STEEL BARS

In the winter of 1988, a reporter for a regional newspaper wrote, "While most local residents fight freeway traffic, rising housing costs and smog as they try to make this valley a place to call home, about 12,000 men and women are fighting demons of a different sort."[98] From this opening line in the local section of the *Pomona Progress Bulletin,* the story spoke of the massive rise in the Pomona Valley's prison population since the 1970s. Including four state correctional institutions and three fire camps—where the Department of Corrections contracted inmates for fire service in the foothills and mountains—the valley's prison complex was a regional growth engine.[99] It employed 3,000 local staff members as correctional officers, staffers, and counselors; spent hundreds of thousands of dollars on medical services at local hospitals; and contracted with local plumbers, mechanics, and teachers at costs in the millions. Many people of color living in this region moved into the middle class precisely because of the economic opportunities available at local correctional institutes, where they benefited from equal employment opportunity legislation.[100] But where suburbs have often been understood as entry points for upward mobility and protection of the single-family household, the case of the Pomona Valley further reveals the ways suburbia's growth depended on the imprisonment of those with the least motility capital (economically, socially, and geographically) throughout the state. The article continued, "They've been told this is home—for the next 60 days, 60 months or the rest of their lives. They have no choice."[101] Examining the rise of "Prison Valley" brings into focus prisoners' forced mobility into suburbs and their increasing immobilization by state forces. This examination reveals not only the vast concerns of local officials and residents with nonwhite bodies, including escaped inmates and the potential reach of prison gangs, but also prisoners' innovative mobility strategies.

Throughout early statehood, California's southern regions existed without a state prison. Inmates were sent to one of two prisons in Northern California: San Quentin near San Francisco (established in 1852) and Folsom Prison in the vicinity of Sacramento (established in 1880). It was not until the 1930s that the California state legislature authorized construction of a third prison, this time in Southern California, to aid with overcrowding and to ease increasing tension among prisoners. Unlike the maximum-security prisons up north, the Southern California prison was to be a minimum-security institution with the aim of rehabilitation. Inmates would have access to vocational, farming, and industrial training that would help ease their transition outside of the prison system. The state chose the city of Chino, whose semi-rural farmlands and proximity to Los Angeles, just forty miles to the west, made this suburbanizing community an ideal site for the Department of Correction's open-campus facility.[102]

The directors of the state Board of Prisons selected a former sugar beet property surrounded by farms and dairies for the new prison site. Built without high barbed wire fences, run by "supervisors" instead of "prison guards," and managed by an "executive supervisor" instead of a "warden," the prison was a model of liberal reform. As described by Governor Culbert Olson at the prison's 1941 dedication, "Chino is not a venturesome step that will not succeed, it is a noble advance in prison reform based on the real foundation of society, the brotherhood of men."[103] Of the first fifty supervisor positions, each handpicked by the executive supervisor, Kenyon J. Scudder, 90 percent were college graduates and zero were chosen from among staff at San Quentin and Folsom, where guards had a reputation for harsh treatment of inmates. Likewise, each of the first thirty-four inmates were personally interviewed, selected, and escorted from San Quentin to Chino. This inaugural group was racially mixed and had been imprisoned for infractions ranging from burglary to murder. Rather than their personal backgrounds or criminal histories, the inmates were selected for their potential for rehabilitation. The focus of their time was to be on "personal responsibility" and "freedom of choice," rather than punitive measures.[104] The facility's integrationist aim was notably successful in this early period. Upon parole, almost 70 percent of former inmates found employment with competitive wages. Their placement was aided by professional training. The prison sponsored daily classes through the Chino Unified School District and a vocational program—in welding, auto mechanics, machine operation, and bricklaying—that provided preparation for private industries.[105] Reflecting its focused aim on reformation, the site's name was changed from Southern California State Prison to the California Institute for Men (CIM).

Our understanding of the Citrus Belt's development into an Inland Empire cannot be divorced from the entrance of the carceral state. Fully operational by World War II, CIM provided an important source of forced labor that helped alleviate the shortage caused by war service. Many prisoners were assigned to a forestry camp in San Bernardino County, where they aided in fire prevention and received a salary of $3.50 a day. In the following years, many other camps, spanning distances from San Diego County in California to Yuma County in Arizona, were constructed where prisoners provided essential civil services. Others labored nearby, in towns like Mira Loma where they loaded and unloaded military supplies. In these endeavors, they often worked alongside Italian prisoners of war. Notably, Pomona was also the site of a Japanese American Assembly/Detention Center, where 5,400 internees were temporary located at the Los Angeles County Fairground.[106] In the post World War II era, the carceral system continued to expand with the addition of the California Institution for Women in 1952, the Youth Training School in 1960, and the California Rehabilitation Center in 1962. It was through those who were imprisoned in the Pomona Valley and its environs that the region found itself on the competitive edge of regional development and militarization.

Throughout the 1960s, CIM maintained a campus-like environment. Then in the 1970s significant changes in the prison's operation would shift the relationship among prisoners, their place in the Inland Empire, and mobility. The major catalyst for these changes was the Uniform Determinate Sentencing Act of 1976, or Senate Bill 42. Berkeley law professors Sheldon L. Messinger and Phillip E. Johnson's explanation for the radical shift in sentencing at the time of the bill's passing is worth quoting at length:

> [Before 1976, California] laws implied or said that the length of imprisonment should depend more on the individual characteristics of the criminal than on the nature of the crime; maximum discretion over length of sentences should be given to an administrative agency shielded from public accountability; the purpose of imprisonment is to rehabilitate the offender and to protect from his further misdeeds; and the released prisoner should be subjected to a lengthy period of parole supervision to protect the public and

to insure his rehabilitation ... [SB 42] seems to be based on the opposite assumption ... it provided a relatively narrow range of fixed penalties for each crime; replaced Adult Authority discretion over release with a complex system of "good time" credits; greatly lessened the period of parole and the importance of parole supervision; and, perhaps most significantly, stated flat out that *the* purpose of imprisonment is punishment.[107]

With the passage of SB 42, California corrections moved into a new period, one that changed the official purpose of prisons and further exacerbated statewide overcrowding.[108] The maturation of these changes was marked by the prison system's growth across the state into the 1980s, particularly in rural California. Geographer and ethnic studies scholar Ruth Gilmore has termed this response to the crisis of surplus land, capital, labor, and state capacity as the "prison fix," whereby farm communities turned to prisons as an alternative to struggling croplands.[109]

After the passage of SB 42, CIM became a far cry from the "state reformatory" of its early years. Chino inmates found themselves in progressively more violent and repressive surroundings as overcrowding worsened.[110] Prisoners' deaths were increasingly frequent, such as that of Gary Lee Schultz, a San Diego man who was beaten to death by multiple unknown assailants after only a twenty-day stay at the institution. In another widely publicized case, an inmate named William Gonzalez was fatally stabbed in a dispute involving rival prison gangs—on his first day. The racial minefield of Chino prison gangs even provided a central setting for the neo-Nazi crime drama *American History X*. The Aryan Brotherhood, La Nuestra Familia, and the Mexican Mafia were among those linked to increasing altercations among prisoners, as they battled for control over drug trafficking and the prison sex trade.[111]

Both prison growth advocates and detractors were concerned with overcrowding. Officials responded by double-bunking prisoners in single cells and expanding makeshift bunking into the dayrooms and gymnasium, resulting in a near total loss of prisoner privacy. This problem was most rampant for medium and maximum security prisoners. As described before the California legislature, "[Our reception center holds] 1,141 and it's designed to hold 618. Our east facility is designed for 400 people, and it has 783 in it. And, west ... is designed for 640 and it has 1,067 this morning. So we're packed everywhere except minimum."[112] Responding to overcrowding, insufficient counseling services, poor food quality, and insufficient health services, prisoners staged a one-day walkout, but without gaining any concessions.[113] By 1980, the State Bar's board of governors declared the institution "unfit for humans," with stifling density, oppressive heat, inadequate lighting, and no outside exercise.[114] The CIM of the 1970s and 1980s was far from the liberal model envisioned at its inception.[115]

It was under these worsening conditions that prisoners tapped into their mobility options, however limited. In addition to their one-day walkout, prisoners more frequently turned to unauthorized flight, abandoning local penal institutions for a fugitive life. Previously at this institution, prisoners were expected to serve their time largely of their own accord without the militarized surveillance apparatus of other prisons, like gun towers and encompassing walls. Recall that CIM's original aim was rehabilitation in an open-campus setting. However, as the prison became more dangerous, uncomfortable, and repressive, inmates used their feet to seek reprise. Rejecting their own immobility in the form of physical confinement to prison grounds, inmates abandoned their work details for the streets, often simply walking away. Herschell Ballinger left while laboring on an irrigation crew in a nearby cornfield; Fred Salazar abandoned the prison while on work detail in CIM's minimum custody section; and in one incident, ten prisoners escaped on the same night by cutting through a chain link fence. The California Institution for Women (CIW) in Corona likewise saw an increase in escapes from previous years, but in much smaller numbers and with less attention compared to those at CIM. In total, 694 prisoners escaped from California Department of Corrections institutions in 1972. That for many escaped inmates parole was only a few months away, and that they would trade those remaining months for the uncertainties of flight, further underscores how unbearable the prisons had become.[116] It is interesting to think here of a context in which prisoners of color more closely blended into their suburban surroundings in this multiracial site, somewhat reducing their risk of detection. Prison authorities responded to inmates' unauthorized movements by arming the prison's guards and fortifying its walls, thus formally limiting prisoners' mobility for the first time.[117]

Even before fortified walls went up in the 1980s, inmates aimed to make meaning within their multiracial suburban context, in part by navigating their physical immobility to achieve some social mobility. CIM self-help groups, which met regularly with administrative recognition, offer a poignant example of these efforts. Chicanos Organizados Pintos de Aztlán (COPA), the Black Awareness Community Development Organization, and the Red Hawk Native American Society each stressed aspects of cultural pride, community integration, and educational assistance. The Senior Citizens

Fellowship Group and Prison Preventers focused their efforts on community service, such as repairs of donated toys and inmate presentations to area youth about the negative effects of drugs and alcohol on their lives.[118] In each case, members of these groups embraced open dialogue, introspection, and public outreach as forms of rehabilitation and eventual reintegration in life outside the prison.[119]

Chicana and Chicano self-help groups formed a nodal network throughout the California prison system, such as Mujeres Unidas Juntas en Revolución at Terminal Island, La Raza Unida at Tehachapi, and El Mejicano Preparado Listo Educado y Organizado at San Quentin. Others formed through partnerships initiated outside of prisons, such as the Mexican American Research Association (MARA), an alliance of students, teachers, community members, and Chicana inmates held at CIW. Of the prison-based self-help groups, Chino's COPA was particularly active, with frequent meetings, formal prison sponsorship, large cultural celebrations, and classes. As described in COPA's self-published newsletter, "the group's main objectives are in higher education in all fields of society; economics, management, skilled professions, and in being an asset to the communities we will be paroled to."[120] At the time of its founding in 1971, the organization already held a sizable membership. Of about 150 Chicanos incarcerated at CIM, COPA claimed a third. It is likely that members may have also included other Latino-origin members, as was the case in other Chicano-affinity groups in California. Most were single men in their thirties or older, without dependents, who had spent time in other state institutions, were recovering from drug addiction, and were serving five or more years on their current offense.[121]

COPA's network building with nonincarcerated allies is a compelling example of how a largely immobile population navigated their captivity within the place-based context of Pomona Valley. Even where inmates experienced limited mobility, prisoners keenly created networks by connecting to local institutions staffed by a rising Chicana/o middle class. Through their print campaigns and letter writing, for instance, COPA actively created links to suburban colleges that had emerging support resources aimed towards Chicana/o students. As a result of these efforts, inmates gained access to weekly Chicano Studies courses via the resources of the nearby Claremont Colleges. The assistant director of the Chicano Recruitment Office, Osvaldo Romero, and student members of United Mexican American Students, visited CIM each Saturday morning, and discussed the poetry of Octavio Paz, Carey McWilliams's classic survey of Mexican American history, and articles concerning Mexican American literature in *El Grito*.[122] COPA's efforts helped craft a pipeline between prisons and the area's colleges, particularly through Upward Bound and Equal Opportunity Programs (EOP) seeking to diversify the student body. As a few examples: the director of Upward Bound at the Claremont Colleges, Octavio Boubion, held weekly college guidance classes at the prison; the associate director of EOP at California State University Long Beach, Ruben Pardo, worked to place COPA members at the university upon release; and COPA president Rudy Alanis coached COPA members for interviews to San Diego State College's Chicano Studies Center. Educational grants from organizations such as the L.A.-based League of United Citizens to Help Addicts and the Youth Opportunity Foundation further helped materialize these networks.[123]

Groups like COPA articulated clear links between the work they did in prisons and life beyond the chain-linked fence. COPA projects such as the youth program, job development, and public relations aimed to connect the group to "all the Chicano organizations out-side and in-side the walls."[124] The vocational training earlier established at CIM was instrumental here, allowing for the production of print materials that moved with a freedom denied prisoners themselves. Most notably, COPA self-published a newsletter—through CIM's print program—titled *La Raza Habla de Chino*. Articles throughout the newsletter reflect affinities with the larger Chicano movement, service to "nuestra comunidad Mexicana," and prison reform.[125] Further, COPA members advocated for halfway houses in Los Angeles and underscored systematic discrimination within the legal system. As one member explained, "they tell us we are a part of the American System, but yet . . . their flag will not extend over us . . . nor protect us . . . in their courtrooms."[126] Through profits earned by selling self-made crafts at the prison store, COPA members purchased envelopes and stamps through which they circulated their words and fostered critical networks among allies, despite their physical captivity. In some cases, COPA members even received permission to accept invitations from nearby campuses to speak about their cause. That is, they could literally leave the prison, albeit temporarily. And, upon parole, many Chicano prisoners worked in their home neighborhoods on antidrug campaigns and in community-based programming.[127]

Another example of how Chicano inmates navigated their own immobility in this particular spatial context can be found in their efforts to manage their home lives. Of all their worries while in prison, COPA members reported concern for their families as their greatest stress (64 percent).[128] In terms of familial separation, they faced some parallel challenges to other working class suburbanites who had (voluntarily) relocated from the central city to its exurbs. Although places like Chino were connected to Los Angeles by highway, the area was largely auto-oriented with little in the way of public transportation.[129] To alleviate this disconnect, prisoners advocated for improved bus services between Los Angeles and Chino. And, to encourage visitation by friends and family across this spatial divide—a considerable emotional and time investment—Chicano inmates held special events like El Dia del Chicano, which commemorated the 1970 Chicano Moratorium protesting the Vietnam War, alongside more traditional Mexican American celebrations, such as Cinco de Mayo and Mexican Independence Day. In the former, special invitations were mailed to inmates' families, as well as to local entertainers and community groups, attracting popular radio stations and celebrities such as Lalo Guerrero.[130]

Nonincarcerated residents also worked to close the gap between prisoners and their families. For instance, relatives traveling with children or from long distances could find support in the Chino branch of Friends Outside. The hospitality center was a mobile unit with a fenced play area, largely financed by donations and administered by volunteers. It offered access to food, showers, and three-hour child care while adult family members visited the prison; provided transportation between bus depots and prison grounds, which could span seven miles; and offered support to those intimidated by visiting procedures. Located in a multiracial community with a sizable Latina/o population and directed by Helen Fayloga, prisoners and their families found diverse forms of support that helped address the challenge of geographic separation where only one party could move.[131]

After prison sentences were extended in the 1970s, sometimes by decades, special events and visitation were no longer sufficient to sustain unification between prisoners and their families. Seeking to mitigate their immobility, some prisoners fully relocated their families to Chino—a long-term mobility solution viewed with suspicion by some local leaders. City manager John Gerardi spoke of this movement with wariness, claiming that prisoners who settled in the town upon release increased police costs and rates of recidivism. Local law enforcement blamed the prison gang Nuestra Familia for the local narcotic and sex work activities of a Mexican American gang, the Chino Sinners. Although there was debate among police officials, prison administrators, government officials, and nonincarcerated residents over the exact relationship between inmates and street gangs, the perception that prison life

Gonzales family: (left to right) Dora Gonzales, Ruben Gonzales, Lupe Torres-Rico, and Evangeline Gonzales-Flores at visiting day for California Institution for Men, ca. 1940s. Used by permission of the Board of Trustees of the Corona Public Library.

and residential life were fluid served to exacerbate local concern over inmates and their families.[132]

The Pomona Valley was inextricably linked to its place as "Prison Valley," further complicating the equation between residential mobility and social mobility for Latina/o suburbanites. On the one hand, Chino and surrounding areas maintained a sizable proportion of Latina/o families from the postwar period forward. Many of them maintained a middle class lifestyle because of the economic opportunities available to them through local correctional institutes and related spending. Notably, at CIM, nearly 25 percent of all staff identified as Hispanic by 1991.[133] On the other hand, prisons catalyzed a significant exurban migration through coercive means. As prison conditions worsened after SB 42, inmates engaged new mobility strategies to help alleviate their own physical confinement. In extreme cases, some fully rejected state restrictions on their bodies and chose life on the run. Others fostered reciprocal networks between self-help groups and suburban educational opportunities, and some worked to shrink geographic divides for families. Perhaps the most quintessentially immobile population, inmates consistently leveraged mobility in deliberate and strategic ways: because of, rather than despite of, their own spatial fixity.

THE LONG COMMUTE

Developers like the Lewis family transformed the Inland Empire into an affordable alternative to urban living. Their colorblind strategy of home sales attracted a multiracial population, creating the foundation for post–World War II era, mixed-use development in the Inland Empire. The legacy of long-distance commerce, with roots in Indigenous networks and the citrus era, made this transition possible. Private developers and government officials alike imagined the postwar Inland Empire as a new frontier marked by eastward metropolitan expansion, sprouting tracts of affordable housing and smart growth. Fair housing efforts helped support the residential mobility of Latinas/os and African American Angelenos into the exurbs of Greater Los Angeles. Paradoxically, the region's welfare was dependent on the enforced immobility of a racialized surplus workforce, relocated to the Inland Empire through the California prison system's spreading network. In the years to follow, hopes for the Inland Empire were deflated by mass foreclosures, environmental devastation, and unwavering anti-immigrant policies, prompting scholar-activist Mike Davis in 1990 to describe the Inland Empire as "the regional antipode to the sumptuary belts of West L.A. or Orange County."[134]

The process of suburban ghettoization that occurred in Pomona is a preamble to the contemporary racial geographies of suburban development in the Inland Empire. Despite the continued prevalence of colorblind rhetoric, resegregation is occurring throughout the metropolitan United States. Examining population change in the nation's fifty largest metropolitan areas between 1980 and 2005–2009, for instance, metropolitan studies experts have found that over time integrated neighborhoods become majority non-white neighborhoods.[135] The national housing collapse is further evidence of the continuing ambivalence of the suburban promise. Although the housing crisis of 2005–2009 was widely devastating, African American and Latina/o homeowners were the hardest hit and collectively lost more than half of their household wealth in those five years.[136]

The edges of Greater Los Angeles continue to represent the promise of the suburban ideal for African American and Latina/o populations. But people of color have had to travel further and further from the city core, beyond the exurbs of the metropolitan borderlands and into its periphery in this pursuit. There is still much uncertainty for African American and Latina/o suburbanites, but one thing is clear. Spatial inequality continues to be inscribed in the interracial metropolis, even as diverse populations continue to search for the suburban ideal in its expanding edges.[137]

Conclusion

THE REEMERGENCE OF THE ANGLO FANTASY PAST

In the spring of 2008, the Pomona Latino Chamber of Commerce hosted their annual Cinco de Mayo festival. The event was a fitting reflection of Pomona's changing demographics, which like many suburbs in inland Southern California had become a gateway for Latina/o immigrants.[1] As residents ended a day celebrating Mexican music, food, and arts, drivers found themselves trapped by blue and red lights, experiencing something else that has become all too common in Latina/o communities. The festival celebrants waited at a four-way checkpoint as police officers stopped each car. Drivers were checked for sobriety, proof of insurance, and their driver's license. Although police were ostensibly operating a sobriety checkpoint, they cited anyone without a license and impounded their car for a mandatory thirty days. Dozens of families were left stranded on the sidewalk with whatever possessions they could carry as they watched tow trucks drag their automobiles off to the impound lot by order of the Pomona Police Department.[2]

Pomona's 2008 checkpoint on Cinco de Mayo was just one of many erected throughout California that year. The National Highway Association had distributed grants providing funding for police checkpoints throughout the state. In Pomona, residents argued that by planning a checkpoint following the Mexican-oriented festival the police deliberately intended to terrorize immigrants in the majority Latina/o city. Their protests joined a chorus of advocates organized under the name Pomona Habla, a coalition of residents, community leaders, and students who asserted that traffic checkpoints targeted undocumented immigrants, who at the time were prohibited from attaining a license in the State of California. Statistics revealing the tiny number of violations for driving under the influence (DUI) identified by the checkpoints support their conclusion. In a series of six checkpoints held on

Valley Boulevard in Pomona, only 0.04 percent resulted in a DUI citation.[3] These sobriety checkpoints were a guise under which all residents were subject to search and undocumented immigrants were made vulnerable to seizure of their assets.

Traffic checkpoints are one manifestation of the larger history explored in this book, in which policies regulate mobility in order to sort, manage, and dominate racialized bodies. But their hegemony has not been uncontested. Rather, protests by Pomona Habla and the efforts by lowrider drivers to claim space on Route 66 point towards residents' continued efforts to disrupt regional campaigns set on popularizing the selective traditions of white settler colonialism and normalizing the criminalization of nonwhite settlement.[4] For instance, following San Bernardino's ban on lowriders' participation in the Rendezvous festival, Mexican American motorists organized a counterprotest called Salute to the Route that drew hundreds of custom cars and thousands of spectators to San Bernardino in an alternative celebration of regional car culture. After six years of organizing the festival and petitioning city leaders, the no-lowrider clause was ultimately removed from the Rendezvous application. From four devoted lowriders and their families to 5,000 people on the multiracial Westside, Salute to the Route became the medium through which lowriders—as a symbolic extension of Mexican Americans—would be included in the downtown festival. Moreover, lowriders' claims to Route 66 became a rallying cry for increased municipal investment in the Westside community, resulting in increased political representation in city government, an upsurge in community organizing, and the development of a Westside task force.[5] *Collisions at the Crossroads* offers an analysis of prohibitions and permissions on movement over the broad stretch of the twentieth century. Foremost, this analysis has aimed to uncover the ways contests over settlement, mobility, and immobility have been used to manage various waves of racial change in California and how targeted groups have responded.

Throughout the twentieth century, mobility has been contested with aims as different as regulating, celebrating, criminalizing, and undermining racial change. While this book focuses on the first half of the twentieth century, these connections span well into the present day. Like the efforts of early Anglo American settlers to carve a dominant place in a multiracial inland Southern California, memory remains an active site where complicated histories are erased and replaced with selective traditions that romanticize an Anglo Fantasy Past. The popular slogan of Donald Trump's 2016 presidential campaign, "Make America Great Again"; Iowa representative Steve King's public comment about Western civilization, "Where are these contributions that have been made by these other categories of people . . . where did any other [non-European] subgroup of people contribute more to civilization?"; and prominent white supremacist Richard B. Spencer's announcement that "America was until this past generation a white country designed for ourselves and our posterity. . . . It is our creation, it is our inheritance, and it belongs to us"—are all evidence of the reemergence of selective discourse.[6] The dominant narratives of the past, including regional histories of travel and migration, present uneven power relations between whites and nonwhites as natural, linear, and inevitable. Through the circulation of white possessive logics, Indigenous dispossession is erased and questions over the place of nonwhites are framed as commonsense protections against unwanted, or even criminalized, racial and social changes.[7] Analysis of the historical record and the interdisciplinary examination by scholars of ethnic studies, geography, and history unsettle the "commonsense" assumptions that would link whiteness to regional ownership.[8]

Combining the tools of racial formation and mobility studies provides a new way to understand spatial relations in gateway regions. The long-standing presence of multiracial populations and contests over their movements in places like inland Southern California is far more consistent to regional history than dominant narratives have suggested. This elision is not by accident. Rather, the erasure of contests over mobility requires extensive and deliberate efforts by regional elites, as well as by marginalized players seeking to claim space by exercising a possessive investment in whiteness.[9] These efforts recast the past in terms that legitimize the present. They cast immigrants as economic threats, nonwhites as indelible outsiders, and working class laborers as forces whose movements should be managed by business interests, neighbors, and the state. The arguments laid out in this book explain why it is troubling that both governmental and private forces are reviving this rhetoric today. It also underscores why this hidden multiracial history of contested movements needs to be embraced by all, including nonwhite conservatives and white allies, if we hope to heal deep divides over race, metropolitan development, and belonging in the United States. When we draw upon these historical geographies, we are better able to question policies targeting marginalized people, identify innovative strategies towards equity, and celebrate the victories that allow people to forge their own paths.

In inland Southern California, there is a palatable reemergence of white settler colonialism and a reinvigoration of racial capitalism through the mythology of driving. The core of this revitalization has been the celebration of white
migration and the erasure of nonwhite populations within the Route 66 heritage. This permutation of the Anglo Fantasy Past adopts core elements of
narratives earlier employed in Riverside's founding, such as linking regional
development to Anglo American arrival and erecting monuments celebrating
this migration, and adapts them to the westbound journey of Dust Bowl
migrants. In a modern settler colony, marked by fast population growth and
new residential development, travelers on the Route 66 corridor are seen as
retracing the steps of white pioneers and thus reenacting a selective tradition
in which Anglo Americans are the rightful inheritors of the region. By recy-
cling the Anglo Fantasy Past within the newly suburbanized and quickly
growing communities of the Inland Empire, regional boosters draw on not
only an incorrect set of historic tropes, but more dangerously ascribe to them
the same racial logics of frontier mythology. Regardless of intention, through
the seamless integration of fact and fiction these scripts once again reassign
people of color the roles either of consolidating enemy (threatening inhabitants) or late arrivals (undeserving immigrants).[10] This revival is powerfully
evident in the reconstruction of inland Southern California's Route 66 corridor and its bejeweled apex, a regional mall called Victoria Gardens.

The reemergence of the Anglo Fantasy Past was born out of inland
Southern California's depressed regional conditions and developers' attempts
to maximize its economic location as a transportation gateway in the 1980s.
Boosters had envisioned a real estate boom along the Inland Empire's central
travel arteries, investing in mixed-use developments that balanced office,
industrial, and retail uses. Illustrative of this agenda was a regional mega-
project called the Ontario Center, a project of the Chevron Land and
Development Company, envisioned as a cityscape around the bustling goods
movement in and out of the Ontario airport. But developers' hopes were
largely unsuccessful. The dream of prosperous mixed-use development was as
dilapidated as the Ontario Center's landmark sign, perched on the side of
the Interstate 10 freeway. Peeling and cracked, the once proud symbol of
regional development was now an indicator of blight. That is—until 1998,
when inland developers revived their dreams of a regional hub.[11] This

time, they would draw inspiration from the original orange magnates in a re-visioning of agricultural heritage in the logistics age. The culmination of this plan was the Victoria Gardens regional lifestyle center in Rancho Cucamonga.

Best known for its melodic name—made infamous as a Looney Tunes' travel stop—Rancho Cucamonga is one of the fastest growing cities within one of the most rapidly growing regions in the United States.[12] Rancho Cucamonga was incorporated as a city in 1977 by consolidating the inland communities of Alta Loma, Etiwanda, and Cucamonga. While the Inland Empire as a whole has experienced a significant growth in its Latina/o population and a decrease in its white population in recent years, Rancho Cucamonga has maintained a smaller percentage of Latinas/os than surrounding cities. In 2010, 42.7 percent of city residents identified as white non-Hispanic compared to 33.3 percent in San Bernardino County, in which Rancho Cucamonga resides. Only 34.9 percent of the population identified as Hispanic, compared to 49.2 percent in the county. Conversely, the proportions of the African American, Asian, American Indian, and Alaskan Native populations were slightly higher than that of the wider region.[13] That is, the City of Rancho Cucamonga had a smaller Latina/o population in a predominantly Latina/o region, a larger white population in a region with a declining white population base, and was slightly more racially diverse than surrounding cities.

Much of this growth has been new. Between 2000 and 2010, the city's population grew by a leap of 30 percent.[14] With among the highest median household incomes in the Inland Empire, moving to "Rancho" has signified upward mobility for many newcomers. For instance, in rapper Ice Cube's comedy sequel *Next Friday,* he describes moving from Los Angeles to the suburbs with his uncle who has bought a home in Rancho Cucamonga after winning the lottery.[15] It is this rapid demographic change and population growth that has set the backdrop for a nascent nostalgia of semirural agriculturalism that permeates the young city.

Resembling an early Riverside, Rancho Cucamonga is a settler colony in the process of laying claim to a majority-minority region. And like Riverside, as well as settler communities similar to it, Rancho Cucamonga's business interests, municipal leaders, and residents have done so through the historical erasure of prior nonwhite inhabitants and a focused celebration of white settlement. Rather than occurring through nefarious decision making by white supremacists behind closed doors, these moral geographies are often taken for granted. Even absent malicious intent, white privilege is often inscribed in the name of regional development, where planning agendas invest in narratives of Route 66 whose potency continues to rest in whiteness and masculinity. Much of this revitalization is evident in city development campaigns initiated in the 1990s, a period of general economic recession.[16] Moreover, from the 1990s forward, a climate of escalated anti-immigrant sentiment has been prevalent throughout San Bernardino County. For instance, the county is hometown to Minuteman Project founder Jim Gilchrist, the former base of the anti-immigration hate group Save Our State, and an early testing ground for voluntary county-federal agreements enabling local police to enforce immigration law.[17]

In particular, two threads of regional development characterize local efforts to distinguish the city from surrounding municipalities. First, the city has concerned itself with community design efforts (streetscapes) that differentiate the town from proximate suburbs, especially those that are both less affluent and predominantly Latina/o. Second, municipal planners have adopted a development strategy that promotes a sense of origin for its residents, many of whom are regional newcomers for whom fictive nostalgia creates their understanding of the region's past. Through celebrating the city's white agricultural heritage and embedding agrarian iconography into the built environment, city planners and developers celebrate Anglo routes and institutionalize the erasure of multiracial roots in inland southern California.[18]

Planners chose a road to anchor the city's past, foregrounding the centrality of mobility to the identity of the region. Consistent with a regional history in which public and private efforts actively differentiated celebratory from deviant movements, a key role in Rancho Cucamonga's development strategy has been creating a heritage statement for its Route 66 corridor (Foothill Boulevard). Much thought has been put into defining community character, foremost of which are architectural characteristics reminiscent of inland Southern California's agricultural history, including mission, winery, barn, and farm designs. These community-defining characteristics have been further historicized through earth elements, such as arbors wrapped in vines, and splashes of river-washed cobble that lend an aged effect to newer construction. This purposeful maturing of the landscape makes it difficult to discern reality from design, as does the dominance of agrarian iconography. Several architectural features were rejected in favor of these design elements.[19] As outlined in the city's Foothill Boulevard Specific Plan (1987), art deco and modern styles were prohibited on the corridor, as was the use of industrial materials, such as steel, metal sidings, plastic sidings, reflective glass, and modernist window shapes. The built environment was to reflect a historic farm town to the exclusion of competing design statements.

Notably, in its efforts to promote a sense of regional roots, planners drew upon a popular set of globally recognizable tropes related to western mobility. That is, divorced from its multiracial history, the iconography of a rural Route 66 provided the city a community heritage statement that would have been familiar to even the newest suburbanite. As noted in the Foothill Boulevard Specific Plan:

> Remember the vagabond Corvette cruising along Route 66 on TV in the early 60s and even further back when your Aunt and Uncle made the "big move" from the Midwest to Southern California along that same road. Well, a part of that memorable highway is alive and well as it passes through Rancho Cucamonga's history.[20]

By utilizing a Depression-era narrative of midwestern migration to the region, the excerpt above implicitly affiliates Rancho Cucamonga with whiteness. As described in previous chapters, progressives had earlier divorced the tropes of Depression-era migration from nonwhite (im)migrants, instead deliberately tying white migrants to earlier Anglo American pioneers. An extension of the frontier myth, the city's plan for the Route 66 corridor privileged the east-to-west migration of Anglo Americans. Further, the centering of Route 66 heritage above all other migration stories—from the Pacific Rim, Latin America, and the American South—deemphasized earlier waves of migration and immigration, as well as long-present Indigenous communities. Through streamlined design elements naturalizing this narrative, such as faux ranch architecture and honorific Route 66 signage, city planners hoped to promote "a balanced mixture of commercial and residential uses, with safe, efficient circulation and access" within a deliberately crafted community identity.[21]

Rancho Cucamonga's efforts to provide a linear narrative of white settlement anchored to Route 66 is distinctly tied to the context of the Inland Empire, a historic Citrus Belt with pronounced labor migrations from diverse sources. Similar efforts are evident throughout the region, as classic car shows and vintage citrus signage have sprouted across the valley. However, the Route 66 renaissance also reflects larger national mythologies concerning the travel corridor. Numerous films, travel books, and small museums have appeared that commemorate the historic highway. In recent years, the release

Honorific signage for Route 66 corridor, Rancho Cucamonga. Photograph by Luis Camas, 2018.

of the popular Pixar movie *Cars,* the opening of Cars Land at Disney's California Adventure Theme Park, and the National Park Service Route 66 Corridor Preservation Project have introduced Route 66 nostalgia to a new generation. Urban landscapes have a powerful capacity to foster a sense of cultural belonging or exclusion.[22] In its dominant representations, the Route 66 corridor provides a journey through the past in which travelers consume a built landscape embedded with a selective tradition of white migration. That is, the Route 66 corridor has been to the Anglo Fantasy Past what El Camino Real has been to the Spanish Fantasy Past: a pilgrimage in which travelers retrace the steps of the pioneers and, by doing so, reenact an origin myth in which Anglo Americans are the rightful inheritors of the region.[23]

Alongside planners, developers have worked to construct a believable, but nevertheless fictive, heritage statement for the Route 66 corridor since the 1980s. In line with this vision, Rancho Cucamonga's planning department envisioned a regional commercial center that would operate as a public-private venture, simultaneously generating revenue for the city and functioning as a civic plaza.[24] Deemed a "less urbanized" area without "strong architectural style," the meeting place of Route 66 and Interstate 15 offered planners and developers a prime site to recreate an idealized community design and to manufacture a sense of place that could integrate a growing population of newcomers into the nascent city.[25] It was Lewis Homes, managed by the same Lewis family who had championed fair housing and now operating as the Lewis Group of Companies, who delivered this vision.

In a $554 million deal made during the fall of 1998, the Lewis brothers sold their residential operations to Kaufman and Broad (KB Home). Where Lewis Homes had built about 3,000 single-family homes in 1998, an already impressive development portfolio, KB Home is estimated to have sold five to six times that amount. Mega-builders like KB Home—who benefited from an economy of scale, volume pricing on appliances and building materials, as well as lower loan rates—were outpacing medium-sized builders like the Lewis family. In the midst of the Inland Empire's housing boom, even a top company like Lewis Homes needed a new development approach if it hoped to keep pace with the expansion it had helped initiate. The opportunity to invest in master-planned communities provided the answer to their search. Money in hand, as well as a share of KB Home's stock, the Lewis family embarked on a career of mixed-use development that included the construction of Victoria Gardens, the grand culmination of city planners' vision for the Route 66 corridor.[26]

With about 16 million visitors annually, Victoria Gardens opened to the public in 2004 and has since been a primary anchor for the Inland Empire's regional identity. A venture involving the City of Rancho Cucamonga, the Lewis Investment Company, and mixed-use developer Forest City, the development has been marketed as a "regional life-style center" for its commercial, public, and residential amenities. Higher-end chain retailers, such as Crate and Barrel, Pottery Barn, Anthropologie, and White House Black Market, anchor the shopping district and pull in a regional base of consumers.[27] Booming today, the open-air nature of the mall connects it to similar entertainment-retail centers prevalent throughout Southern California, such as Paseo Colorado in Pasadena, the Grove in Los Angeles, and the Americana in Glendale. However, it is unique to the degree in which it operates as a public-private venture. To the north of a Main Street retail district is a town center, complete with public library, police substation, playground, and playhouse. Located just north of these public services is a residential complex, with townhouses for purchase. As an Urban Land Institute's recipient of an Award for Excellence in the Americas (2006), Victoria Gardens has been deemed a model for similar commercial developments throughout the nation.[28] That is, what happens in the Inland Empire has not been confined to Southern California, but rather has served as a testing ground for developmental schemes with wide implementation.

A central goal of Victoria Garden's design is providing visitors the experience of community heritage through an immersive, walkable tableau of regional history. As stated by Forest City president Brian Jones, "We realized there was no sense of place here—no essence of any identifiable downtown."[29] In order to evoke an impression of change over time, like one would see in a traditional downtown where varied epochs of construction interweave, the company hired multiple design teams to create four subdistricts framing the mall. Organized around a village green, these subdistricts are united by design elements that refer to the region's agricultural history and differentiated from one another by their architecture and landscaping. Each followed a fictive history written by developers intent on providing "some instant heritage."[30] As described by Urban Land Institute's senior resident fellow, Robert Dunphy:

> The project's detailed, historically inspired design is based on a postmodern storyboard for how a southern California downtown *might have* organically evolved from a modest grouping of agricultural structures along a farm road to Main Street buildings designed in art deco, modern, and contemporary styles.[31]

Developers had originally imagined the project as a one-theme design with community-oriented retailers like locksmiths, grocery stores, and pharmacies. Instead, Victoria Gardens ultimately provided a storyboard for a fictive city, a town that "might have organically evolved"—one that has come to serve as an origin tale in-situ not only for the growing town, Rancho Cucamonga, but also its surrounding hinterland, the Inland Empire.

Through the act of walking, the Victoria Gardens visitor subliminally consumes a chronological history of the Inland Empire that begins at a rural packinghouse and ends at a modern Main Street, set apart by art deco styles otherwise prohibited on the Foothill corridor. The story is embedded in the built environment. Spanish place names, bronze plaques, and historic signage all create a sense of roots in this postmodern town square. At times, this signage is purposely distressed, such as the prominent but faded "California's Best Lemons" painted on the metal siding of a storefront. Superimposed signage such as this contributes an aged quality to the building and lends a sense of authenticity to the narrative of the past portrayed by developers.

Faux historical signage at Victoria Gardens, Rancho Cucamonga. Photograph by Luis Camas, 2018.

Visual iconography reaffirms this sense of place. In a food hall designed to resemble a citrus packinghouse, such as those that dotted the Citrus Belt before World War II, the visitor consumes images of agricultural heritage just as easily as warm dishes from Panda Express or Hot Dog On a Stick. Vibrant orange crate labels, wooden picnic tables, colorful ladders, and large images of groves and vineyards bombard the visitor as they walk from one end to the other. Entering the food hall, the visitor is transported to a visual chorus of the Citrus Belt's heyday itself.[32]

Although drawing upon the region's citrus heritage, connections to this local history have been selectively featured and omitted. For instance, large prints of digital murals in the food hall feature images of the white farmer.[33] Through visual consumption, the built environment of the food hall presents a regional landscape with small ranches and enterprising farmers reminiscent of Jeffersonian mythology. This feature contributes to the erasure of both the multicultural work force who produced these fruits and the industrialized agriculture that characterized much of California. Moreover, it sidesteps the contribution of women's agricultural labor, which dominated packinghouse work.

The line between history and mythology is difficult to untangle within the space of the mall. The food hall, for one, mimics the architecture of a citrus packinghouse, including features like high ceilings, natural light, exposed beams, and a long narrow central corridor. However, unlike regional adaptive reuse projects, such as the Claremont Packinghouse and Anaheim Packing District, "Rancho Victoria" never existed. Nevertheless, at Victoria Gardens, facsimiles of a Rancho Victoria citrus label are integrated into a collage of historical citrus label art, leading to a seamless integration of fact and fiction. While these spaces required careful and intense planning, they are successful because they appear effortless. They use concepts of space that most people take for granted: color schemes, walkways, and music, each strategically applied towards their specific storyboard. Through "imagineering," they create a past that never happened.[34]

For visitors commuting by car or leisurely shopping on foot, the Route 66 Corridor Project and Victoria Gardens each reinforce a fictive heritage statement that suggests a linear progression from a rural agricultural community to a modern Main Street, one that marks nonwhite migration as ahistorical. In each case, Anglo Americans occupy center stage in the regional history and development narrative. By extension, nonwhites are deemed outsiders. The exclusion of Indigenous populations, people of color, and immigrants from this regional story echoes the selective traditions that legitimized the broad enforcement of the Geary Act by Chinese inspectors at the turn of the century, discourses surrounding Japanese bicyclists and housing integration near World War I, immigration debates concerning Mexican, Puerto Rican, and Filipino migrants in the interwar years, and depictions of Mexican automobility during the Depression. Together, these mythologies reinforce a selective history that celebrates white migration and falsely denaturalizes nonwhite movement.

Many Inland Empire residents, including people of color, engage these mythologies by participating in their construction, it is true; many other residents also participate in ways that challenge a possessive investment in whiteness. The Salute to the Route movement, for example, evolved into not only an alternative to the exclusionary downtown San Bernardino's Rendezvous festival, but also as a gathering place in which Mexican American lowriders could display icons of cultural pride, such as Mexican flags, sarapes, and airbrushed murals of Mexican heroes. Another example of Inland Empire residents challenging the status quo narrative, the Harada case has become the basis for a historic walking tour of the Japanese American community and proposals for an interpretive center examining California's civil rights history. Also, Inland Mexican Heritage emerged as a grassroots effort by a local historian and a handful of volunteers to gather the stories of Indigenous and Mexican elders. In each case, people of color and their allies, including activists, nonprofits, historians, and students, work to remap belonging in the region.

When viewed within the context of multiracial growth and white decline in the region as a whole, narratives erasing nonwhite mobility take on an added significance. Regional heritage and their selective traditions are rarely preserved for the sake of historical knowledge alone. Rather, they are fundamentally concerned with the present, from concerns with economic development to contests over insiders and outsiders.[35] In recent years, nostalgia has assumed a more prominent role in erasing the majority nonwhite population from the Inland Empire even as, or perhaps especially as, it has become majority-minority. Enforced by city planning and design review, the Route 66 Corridor Project and Victoria Gardens omit the historical presence and flows of multiracial communities that long moved between the Inland Empire and the rest of the world. These histories are buried in the reinvented landscape of these manufactured environments, which bypass people of color altogether and reestablish Anglos as pioneers in an increasingly nonwhite region through the origin myth of Route 66.

DRIVING IN REVERSE

In 1893, historian Fredrick Jackson Turner placed internal migration at the center of American identity in his infamous treatise, *The Significance of the Frontier in American History*. He wrote, "This perennial rebirth, this fluidity of American life, this expansion westward with its new opportunities, its continuous touch with the simplicity of primitive society, furnish the forces dominating American character."[36] By Turnerian logic, western movement across the open continent had transformed a diverse group of European immigrants into American settlers and an underdeveloped wilderness into U.S. civilization. Speaking of one such representative migrant he continued, "Little by little he transforms the wilderness, but the outcome is not the old Europe ... here is a new product that is American."[37] When practiced by European Americans, mobility signified release from the influence of Europe, an independent spirit, and the pursuit of opportunity in the face of harsh obstacles. Turner credits mobility, explicitly, to the flowering of nationalism and "death to localism."[38] From the eastern reaches of the United States to the western edges of Southern California, Turnerian logic placed mobility at the center of American nationhood and white citizenship.

But what of those already here? Or those who immigrated after the closing of the frontier?[39] For Turner, it was the "common danger" of the American Indian that served as the "consolidating agent" of American colonists, thus forming a "composite nationality for the American people."[40] That is, it was through encounters with Indigenous people and the ultimate advancement of "civilization" that a hodgepodge of Europeans became American "natives." Nonwhite immigrant newcomers were denied a space within this melting pot. Where westward movement stood as the "dominant fact" of American life until 1890, Turner's treatise declared its end. He wrote, that "the frontier has gone, and with its going has closed the first period of American history."[41]

When immigrant and resident nonwhites attempted to find a place within the U.S. nation, their migration and settlement could not be imagined as American. Instead, for white Americans, the mobility of nonwhite residents served as a racial threat. Whereas East Coast concerns with migration at the beginning of the twentieth century were directed at eastern and southern European immigrants, it was to a multiracial workforce of agricultural workers with diverse origins in Asia and Latin America and, later, African American suburbanites that the settler colonists of inland Southern California turned their attention. Those who leveraged their personal mobility in order to find a place in the promised cornucopia of inland Southern California found that they were not only excluded as "late arrivals," now deemed threatening to the rewards of white pioneer development, but also subject to legal, political, and social restraints on their movements.[42] Land laws, city planning, housing programs, immigration policy, violence, and incarceration were each employed with the aim of dominating people of color and their movement, on whom the agricultural economy relied.

But Turner had it wrong. Rather than the victory of white pioneers over an undeveloped wilderness, an Anglo Fantasy Past seeping into frontier mythologies gave racial logic to a coercive state process of subordinating alternative economic systems already established by resident populations. For instance, when the Riverside colonists arrived in inland Southern California in 1870, they carved a space for themselves out of a multiracial region of Indigenous, Mexican, and New Mexican people. In their efforts, white settlers employed the tools of the state, such as mapping, and the power of selective tradition. Through subsequent and ongoing processes of conquest, the dominant Mexican ranch economy was remade in the image of U.S. capitalism.

At the inception of these Anglo American colonies, heritage campaigns consistently placed the origins of regional development exclusively at the arrival of white colonists. Native populations and nonwhite migrants were consistently erased from the history of this multiracial region—from the placement of Indigenous children in the Sherman Institute in the early 1900s, to the rising incarceration of Mexican Americans and African Americans in the 1970s. But these efforts to keep marginalized populations in place have not been without resistance. Groups targeted for their mobility met the constraints levied by government officials, their neighbors, and the media with movements of their own, from the Japanese racers of Riverside's early bicycling circuits to the deviant Latina drivers who took to the streets in Depression-era Los Angeles.

The reemergence of the Anglo Fantasy Past betrays the acute danger from the ways regional development remains tied to racially exclusive ideas of white migration in the Inland Empire. The history put forth in this book underscores the virility of settler colonialism, white supremacy, and possessive investment in whiteness stemming from similar contests over mobility and race making across the twentieth century. The Citrus Era and its decline from the 1870s to the 1970s are defined by these developments. Namely, Anglo American settler colonists arriving in inland Southern California carved a place for themselves in a multiracial region through the articulation of an Anglo Fantasy Past. These settlers and their descendants, aided by government officials, constructed policies at multiple scales of governance with the aim of regulating the mobility and immobility of a multiracial agricultural workforce. And, throughout these efforts, white supremacy was consistently reaffirmed and challenged through vivid contests among Anglo American settlers, Indigenous and non-Indigenous inhabitants, and new migrants over the right to mobility and the right to stay put. Looking to these developments reveals how mobility (specifically, constrained movement) has to be factored into racial formation, spatial formation, and contests over unequal power relations in twentieth-century inland Southern California.

When approaching the final destination of a journey, the road traveled comes into focus in the rear-view mirror. Whether for the driver or a passenger, the images of where one is going and where one has been cannot be divorced from one another. Likewise, the histories interweaved in this book are revisited here with ties made to the road ahead. The story begins with the symbolic replanting of the first navel orange tree in the city of Riverside, where white settler colonists christened the heart of a booming Citrus Belt and memorialized regional development efforts by Anglo Americans in the American West. This Anglo Fantasy Past dominated regional development despite counternarrative-based claims to place by American Indian child runaways, San Salvador parishioners, and Chinese migrant farmers.

Following the Chinese Exclusion Act of 1892, regional demography shifted rapidly to include new migrant streams to California and the diversification of laborers within the agricultural hinterland of the Los Angeles metropolitan region. Global migrations to the Citrus Belt were met by staunch efforts to restrict local mobility, particularly where it threatened the perception of a strict racial and spatial order. In the thirty years between the 1892 Geary Act and the 1920 Alien Land Law, residents found themselves at the center of far-reaching debates over mobility and immobility. Of foremost concern were Japanese laborers, who moved through the region in search of work opportunities, started collective farms, and sought residential integration. Although Asian mobility was criminalized in both federal and state laws, it was at the municipal level that officials and marginally white residents enforced racial divisions. An approach grounded in relational racial formation reveals the complex strategies adopted by Japanese residents seeking to defend their right to mobility, ranging from public displays of sportsmanship in high-profile bicycle races to fighting for the right to live in the neighborhood of one's own choosing.

The meanings attributed to Asian mobility had long-lasting ramifications, but they were also flexible, recycled, and rewritten in response to pressing economic and political needs. For instance, during the long immigration debate era of the 1920s, after World War I, Mexican workers in Southern California experienced two very different forms of racialization tied to their movements. In the earlier years, Mexican immigrants were positioned as ideal settlers, largely against the prevailing racial formation of Asian workers and white ethic tramps as unreliable single male migrants. As national critiques of Mexican immigration heightened at the end of the decade, the agriculturalists who had relied on Mexican workers in World War I citrus housing campaigns now strategically flipped the script. In a stark recasting, Chambers of Commerce and southwestern industrial leaders contended that Mexican workers were "birds of passage," innately mobile and habitually drawn back to Mexico at the end of the picking season. Conversely, agriculturalists strategically leveraged larger fears of permanent settlement by "negro" colonial subjects from Puerto Rico and the Philippines in order to position Mexicans as the lesser threat. Although both Mexicans and colonial subjects were exempt from quotas under the Immigration Act of 1924, they were effectively placed on opposite sides of a racial hierarchy that ranked them by their ability to move freely.

The construction of Mexicans as racial homers had reverberating consequences in the Depression years that followed. In the early decades of the twentieth century, Mexican "automobility" underwent a series of profound transformations. For instance, Mexican residents had significantly higher rates of automobile ownership than Californians as a whole. However, by the onset of the Great Depression there were stark changes in public attitudes towards them. Mexican immigrant and Mexican American drivers, as well as Latinas/os more broadly, were actively portrayed as both incapable of self-control and as a danger to the white public. Impoverished Dust Bowl migrants too were at risk of this blackening; however, agrarian partisans successfully recast white Dust Bowl migrants as yeoman within progressive circles. Even if denigrated upon arrival, Route 66 migrants would eventually be able to move past their marginalization and reintegrate into Anglo America. Conversely, ethnic Mexicans, as well as a broad range of Latina/o and Asian-origin populations, were marked as perpetually migrant.

Although encountering staunch efforts to regulate their mobility, people of color often sought social mobility through physical movement, including suburbanization. World War II marked the demise of the celebrated citrus industry on which regional identity had been founded. In the place of the Citrus Belt would emerge the Inland Empire, a suburban hinterland with burgeoning military, logistics, and prison industries. A multiracial population took advantage of postwar opportunities for integrated housing in the exurbs, but found themselves subsumed in a process of suburban ghettoization. White flight and disinvestment in places like Pomona provide a preamble to the contemporary racial geographies of suburban development in the Inland Empire and beyond. Spatial inequality continues to be inscribed in the interracial metropolis, even as diverse populations search for the suburban ideal in its expanding edges.

This analysis demonstrates that mobility is a key modality through which race is lived and contested.[43] Struggles between elites and subaltern subjects over mobility have been steadfast, particularly in times of demographic and economic change. How racial meaning is attributed to mobility at these moments has shifted in response. Yet, within the capitalist landscape of

Southern California, the purpose behind attributing racial meaning to mobility has remained constant: it has served to foster white claims to Indigenous territories and to maintain control over diverse sources of labor in a multiracial region. In this light, contests over mobility today can be viewed as more than isolated responses to contemporary debates over immigration and shifting suburban demographics. Rather, efforts to control and give meaning to mobility are extensions of historical efforts to identify, target, and regulate the movement of racialized people. Whereas whiteness has operated through choice over one's own mobility and the mobility of others, the racialization of nonwhites has been experienced in the multiple ways their mobility and fixity have been coerced through systems of power. In each case, those most affected by these policies and practices have responded by asserting their right to mobility and, likewise, their right to stay put.[44]

As we stand firmly in the twenty-first century, clashes between bodies on the move and those who would regulate their flows seem to be appearing with increased frequency. Across the United States, smart phones and social media place these occurrences at our fingertips. The large range of mobile catalysts and actions linked to Arizona SB1070's mandate of local immigration enforcement; the death of Trayvon Martin at the hands of a neighborhood watch volunteer while walking from a convenience store; the death of Jessie Hernandez while parked in an alley; and protest against proposed immigration policy and border securitization—all underscore the deep importance of mobility in constructing racial meaning. In each instance, movement can function to fuel a discourse of deviancy in a multiracial landscape or to reaffirm cultural citizenship through mass action. The contests over racial lines evident in the first half of the twentieth century have not dissipated. Rather, they have evolved.

The story of mobility and race making in inland Southern California opens up critical issues related to historical geography. Once we employ a historical view of mobility in multiracial places, two developments become clear. First, mobility has always been a contested ground where struggles over power and racial meaning are fiercely fought. These struggles have shaped settler colonial spaces, both ideologically and spatially. It is understandable that historical attention has focused on place-based meanings, as evidenced by the rich analysis of specific spaces of racial difference like Chinatowns and Latina/o barrios. However, in doing so, we have overrepresented the firmness of spatial and racial boundaries, even as we seek to disrupt them. An approach rooted in racial formation and mobility foregrounds an often overlooked dimension of spatial development—the flows and stoppages that seek to reinforce lines of racial difference.

Second, migrants entering the multiracial landscape of inland Southern California have consistently attempted to navigate regional racial hierarchies through their mobility. Organizing for their familial, ethnic, and neighborhood interests, multiracial communities have responded across time to outside forces seeking to regulate their movements through their bodies, the courts, media, photography, and, at times, reinvestment in whiteness, each with varying effectiveness. Gender, class, and citizenship have been implicated in these processes, from Japanese men's claims to manhood and national belonging through cycling to the efforts of agrarian progressives to recast Okies as pioneer families in search of refuge. Race making and mobility do not explain every dimension of power in the twentieth-century United States. However, this linkage is more critical to the evolution of uneven power relations and spatial development than has previously been suggested. We need more research at this intersection and more attention to the ways mobility informs racialization, as well as how race informs the field of mobility studies, as scholars investigate the long-distance immigrations, regional migrations, and shifting technologies of travel across time.

People of color and their allies continue to negotiate and contest their place within these meaning systems. A 2010 forum at the Universalist Unitarian Church in Riverside, called "The Empire Strikes Back: Organizing Inland," represents one such effort. The forum brought together a myriad of residents from across the region to advocate "for a just and sane economy in the Inland Empire and beyond."[45] A comment made by a representative of Warehouse Workers United, Sheheryar Kaoosji, struck an important note about the myth of inevitability that permeates regional inequality. He firmly stated, "This is not an accident."[46] I had heard a similar comment made in Los Angeles two years earlier. In her discussion of inequality, gentrification, and the right to the city, public intellectual Gilda Haas explained that "once you know that it wasn't the 'market,' that it wasn't a 'natural cycle,' that it wasn't inevitable, then you can believe in change. You can witness and know and believe that other human decisions can make it right, take it back, and produce justice."[47]

The empirical evidence presented in this book underpins an analytical unraveling of these unnatural forces. From an interdisciplinary lens that foregrounds the relationship between mobility and race making, we are better able to see the creation of regional inequality, from the impactful efforts of Riverside settlers anxious to carve a white space for themselves in a multi-racial region at the beginning of the twentieth century to the ambivalent experiences of suburbanization for people of color in the postwar period. Such an understanding, and the tensions it reveals, can help us uncover the means by which race, place, and mobility have shaped California. The people in this book are defining a new form of belonging, one insistent on the ability to be in control of one's own movements. From this perspective, mobility is a right, and is tied to the daily experiences of our social, economic, and political lives. We have not quite reached our destination yet. But we remain people on the move.

NOTES

Sources for maps: Militant Angeleno, "Pacific Electric Archaeology Map," http://
militantangeleno.blogspot.com/2015/11/pacific-electric-week-militants-pacific
.html; "Native Land," https://native-land.ca/api-docs/; CKAN, "Early California
Cultural Atlas," http://ecaidata.org/dataset/spanish-and-mexican-land-grants-in-
california; National Park Service, "Old Spanish Trail," https://www.nps.gov/olsp
/planyourvisit/maps.htm; "Streets, Cities, River," © OpenStreetMap; California
Department of Transportation, "Highways, Railways," http://www.dot.ca.gov/hq
/tsip/gis/datalibrary/; Esri, USGS, NOAA, "ESRI World Terrain Base," https://
www.arcgis.com/home/item.html?id=c61ad8ab017d49e1a82f580ee1298931.

INTRODUCTION

1. I use the term "Mexican American" to refer to Mexican-descent people born
in the United States and the term "Mexican immigrant" for those born in Mexico.
"Mexican" refers to both Mexican Americans and Mexican immigrants.

2. Danny Flores interviewed by Robert Gonzalez and Matt Garcia, 15 June
2004, transcript, p. 10, Inland Mexican Heritage, Redlands; "'Route 66 Rendezvous': S.B.'s Salute to Bygone Era," *San Bernardino County Sun,* September 8, 1990;
James Folmer, "Alternate Show Calling All Cars," *San Bernardino County Sun,*
September 16, 1997.

3. On the Inland Empire's deindustrialization, see Juan D. De Lara, *Inland Shift:
Race, Space, and Capital in Inland Southern California* (Oakland: University of
California Press, 2018); and Mike Davis, *City of Quartz: Excavating the Future in
Los Angeles* (London: Verso, 1990). On rising crime and policing, see Miles Corwin
and Tom Gorman, "Bad Rap?: Despite Crime Image, L.A. Fails to Make Worst 15
Cities, but San Bernardino Does," *Los Angeles Times,* May 25, 1994; Joe Mozingo,
"San Bernardino: Broken City," *Los Angeles Times,* June 14, 2015.

4. U.S. Census Bureau, "Table 5. Race and Hispanic Origin: 1990," Census of Population, General Population Characteristics (1990), 99; Dowell Myers and Julie Park, "Racially Balanced Cities in Southern California, 1980–2000," Race Contours 2000 Study, Public Research Report No. 2001–05 (Los Angeles: Population Dynamics Group, May 23, 2001).

5. I use the term "Latina/o" when referring to people of Latin American-descent living in the United States, combining the feminine "a" and masculine "o" from Spanish. In electing to use this term, I seek to draw attention to the intersecting racial and gender constructions that have shaped mobility in the past. That is, experiences of race and mobility were very much shaped by whether a person was gendered as male or female. There is currently a shift towards "Latinx" as a more inclusive sociopolitical category term, one that disrupts gender binaries in the contemporary moment. For a genealogy of these terms, see Nicole M. Guidotti-Hernández, "Affective Communities and Millennial Desires: Latinx, or Why My Computer Won't Recognize Latina/o," *Cultural Dynamics* 29, no. 3 (August 2017).

6. Daniel Martinez HoSang, *Racial Propositions: Ballot Initiatives and the Making of Postwar California* (Berkeley: University of California Press, 2010); George Sánchez, "Face the Nation: Race, Immigration, and the Rise of Nativism in Late Twentieth Century America," *International Migration Review* 31 (Winter 1997).

7. Jodi Melamed, "The Spirit of Neoliberalism: From Racial Liberalism to Neoliberal Multiculturalism," *Social Text* 24 (Winter 2006); David Harvey, "Globalization and the 'Spatial Fix,'" *Geographische Revue* 2 (February 2001); David Harvey, *A Brief History of Neoliberalism* (New York: Oxford University Press, 2005).

8. Developers have explicitly stated that new housing developments were not designed to target the current (majority-Latina/o) population. See Urban Land Institute, "San Bernardino California: Crossroads of the Southwest," An Advisory Services Panel Report (Washington, DC, June 24–29, 2007), 15. Such efforts to reconfigure downtown development have consistently masked racial difference. Eugene McCann, "Race, Protest, and Public Space: Contextualizing Lefebvre in the U.S. City," *Antipode* 31, no. 2 (2002); Neil Smith, *Uneven Development: Nature, Capital, and the Production of Space,* 3rd ed. (1984; Athens: University of Georgia Press, 2008). On current struggles against gentrification, see "Anti-Eviction Mapping Project: Visualizing Bay Area Displacement and Resistance," last accessed September 6, 2017, https://www.antievictionmap.com.

9. Mimi Sheller and John Urry provide a thorough introduction to the field in their "The New Mobilities Paradigm," *Environment and Planning A,* 38 (2006); see also Mei-Po Kwan and Tim Schwanen, "Geographies of Mobility," *Annals of the American Association of Geographers* 106 (March 2016). For notable book-length works, see Tim Cresswell, *On the Move: Mobility in the Modern Western World* (New York: Routledge, 2006); John Urry, *Mobilities* (Oxford: Polity Press, 2007); Mimi Sheller, *Aluminum Dreams: The Making of Light Modernity* (Cambridge, MA: MIT Press, 2014).

10. Throughout this book, I use the term "Indigenous" to refer to American Indian populations originating in what is now Southern California and the term

"American Indian" as a pan-ethnic term referring to the earliest arriving peoples to what is now the United States, unless otherwise indicated. Readers should look for shifts in my use of the terms "Native" and "native" in the text. In the period covered in this book, settler colonial regimes worked to eliminate Indigenous populations in Southern California. To denaturalize the elision of this violence, I use "native" when referring to white colonists who sought to identify themselves with the region by displacing "Native" claims to the region. Beth Piatote, *Domestic Subjects: Gender, Citizenship, and Law in Native American Literature* (New Haven: Yale University, 2013).

11. My understanding of everyday life is rooted in the work of Henri Lefebvre, *Critique of Everyday Life,* trans. John Moore (London: Verso, 1991). Also influential for his focus on everyday materiality has been Michel de Certeau, *The Practice of Everyday Life,* trans. Steven Rendall (Berkeley: University of California Press, 1984).

12. For more on the ways restrictive immigration measures operated at the local level in their earliest iterations, see Natalia Molina, *Fit to Be Citizens?: Public Health and Race in Los Angeles, 1879–1939* (Berkeley: University of California Press, 2006).

13. I draw inspiration here from Stuart Hall et al., *Policing the Crisis: Mugging, the State, and Law and Order* (New York: Holmes and Meier, 1978).

14. Monica Rodriguez, "Federal Lawsuit Filed Against Pomona Police Involving August 2008 Checkpoint Meeting," *Inland Valley Daily Bulletin,* September 8, 2009. For more on traffic checkpoints and their impact on immigrant communities, see Genevieve Carpio, Clara Irazábal-Zurita, and Laura Pulido, "Right to the Suburb? Rethinking Lefebvre and Immigrant Activism," *Journal of Urban Affairs* 33, no. 2 (May 2011).

15. Video available at Laotrapomona, "Pomona PD Attempts to Infiltrate Checkpoint Forum," August 21, 2008, http://www.youtube.com/watch?v =xjPCDwc9jmo. Notable parallels can be drawn to Arizona's SB1070, which proposed state-level immigration requirements and led to massive racial profiling in the state.

16. This fluidity reflects the structure of capitalism, in which regions are dynamic units whose coherence is shaped and reshaped by the production of specific commodities or services; Smith, *Uneven Development.* Geographer Anssi Paasi makes an important distinction between the identity of a region, referring to those features that are used in regional marketing and governance to distinguish one region from others, and a regional identity, referring to the multiple identifications of people with the institutionalized region. Although I use the term "regional identity" throughout the text, I use it to denote what Paasi calls the "identity of the region." See Anssi Paasi, "Region and Place: Regional Identity in Question," *Progress in Human Geography* 27, no. 4 (2003).

17. Clyde Woods, *Development Arrested: The Blues and Plantation Power in the Mississippi Delta* (London: Verso Press, 1998); Clyde Woods, "Life After Death," *Professional Geographer* 54, no. 1 (2002). On the relationship between racial formation and region in its California context, see Laura R. Barraclough, "South Central

Farmers and Shadow Hills Homeowners: Land Use Policy and Relational Racialization in Los Angeles," *Professional Geographer* 61, no. 2 (2009); Laura R. Barraclough, *Making the San Fernando Valley: Rural Lands, Urban Development, and White Privilege* (Athens: University of Georgia Press, 2011); Wendy Cheng, *The Changs Next Door to the Diazes: Remapping Race in Suburban California* (Minneapolis: University of Minnesota Press, 2013).

18. On mobility, regions, and capital flows, see Doreen Massey, *Space, Place and Gender* (Minneapolis: University of Minnesota Press, 1994); and Anssi Paasi, "Bounded Spaces in the Mobile World: Deconstructing 'Regional Identity,'" *Tijdschrift Voor Economische En Sociale Geografie* 93, no. 2 (2002): 137–148.

19. Douglas Cazaux Sackman, *Orange Empire: California and the Fruits of Eden* (Berkeley: University of California Press, 2005).

20. Based on author's analysis of lemon-shipping records. "Cucamonga Citrus Fruit Growers. Supplements and Returns," 1908, Cucamonga Citrus Fruit Growers' Association Records, 1896–1927, Huntington Library.

21. Sackman, *Orange Empire;* Catherine Merlo, *Heritage of Gold: The First 100 Years of Sunkist Growers, Inc., 1893–1993* (Van Nuys: Sunkist Growers Inc., 1994); Esther Klotz, Harry W. Lawton, and Joan H. Hall, eds., *A History of Citrus in the Riverside Area* (Riverside: Riverside Museum Press, 1969).

22. William Cronon, *Nature's Metropolis: Chicago and the Great West* (New York: W. W. Norton, 1991), 371–378; Andrew F. Burghardt, "A Hypothesis About Gateway Cities," *Annals of the Association of American Geographers* 16 (June 1971).

23. Quote from William Rankin, "Choke Points in a Fragile Network" [map] (New York: Center for Urban Pedagogies. 2001). Edna Bonacich and Jake B. Wilson, *Getting the Goods: Ports, Labor, and the Logistics Revolution* (Ithaca: Cornell University Press, 2008); Carola Hein, ed., *Port Cities: Dynamic Landscapes and Global Networks* (London: Routledge, 2011).

24. Gabriel Thompson, "The Workers Who Bring You Black Friday," *The Nation,* December 16, 2013.

25. On the production of scale as a politicized site of resistance, see Neil Smith, "Contours of a Spatialized Politics: Homeless Vehicles and the Production of Geographic Scale," *Social Text* 33 (1992); Massey, *Space, Place and Gender;* Andrew Herod and Melissa W. Wright, *Geographies of Power: Placing Scale* (Oxford: Wiley-Blackwell, 2002); Laura Pulido, "Rethinking Environmental Racism: White Privilege and Urban Development in Southern California," *Annals of the Association of American Geographers* 90, no. 1 (2000).

26. Margaret D. Jacobs provides an extensive review of this literature in her recent call to twentieth-century U.S. historians to engage Indigenous histories: Margaret D. Jacobs, "Seeing Like a Settler Colonial State," *Modern American History* 1, no. 2 (2018). For select works drawn upon in this book, see Patrick Wolfe, "Settler Colonialism and the Elimination of the Native," *Journal of Genocide Research* 8, no. 4 (2006); Sherene Razack, ed., *Race, Space, and the Law: Unmapping a White Settler Society* (Toronto: Between the Lines, 2002); Penelope Edmonds, *Urbanizing Frontiers: Indigenous Peoples and Settlers in 19th-Century Pacific Rim*

Cities (Vancouver: University of British Columbia Press, 2010); Kelly Lytle Hernández, *City of Inmates: Conquest, Rebellion, and the Rise of Human Caging in Los Angeles, 1771–1965* (Chapel Hill: University of North Carolina Press, 2017). My approach to mapping is influenced by critical cartography, foremost, by Laura Pulido, Laura Barraclough, and Wendy Cheng, *A People's Guide to Los Angeles* (Berkeley: University of California Press, 2012).

27. On race and racial formation, see Michael Omi and Howard Winant, *Racial Formation in the United States: From the 1960s to the 1990,* 2nd ed. (New York: Routledge, 1994). On shifting categories of whiteness, see David Roediger, *The Wages of Whiteness: Race and the Making of the American Working Class* (London: Verso, 1991); Matthew Frye Jacobson, *Whiteness of a Different Color: European Immigrants and the Alchemy of Race* (Cambridge, MA: Harvard University Press, 1998); Linda Gordon, *The Great Arizona Orphan Abduction* (Cambridge, MA: Harvard University Press, 1999); on "nonwhite" as an analytical category, see Cheng, *The Changs Next Door to the Diazes.*

28. Kimberlé Crenshaw, "Mapping the Margins: Intersectionality, Identity Politics, and Violence against Women of Color," *Stanford Law Review* 43, no. 6 (1991).

29. This project adopts a relational racial analysis. In this work, I draw upon Chicana/o studies scholarship on relational racialization, including Luis Alvarez, "From Zoot Suits to Hip Hop: Towards a Relational Chicana/o Studies," *Latino Studies* 5, no. 1 (2007); Natalia Molina, "Examining Chicana/o History through a Relational Lens," *Pacific Historical Review* 82, no. 4 (2013); Gaye Theresa Johnson, *Spaces of Conflict, Sounds of Solidarity: Music, Race, and Spatial Entitlement in Los Angeles* (Berkeley: University of California Press, 2013); and Natalia Molina, *How Race Is Made in America: Immigration, Citizenship, and the Historical Power of Racial Scripts* (Berkeley: University of California Press, 2014). Another influential text is Tomás Almaguer, *Racial Fault Lines: The Historical Origins of White Supremacy in California* (Berkeley: University of California Press. 1994).

30. Quoted material from Melanie McAlister, *Epic Encounters: Culture, Media, and U.S. Interests in the Middle East, 1945–2000* (Berkeley: University of California Press, 2001), 4; Michael J. Shapiro, "Moral Geographies and the Ethics of Post-Sovereignty," *Public Culture* 6, no. 3 (1994). On "moral geographies of differentiated space," see George Lipsitz, *How Racism Takes Place* (Philadelphia: Temple University Press, 2011), 60.

31. For more on global trade and warehousing in the Inland Empire, with its local/global catalysts and ramifications, see De Lara, *Inland Shift.*

32. Henri Lefebvre, *The Production of Space,* trans. Donald Nicholson-Smith (Hoboken: Wiley-Blackwell, 1991).

33. Kay J. Anderson, *Vancouver's Chinatown: Racial Discourse in Canada, 1875–1980* (Montreal: McGill-Queen's University Press, 1995).

34. There is a broad literature on "place" as an analytic concept. For an introduction to these debates, see Tim Cresswell, *Place: An Introduction,* 2nd ed. (West Sussex, UK: John Wiley and Sons Ltd., 2015). For representative humanities texts addressing the spatial turn that influence this book see Lisbeth Haas, *Conquests and*

Historical Identities in California, 1769–1936 (Berkeley: University of California Press, 1995); José Saldívar, *Border Matters: Remapping American Cultural Studies* (Berkeley: University of California Press, 1997); Matt Garcia, *A World of Its Own: Race, Labor, and Citrus in the Making of Greater Los Angeles, 1900–1970* (Chapel Hill: University of North Carolina Press, 2001); David Delaney, "The Space that Race Makes," *Professional Geographer* 54, no. 1 (2002).

35. Mobility centers include the Center for Mobilities Research and Policy at Drexel University, Mobilities.lab at Lancaster University, and the European Cosmobilities Network. One hundred and fourteen papers mentioned "mobility" and "mobilities" in their titles for the 2018 American Association of Geographers's annual meeting in New Orleans. "Geographies of Mobility," published in *Annals of the American Association of Geographers,* March 2016.

36. This gap is noticeable in *Mobilities,* the leading mobility studies journal. See data visualization conducted by global historian Donna Gabaccia, "From Immigration Studies to Mobilities Studies," paper presented at the American Studies Association Annual Conference, 2015. Exceptions to this gap include book-length work on African American automobility: Cotten Seiler, *Republic of Drivers: A Cultural History of Automobility in America* (Chicago: University of Chicago Press. 2008); Jeremy Packer, *Mobility without Mayhem: Safety, Cars, and Citizenship* (Durham: Duke University Press, 2008). For other notable exceptions, see Derek H. Alderman and Joshua Inwood, "Mobility as Antiracism Work: The 'Hard Driving' of NASCAR's Wendell Scott," *Annals of the American Association of Geographers* 106, no. 3 (2016); Tim Cresswell, "Race, Mobility, and the Humanities: A Geospatial Approach," in *Envisioning Landscapes, Making Worlds: Geography and the Humanities,* ed. Stephen Daniels et al. (New York: Routledge, 2011).

37. Angela Pulley Hudson, *Creek Paths and Federal Roads: Indians, Settlers, and Slaves and the Making of the American South* (Chapel Hill: University of North Carolina Press, 2010); David Delaney, *Race, Place, and the Law, 1836–1948* (Austin: University of Texas Press, 1998): Nayan Shah, *Stranger Intimacies: Contesting Race, Sexuality, and the Law in the North American West* (Berkeley: University of California Press, 2012); Kelly Lytle Hernández, *Migra! A History of the U.S. Border Patrol* (Berkeley: University of California Press, 2010).

38. Rhacel Salazar Parrenas, *Servants of Globalization: Migration and Domestic Work,* 2nd ed. (Stanford: Stanford University Press, 2015); Pierrette Hondagneu-Sotelo, *Domestica: Immigrant Workers Cleaning and Caring in the Shadows of Affluence* (Berkeley: University of California Press, 2001); Donna Gabaccia, *Foreign Relations: American Immigration in Global Perspective* (Princeton: Princeton University Press, 2012); Leisy J. Abrego, *Sacrificing Families: Navigating Law, Labor, and Love Across Borders* (Stanford: Stanford University Press, 2014).

39. Of course, mobility studies have also drawn insight into places and processes quite distant from each other. See, for instance, Sheller, *Aluminum Dreams.*

40. George Lipsitz, *The Possessive Investment in Whiteness: How White People Benefit from Identity Politics,* revised and expanded (Philadelphia: Temple University Press, 2006), 3.

41. Omi and Winant, *Racial Formation in the United States*, 55.

42. Alvarez, "From Zoot Suits to Hip Hop"; Molina, "Examining Chicana/o History through a Relational Lens"; Johnson, *Spaces of Conflict, Sounds of Solidarity;* Molina, *How Race Is Made in America;* Almaguer, *Racial Fault Lines.*

43. For Trouillot, silences enter at four crucial moments: "the moment of fact creation (the making of *sources*); the moment of fact assembly (the making of *archives*); the moment of fact retrieval (the making of *narratives*); and the moment of retrospective significance (the making of *history* in the final instance)." Michel-Rolph Trouillot, *Silencing the Past: Power and the Production of History* (Boston: Beacon Press, 1995), 26.

44. I draw here on Blues epistemology, Black spatial imaginary, and the ethics of postsovereignty. Woods, *Development Arrested;* Lipsitz, *How Racism Takes Place;* Shapiro, "Moral Geographies and the Ethics of Post-Sovereignty."

45. Lytle Hernández, *City of Inmates.*

46. Antonio González Vasquez and Genevieve Carpio, *Mexican Americans in Redlands* (Charleston: Arcadia Press, 2012). The full collection is now held in Casa de Culturas in Joshua Tree, directed by the founder of Inland Mexican Heritage, Antonio González Vasquez.

47. On maps as texts open to deconstruction and close reading, see John B. Harley, "Deconstructing the Map," *Cartographica* 26, no. 2 (Spring 1989); on regions, mapping, and countermapping, see Joe Painter, "Cartographic Anxiety and the Search for Regionality," *Environment and Planning A,* 40 (2008); for a list of mapping resources and projects, see Genevieve Carpio and Andrzej Rutkowski, "Mapping LA-tinx Suburbs," *Boom California* (July 2017).

48. On selective tradition, see Raymond Williams, *Marxism and Literature* (New York: Oxford University Press, 1977).

49. On racial scripts see Molina, *How Race Is Made in America.*

CHAPTER ONE. THE RISE OF THE ANGLO FANTASY PAST

1. California Promotion Committee, *California Addresses by President Roosevelt* (San Francisco: Tomoyé Press, 1903), 17.

2. Quoted material from "Picture Showing Ex-President Roosevelt Planting Famous Navel Orange Tree in Court of Mission Inn," *Riverside Daily Press,* January 6, 1919, 7; "Good Bye and Good Luck Was the Farewell Greeting," *Riverside Daily Press,* May 8, 1903; "President Roosevelt Replanting Original Navel Trees," *Citrograph* (Redlands), May 23, 1903. Original copies of the *Citrograph,* also titled *The California Citrograph,* are available in the Riverside Public Library's noncirculating collection.

3. On selective tradition, see cultural-materialist Raymond Williams, *Marxism and Literature* (New York: Oxford University Press, 1977), 115; on memory and its role in shaping social identity, see Jill Lepore, *The Name of War: King Phillip's War and the Origins of American Identity* (New York: Vintage Books, 1998); on local

narratives in their settler colonial context, see Jean M. O'Brien, *Firsting and Lasting: Writing Indians Out of Existence in New England* (Minneapolis: University of Minnesota Press, 2010); on the shaping effects of memory on race in its California context, see Phoebe S. Kropp, *California Vieja: Cultural Memory in a Modern American Place* (Berkeley: University of California Press, 2006).

4. My understanding of everyday life is rooted in Henri Lefebvre, *Critique of Everyday Life,* trans. John Moore (London: Verso, 1991); Kanishka Goonewardena et al., eds., *Space, Difference, Everyday Life: Reading Henri Lefebvre* (New York: Routledge, 2008). Also influential for his writings on everyday materiality and walking has been Michel de Certeau, *The Practice of Everyday Life,* trans. Steven Rendall (Berkeley: University of California Press, 1984).

5. Margaret D. Jacobs provides an extensive review of this literature in her recent call to historians of the United States to engage Indigenous histories, "Seeing Like a Settler Colonial State," *Modern American History* 1, no. 2 (2018). For select works drawn upon in this book, see Patrick Wolfe, "Settler Colonialism and the Elimination of the Native," *Journal of Genocide Research* 8, no. 4 (2006); Sherene Razack, ed., *Race, Space, and the Law: Unmapping a White Settler Society* (Toronto: Between the Lines, 2002); Penelope Edmonds, *Urbanizing Frontiers: Indigenous Peoples and Settlers in 19th-Century Pacific Rim Cities* (Vancouver: University of British Columbia Press, 2010); Kelly Lytle Hernández, *City of Inmates: Conquest, Rebellion, and the Rise of Human Caging in Los Angeles, 1771–1965* (Chapel Hill: University of North Carolina Press, 2017).

6. Estimates vary as to when Indigenous Californians first settled in the region, but sources agree members of the Uto-Aztecan or Shoshonean language family comprised a linguistically diverse, dispersed, and dense population by the time of Spanish arrival in the sixteenth century. See Malcom Margolin, ed., *The Way We Lived: California Indian Stories, Songs, Reminiscences* (Berkeley: Heyday Books, 1993); Thomas C. Patterson, *From Acorns to Warehouses: Historical Political Economy of Southern California's Inland Empire* (Walnut Creek: Left Coast Press, 2015).

7. For detailed local histories of Riverside and San Bernardino Counties, see John Brown and James Boyd, *History of San Bernardino and Riverside Counties with Selected Biography of Actors and Witnesses of the Period of Growth and Achievement* (Chicago: The Lewis Publishing Company, 1922); Tom Patterson, *A Colony for California: Riverside's First Hundred Years* (Riverside: Press-Enterprise Co., 1971); Joyce Vickery, *Defending Eden: New Mexican Pioneers in Southern California, 1830–1890* (Riverside: Riverside Museum Press, 1977); Patterson, *From Acorns to Warehouses.*

8. Tomás Almaguer, *Racial Fault Lines: The Historical Origins of White Supremacy in California* (Berkeley: University of California Press, 1994); Reginald Horsman, *Race and Manifest Destiny: The Origins of American Racial Anglo Saxonism* (Cambridge, MA: Harvard University Press, 1981).

9. On regional formation, see Anssi Paasi, "Bounded Spaces in the Mobile World: Deconstructing 'Regional Identity,'" *Tijdschrift Voor Economische En Sociale Geografie* 93, no. 2 (2002): 137–148.

10. "A Colony for California," Knoxville, TN, March 17, 1870; reproduced in Brown and Boyd, *History of San Bernardino and Riverside Counties*, 25. For a biography of John North and his efforts at building model colonies, see Merlin Stonehouse, *John Wesley North and the Reform Frontier* (Minneapolis: University of Minnesota Press, 1965).

11. Ibid.

12. On the expansion of the United States in the nineteenth century, particularly discourses of Manifest Destiny and its gendered dimensions, see Amy Greenberg, *Manifest Manhood and the Antebellum American Empire* (New York: Cambridge University Press, 2005).

13. Original leaflet reprinted in Patterson, *A Colony for California*, 20; Brown and Boyd, *History of San Bernardino and Riverside Counties*.

14. Stonehouse, *John Wesley North and the Reform Frontier;* Kent G. Lightfoot, *Indians, Missionaries, and Merchants: The Legacy of Colonial Encounters on the California Frontiers* (Berkeley: University of California Press, 2006), 63–66; Albert Hurtado, *Intimate Encounters: Sex, Gender, and Culture in Old California* (Albuquerque: University of New Mexico Press, 1999); Lisbeth Haas, *Saints and Citizens: Indigenous Histories of Colonial Missions and Mexican California* (Berkeley: University of California Press, 2014); for a dynamic, crowd-sourced mapping project recognizing the traditional territories of Indigenous nations, see *Native Land,* accessed October 14, 2018, https://native-land.ca/about/

15. Quoted material from Section 1 of Cal. Stat. 175 in *Statutes of California* (1855). See also "Act for the Government and Protection of Indians" (April 22, 1850).

16. This is not to elide the drastic population drop at the end of the nineteenth century. Scholars estimate a Native Californian population of 30,000 by 1870, an 80 percent decrease following the Mexican American War. Brendan Lindsay, *Murder State: California's Native American Genocide, 1846–1873* (Lincoln: University of Nebraska Press, 2012), 336.

17. Haas, *Saints and Citizens;* Steven W. Hackel, *Children of Coyote, Missionaries of Saint Francis: Indian-Spanish Relations in Colonial California, 1769–1850* (Chapel Hill: University of North Carolina Press, 2005); Miroslava Chávez-García, *Negotiating Conquest: Gender and Power in California, 1770s to 1880s* (Tucson: University of Arizona Press, 2004).

18. George Harwood Phillips, *Chiefs and Challengers: Indian Resistance and Cooperation in Southern California* (Berkeley: University of California Press, 1975), 81–84.

19. Ned Blackhawk, *Violence Over the Land: Indians and Empires in the Early American West* (Cambridge, MA: Harvard University Press, 2006); Aileen Moreton-Robinson, *The White Possessive: Property, Power, and Indigenous Sovereignty* (Minneapolis: University of Minnesota Press, 2015).

20. Stonehouse, *John Wesley North and the Reform Frontier,* 226.

21. Vickery, *Defending Eden,* 15.

22. Angela Pulley Hudson, *Creek Paths and Federal Roads: Indians, Settlers, and Slaves and the Making of the American South* (Chapel Hill: University of North

Carolina Press, 2010), 163–166. I employ Lisbeth Haas's definition of conquest as "the process that extends the political, economic, and social dominion of one empire, nation, or society over another one." Lisbeth Haas, *Conquests and Historical Identities in California, 1769–1936* (Berkeley: University of California Press, 1995), 2.

23. On Hispano culture and identity, see John M. Nieto-Phillips, *The Language of Blood: The Making of Spanish-American Identity in New Mexico, 1880s-1930s* (Albuquerque: University of New Mexico Press, 2004); Ramón Gutiérrez, *When Jesus Came, the Corn Mothers Went Away* (Stanford: Stanford University Press, 1991); Laura E. Gómez, *Manifest Destinies: The Making of the Mexican American Race* (New York: New York University Press, 2008).

24. R. Bruce Harley, "Abiquiu, New Mexico: Ancestral Home of the Agua Mansa Pioneers," *San Bernardino County Museum Association* 39 (Winter 1991). For more on Abiquiú, a Southwestern gateway of trade in its own right, see Haas, *Saints and Citizens.*

25. The most comprehensive explorations of the Agua Mansa community are by Dr. R. Bruce Harley, archivist of the San Bernardino Catholic Diocese. Among his works are *The Story of Agua Mansa: Its Settlement, Churches, and People; First Community in San Bernardino Valley 1842–1893* (San Bernardino: Diocese of San Bernardino, 1995), in Rare Book F868.S14H341998, University of Southern California Special Collections; "An Early Riverside Suburb at La Placita," *Journal of the Riverside Historical Society,* 7 (2003), in History Collection, San Bernardino County Museum; and "Abiquiu, New Mexico: Ancestral Home of the Agua Mansa Pioneers." Relevant works by other scholars include Tom Patterson, "Life and Death of a Unique Settlement," *Riverside Press-Enterprise,* October 11, 1998; Harold Whelan, "Eden in Jurupa Valley: The Story of Agua Mansa," *Southern California Quarterly* 55, no. 4 (1973): 413–429; see also Vickery, *Defending Eden.*

26. On these raids, see Vickery, *Defending Eden,* especially chapter 4. For more on Mormon settlement in San Bernardino, see Joseph Snow Wood, "The Mormon Settlement in San Bernardino" (PhD diss., University of Utah, 1968), 92–128.

27. On how this dispossession played out in California, see Chávez-García, *Negotiating Conquest;* Leonard Pitt, *Decline of the Californios: A Social History of the Spanish-Speaking Californians, 1846–1890* (Berkeley: University of California Press, 1999); Haas, *Conquests and Historical Identities in California.*

28. For examples of how dispossession occurred in other southwestern regions, see María Montoya, *Translating Property: The Maxwell Land Grant and the Conflict over Land in the American West, 1840–1900* (Berkeley: University of California Press, 2002); Andrés Reséndez, *Changing National Identities at the Frontier: Texas and New Mexico, 1800–1850* (New York: Cambridge University Press, 2004); David Montejano, *Anglos and Mexicans in the Making of Texas, 1836–1986* (Austin: University of Texas Press, 1987).

29. Almaguer, *Racial Fault Lines;* Patterson, *A Colony for California,* 113–118 and 369–370.

30. Quoted material from Moreton-Robinson, *The White Possessive,* xii.

31. As one important example, Maria Montoya expands the story of U.S. imperialism to before 1898 through the history of land loss in the American West. Montoya, *Translating Property*.

32. See John B. Harley, "Deconstructing the Map," *Cartographica* 26, no. 2 (Spring 1989).

33. Quoted materials from Brown and Boyd, *History of San Bernardino and Riverside Counties*, 378; Stonehouse, *John Wesley North and the Reform Frontier*, 211–232; Patterson, *A Colony for California*.

34. For a helpful compilation of key texts on the representational power of maps, see Martin Dodge, Rob Kitchin, Chris Perkins, eds., *The Map Reader: Theories of Mapping Practice and Cartographic Representation* (West Sussex: Wiley-Blackwell, 2011). On alternative forms of mapping Indigenous Southern California today, see Maylei Blackwell, Mishuana Goeman, and Wendy Teeter, "Mapping Indigenous Los Angeles," UCLA, accessed September 21, 2017, https://mila.ss.ucla.edu.

35. On moral geographies, see Michael J. Shapiro, "Moral Geographies and the Ethics of Post-Sovereignty," *Public Culture* 6, no. 3 (1994); George Lipsitz, *How Racism Takes Place* (Philadelphia: Temple University Press, 2011), 60.

36. Joan Hall, "Riverside's Historical Societies Centennial," *Journal of the Riverside Historical Society* 7 (February 2003); Brown and Boyd, *History of San Bernardino and Riverside Counties*.

37. Non-English terms appear without italics to reflect the fluidity of people and languages from the Américas and to emphasize their equal status among each other. See Alicia Schmidt Camacho, *Migrant Imaginaries: Latino Cultural Politics in the U.S.-Mexico Borderlands* (New York: New York University Press, 2008).

38. "Selected Orange and Lemon Buds," *California Citrograph*, December 1924, 60; Archibald Shamel, Charles Pomeroy, and R. E. Caryl, "Bud Selection in the Washington Navel Orange," *California Citrograph*, 1929, p. 198; *The Gardeners' Chronicle: A Weekly Illustrated Journal of Horticulture and Allied Subjects* (London: Bradbury, Agnew, and Co., 1906), 423; Letter from E. S. Hubbard to C. S. Pomeroy, August 1, 1924, box 6, Tomás Rivera Library, University of California Riverside; Letter from Pomologist to Mr. Has A. Harris, August 4, 1924, box 6, Tomás Rivera Library, University of California Riverside.

39. For a sample of publications relating the navel origin story, see "A Produção De Laranjas Sem Sementes" (The Production of Oranges Without Seeds), *Bulletin of the Pan American Union* (Washington, DC, January–June 28, 1900); Archibald Shamel, "Semi Centennial of the Washington Navel Orange in California," *Citrograph* 9, no. 2 (December 1913), box 6, folder 6, Archibald Shamel Papers, Tomás Rivera Library, University of California Riverside; Riverside Chamber of Commerce, "Riverside: The Birthplace of the Navel Orange," ephemera, 1926, box 6, folder 6, Tomás Rivera Library, University of California Riverside; Archibald Shamel and C. S. Pomeroy, *The Washington Navel Orange* (Riverside: Riverside Chamber of Commerce, 1933), box 2, folder 2, Riverside Chamber of Commerce Collection, Riverside Public Library; Anonymous, "Riverside-Home of the Navel," *California Citrograph* (1943), box 6, folder 3, Archibald Shamel Papers, Tomás

Rivera Library, University of California Riverside; Esther H. Klotz, "Eliza Tibbets and her Washington Navel Orange Trees," in *A History of Citrus in the Riverside Area,* ed. Esther H. Klotz, Harry W. Lawton, and Joan H. Hall (Riverside: Riverside Museum Press, 1989). On the Tibbets, see Patricia Ortlieb and Peter Economy, *Creating an Orange Utopia: Eliza Lovell Tibbets and the Birth of California's Citrus Industry* (West Chester, PA: Swedenborg Foundation, 2011).

40. Hall, "Riverside's Historical Societies Centennial," 8.

41. Ron Goff, "Reprint of a 1903 Newspaper Story: 'New Society of Historians,'" *Journal of the Riverside Historical Society* 7 (February 2003), 10; for select member biographies, see Elmer Wallace Holmes, *History of Riverside County, California: With Biographical Sketches of Men and Women of the County Who Have Been Identified with Its Growth and Development from the Early Days to the Present* (Riverside: Historic Record Company, 1912).

42. The Riverside Historical Society adopted the constitution and bylaws from Historical Society of Southern California, "Constitution, Adopted September 4, 1897," *Publications* 4 (Los Angeles:Los Angeles County Pioneers of Southern California, 1898), 92.

43. In areas of the Southwest where the Hispano elite maintained economic and political power, they remained active in commemorations of public history; Nieto-Phillips, *The Language of Blood.* On the relationship between public history and lines of difference, see Kropp, *California Vieja,* esp. 47–102; Richard R. Flores, *Remembering the Alamo: Memory, Modernity, and the Master Symbol* (Austin: University of Texas Press, 2002), esp. 61–92.

44. For detailed histories of the Sherman Institute, see Clifford Trafzer, Jean Keller, and Lorene Sisquoc, eds., *Boarding School Blues: Revisiting American Indian Educational Experiences* (Lincoln: University of Nebraska Press, 2006); Clifford Trafzer, Matthew Sakiestewa Gilbert, and Lorene Sisquoc, eds., *The Indian School on Magnolia Avenue: Voices and Images from Sherman Institute* (Corvallis: Oregon State University Press, 2012).

45. Quoted material from A.C. Tonner, "Address," 1903, Binder 1, Sherman Indian Museum Collection; see also "Big Day Coming for Riverside," *Los Angeles Herald,* July 8, 1901.

46. S.L. Welsh, *Southern California Illustrated: Containing an Epitome of the Growth and Industry of the Three Southern Counties* (Los Angeles: Warner Brothers, 1887), 8, Rare Book 248657, Huntington Library.

47. O'Brien, *Firsting and Lasting.*

48. On settler colonialism and its "logic of elimination," see Wolfe, "Settler Colonialism and the Elimination of the Native"; Margaret D. Jacobs, *White Mother to a Dark Race: Settler Colonialism, Maternalism, and the Removal of Indigenous Children in the American West and Australia, 1880–1940* (Lincoln: University of Nebraska, 2009). On colonialism and Indigenous erasure, see Bonita Lawrence, "Rewriting Histories of the Land: Colonization and Indigenous Resistance in Eastern Canada," in Razack, *Race, Space, and Law.*

49. U.S. Department of the Interior, "Pupils Register, 1911–1912," Riverside, CA, Student Registration Records 1892–1970s, Sherman Indian Museum, Riverside; U.S. Department of the Interior, "Pupils Register: 1912–1913," Riverside, CA, Student Registration Records 1892–1970s, Sherman Indian Museum, Riverside.

50. For more on the criminalization of youth of color and a history of juvenile facilities in California, including Preston, see Miroslava Chávez-García, *States of Delinquency: Race and Science in the Making of California's Juvenile Justice System* (Berkeley: University of California Press, 2012); on the ways incarceration reproduces settler society, see Lytle Hernández, *City of Inmates.*

51. See "Sherman Institute Cemetery," in Binder 1, Sherman Indian Museum, Riverside; on "empty land" and terra nullius in its settler colonial contexts, see Razack, *Race, Space, and the Law.* On Sherman students' mobility and agency, see Kevin Whalen, "Beyond School Walls: Indigenous Mobility at Sherman Institute," *Western Historical Quarterly* 49, no. 3 (2018).

52. Quoted material from Brown and Boyd, *History of San Bernardino and Riverside Counties,* 376.

53. R. Bruce Harley, "Reminiscences of David Santiago Garcia as Told to Helen Loehr, with Notes and Comments by R. Bruce Harley," *San Bernardino County Museum Association Quarterly* 40 (Fall 1993); on the history of charrería in the U.S. Southwest, see Laura R. Barraclough, *Charros: How Mexican Cowboys Are Remapping Race and American Identity* (Oakland: University of California Press, forthcoming).

54. Bishop Peter Verdaguer, "Reminiscences of 'Father Peter,'" in *Ingersoll's Century Annals of San Bernardino County, 1769–1904,* ed. Luther Ingersoll (Los Angeles: L.A. Ingersoll, 1904).

55. Quoted material from Verdaguer, "Reminiscences of 'Father Peter,'" 355; Harley, *The Story of Agua Mansa;* "General Items," *Harvard Daily Echo* 5, no. 62 (December 12, 1881).

56. R. Bruce Harley, "From New Mexico to California: San Bernardino Valley's First Settlers at Agua Mansa," *San Bernardino County Museum Association Quarterly* 47, nos. 3 and 4 (2000), History Collection, San Bernardino County Museum, San Bernardino, CA; R. Bruce Harley, ed., "The Agua Mansa History Trail," *San Bernardino County Museum Association Quarterly* 43 (Summer 1996), History Collection, San Bernardino County Museum, San Bernardino, CA.

57. Harley, *The Story of Agua Mansa;* Harley, "From New Mexico to California"; Harley, "The Agua Mansa History Trail."

58. On Hispanophilia and the Spanish Fantasy Past at this time, see William Deverell, *Whitewashed Adobe: The Rise of Los Angeles and the Remaking of Its Mexican Past* (Berkeley: University of California Press, 2004); Kropp, *California Vieja.*

59. In doing so, Hayden borrows from historians Jack Tchen and Michael Wallace. Dolores Hayden, *The Power of Place: Urban Landscapes as Public History* (Cambridge, MA: MIT Press, 1997), 46.

60. See William Andrew Spalding, *The Orange: Its Culture in California, With a Brief Discussion of the Lemon, Lime, and Other Citrus Fruits* (Riverside Press and

Horticulturist Steam Print, 1885); Iris Wilson Engstrand, *William Wolfskill, 1798–1866: Frontier Trapper to California Ranchero* (Glendale: A. H. Clark, 1965).

61. See Carey McWilliams, *Southern California: An Island on the Land,* 9th ed. (1946; Salt Lake City: Gibbs Smith, 1980).

62. Cedric J. Robinson, *Black Marxism: The Making of the Black Radical Tradition,* 2nd ed. (1983; Chapel Hill: University of North Carolina Press, 2000).

63. See "A Produção De Laranjas Sem Sementes"; Shamel, "Semi Centennial of the Washington Navel Orange in California"; Riverside Chamber of Commerce, "Riverside: The Birthplace of the Navel Orange"; Shamel and Pomeroy, *The Washington Navel Orange;* Anonymous, "Riverside—Home of the Navel,"; Klotz, "Eliza Tibbets and her Washington Navel Orange Trees."

64. *Practical Common Sense Guide Book Through the World's Industrial and Cotton Centennial Exposition at New Orleans* (Harrisburg, PA: L.S. Hart, 1885); Shamel and Pomeroy, *The Washington Navel Orange;* Catherine Merlo, *Heritage of Gold: The First 100 Years of Sunkist Growers, Inc., 1893–1993* (Van Nuys: Sunkist Growers Inc., 1994).

65. Douglas Cazaux Sackman, *Orange Empire: California and the Fruits of Eden* (Berkeley: University of California Press, 2005); George Harold Powell, *Letters from the Orange Empire,* ed. Richard Gordon Lillard and Lawrence Clark Powell (Los Angeles: Historical Society of Southern California, 2001).

66. W.W. Robinson, *The Story of San Bernardino County* (San Bernardino: Pioneer Title Insurance Company, 1958); Merlo, *Heritage of Gold.*

67. Neil Smith, *Uneven Development: Nature, Capital, and the Production of Space,* 3rd ed. (Athens: University of Georgia Press, 2008), 86; William Cronon, *Nature's Metropolis: Chicago and the Great West* (New York: W. W. Norton, 1991); Richard White, *The Organic Machine: The Remaking of the Columbia River* (New York: Hill and Wang, 1996); Sackman, *Orange Empire.*

68. Based on author's analysis of the Pomona Citrus Label Collection, Pomona Public Library, http://content.ci.pomona.ca.us/databases.php. Labels with duplicates were counted once.

69. Sackman, *Orange Empire,* 19.

70. See Clyde Woods, *Development Arrested: The Blues and Plantation Power in the Mississippi Delta* (London: Verso Press, 1998), esp. chapter 5; Chris Wilson, *The Myth of Santa Fe: Creating a Modern Regional Tradition* (Albuquerque: University of New Mexico Press, 1997); Flores, *Remembering the Alamo.*

71. Alfred Henry Lewis, ed., *A Compilation of the Messages and Speeches of Theodore Roosevelt, 1901–1905* (New York: Bureau of National Literature and Art, 1906).

72. By the 1920s, the tree was protected by an iron gate, adorned with a bronze plaque, and had become a popular tourist site. It was among the first to receive highway designation by the State Historical Society and it continues to bloom at the corner of Arlington and Magnolia. Photographic record of the replanting in box 6, folder 6, Archibald Shamel Papers, Tomás Rivera Library, University of California Riverside.

73. Barbara Moore, ed., *Historic Mission Inn, Riverside, California* (Riverside: Friends of the Mission Inn, 1998); James Rawls, "The California Mission as Symbol and Myth," *California Historical Society* 71, no. 3 (Fall 1992).

74. Kropp, *California Vieja;* Rawls, "The California Mission as Symbol and Myth"; Phoebe S. Kropp, "Citizens of the Past? Olvera Street and the Construction of Race and Memory in 1930s Los Angeles," *Radical History Review* 81 (Fall 2001): 35–60; McWilliams, *Southern California.*

75. Riverside Land and Irrigating Company, *Southern California: Riverside Land and Irrigating Company of San Bernardino, California* (San Francisco: Frank Eastman, 1877), 19, Rare Book 267134, Huntington Library.

76. See Laura Brace, *The Politics of Property: Labour, Freedom, and Belonging* (Hampshire: Edinburgh University Press, 2004); Laura R. Barraclough, *Making the San Fernando Valley: Rural Landscapes, Urban Development, and White Privilege* (Athens: University of Georgia Press, 2011); Razack, *Race, Space, and the Law.*

77. General Services Administration, San Bernardino County, Federal Decennial Census, 1880, RG 029 Records of the Bureau of the Census, National Archives at Riverside.

78. Vincent Moses and Celena Turney, eds., *Our Families Our Stories: From the African American Community Riverside, California 1870–1960* (Riverside: Riverside Museum Press, 1997); Ortlieb and Economy, *Creating an Orange Utopia,* 25–40.

79. Harry Lawton, "Riverside's First Chinatown and the Boom of the Eighties," in *Wong Ho Leun: An American Chinatown,* ed. The Great Basin Foundation, vol. 1, 1–52 (San Diego: The Great Basin Foundation, 1987); Esther H. Klotz, "Griffin and Skelley, Packers and Shippers," in *A History of Citrus in the Riverside Area,* ed. Esther Klotz, Harry W. Lawton, and Joan H. Hall (Riverside: Riverside Museum Press, 1969). Deborah Wong has curated an important website, *Asian American Riverside,* compiled in part by undergraduates at the University of California Riverside. See *Asian American Riverside,* University of California Riverside, last modified 2006, last accessed July 9, 2018, http://www.asianamericanriverside.ucr.edu.

80. Riverside Land and Irrigating Company, *Southern California,* 14.

81. Based on author's analysis of *City Directory,* City of Riverside, 1898, and *City Directory,* City of Riverside, 1905, both in Local History Collection, Riverside Public Library.

82. Analysis of Sanborn Insurance maps from 1885 to 1920, Sanborn Map Collection, Riverside Metropolitan Museum, Riverside, CA.

83. Lawton, "Riverside's First Chinatown"; Wong, *Asian American Riverside;* Michael Moreau, "Drive May Pave Way for Dig at Ruins of Old Riverside Chinatown," *Los Angeles Times,* August 4, 1984.

84. George Anthony Peffer, *If They Don't Bring Their Women Here: Chinese Female Immigration before Exclusion* (Urbana: University of Illinois Press, 1999); George Anthony Peffer, "Forbidden Families: Emigration Experiences of Chinese Women under the Page Law, 1875–1882," *Journal of American Ethnic History* 6 (Fall 1986).

85. On "citriscape," see Matt Garcia, *A World of Its Own: Race, Labor, and Citrus in the Making of Greater Los Angeles, 1900–1970* (Chapel Hill: University of North Carolina Press, 2001).

86. Avenue Brand, lithograph, San Francisco: Schmidt Litho Co., n.d., Citrus Label Collection, Pomona Public Library, Pomona, CA. On Victoria Avenue and other citriscape landmarks, see Brown and Boyd, *History of San Bernardino and Riverside Counties,* 1922; and Riverside Planning Department, *Landmarks of the City of Riverside* (Riverside: City of Riverside, 2002).

87. For an analysis in residential spaces, see Anthea Hartig, "'In a World He Has Created': Class Collectivity and the Growers' Landscape in the Southern California Citrus Industry, 1890–1940," *California History* 74 (Spring 1995). On the suburban ideal in Southern California's agricultural colonies, see Paul Sandul, *California Dreaming: Boosterism, Memory, and Rural Suburbs in the Golden State* (Morgantown: West Virginia University Press, 2014). For more on high-modernist agriculture, see James C. Scott, *Seeing Like a State: How Certain Schemes to Improve the Human Condition Have Failed* (New Haven: Yale University Press, 1998).

88. Shamel and Pomeroy, *The Washington Navel Orange,* 31–32.

89. For a discussion of California's produced "landscape" and its contests by migrant farmworkers, see Don Mitchell, *The Lie of the Land: Migrant Workers and the California Landscape* (Minneapolis: University of Minnesota Press, 1996); on gardens, migration, and labor in California, see Pierrette Hondagneu-Sotelo, *Paradise Transplanted: Migration and the Making of California Gardens* (Berkeley: University of California Press, 2014).

90. Kay J. Anderson, "The Idea of Chinatown: The Power of Place and Institutional Practice in the Making of a Racial Category," *Annals of the Association of American Geographers* 77, no. 4 (1987): 580–598. On Chinatown ordinances, see R. S. Malloch, "When Asked to Put It on Paper . . ." in *Inlandia: A Literary Journey Through California's Inland Empire,* ed. Gayle Wattawa (Santa Clara: Santa Clara University, 2006), 72. As a precursor, by 1873 the City of San Francisco had passed policies requiring high fees from Chinese launderers. See Charles J. McClain, *In Search of Equality: The Chinese Struggle against Discrimination in Nineteenth-Century America* (Berkeley: University of California Press, 1994), chapter 2. In a later example, public health officers condemned Chinese proprietors in an attempt to characterize Los Angeles's Chinatown as a "rotten spot." Natalia Molina, *Fit to Be Citizens?: Public Health and Race in Los Angeles, 1879–1939* (Berkeley: University of California Press, 2006). On the *Riverside Daily Press* newspaper, see Brown and Boyd, *History of San Bernardino and Riverside Counties,* 605; and Patterson, *A Colony for California,* 194–195.

91. "Chinese" appeared as a racial marker on individual residences on the 1884 and 1885 Sanborn maps. Sanborn Map Collection, Riverside Metropolitan Museum, Riverside, CA.

92. The first Sanborn map surveying Chinatown is dated February 1895. It places the majority of Chinese merchants in the new Chinatown at the intersection of Brockton and Tequisquite Avenues. A review of city directories for 1895 lacks any

Chinese surname residences in downtown Riverside at this time. Reviewing directories in later years confirms that Chinese merchants concentrated in Chinatown with few exceptions. See city directories, City of Riverside, 1898 and 1905, Local History Collection, Riverside Public Library. The Save Our Chinatown Committee has developed a compelling public history site on Chinese American heritage and Riverside's Chinatown at http://www.saveourchinatown.org.

93. Paul Wormser, "Chinese Agricultural Labor in the Citrus Belt of Inland Southern California," in *Wong Ho Leun: An American Chinatown,* ed. The Great Basin Foundation, vol. 1, 173.

94. Cecilia Tsu underscores the tension between the claims by white orchard farmers in the Santa Clara Valley, who promoted a life free of Chinese labor in booster materials, and Chinese farmers, who carved out a central place as labor, merchants, and specialists within the industry. Cecilia M. Tsu, *Garden of the World: Asian Immigrants and the Making of Agriculture in California's Santa Clara Valley* (New York: Oxford University Press, 2013). For more on the anti-Chinese movement in the San Bernardino Valley, see Harry Lawton, "Denis Kearney among the Orange Groves: The Beginnings of the Anti-Chinese Movement in the Citrus Belt (1876–1880)," in *Wong Ho Leun: An American Chinatown,* ed. The Great Basin Foundation, vol. 1, 193–203.

95. For instance, Molina describes the collective efforts of public health professionals to regulate the flow of Mexican laborers through quarantine zones. See Molina, *Fit to Be Citizens?;* see also border agents' efforts to regulate immigrant labor in border communities, as described in Kelly Lytle Hernández, *Migra! A History of the U.S. Border Patrol* (Berkeley: University of California Press, 2010).

96. In 1882, the Chinese Exclusion Act suspended the immigration of Chinese laborers for ten years, prohibited naturalization (an extension of the Naturalization Act of 1790), and required exempted classes such as teachers, students, merchants, and casual travelers to present a certificate from the Chinese government upon arriving in the United States. It also required that Chinese nationals already legally in the United States obtain a certificate of reentry in order to return to the United States upon the conclusion of international travel. See "An Act to Execute Certain Treaty Stipulations Relating to the Chinese," May 6, 1882, Enrolled Acts and Resolutions of Congress, 1789–1996; RG 11 General Records of the United States Government, National Archives at Riverside; on the Page Act, see note 84.

97. Act to Prohibit the Coming of Chinese Persons into the United States, 27 Stat. 25 (May 1892); "Enforcement of the Geary Law: Letter from the Acting Secretary of the Treasury" (Washington, DC: Government Printing Office, September 27, 1893); quoted material from McClain, *In Search of Equality,* 203.

98. Erika Lee's use of "shadows of exclusion" describes the extension of the 1882 Chinese Exclusion Act to "not only legal and illegal Chinese immigrants but also to native-born Chinese American citizens, whose plight was inextricably connected to that of their immigrant brethren." See Erika Lee, *At America's Gates: Chinese Immigration During the Exclusion Era, 1882–1943* (Chapel Hill: University of North Carolina Press, 2003), 223.

99. Mae M. Ngai, *Impossible Subjects: Illegal Aliens and the Making of Modern America* (Princeton: Princeton University Press, 2004).

100. Act to Prohibit the Coming of Chinese Persons into the United States, 27 Stat. 25 (May 1892); "Resolution Introduced by Senator Henry Clay in Relation to the Adjustment of All Existing Questions of Controversy Between the States Arising Out of the Institution of Slavery," 29 January 1850, Senate Simple Resolutions, Motions, and Orders of the 31st Congress, ca. 03/1849-ca. 03/1851, RG 46 Records of the United States Senate, 1789–1990, National Archives at Riverside; Sally E. Hadden, *Slave Patrols: Law and Violence in Virginia and the Carolinas* (Cambridge, MA: Harvard University Press, 2001); David Delaney, *Race, Place, and the Law, 1836–1948* (Austin: University of Texas Press, 1998).

101. Opinion of Justice Antonin Scalia, Supreme Court of the United States, No. 11–182, Arizona, et al., *Petitioners v. United States,* On Writ of Certiorari to the United States Court of Appeals for the Ninth Circuit, June 25, 2012, p. 4.

102. Opinion of Justice Antonin Scalia, 2012; Arizona Senate, Senate Bill 1070, 49th legislature, 2nd sess. (2010).

103. On relational racialization and racial scripts, see Natalia Molina, *How Race Is Made in America: Immigration, Citizenship, and the Historical Power of Racial Scripts* (Berkeley: University of California Press, 2014).

104. Hadden, *Slave Patrols;* Delaney, *Race, Place, and the Law, 1836–1948.*

105. See Waverly B. Lowell, ed., "Chinese Immigration and Chinese in the United States," Reference Information Paper 99, Records in the Regional Archives of the National Archives and Records Administration, 1996; Anna Pegler-Gordon, *In Sight of America: Photography and the Development of U.S. Immigration Policy* (Berkeley: University of California Press, 2009), 30–33; *Lew Moy et al. v. United States* (237 Fed. 50).

106. "Daring Officer Called Beyond," *Los Angeles Times,* November 22, 1904, p. 6.

107. "Appointed Chinese Inspector," *San Francisco Call* 76, no. 80, August 1898 p. 19; "Many Attend Funeral," *Los Angeles Herald* 32, no. 53, November 23, 1904; John McGroarty, *Los Angeles from the Mountain to the Seas* (Chicago and New York: American Historical Society, 1921), 365–366.

108. "Goes to El Paso: Chinese Inspector Putnam Transferred to Los Angeles," *Los Angeles Times,* June 16, 1899, p. 7.

109. Lee, *At America's Gates,*193–198; Lytle Hernández, *Migra!;* Robert Chao Romero, *The Chinese in Mexico, 1882–1940* (Tucson: University of Arizona Press, 2010).

110. "Evidence of Sam Gong" in Statement of He Tie, 3 August 1896, box 2, folder 77; "Evidence of Hom Oie" in Statement of Wong Hong, August 19, 1897, box 6, folder 242; "Evidence of Lee Quong," in Statement of Mee Kee, December 21, 1896, box 4, folder 170—all in RG 85 Records of the Immigration and Naturalization Service, Los Angeles District Office, Segregated Chinese Case Files, 1893–1935, National Archives at Riverside.

111. For more on Chinese agricultural endeavors in California during this period, see Sucheng Chan, *The Bittersweet Soil: The Chinese in California Agricul-*

ture, 1860–1910 (Berkeley: University of California Press, 1989). For an itemized cost of managing a ten-acre orange crop, see S. L. Welsh, *Southern California Illustrated: Containing an Epitome of the Growth and Industry of the Three Southern Counties* (Los Angeles: Warner Brothers, 1887), Rare Book 248657, Huntington Library.

112. Based on review of RG 85 Records of the Immigration and Naturalization Service, Los Angeles District Office, Segregated Chinese Case Files, 1893–1935, National Archives at Riverside; for one example, see "Evidence of Sam Gong," in Statement of He Tie, August 3, 1896, box 2, folder 77.

113. Likewise, in California's Santa Clara Valley, historian Cecilia Tsu has found that stark ideological lines demarcated the racial boundaries of crop production, where promoters suggested Chinese laborers were relegated to hand labor and orchard farming was tied to a white family farm ideal. See Tsu, *Garden of the World,* 2013.

114. "Opinion of the Court," *United States of America vs. Wong Fong,* n.d., box 41, RG 85 Records of the Immigration and Naturalization Service, Los Angeles District Office, Segregated Chinese Case Files, 1893–1935, National Archives at Riverside. My attention was first brought to this case by Harry Lawton, "Two Riverside Chinatown Merchants Describe Their Operations During a Geary Act Deportation Hearing," in *Wong Ho Leun: An American Chinatown,* ed. The Great Basin Foundation.

115. Yield based on evidence of Wong Yee, May 22, 1897, box 5, folder 213, Records of the Immigration and Naturalization Service Los Angeles District Office Segregated Chinese Case Files, 1893–1935, National Archives at Riverside.

116. *United States of America vs. Wong Fong,* General Case #763–773, 12 September 1895, box 40, RG 21 Records of U.S. District Courts, Southern District of California, Southern Division 1887–1907, National Archives at Riverside; "Application of Lawfully Domiciled Chinese Merchant, Teacher, or Student for Preinvestigation of Status," RG 85 Records of the Immigration and Naturalization Service, Los Angeles District Office, Segregated Chinese Case Files, 1893–1935, box 138, National Archives at Riverside; for a similar arrest, see *United States of America vs. Wong Haung,* General Case #773, box 30, RG 21 Records of U.S. District Courts, Southern District of California, Southern Division 1887–1907, National Archives at Riverside.

117. Gabriel J. Chin, "'A Chinaman's Chance' in Court: Asian Pacific Americans and Racial Rules of Evidence," *UC Irvine Law Review* 3, no. 965 (December 2013).

118. Testimony of P. T. Evans, *United States of America vs. Wong Fong,* General Case #763–773, 12 September 1895, box 40, RG 21 Records of U.S. District Courts, Southern District of California, Southern Division 1887–1907, National Archives at Riverside.

119. *United States of America v. Wong Hong* (September 12, 1895).

120. *Wong Fong v. United States.* Circuit Court of Appeals, Ninth Circuit, October 6, 1896, no. 297; "At the U.S. Building, 1896," *Los Angeles Times,* December 2, 1896.

121. *United States of America v. Wong Hong* (September 12, 1895).

122. Grace Delgado, *Making the Chinese Mexican: Global Migration, Localism, and Exclusion in the U.S.-Mexico Borderlands* (Stanford: Stanford University Press, 2012), 88.

123. For a few examples, see "Hobo Rode on Train," *Riverside Daily Press,* April 25, 1903; "All Ready for the Day," *Riverside Daily Press,* May 6, 1903; "Riverside Welcomes Nation's Executive," *Riverside Daily Press,* May 7, 1903; "President Roosevelt's Welcome to California," *Riverside Daily Press,* May 7, 1903; "Riverside Welcomes the President," *Riverside Daily Press,* May 7, 1903; for a retrospective, see "City Welcomed Teddy Roosevelt in Gala Fashion: Just Thirty Years Ago Great President Was Riverside Guest," *Riverside Press Enterprise,* May 8, 1933.

124. Gail Bederman, *Manliness and Civilization: A Cultural History of Gender and Race in the United States, 1880–1917* (Chicago: University of Chicago Press, 1995), 172; Thomas G. Dyer, *Theodore Roosevelt and the Idea of Race* (Baton Rouge: Louisiana State University Press, 1980); Amy Kaplan and Donald E. Pease, eds., *Cultures of United States Imperialism* (Durham: Duke University Press, 1994); Theodore Roosevelt, *The Winning of the West* (New York: Putnam's, 1889).

125. California Promotion Committee, *California Addresses by President Roosevelt,* 7; "Welcome to California," *Riverside Daily Press,* May 7, 1903; Stephen Ponder, "Publicity in the Interest of the People: Theodore Roosevelt's Conservation Crusade," *Presidential Studies Quarterly* 20, no. 3 (Summer 1990).

126. Thomas C. Leonard, "Retrospectives. Eugenics and Economics in the Progressive Era," *Journal of Economic Perspectives* 19 (Fall 2005), 210; Bederman, *Manliness and Civilization,* 178; Dyer, *Theodore Roosevelt and the Idea of Race.*

127. California Promotion Committee. *California Addresses by President Roosevelt,* 7; "Welcome to California," *Riverside Daily Press,* May 7, 1903.

128. "Successful Parade Its Striking Features," *Riverside Daily Press,* May 7, 1903.

129. "Riverside Welcomes Nation," *Riverside Daily Press,* May 7, 1903; "President Roosevelt's Welcome to California," *Riverside Daily Press,* May 6, 1903. On this exchange, see Bederman, *Manliness and Civilization,* 203.

130. "Roosevelt Reception and Addresses," *Citrograph,* May 23, 1903.

131. Ibid.

132. Theodore Roosevelt, "At Ventura California, May 9, 1903," in Louis, *A Compilation of the Messages and Speeches of Theodore Roosevelt.*

133. Quoted material from "Picture Showing Ex-President Roosevelt Planting Famous Navel Orange Tree in Court of Mission Inn," *Riverside Daily Press,* January 6, 1919, 7; "President Roosevelt Replanting Original Navel Orange Tree," *Citrograph,* May 23, 1903. There was extensive coverage in both the *Riverside Daily Press* and the *Citrograph.*

134. "Good Bye and Good Luck was the Farewell Greeting," *Riverside Daily Press,* May 8, 1903.

135. Quoted material from "Picture Showing Ex-President Roosevelt Planting Famous Navel Orange Tree in Court of Mission Inn," *Riverside Daily Press,* January 6, 1919, 7; emphasis added.

136. For a comparative example of how ideologies of race suicide manifested through conservation campaigns for the California redwood, see Alexandra Minna Stern, *Eugenic Nation: Faults and Frontiers of Better Breeding in Modern America* (Berkeley: University of California Press, 2005). The heading for concluding section is a reference to the work of anthropologist James Clifford, *Routes: Travel and Translation in the Late Twentieth Century Literature* (Cambridge, MA: Harvard University Press, 1997).

137. Frederick Jackson Turner, *The Significance of the Frontier in American History* (1894; Penguin Books, 2008). For a discussion of the frontier thesis and its significance for analysis of the American West, see Patricia Limerick, *The Legacy of Conquest: The Unbroken Past of the American West* (New York: W.W. Norton, 1987).

138. S. Craig, "Some of the Men I Have Known Who Have Helped to Make California History," *Citrograph,* May 30, 1903; "Welcome to California," *Riverside Daily* Press, May 7, 1903; "Roosevelt's Praise for Riverside," *Riverside Daily Press,* May 11, 1903.

139. My analysis here is influenced by work on white settler mythologies and analysis of spatial containment as a means of enforcing racial lines. See Razack, *Race, Space, and the Law.*

CHAPTER TWO. ON THE MOVE AND FIXED IN PLACE

1. Gene Stratton-Porter, *Her Father's Daughter* (Garden City: Doubleday, Page and Company, 1921), 6. On the connection between the novel and policies levied at Japanese immigrants, see "Her Father's Daughter and anti-Japanese Legislation," Deborah Wong, ed., *Asian American Riverside,* University of California, Riverside, last modified 2006, last accessed July 9, 2018, http://www.asianamericanriverside .ucr.edu/HerFathersDaughter/index.html.

2. "Class Sixteen in Riverside," *Los Angeles Times,* June 21, 1905; Tom Patterson, "Japanese in Riverside Area: New Mystery About Old Tragedy," *Riverside Press Enterprise,* February 21, 1971. Born in Japan, Arthur Kaneko was naturalized as an extension of his father, Ulysses Kaneko's, successful petition for naturalization in 1896. See "Honorable George Otis to Ulysses Kaneko," Naturalization Certificate, 27 March 1896, box 1, Superior Court of the County of San Bernardino, State of California, Iwata (Masakazu) Collection, Japanese American National Museum, Los Angeles.

3. Stratton-Porter, *Her Father's Daughter,* 115.

4. Mary Louise Pratt, *Imperial Eyes: Travel Writing and Transculturation* (New York: Routledge, 1992). See also Mary Louise Pratt, "Arts of the Contact Zone," *Profession* (1991).

5. California State Board of Control, *California and the Oriental: Japanese, Chinese, and Hindus,* revised (Sacramento: California State Printing Office, 1922; first published in 1920 by California State Board of Control), 7.

6. David Harvey describes the "spatial fix" as "capitalism's insatiable drive to resolve its inner crisis tendencies by geographical expansion and geographical restructuring." Harvey builds on Neil Smith's work to discuss the "temporal" and "spatio-temporal" as interrelated fixes, analysis which in turn has been built on by Bob Jessop, who views them as interactive, rather than additive. See David Harvey, "Globalization and the 'Spatial Fix,'" *Geographische Revue* 2 (February 2001), 24; Neil Smith, *Uneven Development: Nature, Capital, and the Production of Space* (Athens: University of Georgia Press, 2008); Bob Jessop, "Spatial Fixes, Temporal Fixes and Spatio-Temporal Fixes," in *David Harvey: A Critical Reader*, ed. Noel Castree and Derek Gregory (Malden: Blackwell Publishing, 2006).

7. From the colonial lens, the black body (Native) and white body (settler) have been signified through their immobility and mobility, respectively. Radhika Mohanram, *Black Body: Women, Colonialism, and Space* (Minneapolis: University of Minnesota Press, 1999).

8. Tim Cresswell, *In Place/Out of Place: Geography, Ideology and Transgression* (Minneapolis: University of Minnesota Press, 1996); Renisa Mawani, "In Between and Out of Place: Mixed-Race Identity, Liquor, and the Law in British Columbia, 1850–1913," in Sherene Razack, ed., *Race, Space, and the Law: Unmapping a White Settler Society* (Toronto: Between the Lines, 2002).

9. In this work, I draw upon a framework of relational racialization. See Claire Jean Kim, "The Racial Triangulation of Asian Americans," *Politics and Society* 27 (March 1999); Natalia Molina, *How Race Is Made in America: Immigration, Citizenship, and the Historical Power of Racial Scripts* (Berkeley: University of California Press, 2014); and Tomás Almaguer, *Racial Fault Lines: The Historical Origins of White Supremacy in California* (Berkeley: University of California Press, 1994).

10. Figures for the Chinese population are unavailable for Riverside County in 1890, but Census records for San Bernardino County record over a 50 percent drop within the first ten years of the second Chinese Exclusion Act. See U.S. Census Bureau, "Indian, Chinese, and Japanese Population, by Counties," Table 17 (1910), 166.

11. Harry Lawton, "The Pilgrims from Gom-Benn: Migratory Origins of Chinese Pioneers in the San Bernardino Valley," in *Wong Ho Leun: An American Chinatown*, ed. The Great Basin Foundation, vol. 1 (San Diego: The Great Basin Foundation, 1987), 148; Rebecca Lum and Suanne Yamashita, "The Chinese Population of Riverside County in 1900: Data from the Twelfth Federal Census," in *Wong Ho Leun*.

12. "Chinatown Burned Out," *San Francisco Chronicle*, July 31, 1893, 2; "Riverside County," *Los Angeles Times*, August 1, 1893, p. 6; Harry Lawton, "Riverside's First Chinatown and the Boom of the Eighties," in *Wong Ho Leun*, 22. For more on the use of fire as a means of racial removal see Connie Chiang's work on a Chinese fishing village near Monterey in the spring of 1906. Connie Y. Chiang, *Shaping the Shoreline: Fisheries and Tourism on the Monterey Coast* (Seattle: University of Washington Press, 2008).

13. Reviewing case files of Chinese immigrants between 1893 and 1935 in the records of the Immigration and Naturalization Service shows that following the Geary Act, many Chinese business owners returned to China while others moved

to Los Angeles and invested in new ventures. As one example, see evidence provided by Wong Chet in the case of Wong Yee, Box 5, Folder 213, Record Group 85, Records of the Immigration and Naturalization Service, Los Angeles District Office, Segregated Chinese Case Files, 1893–1935, National Archives at Riverside; Census records further confirm stark dips in the California Chinese population, while showing that those who remained increasingly urbanized between 1890 and 1910. See U.S. Census Bureau, "Population of Minor Civil Divisions: 1910, 1900, and 1890," Table 1 (1910), 157. Mary Paik Lee's autobiographical account of this time suggests that the Chinese merchants who stayed in Riverside worked as intermediaries with new immigrants. See Mary Paik Lee, *Quiet Odyssey: A Pioneer Korean Woman in America* (Seattle: University of Washington Press, 1990), 14.

14. Challenging common portrayals of Pacific colonies as "stepping-stones," Kornel Chang examines these colonies as nodes crucial to the expansion of American imperialism. Kornel Chang, *Pacific Connections: The Making of the U.S.-Canadian Borderlands* (Berkeley: University of California Press, 2012).

15. Douglas Cazaux Sackman, *Orange Empire: California and the Fruits of Eden* (Berkeley: University of California Press, 2005).

16. The Asian-descent population (including Indian, Chinese, Japanese, and other) was enumerated as both a single category and as separate populations. See U.S. Census Bureau, "Composition and Characteristics of the Population for the State and for Counties," Table 1 (1910), 168; U.S. Census Bureau, "Population-California-Indian, Chinese, and Japanese Population by Counties," Table 17 (1910), 166; U.S. Census Bureau, "Indian Populations of the United States by County: 1910, 1900, 1890," Table 11 (1910), 25.

17. See Scott Kurashige, "Between 'White Spot' and 'World City': Racial Integration and the Roots of Multiculturalism," in *A Companion to Los Angeles,* ed. Bill Deverell and Greg Hise (Malden: Wiley-Blackwell, 2014).

18. Historian Mark Rawsitch and sociologist Morrison Wong provide detailed portraits of Riverside's Japanese population in Rawsitch, *The House on Lemon Street: Japanese Pioneers and the American Dream* (Boulder: University of Colorado Press, 2012), 51; and Wong, "The Japanese in Riverside, 1890 to 1945: A Special Case in Race Relations" (PhD diss., University of California, Riverside, 1977).

19. George Sánchez built on David Harvey's "geography of difference" in his discussion of multiracialism in Boyle Heights. See George J. Sánchez, "What's Good for Boyle Heights Is Good for the Jews: Creating Multiracialism on the Eastside during the 1950s," *American Quarterly* 56, no. 3 (2004), 634–640. For more on multicultural neighborhoods germinating from shared racial segregation, as well as efforts to reengineer racial difference, see George J. Sánchez, "Face the Nation: Race, Immigration, and the Rise of Nativism in Late Twentieth Century America," *International Migration Review* 31 (Winter 1997).

20. Author's analysis of Sanborn Map Collection, Riverside Metropolitan Museum, Riverside, CA. As a notable exception, in 1887 the area bounded by 10th, 11th, Vine, and Olive Streets was titled "Spanish Town," but even this label was dropped the following year.

21. On postings as spatial/meaning propositions in a sign plane, see Denis Wood, *Rethinking the Power of Maps* (New York: Guilford Press, 2010). On maps as texts open to deconstruction and close reading, see John B. Harley, "Deconstructing the Map," *Cartographica* 26, no. 2 (Spring 1989).

22. Analysis of Sanborn Insurance maps from 1895 and 1908, Sanborn Map Collection, Riverside Metropolitan Museum, Riverside, CA.

23. California State Board of Control, *California and the Oriental*.

24. Based on author's analysis of *City Directory,* City of Riverside, 1898, and *City Directory,* City of Riverside, 1905, both in Local History Collection, Riverside Public Library.

25. Kay J. Anderson, *Vancouver's Chinatown: Racial Discourse in Canada, 1875–1980* (Montreal: McGill-Queen's University Press, 1991); Mary Ting Yi Lui, *The Chinatown Trunk Mystery: Murder, Miscegenation, and Other Dangerous Encounters in Turn-of-the-Century New York City* (Princeton: Princeton University Press, 2005).

26. Donna Graves, "Japanese American Heritage and the Quest for Civil Rights in Riverside California, 1890s–1970s," in National Park Service, *National Register of Historic Places Multiple Property Documentation Form,* 31 May 2012, p. 29, Collection IA 20017: Reports from Recipients of Conservation Grants, Getty Research Institute, Los Angeles.

27. Catherine Gudis, "Reconnaissance Survey and Context Statement for the Marketplace Specific Plan, City of Riverside, California," prepared for the City of Riverside Community Development Department, July 2012.

28. Alice Kanda interview by Deborah Wong, transcript, 18 August 1999, Asian American Riverside, University of California Riverside, http://www.asianamericanriverside.ucr.edu/NotableAsianAmericans/AliceKanada.html.

29. Chang, *Pacific Connections,* 13.

30. In 1905, Japan claimed Korea as a protectorate; in 1910, Japan officially annexed the territory and Koreans became Japanese subjects. See Alexis Dudden, *Japan's Colonization of Korea: Discourse and Power* (Honolulu: University of Hawai'i Press, 2005).

31. Quoted material from "Korean Labor Bureau," *Riverside Daily Press,* April 29, 1905, 7. In these early years of settlement, Lee recalls that her family crossed the street whenever they saw a Japanese person walking nearby. Lee, *Quiet Odyssey.*

32. There was extensive news coverage of the incident. For two informative samples, see "Expulsion Koreans Creates an International Situation," *Riverside Daily Press,* June 27, 1913, p. 6; "Hemet Inquiry Stopped," *Springfield Daily Republican,* July 2, 1913.

33. Works examining the relational aspects of racialization in multiracial suburbs in the postwar period have uncovered multiracial communities comprised of majority-minorities, panethnic solidarity, relational racialization among multiracial neighbors, resilient racial and class divides despite proximity, as well as a nonwhite racial ideology shaped by place. Notable examples include Leland Saito, *Race and Politics: Asian Americans, Latinos, and Whites in a Los Angeles Suburb* (Urbana:

University of Illinois Press, 1998); Allison Varzally, *Making a Non-White America: Californians Coloring Outside Ethnic Lines, 1925–1955* (Berkeley: University of California Press, 2008); Scott Kurashige, *The Shifting Grounds of Race: Black and Japanese Americans in the Making of Multiethnic Los Angeles* (Princeton: Princeton University Press, 2008); and Wendy Cheng, *The Changs Next Door to the Diazes: Remapping Race in Suburban California* (Minneapolis: Minnesota University Press, 2013).

34. On mental maps or cognitive mapping, see Kevin Lynch, *The Image of the City* (Cambridge, MA: MIT Press, 1960); Nedra Reynolds, *Geographies of Writing: Inhabiting Places and Encountering Difference* (Carbondale: Southern Illinois University Press, 2004), esp. chapter 3.

35. Lee, *Quiet Odyssey*, 14; for another autobiographical account, see Easurk Emsen Charr, *The Golden Mountain: The Autobiography of a Korean Immigrant, 1895–1960*, ed. Wayne Patterson (Urbana: University of Illinois Press, 1996).

36. Similarly, Paul Wormser explains that subsequent waves of Japanese and Mexican immigrant workers occupied barracks originally built for Chinese laborers. Paul Wormser, "Chinese Agricultural Labor in the Citrus Belt of Inland Southern California," in *Wong Ho Leun*, 176.

37. "Casa Blanca Has a Kick," *Riverside Daily Press,* October 26, 1905, p. 2.

38. Ibid.

39. D.W. Pontius, "Lines of the Pacific Electric Railway in Southern California," Los Angeles, Pacific Electric Rail Co., 1912 [map], David Rumsey Historical Map Collection, Stanford Library; Kenyon Co. Mapmakers, "Map of the City of Riverside," 1920 [map], Map Collection, Yale University. Prior to the arrival of the Pacific Electric in 1911, Riverside was served by the Riverside & Arlington Railway.

40. C.F. Gates, "Cycling in the Southwest," *Land of Sunshine* vol. 5, June to November, 1896, p. 48.

41. C.F. Gates, "Racing and Racing Men: The Wheel in Southern California," *Overland Monthly* 28, no. 167, 2nd series (San Francisco, November 1896): 539.

42. "All the Year Riding," *The Land of Sunshine: A Southern California Magazine* 5 (June to November 1896); "Another Union Run," *Riverside Daily Press,* August 16, 1895; "Getting Ready: Riverside Wheelmen Busy in Preparing for September 9," *Riverside Daily Press,* August 29, 1895. For a brief retrospective on cycling in Riverside, see "Recorder Logan Has Cycle Club History," *Riverside Enterprise,* April 10, 1917.

43. Gail Bederman, *Manliness and Civilization: A Cultural History of Gender and Race in the United States, 1880–1917* (Chicago: University of Chicago Press, 1995); R. Marie Griffith, "Apostles of Abstinence: Fasting and Masculinity during the Progressive Era," *American Quarterly* 52 (December 2000).

44. "A Puzzle for the L.A.W.: The Color Line Question Likely to Result in Serious Complications," *New York Herald,* March 15, 1894. For more on African American cycling teams in the United States, see Robert Smith, *A Social History of the Bicycle: Its Early Life and Times in America* (New York: American Heritage Press, 1972), esp. chapters 8 and 9, pp. 162–171. On baseball and the color line, see

Adrian Burgos, *Playing America's Game: Baseball, Latinos, and the Color Line* (Berkeley: University of California Press, 2007).

45. Two Spanish-surnamed participants are recorded in the 1896 Riverside Admissions Day road race. Furthermore, another undated ledger of Riverside race participants details a W. Rodriguez registered with the Duarte Wheelmen and a John Tafoya racing unattached to a league. See "Didn't Get But One Smell," *Pacific Field* 7, no. 11 (12 September 1896), Riverside Wheelmen Folder, Riverside Metropolitan Museum; and Ledger in Riverside City, Clubs and Associations, 1890, Riverside Wheelmen Folder, Riverside Metropolitan Museum.

46. On the role of stadiums in racialized struggles over civic identity in the postwar period, see Priscilla Leiva, "Stadium Struggles: The Cultural Politics of Difference and Civic Identity in Postwar Urban Imaginaries" (PhD diss., University of Southern California, 2014).

47. Journalist Tom Patterson authored several articles on cycling in Riverside between 1968 and 1988. Tom Patterson, "Bike Racing Once Drew Excited Crowds in Riverside," *Press Enterprise*, May 5, 1968; Tom Patterson, "The Bicycle Mania that took Riverside by Storm," *Press Enterprise*, 25 May 1980; Tom Patterson, "Czar White Got Biking Fad Rolling in Riverside," *Press Enterprise*, November 27, 1988—all in Vertical File: Riv City–Sports and Recreation–Bicycling, Local History Collection, Riverside Public Library.

48. Paul Smethurst, *The Bicycle—Towards a Global History* (New York: Palgrave Macmillan, 2015); David Herlihy, *Bicycle: The History* (New Haven: Yale University Press, 2004), esp. 310 and 316.

49. See Donald Roden, "Baseball and the Quest for National Dignity in Meiji Japan," *American Historical Review* 85 (June 1980).

50. "General Wheelman Notes," *The Riverside Wheel* 1, no. 5 (July 29, 1895); and "General Wheelman Notes," *The Riverside Wheel* 1, no. 23 (December 5, 1895), both in Bicycling folder, Riverside Metropolitan Museum.

51. Eiichiro Azuma, *Between Two Empires: Race, History, and Transnationalism in Japanese America* (New York: Oxford University Press, 2005); Mari Yoshihara, "The Flight of the Japanese Butterfly: Orientalism, Nationalism, and Performances of Japanese Womanhood," *American Quarterly* 56 (December 2004); Harry Harootunian, *Overcome by Modernity: History, Culture, and Community in Interwar Japan* (Princeton: Princeton University Press, 2000).

52. "Japanese Are Building Bicycle Race Track," *Riverside Daily Press*, October 13, 1905; "Japanese Race Meet," *Riverside Press and Horticulturist*, October 27, 1905, Bicycling folder, Riverside Metropolitan Museum; "Bicycle Races Were Enjoyed by Japanese," *Riverside Daily Press*, November 11, 1905.

53. "Japanese Race Meet," *Riverside Press and Horticulturalist*, October 27, 1905. For additional accounts of the race track and the Japanese emperor's birthday, see "Japanese Are Building Bicycle Race Track," *Riverside Daily Press*, October 13, 1905; "Another Prize," *Riverside Daily Press*, November 2, 1905; "Big Celebration by Japanese," *Riverside Press and Horticulturist*, November 3, 1905; "The Japanese Will Celebrate," *Riverside Daily Press*, November 2, 1905.

54. "Sports," *Riverside Enterprise,* January 2, 1906, 4; Wong, "The Japanese in Riverside," 75; Rawsitch, *The House on Lemon Street.*

55. Quoted material from "Big Celebration by Japanese," *Riverside Daily Press,* November 1, 1905, 5; "Japanese Honor Mikado Birthday," *Riverside Enterprise,* November 4, 1906; Asian American studies scholar Eiichiro Azuma describes such politics among Japanese immigrants, bound to two nation states, as an "inter-National perspective." Azuma, *Between Two Empires,* 5.

56. On cultural citizenship, see Raymond Rocco, "Citizenship, Culture, and Community: Restructuring in Southeast Los Angeles," in *Latino Cultural Citizenship: Claiming Identity, Space, and Rights,* ed. W. Flores and R. Benamayor (Boston: Beacon Press, 1997).

57. Neither Latina/o nor African American riders were noted in newspaper accounts.

58. "Big Celebration by Japanese," *Riverside Press and Horticulturalist,* November 3, 1905; "Bicycle Races were Enjoyed by Japanese," *Riverside Daily Press,* November 4, 1905; "Japanese Bicycle Races," *Riverside Independent Enterprise,* November 5, 1905, p. 8; "Fencing, Wrestling, and Bicycle Races on New Year's Day," *Riverside Daily Press,* December 30, 2005; "Prizes Awarded for Bicycle Day Events," *Riverside Independent Enterprise,* May 18, 1918.

59. Cotten Seiler, *Republic of Drivers: A Cultural History of Automobility in America* (Chicago: University of Chicago Press, 2008); Ben Chappel, *Lowrider Space: Aesthetics and Politics of Modern Custom Cars* (Austin: University of Texas Press, 2012).

60. *First Motorcycle Run Out of Riverside, California,* 1907, Roy L. Haglund Collection, Riverside Metropolitan Museum. Motorbike use was heavily regulated beginning the following year; see "An Ordinance Regulating the Use of Motor Cycles and Motor Bicycles on the Public Streets in the City of Riverside," Ordinance No. 19, January 1908, Ordinance Files, Records of the City Clerk, City of Riverside.

61. My analysis draws on Robin D.G. Kelley, *Yo' Mama's Disfunktional!: Fighting the Cultural Wars in Urban America* (Boston: Beacon Press, 1998).

62. Nayan Shah, *Contagious Divides: Epidemics and Race in San Francisco's Chinatown* (Berkeley: University of California Press, 2001).

63. Roden, "Baseball and the Quest for National Dignity in Meiji Japan"; Burgos, *Playing America's Game;* José M. Alamillo, *Making Lemonade Out of Lemons: Mexican American Labor and Leisure in a California Town, 1880–1960* (Chicago: University of Illinois Press, 2006), chapter 5.

64. Smethurst, *The Bicycle;* Herlihy, *Bicycle,* chapter 3.

65. Rebecca Copeland, "Fashioning the Feminine: Images of the Modern Girl Student in Meiji Japan," *U.S.-Japan Women's Journal* 30/31 (2006); Yoshihara, "The Flight of the Japanese Butterfly," 978. For a modern take, see Robin LeBlanc, *Bicycle Citizens: The Political World of the Japanese Housewife* (Berkeley: University of California Press, 1999).

66. For examples of the diminutive language used to describe Japanese cyclists, see "Japanese Are Building Bicycle Race Track," *Riverside Daily Press,* October 13,

1905; and "Japanese Race Meet," *Riverside Press and Horticulturist,* October 27, 1905. For examples of language used to describe white cyclists, see "Riverside Wins the Team Race," *Los Angeles Herald,* October 4, 1893; "Bicycle Meet," *Riverside Daily Press,* August 12, 1895; "Sporting News: A Bicycle Relay Race—From Los Angeles to San Diego—Notes," *Riverside Independent,* July 8, 1892.

67. "Bicycle Races Were Enjoyed by Japanese," *Riverside Daily Press,* November 4, 1905.

68. Photographs from Riverside's Bicycle Day events can be found in "Riverside City-Fairs and Pageants—Parades," Photographic Collection, Browsing Books, vol. 10, Riverside Public Library. For representative examples, see "Marked Revival in Bicycling Celebrated Feb. 28," *Riverside Independent Enterprise,* February 28, 1916; "Good Old Days of Bicycling Are Coming Back," *Riverside Independent Enterprise,* February 28, 1916; "Slogan, 'Million Bicycles in 1916,' for Big Day," *Riverside Independent Enterprise,* February 28, 1916; "Bicycle Association Meets Last Night," *Riverside Daily Press,* March 22, 1917; "Prizes Awarded for Bicycle Day Events," *Riverside Independent Enterprise,* May 18, 1918.

69. Hal Barron, *Mixed Harvest: The Second Great Transformation in the Rural North, 1870–1930* (Chapel Hill: University of North Carolina Press, 1997), 28.

70. Chinese cycling has been traced to 1892 in Riverside and to 1893 in San Bernardino. See Harry Lawton, "A Selected Chronological History of Chinese Pioneers in Riverside and the Southern California Citrus Belt," in *Wong Ho Leun,* 99, 102.

71. "Prizes Awarded for Bicycle Day Events," *Riverside Independent Enterprise,* May 18, 1918, p. 5.

72. For more on labor mobility and conflict in California agriculture, see Don Mitchell, *The Lie of the Land: Migrant Workers and the California Landscape* (Minneapolis: University of Minnesota Press, 1996); on motility, see Vincent Kaufmann, *Re-Thinking Mobility: Contemporary Sociology* (Burlington, VT: Ashgate 2002).

73. Based on author's analysis of data from Riverside County Justice Dockets between 1897 and 1913. See Justice Docket 6, Criminal Cases January 1897–April 903; Justice Docket 7, Criminal Cases March 1903–February 1905; Justice Docket 8, Criminal Cases January 1907 to February 1911; Justice Docket 9, Criminal Cases March 1911 to January 1913; Justice Docket 10, Criminal Cases January 1913 to March 1913—all in Riverside Metropolitan Museum's archival collection.

74. "Japanese Must Obey Laws," *Riverside Independent Enterprise,* April 20, 1912.

75. Generated from data collected by Morrison Wong, who examined the police court docket from 1907 to 1913 to assess the number of arrests of persons of Japanese ancestry in Riverside. Wong, "The Japanese in Riverside," 75.

76. Quoted materials from "To Curtail Joy Rides," *Riverside Daily Press,* July 26, 1910 and "Validity of City's 'Clean-Up' Ordinance to be Put to Test," *Riverside Independent Enterprise,* July 27, 1910, respectively.

77. Multiple city ordinances were passed regulating vehicle use, including bicycles, tricycles, and velocipedes, in Riverside. Most sections applied to all vehicles,

with a minority detailing bicycle-specific regulations. City ordinances are archived by the Riverside City Clerk from 1907 onward, with minimal changes occurring between policies from 1907 and 1918. For the base ordinance, see Ordinance No. 86, "An Ordinance Regulating Travel and Traffic Upon the Public Streets," May 17, 1910, Ordinance Files, Records of the City Clerk, City of Riverside. Quoted materials from "Validity of City's 'Clean-Up' Ordinance to be Put to Test," *Riverside Independent Enterprise,* July 27, 1910.

78. Compare to police surveillance and the emergence of cars. Jeremy Packer, *Mobility without Mayhem: Safety, Cars, and Citizenship* (Durham: Duke University Press, 2008).

79. See Ordinance No. 86, "An Ordinance Regulating Travel and Traffic Upon the Public Streets," May 17, 1910; Ordinance No. 191, "An Ordinance of the City of Riverside Amending Section 32 of Ordinance No. 86 (New Series) of the City of Riverside," November 17, 1914; Ordinance No. 208, "An Ordinance of the City of Riverside Amending Ordinance No. 86 (New Series) and Adding Two New Sections Thereto," June 1, 1915; Ordinance No. 223, "An Ordinance Regulating Travel and Traffic Upon the Public Streets of the City of Riverside, California," December 14, 1915—all in Ordinance Files, Records of the City Clerk, City of Riverside.

80. Research and correspondence with the Riverside Public Library, Riverside Metropolitan Museum, and City Clerk suggest the police dockets are no longer archived and have either been destroyed or lost.

81. Wong, "The Japanese in Riverside," 73–78.

82. On joyriding, see David Wolcott, *Cops and Kids: Policing Juvenile Delinquency in Urban America, 1890–1940* (Columbus: Ohio State University, 2005); see also David R. Diaz, *Barrio Urbanism: Chicanos, Planning, and American Cities* (New York, Routledge, 2005). On bicycling, see John Bloom, "'To Die for a Lousy Bike': Bicycles, Race, and the Regulation of Public Space on the Streets of Washington, DC, 1963–2009," *American Quarterly* 69, no. 1 (March 2017).

83. These distinctions were sharpest outside of the American West, where gradations of whiteness were more distinct. On mobility and the tramp, see Tim Cresswell, *The Tramp in America* (London: Reaktion Books, 2001); on the tramp in the Southern California context, see Kelly Lytle Hernández, "Hobos in Heaven: Race, Incarceration, and the Rise of Los Angeles, 1880–1910," *Pacific Historical Review* 83 (August 2014).

84. Based on author's analysis of data from Riverside County Justice Dockets for 1897–1913. See Justice Docket 6, Criminal Cases January 1897–April 903; Justice Docket 7, Criminal Cases March 1903–February 1905; Justice Docket 8, Criminal Cases January 1907 to February 1911; Justice Docket 9, Criminal Cases March 1911 to January 1913; Justice Docket 10, Criminal Cases January 1913 to March 1913—all in Riverside Metropolitan Museum's archival collection. For examples of bicycle theft, see Case 205: Charles Richards, Case 255: Mike Corrides, and Case 257: Paul St. John, in Justice Docket 7.

85. On the production of the western white subject as mobile, see Tim Cresswell, *On the Move: Mobility in the Modern Western World* (New York: Routledge,

2006). On the impulse to fix the nonwhite body in space, see Mawani, "In Between and Out of Place," in *Race, Space, and the Law,* ed. Sherene Razack; and Radhika Mohanram, *Black Body: Women, Colonialism, and Space* (Minneapolis: University of Minnesota Press, 1999).

86. Mitchell, *The Lie of the Land,* 195; on sport and "countermobility work" as a means to navigate and challenge white supremacy, see Derek H. Alderman and Joshua Inwood, "Mobility as Antiracism Work: The 'Hard Driving' of NASCAR's Wendell Scott," *Annals of the American Association of Geographers* 106, no. 3 (2016).

87. On the conflicting symbolic systems of American Indians and cars in the same period, see Philip J. Deloria, *Indians in Unexpected Places* (Lawrence: University Press of Kansas, 2004).

88. For comparative cases in the California Imperial Valley and Santa Clara Valley, see Benny J. Andrés, *Power and Control in the Imperial Valley: Nature, Agribusiness, and Workers on the California Borderland, 1900–1940* (College Station: Texas A&M University Press, 2015); Cecilia M. Tsu, *Garden of the World: Asian Immigrants and the Making of Agriculture in California's Santa Clara Valley* (New York: Oxford University Press, 2013).

89. Cresswell, *The Tramp in America;* Lytle Hernández, "Hobos in Heaven"; Shah, *Stranger Intimacies.*

90. Kelly Lytle Hernández, *City of Inmates: Conquest, Rebellion, and the Rise of Human Caging in Los Angeles, 1771–1965* (Chapel Hill: University of North Carolina Press, 2017); Margaret D. Jacobs, "Seeing Like a Settler Colonial State," *Modern American History* 1, no. 2 (2018). Where the legal right to mobility, such as interstate travel, has been upheld consistently in U.S. courts, the right to stay in place has not. See Tim Cresswell, *On the Move: Mobility in the Modern Western World* (New York: Routledge, 2006), esp. chapter 6.

91. Lee, *Quiet Odyssey.*

92. For more on popular perceptions of migrant workers and boardinghouses, see Shah, *Contagious Divides,* esp. chapter 3 on queer domesticity; see also Shah, *Stranger Intimacy.*

93. "Jap Faces Serious Charges," *Riverside Independent Enterprise,* February 1, 1913, p. 5.

94. Ordinance No. 254, An Ordinance of the City of Riverside Providing for the Registration of Lodgers, Roomers and Guests at Lodging Houses, Rooming Houses and Hotels, and Fixing a Penalty for its Violation, December 19, 1916, Ordinance Files, Records of the City Clerk, City of Riverside.

95. Quoted materials from "Chief of Police States on Clean-Up Crusade," *Riverside Daily Press,* February 1, 1913, p. 4; "Manager Fined $25: Japanese Lodging House Owner Is Released from Charge," *Riverside Independent Enterprise,* February 4, 1913, p. 5; Department of the Interior, "Pupils Register, 1911–1912" and "Pupils Register, 1912–1913," both in Sherman Indian Museum Collection, Riverside, CA. For more on the gendered politics of the Sherman Institute, as well as analysis of the American Indian boarding school experience, see Clifford E. Trafzer, Jean A. Keller,

and Lorene Sisquoc, eds., *Boarding School Blues: Revisiting American Indian Educational Experiences* (Lincoln: University of Nebraska Press, 2006).

96. I am influenced here by Patrick Wolfe, "Settler Colonialism and the Elimination of the Native," *Journal of Genocide Research* 8, no. 4 (2006); Margaret D. Jacobs, *White Mother to a Dark Race: Settler Colonialism, Maternalism, and the Removal of Indigenous Children in the American West and Australia, 1880–1940* (Lincoln: University of Nebraska, 2009); Iyko Day, *Alien Capital: Asian Racialization and the Logic of Settler Colonial Capitalism* (Durham: Duke University Press, 2016).

97. The first Alien Land Law was a state statute that prevented land titles in the name of "aliens ineligible for citizenship," a status ensured by a naturalization act denying citizenship to all residents with the exception of free whites and persons of African descent. See Edwin E. Ferguson, "The California Alien Land Law and the Fourteenth Amendment," *California Law Review* 35, no. 1 (March 1947). On the dismantling of the California Alien Land Law, see Mark Brilliant, *The Color of America Has Changed: How Racial Diversity Shaped Civil Rights Reform in California, 1941–1978* (New York: Oxford University Press, 2010), chapter 2.

98. Mark Rawsitch provides a comprehensive study of the Harada case that begins with the meeting of Ken and Jukichi Harada in Japan and concludes in the post-internment era with Sumi Harada's return to the house. See Rawsitch, *The House on Lemon Street*.

99. Matthew Frye Jacobson, *Whiteness of a Different Color: European Immigrants and the Alchemy of Race* (Cambridge, MA: Harvard University Press, 1998).

100. Linda Gordon, *The Great Arizona Orphan Abduction* (Cambridge, MA: Harvard University Press, 1999), 167.

101. U.S. Census Bureau, "Riverside Ward 1, Riverside, California," Roll: T625_125 Enumeration District: 11 (1920), 10B-11A.

102. Mark Larking, "Japanese Merchant Wages Legal Fight to Occupy Home and Nullify California Land Law," *Evening News* (San Jose), January 18, 1917.

103. For more on white privilege see Cheryl I. Harris, "Whiteness as Property," *Harvard Law Review* 106 (June 1993); George Lipstiz, *The Possessive Investment in Whiteness: How White People Profit from Identity Politics,* revised and expanded (Philadelphia: Temple University Press, 2006).

104. Quoted material from Elmer Wallace Holmes, *History of Riverside County, California,* (Los Angeles: Historic Record Company, 1912), 345; John Brown and James Boyd, *History of San Bernardino and Riverside Counties with Selected Biography of Actors and Witnesses of the Period of Growth and Achievement* (Chicago: The Lewis Publishing Company, 1922), 740–743; John M. Nieto-Phillips, *The Language of Blood: The Making of Spanish-American Identity in New Mexico, 1880s-1930s* (Albuquerque: University of New Mexico Press, 2004).

105. Rose Cuison Villazor, "Rediscovering Oyama v. California: At the Intersection of Property, Race, and Citizenship," *Washington University Law Review* 87 (2010). Mark Brilliant documents a sharp rise in prosecutions between 1944 and 1945. Brilliant, *The Color of America Has Changed,* 38.

106. Interview with Tsurumatsu and Iso Okamoto, handwritten notes, March 25, 1978; Interview with Shotaro Yamaguchi, handwritten notes, March 25, 1978; Interview with K. Shosan, June 30, 1965—all in Folder Upland-Cucamonga 94.58.1, box 1, Iwata (Masakazu) Papers, Japanese American National Museum, Los Angeles.

107. The Haradas owned a home at 233 14th Street, which was occupied by another Japanese family. See "Reconnaissance Survey and Context Statement for the Marketplace Specific Plan, City of Riverside, California," Prepared for the City of Riverside Community Development Department, July 2012, p. 74. Throughout World War II, the Haradas collected rent on two apartments, at 4438 and 4440 Howard Ave. The properties were located just blocks from Lemon Street, but both were on the east side of the Santa Fe tracks. A visit to the site by the author reveals that neither house exists today. For representative correspondence, see Jess Stebler to Sumi Harada, 19 May 1943, Harada Family Collection, Riverside Metropolitan Museum.

108. Quoted material from Rawsitch, *The House on Lemon Street,* 93.

109. *California v. Harada,* No. [7751] California Superior Court (September 17, 1918), 66.

110. In Gudis, "Reconnaissance Survey and Context," 74.

111. Viewing Asian and Latina/o populations together in this earlier era provides precedent for Asian-Latina/o interactions in later years. For more on this, see Cheng, *The Changs Next Door to the Diazes.*

112. Lipsitz, *The Possessive Investment in Whiteness,* 3.

113. On LULAC, see Craig A. Kaplowitz, *LULAC: Mexican Americans and National Policy* (College Station: Texas A&M University Press, 2005); Benjamin Márquez, *LULAC: The Evolution of a Mexican American Political Organization* (Austin: University of Texas Press, 1993).

114. "Minor Children of Japanese Purchase Residence," *Riverside Enterprise,* December 23, 1915, p. 7.

115. Menu, Washington Restaurant, circa 1910, box A1598-AC.108.36, Harada Family Collection, Riverside Metropolitan Museum; Rawsitch, *The House on Lemon Street.*

116. "Minor Children of Japanese Purchase Residence," 7.

117. Likewise, in a later interview, Sumi Harada positioned her family above their Mexican and African American clientele and as aspiring towards "a life similar to the Caucasians." See Interview with Sumi Harada by Charles Kikuchi, "#60. Harada, Sumi," Japanese American Evacuation and Resettlement Study, 7 December 1944, p. 27, Banc MM 67/14, folder T1.989, Bancroft Library, University of California Berkeley. Quoted material from "Minor Children of Japanese Purchase Residence," 7.

118. Claire Jean Kim, "The Racial Triangulation of Asian Americans," *Politics and Society* 27 (March 1999); quoted material from "Minor Children of Japanese Purchase Residence," 7; emphasis added.

119. "Riverside Takes Up the Alien Land Law," *Hemet News,* November 10, 1916, p. 9; emphasis added.

120. Ibid.

121. As quoted in Rawsitch, *The House on Lemon Street,* 68. Speaking of the restaurant, Sumi Harada described the clientele as "the poorer class of people" and "mostly Mexicans and Negroes." Interview with Sumi Harada by Charles Kikuchi, "#60. Harada, Sumi," Japanese American Evacuation and Resettlement Study, 7 December 1944, pp. 39 and 8, respectively, Banc MM 67/14, folder T1.989, Bancroft Library, University of California Berkeley.

122. I am influenced here by Tim Cresswell's work on "dirt" as indicative of an object out of place, "something in the wrong place or wrong time." See Cresswell, *In Place/Out of Place,* esp. chapters 3 and 5. On dirt and pollution, see Mary Douglas, *Purity and Danger: An Analysis of Concepts of Pollution and Taboo* (London: Routledge, 2002). For an extension of this argument to the racialization of non-whites through public health argumentations, see Anderson, *Vancouver's Chinatown;* Natalia Molina, *Fit to Be Citizens?: Public Health and Race in Los Angeles, 1879–1939* (Berkeley: University of California Press, 2006).

123. Azuma, *Between Two Empires,* esp. chapter 2. See also Sidney Xu Lu, "Good Women for Empire: Educating Overseas Female Emigrants in Imperial Japan, 1900–45," *Journal of Global History* 8 (November 2013): 436–460.

124. Lu, "Good Women for Empire."

125. U.S. Immigrant Commission, *Reports of the Immigrant Commission Part 25: Japanese and Other Immigrant Races in the Pacific Coast and Rocky Mountain States,* U.S. Congress, Senate, 61st Cong., 2nd sess., S. Doc. 633 (Washington, DC: Government Printing Office, 1911), 27–30.

126. Peggy Pascoe, *What Comes Naturally: Miscegenation Law and the Making of Race in America* (New York: Oxford University Press, 2010).

127. Interview with Sumi Harada by Charles Kikuchi, "#60. Harada, Sumi," Japanese American Evacuation and Resettlement Study, 7 December 1944, p. 42, Banc MM 67/14, folder T1.989, Bancroft Library, University of California Berkeley.

128. George Sánchez, *Becoming Mexican American: Ethnicity, Culture, and Identity in Chicano Los Angeles, 1900–1945* (New York: Oxford University Press, 1995).

129. Ellen Wu, *The Color of Success: Asian Americans and the Origins of the Model Minority* (Princeton: Princeton University Press, 2013).

130. "Judge Craig Rules This Morning that State Could Make Children Parties to Suit Against J. Harada for Violation of California Alien Land Law," *Riverside Daily Press,* June 30, 1917, p. 8; "Harada Case Is Not to Have Jury," *Riverside Independent Enterprise,* May 25, 1918, p. 5.

131. "Judge Craig Decided that Native Born Japanese May Own Land Here," *Riverside Daily Press,* Riverside, September 17, 1918, p. 3.

132. Ibid.

133. Furthermore, despite their right to home ownership, the Haradas would later be forcefully removed from Lemon Street during the World War II internment of Japanese immigrants and Japanese Americans. Tragically, Ken and Jukichi died

in the Poston camp without news of resettlement. Their daughter Sumi credited their passing to movement between camps and separation from friends and family. Interview with Sumi Harada by Charles Kikuchi, "#60. Harada, Sumi," Japanese American Evacuation and Resettlement Study, 7 December 1944, Banc MM 67/14, folder T1.989, Bancroft Library, University of California Berkeley.

134. Sayye's willingness to alter his appearance using female beauty products alludes to the gender uncertainty surrounding Asian men. Similarly, posing as a youth alluded to a popular fear surrounding the subversion of immigration restrictions set by the Gentlemen's Agreement. See Nayan Shah, *Contagious Divides,* 2001; California State Board of Control, *California and the Oriental.*

135. On relational racialization, see note 9 above; Wendy Cheng's theorization of regional racial formation, further, helps to unpack relational racialization by highlighting the place-specific processes by which regional hierarchies of race are produced, often in tension with national racial ideologies. Cheng, *The Changs Next Door to the Diazes,* 10–13.

136. See Ferguson, "The California Alien Land Law and the Fourteenth Amendment." The California Alien Land Law was reversed through a combination of the *Oyama v. State of California* (1948) and *Fujii v. State of California* (1952). For a discussion, see Villazor, "Rediscovering Oyama v. California"; Yuji Ichioka, "Japanese Immigrant Response to the 1920 California Alien Land Law," *Agricultural History* 58 (April 1984).

CHAPTER THREE. FROM MEXICAN SETTLERS
TO MEXICAN BIRDS OF PASSAGE

1. This account draws upon Box Bill testimony, U.S. Congress, House of Representatives, Committee on Immigration and Naturalization, *Seasonal Agricultural Laborers from Mexico. Hearings January 28 and 29, February 2,9, 11, and 23, 1926 on H.R. 6741, H.R. 7559, H.R. 9036,* 69th Cong., 1st sess. (Washington, DC: Government Printing Office, 1926), 71; and efforts to conserve the agricultural workforce described in David Montejano, *Anglos and Mexicans in the Making of Texas, 1836–1986* (Austin: University of Texas Press, 1987).

2. On racial capitalism, see Cedric J. Robinson, *Black Marxism: The Making of the Black Radical Tradition* (1983; Chapel Hill: University of North Carolina Press, 2000); Nancy Leong, "Racial Capitalism," *Harvard Law Review* 126, no. 8 (June 2013): 2152; Laura Pulido, "Flint, Environmental Racism, and Racial Capitalism," *Capitalism Nature Socialism* 27 (July 2016), https://doi.org/10.1080/10455752.2016.1213013; Laura Pulido, "Geographies of Race and Ethnicity II: Environmental Racism, Racial Capitalism, and State-Sanctioned Violence," *Progress in Human Geography* 41 (May 2016).

3. Vincent Kaufmann, *Re-Thinking Mobility Social Justice* (Burlington, VT: Ashgate, 2002).

4. This unfolded as a relational process, for which I draw upon Chicana/o studies scholarship on relational racialization to analyze. Luis Alvarez, "From Zoot Suits to Hip Hop: Towards a Relational Chicana/o Studies," *Latino Studies* 5, no. 1 (2007); Natalia Molina, "Examining Chicana/o History through a Relational Lens," *Pacific Historical Review* 82, no. 4 (2013); Natalia Molina, *How Race Is Made in America: Immigration, Citizenship, and the Historical Power of Racial Scripts* (Berkeley: University of California Press, 2014).

5. Doreen Massey, *Space, Place and Gender* (Minneapolis: University of Minnesota Press, 1994), 149.

6. See California Fruit Growers Exchange, *Annual Report of the General Manager of the California Fruit Growers Exchange for the Year Closing August 31, 1916* (Los Angeles: Pacific Rural Press, 1916); California Fruit Growers Exchange, *Annual Report of the General Manager of the California Fruit Growers Exchange for the Year Closing August 31, 1917* (Los Angeles: Pacific Rural Press, August 31, 1917); California Fruit Growers Exchange, *Annual Report of the General Manager of the California Fruit Growers Exchange for the Year Closing August 31, 1918* (Los Angeles: Pacific Rural Press, August 31, 1918)—all in General Collection, Huntington Library.

7. Veronica Castillo-Muñoz, "Historical Roots of Rural Migration: Land Reform, Corn Credit, and the Displacement of Rural Farmers in Nayarit Mexico, 1900–1952," *Mexican Studies/ Estudios Mexicanos* 29 (Winter 2013): 36–60.

8. Victor Clark, "Mexican Labor in the United States," *Bulletin of the Bureau of Labor,* no. 78 (Washington, DC: Government Printing Office, 1908); Paul S. Taylor, "Hand Laborers in the Western Sugar Beet Industry," *Agricultural History* 41, no. 1 (January 1967): 19–26; Jim Norris, *North for the Harvest: Mexican Workers, Growers, and the Sugar Beet Industry* (St. Paul: Minnesota Historical Society Press, 2009).

9. Charles Snyder to A.C. Ridgway ("Inspector in Charge"), Investigation Report, 8 November 1909, box 1, RG 85, Records of the Immigration and Naturalization Service, Los Angeles District Office, Alien Case Files 1904–1949, National Archives at Riverside.

10. On the role of standardization in creating commodities see William Cronon, *Nature's Metropolis: Chicago and the Great West* (New York: W.W. Norton, 1991); Quoted material from Douglas Cazaux Sackman, *Orange Empire: California and the Fruits of Eden* (Berkeley: University of California Press, 2005), 83.

11. Immigration Act of 1917, 39 Stat. 874 (1917); Otey M. Scruggs, "The First Mexican Farm Labor Program," *Journal of the Southwest* 2 (Winter 1960).

12. Scruggs, "The First Farm Labor Program": "Statement of Fred Cummings, of Fort Collins, Colo," *Seasonal Agricultural Laborers from Mexico,* 71.

13. Margo McBane, "The House That Lemons Built: Race, Ethnicity, Gender, Citizenship and the Creation of a Citrus Empire, 1893–1919" (PhD diss., University of California, Los Angeles, 2001).

14. Shamel's five-part series, entitled "Housing the Employe[e]s of California's Citrus Ranches," appeared in the February, March, May, June, and October 1918 issues of the *California Citrograph;* historians Gilbert González, Matt Garcia, and Margo McBane have previously analyzed this series. See Gilbert G. Gonzalez, *Labor and*

Community: Mexican Citrus Worker Villages in a Southern California County, 1900–1950 (Urbana: University of Illinois Press, 1994); Matt Garcia, A World of Its Own: Race, Labor, and Citrus in the Making of Greater Los Angeles, 1900–1970 (Chapel Hill: University of North Carolina Press, 2001); McBane, "The House That Lemons Built," 2001.

15. Quoted material from Andrew Herod, "Social Engineering through Spatial Engineering: Company Towns and the Geographical Imagination," in Company Towns in the Americas: Landscape, Power, and Working-Class Communities, ed. Oliver Dinius and Angela Vergara (Atlanta: University of Georgia Press, 2011), 21; see aforementioned series by Shamel, "Housing the Employe[e]s of California's Citrus Ranches."

16. Archibald Shamel, "Housing Employe[e]s of California's Citrus Ranches," California Citrograph, March 1918. The Citrus Belt stretched north of Los Angeles, an expansion made possible when reclamation—or federal water management projects expanding irrigation—transformed the central coast into a fruit basket at the beginning of the twentieth century.

17. Ibid.

18. As critical race theorists and scholars of settler colonialism have noted, the colonization of Indigenous land was accompanied by efforts to eliminate American Indians, dominate African Americans, and deny permanent settlement to a non-white immigrant workforce. Cheryl I. Harris, "Whiteness as Property," Harvard Law Review 106 (June 1993); Kelly Lytle Hernández, City of Inmates: Conquest, Rebellion, and the Rise of Human Caging in Los Angeles, 1771–1965 (Chapel Hill: University of North Carolina Press, 2017); Margaret D. Jacobs, "Seeing Like a Settler Colonial State," Modern American History 1, no. 2 (2018); on the effacement of American Indians and positioning of non-Indians as native, see Jean M. O'Brien, Firsting and Lasting: Writing Indians Out of Existence in New England (Minneapolis: University of Minnesota Press, 2010).

19. Typescript of Japanese Association of America, "Memorial Presented to the President While at San Francisco," 18 September 1919, box 1, p. 6, Iwata (Masakazu) Collection, Japanese American National Museum, Los Angeles.

20. Ralph Burnight, "The Japanese in Rural Los Angeles County," Studies in Sociology 4 (June 1920); Adon Poli, Japanese Farm Holdings on the Pacific Coast, Bureau of Agricultural Economics (Berkeley: U.S. Department of Agriculture, December 1944).

21. U.S. Census Bureau, "Per Cent Distribution of the Population by Color and Nativity, by Divisions and States," Table 36, Vol. 3, Part 1 (1930), 28.

22. Archibald Shamel, "Housing Conditions of the Employe[e]s of California Citrus Ranches," California Citrograph, May 1918, p. 151.

23. Archibald Shamel, "Housing Conditions of the Employe[e]s of California Citrus Ranches," typescript, n.d., p. 7, Archibald Shamel Papers, Tomás Rivera Library, University of California Riverside.

24. Ibid., p. 9.

25. Photograph of "House in Mexican Village," March 1918, Archibald Shamel Papers, Tomás Rivera Library, University of California Riverside; Archibald

Shamel, "Housing the Employe[e]s of California's Citrus Ranches," *California Citrograph,* March 1918.

26. Photographs are dated from 1916 to 1919 and include residence on citrus ranches from Los Angeles, San Bernardino, and Ventura Counties. All in box 4, folders 1, 2 and 3, Archibald D. Shamel Papers, Tomás Rivera Library, University of California Riverside; William Deverell, *Whitewashed Adobes: The Rise of Los Angeles and the Remaking of its Mexican Past* (Berkeley: University of California Press, 2004), 48.

27. Photograph of "House in Mexican Village," March 1918, Archibald Shamel Papers, Tomás Rivera Library, University of California Riverside; Archibald Shamel, "Housing Employe[e]s of California's Citrus Ranches," March 1918, p. 151.

28. Ibid.

29. Author notes from site visit and tour of Limoneira, Santa Paula, CA, December 30, 2011. On women's gardening activities at the Corona Chase Plantation, see José M. Alamillo, *Making Lemonade Out of Lemons: Mexican American Labor and Leisure in a California Town, 1880–1960* (Urbana: University of Illinois Press, 2006), 42–43.

30. Since Japanese farmers generally began as farmworkers, the growth of Japanese property ownership was negatively correlated with the Japanese labor supply. See U.S. Immigrant Commission, *Reports of the Immigrant Commission Part 25: Japanese and Other Immigrant Races in the Pacific Coast and Rocky Mountain States,* U.S. Congress, Senate, 61st Congress, 2nd Session, S. Doc. 633 (Washington, DC: Government Printing Office, 1911); Poli, *Japan Farm Holdings on the Pacific Coast.*

31. Burnight, "The Japanese in Rural Los Angeles County," 9; Typescript of Japanese Association of America, "Memorial Presented to the President While at San Francisco," 18 September 1919, box 1, pp. 6–9, Iwata (Masakazu) Collection, Japanese American National Museum, Los Angeles. On the ways race was used to delegitimize Japanese residents and divert attention away from the structural conditions shaping urban housing in this same period, see Natalia Molina, *Fit to Be Citizens?: Public Health and Race in Los Angeles, 1879–1939* (Berkeley: University of California Press, 2006).

32. On Japanese farm acquisition see Poli, *Japanese Farm Holdings on the Pacific Coast,* 7–10. Amount calculated from the estimated returns of the California Fruit Growers Exchange in 1920 ($81,200,000). California Fruit Growers Exchange, *Annual Report of the General Manager of the California Fruit Growers Exchange for the Year Closing August 31, 1920* (Los Angeles: Pacific Rural Press, 1920), General Collection, Huntington Library.

33. Shamel, "Housing Employe[e]s of California's Citrus Ranches," *California Citrograph,* May 1918, p. 151.

34. Shamel, "Housing Conditions of the Employe[e]s of California Citrus Ranches," typescript, n.d., pp. 3–4.

35. Tim Cresswell, *The Tramp in America* (London: Reaktion Books, 2001); Lytle Hernández, *City of Inmates.*

36. James D. Culbertson, "Housing of Ranch Labor," *First Annual Report of the California Citrus Institute* (1920), 97–105; see also Shamel, typescript, n.d., p. 3.

37. See Mae M. Ngai, *Impossible Subjects: Illegal Aliens and the Making of Modern America* (Princeton: Princeton University Press, 2004), 3; Emergency Quota Act, 43 Stat. 5 (1921); Immigration Act of 1924 (The Johnson-Reed Act), 43 Stat. 153 (1924).

38. As defined in Section 4 (c) of the Immigration Act of 1924, this included "an immigrant who was born in the Dominion of Canada, Newfoundland, the Republic of Mexico, the Republic of Cuba, the Republic of Haiti, the Dominican Republic, the Canal Zone, or an independent country of Central or South America, and his wife, and his unmarried children under 18 years of age, if accompanying or following to join him."

39. Kelly Lytle Hernández, "The Sisyphean Task: Origins of the Modern Border," in *Imaginary Lines: Border Enforcement and the Origins of Undocumented Immigration, 1882–1930,* ed. Patrick Ettinger (Austin: University of Texas Press, 2010); see also Lytle Hernández, *Migra! A History of the U.S. Border Patrol* (Berkeley: University of California Press, 2010).

40. A few examples of these texts include Molina, *How Race Is Made in America;* Garcia, *A World of Its Own;* Marshall Roderick, "The 'Box Bill': Public Policy, Ethnicity, and Economic Exploitation in Texas" (Master's thesis, Texas State University-San Marcos, 2011).

41. For instance, Mexican anthropologist Manuel Gamio identified a 632,777-person discrepancy in immigration figures published by the United States and Mexico, in part due to disparate incentives for registration offered on each side of the border. Manuel Gamio, *Mexican Immigration to the United States* (Chicago: University of Chicago Press, 1930).

42. For Box's critiques, see "Statement of Hon. John C. Box Representative in Congress from the State of Texas," 323–345; quoted material from Chairman in "Statement of E.K. Cumming, Representing the (Ariz.) Chamber of Commerce," 141—both in U.S. Congress, *Seasonal Agricultural Laborers from Mexico.*

43. U.S. Congress, *Seasonal Agricultural Laborers from Mexico,* 17; Dr. E.G. Peterson, "Mexican Immigration," address to the Chamber of Commerce of USA, at the Seventh Western Divisional Meeting, Ogden, Utah, 1 October 1929, Chamber of Commerce folder, Inland Mexican Heritage, Redlands, 2; see also George Clements, "Why Should We Rely Upon 'Bootleg' Labor?" *Los Angeles Times,* July 18, 1926.

44. Peterson, "Mexican Immigration," 5.

45. Quoted from Clements, "Why Should We Rely Upon 'Bootleg' Labor?" 3.

46. Ibid.

47. "Statement of S. P. Frisselle, Kearney Park, Calif," in U.S. Congress, *Seasonal Agricultural Laborers from Mexico,* 6.

48. Frank J. Warne, *The Tide of Immigration* (New York and London: D. Appleton and Company, 1916); Mark Wyman, *Round-trip to America: The Immigrants Return to Europe, 1880–1930* (Ithaca: Cornell University Press, 1996), 74–98;

Mirjana Morokvasic, "Birds of Passage Are Also Women," *International Migration Review* 18, no. 4 (1984); Thierry Rinaldetti, "Italian Migrants in the Atlantic Economies: From the Circular Migrations of the Birds of Passage to the Rise of a Dispersed Community," *Journal of American Ethnic History* 34 (Fall 2014).

49. Committee on Immigration of the National Civic Federation, Washington, DC, 1916, quoted in Warne, *The Tide of Immigration*, 73.

50. My interpretation is influenced by Neil Smith's discussion of spatial scales in his *Uneven Development: Nature, Capital, and the Production of Space*, 3rd ed. (1984; Athens: University of Georgia Press, 2008), 181.

51. "Statement of T.A. Sullivan Representing the Farmers of the Red River Valley, East Grand Forks, Minn," 29; "S. Maston Nixon, Robstown, Tex," 45; "Statement of Howard Ottinger, of Chaska, Minn," 126—all in U.S. Congress, *Seasonal Agricultural Laborers from Mexico*.

52. Mexican Fact-Finding Committee, "Mexicans in California: Report of Governor C. C. Young's Mexican Fact-Finding Committee" (San Francisco: California State Printing Office, 1930), 39 and 180; Louie Bloch, "Facts About Mexican Immigration Before and Since the Quota Restriction Laws," *Journal of the American Statistical Association* 24, no. 165 (March 1929). The Los Angeles Chamber of Commerce estimated the Mexican population in San Bernardino at 35,000 and at 25,000 in Riverside County. See George Clements to Paul Taylor, folder 20, box 10, Paul S. Taylor papers, Bancroft Library, University of California Berkeley.

53. Surveys were sent to packinghouse managers and community leaders, such as a social service worker, elementary school principal, and pastor. Two particularly revealing sources are Survey submitted by Bertha Van de Carr to Chamber of Commerce, Inc., Redlands, CA, 17 September 1929; and Survey submitted by Father Thomas Fitzgerald to Chamber of Commerce, Inc., Redlands, CA, 19 September 1929—both in Chamber of Commerce folder, Inland Mexican Heritage, Redlands.

54. "Chamber of Commerce, Inc," typescript, 19 September 1929; quoted material from N.B. Hinckley to the Redlands Chamber of Commerce, 18 September 1929—both in Chamber of Commerce folder, Inland Mexican Heritage, Redlands.

55. Excerpts of oral histories and photographs from this project are published in Antonio González Vasquez and Genevieve Carpio, *Mexican Americans in Redlands* (Charleston: Arcadia Publishing, 2012).

56. Camille Guerín-Gonzales, *Mexican Workers and American Dreams: Immigration, Repatriation, and California Farm Labor, 1900–1939* (New Brunswick, NJ: Rutgers University Press, 1994); Matt Garcia, *A World of Its Own*; Alamillo, *Making Lemonade Out of Lemons;* Ruth Tuck, *Not With the Fist: Mexican-Americans in a Southwest City* (New York: Harcourt, Brace, 1946).

57. Quoted material from George Clements, "Immigration Bill Big Economic Loss," 1927, Chamber of Commerce folder, Inland Mexican Heritage, Redlands. For similar sentiments, see George Clements, "California Casual Labor Demands," paper presented to Friends of the Mexicans, 13 November 1926, George Pigeon

Clements Papers, Young Research Library, University of California Los Angeles. On Clements, see Frank J. Taylor, "Heretic in the Promised Land: Los Angeles' Own Jiminy Cricket," *Saturday Evening Post,* December 21, 1940.

58. U.S. Congress, *Seasonal Agricultural Laborers from Mexico.*

59. Bloch, "Facts About Mexican Immigration," 60.

60. These figures were repeated in Mexican Fact-Finding Committee, "Mexicans in California" and by Charles Teague in "A Statement on Mexican Immigration," *Saturday Evening Post,* no. 107, March 10, 1928, pp. 45–46; see also Central Chamber of Agriculture and Commerce, "Declaration of Principles," El Paso Conference, 13 and 19 November 1927, Chamber of Commerce folder, Inland Mexican Heritage, Redlands.

61. "Statement of Harry Chandler, President Los Angeles Times Co.," U.S. Congress, House of Representatives, Committee on Immigration and Naturalization, *Western Hemisphere Immigration: Hearings Before the Committee on Immigration and Naturalization on the Bills H.R. 8523, H.R. 8530, H.R.8702 to Limit the Immigration of Aliens to the United States, and for Other Purposes,* 71st Cong., 1st sess. (Washington, DC: Government Printing Office, 1930), 59–74.

62. "California's Farm Labor Situation One Calling for Careful Study," *Los Angeles Times,* May 2, 1926.

63. "Mexico Has Her Own Ideas About 'Quotas,'" *Los Angeles Times,* April 22, 1928; see also "It Must Not Pass," *Los Angeles Times,* January 22, 1928.

64. "Saviors of California," *Los Angeles Times,* December 19, 1929, p. 4.

65. "Get the Facts First," *Los Angeles Times,* April 9, 1930, p. 4.

66. Gamio, *Mexican Immigration to the United States;* Ricardo Romo, "Responses to Mexican Immigration, 1910–1930," *Aztlán* 6 (1975): 178; Ethel Mae Morrison, "A History of Recent Legislative Proposals Concerning Mexican Immigration" (Master's thesis, University of Southern California, 1929).

67. Tomás Almaguer, *Racial Fault Lines: The Historical Origins of White Supremacy in California* (Berkeley: University of California Press, 1994).

68. "Statement of I. D. O'Donnell, Billings, Mont., Representing the Farmers of Wyoming and Montana," 92; "Statement of E. K. Cumming, Representing the Nogales (Ariz.) Chamber of Commerce," 143—both in in U.S. Congress, *Seasonal Agricultural Laborers from Mexico.*

69. "Statement of Mr. C. S. Brown," 183, in U.S. Congress, *Seasonal Agricultural Laborers from Mexico.*

70. "Statement of C. V. Maddux, Labor Commissioner, The Great Western Sugar Co., Denver, Colo," 242–243, in U.S. Congress, *Seasonal Agricultural Laborers from Mexico.*

71. "Statement of E. K. Cumming," 144–145, in U.S. Congress, *Seasonal Agricultural Workers from Mexico.*

72. See John M. Nieto-Phillips, *The Language of Blood: The Making of Spanish-American Identity in New Mexico, 1880s-1930s* (Albuquerque: University of New Mexico Press, 2004); Chris Wilson, *The Myth of Santa Fe: Creating a Modern Regional Tradition* (Albuquerque: University of New Mexico Press, 1997), chapter

2; Laura E. Gómez, *Manifest Destinies: The Making of the Mexican American Race* (New York: New York University Press, 2007).

73. "Statement of Hon. Joseph J. Mansfield, of Texas," 213, in U.S. Congress, *Seasonal Agricultural Laborers from Mexico.*

74. "Statement of C. V. Maddux, Labor Commissioner, The Great Western Sugar Co., Denver, Colo," 243, in U.S. Congress, *Seasonal Agricultural Laborers from Mexico.*

75. "Statement of Hon. C. B. Hudspeth, A Representative in Congress from the State of Texas," 287, 290, in U.S. Congress, *Seasonal Agricultural Laborers from Mexico.*

76. Stuart B. Schwartz, "Hurricanes and the Shaping of Circum-Caribbean Societies," The Florida Historical Quarterly 83, no. 4 (Spring 2005): 381–409.

77. Harwood Hull, "Work with Food Urged in Porto Rico," *New York Times,* September 22, 1928; "Storm Crippled Puerto Rican Trade," *New York Times,* September 25, 1928; Harwood Hull, "Porto Ricans Seek to Avoid Old Errors," *New York Times,* October 14, 1928; Harwood Hull, "Relief Fund Delay Dismays Porto Rico," *New York Times,* September 1, 1929.

78. Gabriel Terrasa, "The United States, Puerto Rico, and the Territorial Incorporation Doctrine: Reaching a Century of Constitutional Authoritarianism," *The John Marshall Law Review* 31, no. 1 (1997): 69–83; Charles R. Venator Santiago, "Race, Space, and Puerto Rican Citizenship," *Denver University Law Review* 78, no. 4 (2001); Carmen Teresa Whalen, "Colonialism, Citizenship, and the Making of the Puerto Rican Diaspora: An Introduction," in *The Puerto Rican Diaspora: Historical Perspectives,* ed. Carmen Teresa Whalen and Victor Vázquez-Hernández (Philadelphia: Temple University Press, 2005).

79. Ngai, *Impossible Subjects,* 100.

80. *Isabella Gonzales v. William Williams,* U.S. Commissioner of Immigration at the Port of New York, 192 US 1, 1903; Sam Erman, "Meanings of Citizenship in US Empire: Puerto Rico, Isabel Gonzales, and the Supreme Court, 1898–1905," *Journal of American Ethnic History* 27, no. 4 (2008).

81. See Jones-Shafroth Act, 39 Stat. 951 (1917).

82. Whalen, "Colonialism, Citizenship, and the Making of the Puerto Rican Diaspora."

83. "Statement of Mr. C. S. Brown," 38, in U.S, Congress, *Seasonal Agricultural Laborers from Mexico;* "Statement of D. B. Wiley, Manager, Arizona Farm Bureau, Phoenix, Arizona." 125, in U.S. Congress, *Western Hemisphere Immigration;* Carey McWilliams, *Ill Fares the Land* (Boston: Little Brown, 1942), 71. On Puerto Rican contract labor, see Edwin Maldonado, "Contract Labor and the Origins of Puerto Rican Communities in the United States," *International Migration Review* 13, no. 1 (Spring 1979).

84. See Jennifer McCormick and Cesar J. Ayala, "Felicita 'La Prieta' Mendez (1916–1998) and the End of Latino School Segregation in California, *Centro: Journal of the Center for Puerto Rican Studies* 19 (Fall 2007); see also Whalen, "Colonialism, Citizenship, and the Making of the Puerto Rican Diaspora," 21.

85. "Statement of D. B. Wiley, Manager, Arizona Farm Bureau, Phoenix, Arizona," 122, in U.S. Congress, *Western Hemisphere Immigration.*

86. "Statement of K. B. McMicken, Representing the Arizona Cotton Growers Association," 136, in U.S. Congress, *Western Hemisphere Immigration.*

87. "Statement of Hon. Felix Cordova Davila, The Resident Commissioner to the United States from Porto Rico," 145–147, in U.S. Congress, *Western Hemisphere Immigration;* Clarence O. Senior, *Puerto Rican Emigration* (Río Pierdas: Social Science Research Center, University of Puerto Rico, 1947); "500 Porto Ricans Lured to Arizona, A. F. of L. Charges," *San Bernardino County Sun,* October 7, 1926, p. 17; "Answer Given on Idle Labor," *Los Angeles Times,* February 26, 1927, p. 2.

88. "Phoenix Labor Council Answers Ariz. Pimacottton Growers Ass'n," *Arizona Labor Journal,* October 9, 1926, p. 1; "Phoenix Labor Council Answers Attack of Cotton Growers," *Arizona Labor Journal,* October 30, 1926.

89. "Statement of Mr. C. S. Brown," 184, in U.S. Congress, *Seasonal Agricultural workers from Mexico.*

90. "The Imported Porto Rican Farm Laborers Still Discontented," *Arizona Labor Journal,* March 5, 1927, p. 2.

91. Ralph Taylor, "Mexican vs. American Farm Labor" address at Seventh Western Divisional Meeting, Chamber of Commerce of USA, Ogden, Utah, typescript, 1 October 1929, p. 16, Chamber of Commerce folder, Inland Mexican Heritage, Redlands.

92. Many Puerto Ricans recruited to Hawaii disembarked in California due to misrepresentations of their working conditions by the Hawaiian Sugar Planters Association. Iris López, "Borinkis and Chop Suey: Puerto Rican Identity in Hawai'i, 1900 to 2000," in *The Puerto Rican Diaspora: Historical Perspectives,* ed. Carmen Teresa Whalen and Victor Vázquez-Hernández (Philadelphia: Temple University Press, 2005), 46–47.

93. "Statement of Fred J. Hart, Managing Editor, California Farm Bureau Monthlies," 207, in U.S. Congress, *Western Hemisphere Immigration.*

94. See "Statement of Ralph H. Taylor, Sacramento, California, Executive Secretary Agricultural Legislative Committee of California," 222, in U.S. Congress, *Western Hemisphere Immigration.* On racial passing, see Carlyle Van Thompson, *The Tragic Black Buck: Racial Masquerading in the American Literary Imagination* (New York: Peter Lang Publishing, 2004); David Delaney, "The Space that Race Makes," *Professional Geographer* 54, no. 1 (2002).

95. "Statement of Harry Chandler, President Los Angeles Times Co," 60–61, in U.S. Congress, *Western Hemisphere Immigration.* For a parallel statement claiming ranchers would be forced to turn to black colonial labor, see "Statement of Ralph H. Taylor, Sacramento, Calif., Executive Secretary Agricultural Legislature Committee of California," 222, 238, in U.S. Congress, *Western Hemisphere Immigration.*

96. Clements, "Immigration Bill Big Economic Loss."

97. On "culture of poverty" narratives directed at Puerto Rican women, see Carmen Teresa Whalen, "Labor Migrants or Submissive Wives: Competing Narratives of Puerto Rican Women in the Post-World War II Era," in *Puerto Rican Women's His-*

tory: New Perspectives, ed. Felix V. Matos Rodriguez and Linda C. Delgado (Armonk: M. E. Sharp, 1998); also see Laura Briggs, *Reproducing Empire: Race, Sex, Science, and U.S. Imperialism in Puerto Rico* (Berkeley: University of California Press, 2003).

98. Harwood Hull, "Work with Food Urged in Porto Rico," *New York Times,* September 22, 1928, p. 10; Harwood Hull, "Porto Ricans Seek to Avoid Old Errors," *New York Times,* October 14, 1928, p. 6.

99. See Ronald Takaki, *Pau Hana: Plantation Life and Labor in Hawaii, 1835– 1920* (Honolulu: University of Hawaii Press, 1983); JoAnna Poblete, *Islanders in the Empire: Filipino and Puerto Rican Laborers in Hawai'i* (Urbana: University of Illinois Press, 2014); Clarence Glick, *Sojourners and Settlers: Chinese Migrants in Hawaii* (Honolulu: University of Hawai'i Press, 1980).

100. Comments by Arthur M. Free in "Statement of Ralph H. Taylor, Sacramento, California, Executive Secretary Agricultural Legislative Committee of California," 222.

101. Ibid.

102. U.S. government officials had a long history of describing Puerto Ricans as black, childlike subjects. Carlos Alamo-Pastrana, *Seams of Empire: Race and Radicalism in Puerto Rico and the United States* (Gainesville: University Press of Florida, 2015). I use the term "black" in lowercase letters to signify a racial status that was placed upon people and that has been accompanied by the systematic denigration of that identity.

103. George Clements, "Mexican Immigration and Its Bearing on California's Agriculture," paper delivered to the Lemon Men's Club, 2 October 1929, box 12, folder 12, p. 6, Ron Lopez Papers, Chicano Studies Research Center, University of California Los Angeles.

104. For more on the Afromexican American diaspora, see David Samuel Torres-Rouff on the founding of the Los Angeles pueblo in *Before L.A.: Race, Space, and Municipal Power in Los Angeles, 1781–1894* (New Haven: Yale University Press, 2013). The whitening of Mexicans was consistent with state-building projects in Mexico. See José Vasconcelos, *La Raza Cosmica: Mision de la Raza Iberoamericana* (Madrid: Agencia Mundial de Libreria, 1948).

105. George Clements, "Mexican Immigration and Its Bearing on California's Agriculture," paper delivered to the Lemon Men's Club, 2 October 1929, box 12, p. 6, Ron Lopez Papers, Chicano Studies Research Center, University of California Los Angeles.

106. On questions of racial passing as related to movement across space, see Delaney, "The Space that Race Makes."

107. Charles Teague in "A Statement on Mexican Immigration," *Saturday Evening Post,* no. 107, March 10, 1928, pp. 45–46.

108. Numerous statements before Congress echoed this sentiment. See also the proceedings of the Central Chamber of Commerce, in particular Ralph Taylor, "Mexican vs. American Farm Labor," 15; and Peterson, "Mexican Immigration," 14.

109. Paul A. Kramer, *The Blood of Government: Race, Empire, the United States, and the Philippines* (Chapel Hill: University of North Carolina Press, 2006).

110. Briggs, *Reproducing Empire;* Carmen Teresa Whalen and Victor Vazquez-Hernández, eds., *The Puerto Rican Diaspora: Historical Perspectives* (Philadelphia: Temple University Press, 2005).

111. "Statement of Frank J. Palomares, Manager, Agricultural Labor Bureau of the San Joaquin Valley," 151; "Statement of Harry Chandler, President Los Angeles Times Co," 69; "Statement of Hon. John N. Garner, A Representative in Congress from the State of Texas (Resumed)," 165–166; "Statement of Fred J. Hart, Managing Editor, California Farm Bureau Monthlies," 192–211—all in U.S. Congress, *Western Hemisphere Immigration.*

112. For questions regarding state surveillance of sexuality and its alternatives in Puerto Rico, see Briggs, *Reproducing Empire;* and Eileen Suárez Findlay, *Imposing Decency: The Politics of Sexuality and Race in Puerto Rico, 1870–1920* (Durham: Duke University Press, 2001). On imperialism, gender, and domesticity, see Laura Wexler, *Tender Violence: Domestic Visions in an Age of U.S. Imperialism* (Chapel Hill: University of North Carolina Press, 2000).

113. Comments by Arthur M. Free in "Statement of Hon. Francis I. Jones, Director General United States Employment Service, Department of Labor, Washington, DC," 283, in U.S. Congress, *Western Hemisphere Immigration.*

114. On a literary analysis of the gendering of movement through the Caribbean as male, see Elizabeth DeLoughry, *Routes and Roots: Navigating Caribbean and Pacific Island Literatures* (Honolulu: University of Hawai'i Press, 2007).

115. The 1920s marked a dramatic increase in Filipino immigration, as Filipino immigrants replaced Chinese, Japanese, Korean, and South Asian laborers who had been excluded in canneries and fields. Most who came to California were single, male, and between the ages of 16 and 30 years old. See Yen Le Espiritu, *Filipino American Lives* (Philadelphia: Temple University Press, 1995), 9–14.

116. For more on fears of relationships between Filipino men and white women, see Ngai, *Impossible Subjects;* Kramer, *The Blood of Government;* Vicente L. Rafael, *White Love and Other Events in Filipino History* (Durham: Duke University Press, 2000).

117. "Statement of Chester B. Moore, Los Angeles, Calif., Manager Western Growers Protective Association," 245; and "Statement of Fred J. Hart, Managing Editor, California Farm Bureau Monthlies," 192–211—both in U.S. Congress, *Western Hemisphere Immigration.* See also Ralph Taylor, "Mexican vs. American Farm Labor," 15.

118. "Filipinos Leave Alta Loma," *Riverside Daily Press,* August 23, 1930; "Filipinos Leave District," *Riverside Daily Press,* August 22, 1930; "Stabbing of Girl Leads to Court," *Los Angeles Times,* September 4, 1930.

119. Quoted material from "Girl-Slasher Sentenced," *Los Angeles Times,* September 30, 1930, p. 6; "Filipino Youth Not Juvenile, Court Rules," *Los Angeles Times,* September 16, 1930, For comparative examples of captivity narratives sensationalizing Native American and Chinese violence against white women, see Birgit Rasmussen, *Queequeg's Coffin: Indigenous Literacies and Early American Literature* (Durham: Duke University Press, 2012); and Mary Lui, *The Chinatown Trunk*

Mystery: Murder, Miscegenation, and Other Dangerous Encounters in Turn-of-the-Century New York City (Princeton: Princeton University Press, 2005).

120. "Filipino Will Face Assault Hearing Today," *San Bernardino County Sun,* September 2, 1930; Raynas's plea prompts consideration of the violent lynchings of African American men across the South, as well as the means by which black communities survived mob violence. See Koritha Mitchell, *Living with Lynching: African American Lynching Plays, Performance, and Citizenship, 1890–1930* (Urbana: University of Illinois Press, 2011).

121. As discussed elsewhere, the Watsonville Riots involved an assault by four hundred white vigilantes at an interracial Palm Beach dance hall earlier that year. For more on white-Filipino relationships, see Valentin R. Aquino, *"The Filipino Community in Los Angeles"* (Master's thesis, University of Southern California, 1952), chapter 4; Ngai, *Impossible Subjects;* Linda España-Maram, *Creating Masculinity in Los Angeles's Little Manila: Working-Class Filipinos and Popular Culture, 1920s-1950s* (New York: Columbia University Press, 2006).

122. "Labor Sponsors Plan to Ban Filipino Workers," *San Bernardino County Sun,* September 24, 1930; "Filipino Laborers Exit," *Los Angeles Times,* August 26, 1930; "Filipino held in Juvenile Court," *Los Angeles Times,* September 12, 1930.

123. "Statement of Harry Chandler, President Los Angeles Times Co," 61, in U.S. Congress, *Western Hemisphere Immigration.*

124. "Statement of Hon. John N Garner, Representative in Congress from the State of Texas," 166, in U.S. Congress, *Seasonal Laborers from Mexico.*

125. "Statement of S. P. Friselle, Kearney Park, Calif," 6, in U.S. Congress, *Seasonal Agricultural Laborers from Mexico.*

126. On racial triangulation, see Claire Jean Kim, "The Racial Triangulation of Asian Americans," *Politics and Society,* 27 (March 1999).

127. Quoted material from "Statement of Fred J. Hart, Managing Editor, California Farm Bureau Monthlies," 209, in U.S. Congress, *Western Hemisphere Immigration.* For comparable accounts, see the testimonies by Fleming, Chandler, and Handler, also in U.S. Congress, *Western Hemisphere Immigration.*

128. "Statement of Henry L. Yates, Brownsville, Tex," 45; and "Statement of Fleming, Elephant-Butte Irrigation District," 50–54—both in U.S. Congress, *Western Hemisphere Immigration.*

129. Rita Radeleff and Lee Richardson interviewed by Robert Gonzalez, 14 June 1997, transcript, Inland Mexican Heritage, Redlands. In his study of San Bernardino, Paul Taylor would count five intermarriages between Anglo Americans and elite Mexicans. See "Field Notes San Bernardino," California Imperial Valley, ca. 1927–1934, folder 17, box 10, Paul S. Taylor papers, Bancroft Library, University of California Berkeley. Consider also the biethnic Punjabi-Mexican community in the Imperial Valley. Karen Leonard, *Making Ethnic Choices: California's Punjabi Mexican Americans* (Philadelphia: Temple University Press, 1992).

130. On national myths of racial homogeneity and their limits, see Rosa-Linda Fregoso, *meXicana Encounters: The Making of Social Identities on the Borderlands* (Berkeley: University of California Press, 2003).

131. Laurence M. Benedict, "Bill Barring Mexicans Goes Through Senate," *Los Angeles Times,* May 14, 1930.

132. U.S. Congress, House of Representatives, Committee on Immigration and Naturalization, *Immigration from Mexico. Hearings Before the Committee on Immigration and Naturalization on H.R. 12382,* 71st Cong., 2nd sess. (Washington, DC: Government Printing Office, May 15, 1930). For further congressional opposition, see the minority reports of Samuel Dickenson, A. M. Free, and Edmind Cooke, "Restriction of Immigration from Republic of Mexico," 71st Congress, 2nd Session, Report No. 1594, Part 2, May 28, 1930.

133. "Restriction of Immigration from Republic of Mexico," 6.

134. Francisco E. Balderrama and Raymond Rodríguez, *Decade of Betrayal: Mexican Repatriation in the 1930s* (Albuquerque: University of New Mexico Press, 1995); Douglas Monroy, *Rebirth: Mexican Los Angeles from the Great Migration to the Great Depression* (Berkeley: University of California Press, 1999).

CHAPTER FOUR. "DEL FOTINGO QUE ERA MIO"

1. Blas Coyazo interviewed by Robert Gonzalez, April 1994, transcript, Inland Mexican Heritage, Redlands.

2. On automobility, see Jeremy Packer, *Mobility without Mayhem: Safety, Cars, and Citizenship* (Durham: Duke University Press, 2008); Cotten Seiler, *Republic of Drivers: A Cultural History of Automobility in America* (Chicago: University of Chicago Press, 2009); and John Urry, *Sociology Beyond Societies: Mobilities for the Twenty-First Century* (New York: Routledge, 2000).

3. Mexican Fact-Finding Committee, "Mexicans in California: Report of Governor C. C. Young's Mexican Fact-Finding Committee" (San Francisco: California State Printing Office, 1930), 159.

4. For more on the trope of charity-seeking Mexicans, see Natalia Molina, *Fit to Be Citizens?: Public Health and Race in Los Angeles, 1879–1939* (Berkeley: University of California Press, 2006), chapter 4.

5. For one important account of this history see Francisco E. Balderrama and Raymond Rodríguez, *Decade of Betrayal: Mexican Repatriation in the 1930s* (Albuquerque: University of New Mexico Press, 1995).

6. Seiler, *Republic of Drivers;* see also, Cotten Seiler, "'So That We as a Race Might Have Something Authentic to Travel By': African American Automobility and Cold-War Liberalism," *American Quarterly* 58, no. 4 (2006).

7. Archibald Shamel, "Housing Conditions of the Employe[e]s of California Citrus Ranches," typescript, n.d., p. 4, Archibald Shamel Papers, Tomás Rivera Library, University of California Riverside.

8. On automotive cultures in this period, see Thomas Weiss, "Tourism in America before World War II," *Journal of Economic History* 64, no. 2 (2004); Marguerite S. Shaffer, *See America First: Tourism and National Identity, 1880–1940* (Washington, DC: Smithsonian, 2001); Virginia Scharff, *Taking the Wheel:*

Women and the Coming of the Motor Age (Albuquerque: University of New Mexico, 1992).

9. Constantine Panunzio and the Heller Committee for Research in Social Economics of the University of California, "Cost of Living Studies V. How Mexicans Earn and Live: A Study of the Incomes and Expenditures of One Hundred Mexican Families in San Diego, California," *University of California Publications in Economics,* 13, no. 1 (1933). In their report, the Mexican Fact-Finding Committee cites the San Fernando figure from an unpublished report by the Los Angeles County Health Department. See Mexican Fact-Finding Committee, "Mexicans in California," 178. See also Scott L. Bottles, *Los Angeles and the Automobile: The Making of the Modern City* (Berkeley: University of California Press, 1987). Statewide statistics for Mexican American motorists are unavailable.

10. Panunzio and the Heller Committee, "Cost of Living Studies v. How Mexicans Earn and Live"; Mexican Fact-Finding Committee, "Mexicans in California."

11. Howard Herrera interviewed by Robert Gonzalez, transcript, 13 April 1994, Inland Mexican Heritage, Redlands.

12. In an interview conducted with my paternal grandfather, Vincent Carpio Sr., he recounted his experience as a foreman and the bonus he received for identifying and transporting workers to the fields surrounding Pomona in the 1940s. He described the effective role of "incentives," such as warm food prepared by my grandmother Consuelo Carpio and cold beer on payday, in retaining workers. Vincent Carpio interviewed by Genevieve Carpio, Spring 2001, Pomona, CA.

13. On the connection of migrant workers, automobiles, and collective action see Don Mitchell, *The Lie of the Land: Migrant Workers and the California Landscape* (Minneapolis: University of Minnesota Press, 1996).

14. Rick Martinez, "Co-Founder of Mitla Lucia Rodriguez Dies," *San Bernardino County Sun,* January 13, 1981; "Route 66 Special," *Access Rewind* [film], IE Media Group, 2011.

15. For more on Latina/o restaurant owners as place-makers, see Natalia Molina, "The Importance of Place and Place-Makers in the Life of a Los Angeles Community: What Gentrification Erases from Echo Park," *Southern California Quarterly* 97, no. 1 (2015): 69–111.

16. Author has worked in consultation on various IMH projects since 2004.

17. A selection of these photographs can be found in Antonio González Vazquez and Genevieve Carpio, *Mexican Americans in Redlands* (Charleston: Arcadia Publishing, 2012).

18. Phil Deloria, *Indians in Unexpected Places* (Lawrence: University Press of Kansas, 2004), 138.

19. For the continuing significance of the corrido in Los Angeles, see "The Corrido of LA," an exhibition by the Los Angeles County Museum of Art in 2010, http://www.lacma.org/art/installation/corrido-la; for sound recordings, see the Strachwitz Frontera Collection of Mexican and Mexican American Recordings, UCLA Chicano Studies Research Center and UCLA Digital Library, http://frontera.library.ucla.edu.

20. Manuel Gamio, *Mexican Immigration to the United States* (Chicago: University of Chicago Press, 1930).

21. Translated by author. Original printed in Gamio, *Mexican Immigration to the United States.*

22. Veronica Castillo-Muñoz, "Historical Roots of Rural Migration: Land Reform, Corn Credit, and the Displacement of Rural Farmers in Nayarit Mexico, 1900–1952," *Mexican Studies/ Estudios Mexicanos* 29 (Winter 2013).

23. "You go around showing off in your big automobile." Translated by author. Original printed in Gamio, *Mexican Immigration to the United States,* 93.

24. Rita Urquijo-Ruiz writes that El Renegade was a character in a popular comedy routine in teatro de carpa, or traveling tent theater, used to poke fun at assimilated Mexicans. See Rita Urquijo-Ruiz, *Wild Tongues: Transnational Mexican Popular Culture* (Austin: University of Texas Press, 2012), 23–25.

25. Original printed in Gamio, *Mexican Immigration to the United States,* 31; the term "fotingo" was often synonymous with Ford motor cars, which Mexican farm laborers frequently owned due to their affordability.

26. Ricardo Romo, "Work and Restlessness: Occupational and Spatial Mobility among Mexicanos in Los Angeles," *Pacific Historical Review* 46 (May 1977): 176.

27. See digital archive of Ford's Mexico City plant at "Ford Mexico City Plant Photographs," The Henry Ford, Dearborn, MI, accessed July 2018, https://www.thehenryford.org/collections-and-research/digital-collections/sets/11598/. See also Ford Motor Company, "Historia de Ford de Mexico," accessed March 29, 2013, http://media.ford.com/article_display.cfm?article_id=4166.

28. Indeed, the vast majority were Ford cars and trucks, at 27 percent of all automotive objects (a category including automobile types and auto parts) brought to Mexico by repatriates. See Gamio, *Mexican Immigration to the United States,* esp. Appendix 5, 224–225; for more accounts of Ford automobiles moving back and forth across the U.S.-Mexico border, see Alice Evans Cruz, "The Romanzas Train Señora Nurse," *The Survey* 60 (August 1928): 468–469, 488; Cara Finnegan, *Picturing Poverty: Print Culture and FSA Photographs* (Washington, DC: Smithsonian Books, 2003).

29. The Social Science Council's Committee on Scientific Aspects of Human Migration distributed grants to social scientists for the study of Mexican migration in the United States. See correspondence from Dean E. D. Merrill to President W. Campbell, Berkeley, CA, 30 August 1927, box 11, Paul S. Taylor Papers, Bancroft Library, University of California Berkeley; Paul S. Taylor, "Mexican Labor in the United States Migration Statistics, II," *University of California Publications in Economics* 12, no. 1 (1933); Abraham Hoffman, "An Unusual Monument: Paul S. Taylor's Mexican Labor in the United States Monograph Series," *Pacific Historical Review* 45 (May 1976).

30. Paul S. Taylor, "Mexican Labor in the United States Migration Statistics, II," p. 1.

31. Paul S. Taylor, "Mexican Labor in the United States Imperial Valley," *University of California Publications in Economics,* 6, no. 1 (December 17, 1928): 39.

Although a minority of workers commuted daily between Mexico and the United States, even this small flow was disrupted by immigration officials at the border. See Kelly Lytle Hernández, *Migra! A History of the U.S. Border Patrol* (Berkeley: University of California Press, 2010).

32. Paul S. Taylor, "Mexican Labor in the United States Migration Statistics, IV," *University of California Publications in Economics,* 12, no. 3 (September 1934).

33. For instance, Congressman John Box entered Paul Taylor's preliminary migration statistics directly into congressional record, and others referenced his study during the 1930 hearings on immigration from the Western Hemisphere. See U.S. Congress, House of Representatives, Committee on Immigration and Naturalization, *Western Hemisphere Immigration: Hearings Before the Committee on Immigration and Naturalization on the Bills H.R. 8523, H.R. 8530, H.R.8702 to Limit the Immigration of Aliens to the United States, and for Other Purposes,* 71st Cong., 1st sess. (Washington, DC: Government Printing Office, 1930), 249, 363, 380, 424–448.

34. Taylor, "Mexican Labor in the United States Migration Statistics, II," p. 2.

35. Taylor, "Mexican Labor in the United States Migration Statistics, IV"; on labor in the San Joaquin Valley's cotton industry, see Devra Weber, *Dark Sweat, White Gold: California Farm Workers, Cotton, and the New Deal* (Berkeley: University of California Press, 1994).

36. The structure of my claim draws on Angela Hudson's work on fugitive slaves' mobility as they traversed Creek paths in the American South, and Neil Smith's writings on the "see saw" effect of capitalism. See Angela Pulley Hudson, *Creek Paths and Federal Roads: Indians, Settlers, and Slaves and the Making of the American South* (Chapel Hill: University of North Carolina Press, 2010); Neil Smith, *Uneven Development: Nature, Capital, and the Production of Space,* 3rd ed. (1984; Athens: University of Georgia Press, 2008). For more on challenges encountered by migrant workers in transit, see Albert Croutch, "Housing Migratory Agricultural Workers in California, 1913–1948" (Master's thesis, University of California Berkeley, 1948), 37.

37. A.C. Fleury to Paul S. Taylor, 2 July 1936, Paul S. Taylor Papers, container 14, Bancroft Library, University of California Berkeley.

38. Paul S. Taylor, "Mexican Labor in the United States Migration Statistics, III," *University of California Publications in Economics* 12, no. 2 (1933): 13.

39. Ibid.

40. Emphasis in original. Seiler, "So That We as a Race Might Have Something Authentic to Travel By," 1111. Jeremy Packer points towards the dangers of "driving while black," and suggests window tinting was intentionally used by African American drivers to obscure their visibility. Packer, *Mobility without Mayhem,* chapter 5.

41. Taylor, "Mexican Labor in the United States Migration Statistics, II," pp. 2–3.

42. In later fieldwork conducted in Rialto, San Bernardino County, as part of his *Mexican Migration Statistics* study, Taylor would distinguish between the "better class" as "Spanish" and "low class" as "Mexican." See "Field Notes San

Bernardino," California Imperial Valley, ca. 1927–1934, folder 17, box 10, Paul S. Taylor papers, Bancroft Library, University of California Berkeley.

43. I adopt Kelly Lytle Hernández's term "Mexican Brown" to indicate the profiling of color and class used by Taylor to compile his migration statistics. This is a widening of the original application of the term. For Lytle Hernández, "Mexican Brown" indicates the racial and economic markers, as well as entanglements with crime and drug enforcement engaged by border patrol personnel from the 1960s onward. See Lytle Hernandez, *Migra!*

44. My analysis here is influenced by Tim Cresswell's work on the invention of the "tramp" in modern America. Tim Cresswell, *The Tramp in America* (London: Reaktion Books, 2001).

45. Tim Cresswell, *In Place/Out of Place: Geography, Ideology and Transgression* (Minneapolis: University of Minnesota Press, 1996).

46. Romo, "Work and Restlessness"; Graciano Gomez interviewed by Robert Gonzalez, 27 January 1995, transcript, pp. 2–3, Inland Mexican Heritage, Redlands.

47. Emory Bogardus to Ron Lopez, 1 February 1968, box 27, folder 17; and Emory Bogardus to Ron Lopez, 15 February 1968, box 27—both in Ron Lopez Papers, Chicano Studies Research Center, University of California Los Angeles.

48. Wally Sanchez interviewed by Robert Gonzalez, 15 July 1994, transcript, Inland Mexican Heritage, Redlands.

49. Margaret Roque Castro and Angeline Sumaya Cosme interviewed by Robert Gonzalez, 17 July 2000, transcript, p. 8, Inland Mexican Heritage, Redlands.

50. J. H. Winslow to Rex Thomson, "Mexicans," 26 January 1934, box 12, Ron Lopez Papers, Chicano Studies Research Center, University of California, Los Angeles.

51. Cruz, "The Romanzas Train Señora Nurse." Despite the author's Spanish surname, Census records list both the author and her husband, Bernard Cruz, as white. U.S. Census Bureau, "Place: O'Neal, San Joaquin, California," Roll 212, Enumeration District 0070 (1930), 2B.

52. Cruz, "The Romanzas Train Señora Nurse," 468.

53. Ibid., 469.

54. Charles Hyde, *Riding the Roller Coaster: A History of the Chrysler Corporation* (Detroit: Wayne State University Press, 2003), chapter 5.

55. Cruz, "The Romanzas Train Señora Nurse," 488.

56. Ibid.

57. Ibid.

58. Louis Hyman, *Borrow: The American Way of Debt: How Personal Credit Created the American Middle Class and Almost Bankrupted the Nation* (New York: Vintage Books, 2012).

59. Charles McGovern, *Consumption and Citizenship, 1890–1945* (Chapel Hill: University of North Carolina Press, 2006); see also Lizabeth Cohen, *A Consumers' Republic: The Politics of Mass Consumption in Postwar America* (New York: Alfred A. Knopf, 2003), 20.

60. Packer, *Mobility without Mayhem*, 206. For primary media sources contextualizing the Los Angeles experience of car shopping, see Los Angeles Cultural Heritage Commission, "Historical-Cultural Monument Application Part 2," May 2006, City of Los Angeles Office of Historic Resources. A notable exception to this racial exclusion was Felix Chevrolet in Los Angeles. Owned by a Mexican American, Winslow Felix, the dealership was known for selling to racial minorities and hiring Latino salesmen. Jon G. Robinson, *Classic Chevrolet Dealerships: Selling the Bowtie* (Hong Kong: Motorbooks International, 2003), 97.

61. John Steinbeck, *Their Blood Is Strong* (San Francisco: Simon J. Lubin Society of California, 1938); quote in heading for next section is from Steinbeck's report, p. 3.

62. Excerpt from Paul S. Taylor's testimony, in U.S. Congress, House of Representatives, Select Committee to Investigate the Interstate Migration of Destitute Citizens, *Interstate Migration*, 76th Cong., 3rd sess., Part 8, November 29, December 2, 3, 1940 (Washington, DC: Government Printing Office, 1941), 3245.

63. See Michael B. Katz, *The Undeserving Poor: From the War on Poverty to the War on Welfare* (New York: Pantheon Books, 1989).

64. H. Mark Wild, "If You Ain't Got That Do-Re-Mi: The Los Angeles Border Patrol and White Migration in Depression-Era California," *Southern California Quarterly* 83 (Fall 2001); McWilliams, *Factories in the Field: The Story of Migratory Farm Labor in California* (Boston: Little, Brown, 1939), 310–312.

65. Wild, "If You Ain't Got that Do-Re-Mi"; McWilliams, *Factories in the Field*, 310.

66. At the conclusion of the pea harvest, one county approved a $2,500 expenditure to fill migrant tanks with just enough gas to get them from one county to the next. See Dorothea Lange and Paul S. Taylor, *An American Exodus: A Record of Human Erosion* (1939; Paris: Jean Michel Place, 1999), 146. Similarly, Santa Barbara and San Luis Obispo Counties appropriated $2,000 to buy gasoline for destitute workers bound for inland counties. McWilliams, *Factories in the Field*, 312–314.

67. See Katz, *The Undeserving Poor*.

68. David Roediger, *The Wages of Whiteness: Race and the Making of the American Working Class* (London: Verso, 1991); Matthew Frye Jacobson, *Whiteness of a Different Color: European Immigrants and the Alchemy of Race* (Cambridge, MA: Harvard University Press, 1998).

69. John Steinbeck, *The Harvest Gypsies: On the Road to the Grapes of Wrath*, with introduction by Charles Wollenberg (1936; Berkeley: Heyday Books, 1988), xiii–4.

70. Eunice Romero Gonzales interviewed by Robert Gonzalez, 8 July 1994, transcript, p. 14, Inland Mexican Heritage, Redlands.

71. Weber, *Dark Sweat, White Gold*. See also Roediger, *The Wages of Whiteness*.

72. Douglas Cazaux Sackman, *Orange Empire: California and the Fruits of Eden* (Berkeley: University of California Press, 2005), 11.

73. See analysis by Sarah Wald, *The Nature of California: Race, Citizenship, and Farming Since the Dust Bowl* (Seattle: University of Washington Press, 2016).

74. Henry Mayer, "The Making of a Documentary Book," in Lange and Taylor, *An American Exodus.*

75. Lange and Taylor, *An American Exodus.*

76. George Caleb Bingham, *Daniel Boone Escorting Settlers through the Cumberland Gap,* 1851–1852, oil on canvas, 36.5 × 50.25 inches, St. Louis, Kemper Art Museum; for a discussion of Bingham in relation to settler colonialism, see Sherene Razack, ed., *Race, Space, and the Law: Unmapping a White Settler Society* (Toronto: Between the Lines, 2002).

77. Paul S. Taylor and Dorothea Lange, "Again the Covered Wagon," *Survey Graphic* 24 (July 1935).

78. Lange and Taylor, *An American Exodus,* 133.

79. Josh Sides, *L.A. City Limits: African American Los Angeles from the Great Depression to the Present* (Berkeley: University of California Press, 2004); Douglas Flamming, *Bound for Freedom: Black Los Angeles in Jim Crow America* (Berkeley: University of California Press, 2006).

80. John Steinbeck, *Their Blood Is Strong* (San Francisco: Simon J. Lubin Society of California, 1938). For an insightful analysis, see Michael Denning, *The Cultural Front: The Laboring of American Culture in the Twentieth Century* (London: Verso, 1998). On Lange's multiple migrant mothers, see Linda Gordon, *Dorothea Lange: A Life Beyond Limits* (New York: W. W. Norton, 2009).

81. Steinbeck, *Their Blood Is Strong,* 3.

82. Ibid., 25–28.

83. "Testimony of Dr. Paul Taylor, Professor of Economics, University of California, Berkeley, Calif," in U.S. Congress, *Investigation of Concentration of Economic Power,* 76th Cong., 3rd sess., Part 30 (Washington, DC: Government Printing Office, 1940), 17043.

84. Ibid., 17055.

85. Over 33 percent of all large-scale farms were located in California, as were 60 percent of all large-scale truck and fruit farms. Paul S. Taylor and Tom Vasey, "Contemporary Background of California Farm Labor," *Rural Sociology* 1 (December 1936): 403.

86. Lange and Taylor, *An American Exodus,* 107.

87. Ibid., 146.

88. Ibid., 141.

89. Steinbeck, *Their Blood Is Strong,* 3.

90. Terms identified by McWilliams, *Factories in the Field,* 197–198, and by Lange and Taylor, *An American Exodus,* 88.

91. On "queer domesticity" see Nayan Shah, *Contagious Divides: Epidemics and Race in San Francisco's Chinatown* (Berkeley: University of California Press, 2001), 104.

92. Lange and Taylor, *An American Exodus,* 130–135.

93. Becky Nicolaides, *My Blue Heaven: Life and Politics in the Working-Class Suburbs of Los Angeles, 1920–1965* (Chicago: University of Chicago Press, 2002); Daniel Jay Cady, "'Southern' California: White Southern Migrants in Greater Los Angeles, 1920–1930" (PhD diss., Claremont Graduate University, 2005).

94. Emphasis in original. Simon J. Lubin Society's Preface in Steinbeck, *Their Blood Is Strong.*

95. Steinbeck, *The Harvest Gypsies,* vii. Similarly, in 1935, Taylor was employed by the California Emergency Relief Administration to "undertake research designed to help in shaping public action toward this human tide." Paul S. Taylor, *On the Ground in the Thirties* (Salt Lake City: Peregrine Smith Books, 1983), xi.

96. "Action Asked on Migrants," *Los Angeles Times,* December 1, 1939.

97. "Legislators Launch Final Rush of Bills," *San Bernardino County Sun,* June 19, 1939.

98. For media coverage of proposed Senate Bill 740, see "Alien Relief Curb Voted: Measure to Save Huge Sum for State Passed, 43 to 28, by Assembly," *Los Angeles Times,* June 19, 1939; "Ralph Swing, Former State Senator Dies," *Los Angeles Times,* February 6, 1961. As a precedent see "Stubbs Wants to Bar Aliens from Relief," *San Bernardino County Sun,* May 1, 1936; "Legislators Launch Final Rush of Bills," *San Bernardino County Sun,* June 19, 1939.

99. "Confiscatory Taxes Seen in Relief Burden," *San Bernardino Country Sun,* June 1, 1939.

100. Chairman of the Oklahoma Highway Commission Cyrus Avery is credited with first referring to Route 66 as the Main Street of America. See Gordon Slethaug, "Mapping the Trope: A Historical and Cultural Journey," in *Hit the Road Jack: Essays on the Culture of the American Road,* ed. Gordon E. Slethaug and Stacilee Ford (Quebec: McGill Queens University Press, 2012), 27.

101. Weiss, "Tourism in America before World War II."

102. Phoebe S. Kropp, *California Vieja: Culture and Memory in a Modern American Place* (Berkeley: University of California Press, 2006), 91.

103. Deloria, *Indians in Unexpected Places.*

104. "Madonna of the Trail Volume 1," scrapbook; "Madonna of the Trail Volume 2," scrapbook; "Madonna of the Trail Volume 3," scrapbook; "Madonna of the Trail Volume 4," scrapbook—all in Daughters of the American Revolution Collection, 1915–2008, drawer 3, Robert E. Ellingwood Model Colony History Room, Ovitt Family Community Library, Ontario, CA; Fern Ioula Bauer, *The Historic Treasure Chest of the Madonna of the Trail Monuments* (Springfield, OH: John McEnaney Printing, 1984).

105. Mrs. William Talbott, "Annual Report of Progress in the Work of the National Old Trails Committee," Proceeding of the Continental Congress of the Daughters of the American Revolution (Washington, DC: National Society of the Daughters of the American Revolution, 1922), 102.

106. Originally appearing in a summer issue of the 1928 *Federal Illustrator,* Leimbach was later quoted in Carla Sanders, "O Pioneers!," *Inland Living Magazine,* clipping (February-March, 2011), p. 16, Daughters of the American Revolution Collection, 1915–2008, Robert E. Ellingwood Model Colony History Room, Ovitt Family Community Library, Ontario, CA.

107. Quoted material from Sanders, "O Pioneers!," 16. On the longevity of the American frontier in the popular imagination see Richard White and Patricia

Limerick, *The Frontier in American Culture* (Berkeley: University of California Press, 1994). For more on German fascination with the American West, especially Native American communities, see H. Glenn Penny, *Kindred by Choice: Germans and American Indians Since 1800* (Chapel Hill: University of North Carolina Press, 2015).

108. Site visit by author to Madonna of the Trail monument, Ontario, on August 14, 2012.

109. For selective works, see William Deverell, *Whitewashed Adobe: The Rise of Los Angeles and the Remaking of Its Mexican Past* (Berkeley: University of California Press, 2004); Kropp, *California Vieja*.

110. Matt Garcia, *A World of Its Own: Race, Labor, and Citrus in the Making of Greater Los Angeles, 1900–1970* (Chapel Hill: University of North Carolina Press, 2001), 17–46.

111. U.S. Census Bureau, "Statistics of Mexican, Indian, Chinese, and Japanese Families," Table 39 (1930), 212; Kelly Lytle Hernández, *City of Inmates: Conquest, Rebellion, and the Rise of Human Caging in Los Angeles, 1771–1965* (Chapel Hill: University of North Carolina Press, 2017), chapter 5.

112. Edward J. Escobar, *Race, Police, and the Making of a Political Identity: Mexican Americans and the Los Angeles Police Department, 1900–1945* (Berkeley: University of California Press, 1999).

113. Miroslava Chávez-García, *States of Delinquency: Race and Science in the Making of California's Juvenile Justice System* (Berkeley: University of California Press, 2012).

114. Natalia Molina, *How Race Is Made in America: Immigration, Citizenship, and the Historical Power of Racial Scripts* (Berkeley: University of California Press, 2014).

115. Based on author's analysis of original enrollment records, which show only 38 Spanish surnamed boys enrolled between 1908 and 1941. Full records are available for 1929–1939, with partial records for 1908–1928 and 1941. Boy's Republic, "California Junior Republic Application for Enrollment," Institutional Records, Chino, 1908–1941.

116. Escobar, *Race, Police, and the Making of a Political Identity;* episodes are archived by the Old Time Radio Researchers Group at https://archive.org/details /OTRR_Calling_All_Cars_Singles. For analysis of the series in the context of radio crime dramas, see Kathleen Battles, *Calling All Cars: Radio Dragnets and the Technology of Policing* (Minneapolis: University of Minnesota Press, 2010).

117. "Missing Mexican Sheiks," Episode 6, *Calling All Cars,* January 3, 1934.

118. On Mexican-Filipina/o relations, as well as shared living conditions, see Rudy Guevarra Jr., *Becoming Mexipino: Multiethnic Identities and Communities in San Diego* (New Brunswick, NJ: Rutgers University Press, 2012).

119. "Missing Mexican Sheiks."

120. Ibid.

121. Rudolph Valentino starred as the titular character in the 1921 film, *The Sheik,* playing an Arab sheik who abducts a white woman but ultimately charms her.

The role cemented his status as a sex symbol. Zaragosa Vargas writes about Mexican American cultural adaptations of *The Sheik* in *Proletarians of the North: A History of Mexican Industrial Workers in Detroit and the Midwest, 1917–1933* (Berkeley: University of California Press, 1999), 165–166.

122. Luis Alvarez, *The Power of the Zoot Suit: Youth Culture and Resistance during World War II* (Berkeley: University of California Press, 2009); Catherine S. Ramirez, *The Woman in the Zoot Suit: Gender, Nationalism, and the Cultural Politics of Memory* (Durham: Duke University Press, 2009).

123. "Missing Mexican Sheiks."

124. "Missing Mexican Sheiks."

125. Compare to the criminalization of Pachucas/os in World War II America. Alvarez, *The Power of the Zoot Suit*. On the criminalization of Mexican youth more broadly, see Escobar, *Race, Police, and the Making of a Political Identity;* and Chávez-García, *States of Delinquency.*

126. Alicia Gaspar de Alba, *[Un]Framing the "Bad Woman": Sor Juana, Malinche, Coyolxauhqui and Other Rebels with a Cause* (Austin: University of Texas Press, 2014).

127. John Fante, *Ask the Dust* (1939; New York: Harper Perennial, 2006), 44, 87, 122. On Bandini's whitening through consent of California's racial hierarchies, see Matthew Elliott, "John Fante's *Ask the Dust* and Fictions of Whiteness," *Twentieth Century Literature* 56 (Winter 2010).

128. This homage to actress Carole Lombard reflects the whitening of Hollywood Latinas and underscores Camilla's efforts to convey an Americanized persona. See Catherine Kordich, "John Fante's *Ask the Dust*: A Border Reading," *Melus* 20 (December 1995): 24.

129. On the presumed social contract of drivers, see Seiler, *Republic of Drivers,* chapter 2.

130. Fante, *Ask the Dust,* 63.

131. Mexican Fact-Finding Committee, "Mexicans in California," 196–207; California Motor Vehicle Act of 1927; Chávez-García, *States of Delinquency;* Lytle Hernández, *City of Inmates.*

132. David Wolcott, *Cops and Kids: Policing Juvenile Delinquency in Urban America, 1890–1940* (Columbus: Ohio State University, 2005); David R. Diaz, *Barrio Urbanism: Chicanos, Planning, and American Cities* (New York: Routledge, 2005).

133. Ruth Tuck, *Not with the Fist: Mexican-Americans in a Southwest City* (New York: Harcourt, Brace, 1946), 51.

CHAPTER FIVE. FROM CITRUS BELT TO INLAND EMPIRE

1. Myra Tanner Weiss, "Vigilante Terror in Fontana: The Tragic Story of O'Day H. Short and His Family," pamphlet, February 1946, box 1, folder 117, American Left Ephemera Collection, 1894–2008, University of Pittsburgh; "Proof of Threat Barred

from Short Inquest," *Los Angeles Sentinel,* January 3, 1946; U.S. Census Bureau, "Place: Los Angeles, Los Angeles, California," Roll: T62_7413, Page: 8B, Enumeration District: 60–490 (1940); Mike Davis, *City of Quartz: Excavating the Future in Los Angeles* (London: Verso, 1990), 399. An important digital project brings together coverage of the incident from historic black newspapers; see Matthew F. Delmont, "February 14, 1946," *Black Quotidian: Everyday History in African-American Newspapers,* last modified February 2, 2018, last accessed June 30, 2018, http://blackquotidian.com/anvc/black-quotidian/february-14-1946.

2. Weiss, "Vigilante Terror in Fontana"; "Proof of Threat Barred from Short Inquest."

3. Quoted material from "Proof of Threat Barred from Short Inquest," 5.

4. I use the term "Black" in capital letters, specifically in the civil rights era and beyond, to signify a racial identity including people of self-acknowledged African descent. See Beverly Tatum, *Why Are All the Black Kids Sitting Together in the Cafeteria?* (New York: Basic Books, 2003), 15.

5. Weiss, "Vigilante Terror in Fontana."

6. Suburban revisionists have pushed for scholarship examining the contexts in which the urban and the suburban are produced together. Greg Hise, *Magnetic Los Angeles: Planning the Twentieth Century Metropolis* (Baltimore: Johns Hopkins University Press, 1997); Robert O. Self, *American Babylon: Race and the Struggle for Postwar Oakland* (Princeton: Princeton University Press, 2003), 1–2; Becky Nicolaides and Andrew Wiese, eds., *The Suburban Reader* (New York: Routledge, 2016).

7. Laura R. Barraclough, *Making the San Fernando Valley: Rural Landscapes, Urban Development, and White Privilege* (Athens: University of Georgia Press, 2011); Wendy Cheng, *The Changs Next Door to the Diazes: Remapping Race in Suburban California* (Minneapolis: University of Minnesota Press, 2013); Jerry González, *In Search of the Mexican Beverly Hills: Latino Suburbanization in Postwar Los Angeles* (New Brunswick, NJ: Rutgers University Press, 2018).

8. For one notable work, see Matt Garcia, *A World of Its Own: Race, Labor, and Citrus in the Making of Greater Los Angeles, 1900–1970* (Chapel Hill: University of North Carolina Press, 2001).

9. On inland Southern California's postwar economy, see Hise, *Magnetic Los Angeles;* and Juan D. De Lara, *Inland Shift: Race, Space, and Capital in Inland Southern California* (Oakland: University of California Press, 2018).

10. Department of Commerce, "Percent Change in Total Population, by States: 1940 to 1950," in Clarence E. Batschelet, ed., *Portfolio of United States Census Maps: 1950. A Selection of Maps Used in the Publications of the 1950 Censuses of Population and Agriculture* (Washington, DC: Government Printing Office, 1953) 4.

11. Francesca Ammon, *Bulldozer: Demolition and Clearance of the Postwar Landscape* (New Haven: Yale University Press, 2016).

12. Ann Frank, "Valley Citrus Industry Braces for Bleak Future," *Los Angeles Times,* March 3, 1963.

13. Paul F. Griffin and Ronald L. Chatham, "Population: A Challenge to California's Changing Citrus Industry," *Economic Geography* 34, no. 3 (1958).

14. Nellie Mae and Sandra Ford Montgomery, "William Ford Montgomery," in *Yuma Mesa Homesteaders 1948 and 1952*, ed. Debra Conrad (Raleigh: Lulu Press, 2007), 173; Catherine Merlo, *Heritage of Gold: The First 100 Years of Sunkist Growers, Inc., 1893–1993* (Van Nuys: Sunkist Growers Inc., 1994).

15. Debra Conrad, ed., *Yuma Mesa Homesteaders 1948 and 1952* (Raleigh: Lulu Press, 2007). For a selection of newspaper articles detailing the boom, see "Yuma Citrus Enjoyed California 'Overflow' and Taxes," *Tiempo,* September 30, 1971; "Citrus Story Continues," *Tiempo,* September 23, 1971; "A Citrus Story," *Tiempo,* October 14, 1971—all in box 2, folder 22, AHS-Rio Colorado Ephemera Collection, Arizona Historical Society-Rio Colorado Division, Yuma, AZ.

16. Griffin and Chatham, "Population," 272–276; Merlo, *Heritage of Gold,* 112; Vaun Skellenger, "Citrus in Yuma," *Arizona Agriculture,* March 1987, in box 2, folder 22, Arizona Historical Society-Rio Colorado Ephemera Collection, Yuma.

17. On the Mississippi Delta and tractoring as a form of eviction, see Clyde Woods, *Development Arrested: The Blues and Plantation Power in the Mississippi Delta* (London: Verso Press, 1998).

18. Quoted material from Woods, *Development Arrested,* 127. For key texts on post–World War II housing and its uneven racial effects, see Thomas Sugrue, *The Origins of the Urban Crisis: Race and Inequality in Postwar Detroit* (Princeton: Princeton University Press, 1996); George Lipsitz, *The Possessive Investment in Whiteness: How White People Profit from Identity Politics,* revised and expanded (Philadelphia: Temple University Press, 2006); Self, *American Babylon.*

19. George Clements, "Why Should We Rely Upon 'Bootleg' Labor?," *Los Angeles Times,* July 18, 1926. On Los Angeles boosters and their attempts to build wealth through an extensive hinterland, including Mexico, see Jessica Kim, *Imperial Metropolis: Los Angeles, Mexico, and the Borderlands of American Empire, 1865–1941* (Chapel Hill: University of North Carolina Press, forthcoming 2019).

20. William Cronon, *Nature's Metropolis: Chicago and the Great West* (New York: W. W. Norton, 1991).

21. Based on author's analysis of the "California Cities, Los Angeles 1900–1969" series in Yale University's map collection. For representative examples, see American Map Company, "Official Transportation and City Map of Los Angeles California and Suburbs: Revised Car Routing," 1927 [map]; H. M. Gousha Company, "Shell Metropolitan Map: Los Angeles and Vicinity," 1933 [map]; H. M. Gousha Company, "Street Guide and Metropolitan Map of Los Angeles," 1936 [map]—all in Map Collection, Yale University.

22. Based on review of the "California Cities, Los Angeles 1900–1969" series in Yale University's map collection. For representative examples, see Rand McNally, "Los Angeles City Map," 76 Union Oil Company, 1949 [map]; and Rand McNally, "Los Angeles Metropolitan Area," 1950 [map]—both in Map Collection, Yale University.

23. U.S. Census Bureau, "Summary of Population Characteristics for Counties: 1950," Table 12, Decennial Census, General Characteristics, California (1950).

24. On the Lewis's development model, see Ralph M. Lewis, *Land Buying Checklist,* 3rd ed. (Washington, DC: National Association of Home Builders, 1988).

For a sample of media reviews covering the family's regional impact, see Andy McCue, "Lewises Made Home Building a Family Affair: Ralph and Goldy Lewis Started the Upland Company in 1957," *Riverside Press-Enterprise,* October 21, 1998; Darren Schenck, "Lewis Homes Co-Founder Dies at 84," *USC News,* March 23, 2006. On John Lusk, see John O'Dell, "John D. Lusk, Pioneering Developer in Southern California, Dies at 91," *Los Angeles Times,* March 2, 1999; "John Lusk, 91, Dies; Built California Suburbs," *New York Times,* March 9, 1999.

25. Chris Ehrlich, "Lewis Family Business Worth $1 Billion," *Inland Valley Daily Bulletin,* December 16, 2001. Shortly before her death, the *Inland Valley Daily Bulletin* dubbed Goldy Lewis "the mother of suburbia" for her role in shaping the Lewis legacy. "Goldy's Vision: A Better Suburbia," *Inland Valley Daily Bulletin,* June 24, 2004, 6; and, Wendy Leung, "Goldy Lewis, Mother of Inland Empire Suburbia, Dies at 84," *Inland Valley Daily Bulletin,* March 14, 2006.

26. Davis, *City of Quartz.* 174. On the extension of these home-building projects along the coastline in this same period, see Sara Fingal, *Turning the Tide: The Politics of Land and Leisure During the Age of Environmentalism* (Seattle: University of Washington Press, forthcoming).

27. On mobility capital, referred to elsewhere as motility, see Vincent Kaufmann, Manfred Max Bergman, and Dominique Joye, "Motility: Mobility as Capital," *International Journal of Urban and Regional Research* 28 (December 2004); Vincent Kaufmann, *Re-Thinking Mobility Social Justice* (Burlington, VT: Ashgate, 2002). This mobility often occurred at the expense of minoritized communities adversely impacted by freeway construction. Eric Avila, *Folklore of the Freeway: Race and Revolt in the Modernist City* (Minneapolis: University of Minnesota Press, 2014).

28. "Brisk Building Pace Revealed," *Los Angeles Times,* February 12, 1956.

29. Homes in the campaign ranged from $10,250 to $35,000. See "Builders Group Launches New Campaign," *Los Angeles Times,* August 19, 1956; "Home Developments' Sales Spur Cited," *Los Angeles Times,* September 9, 1956. In California as a whole, the median home was valued between $9,564 and $15,100 during this decade (1950–1960). U.S. Census Bureau, "Median Home Values: Unadjusted," Census of Housing, last modified August 2012, available at http://www.census.gov /housing/census/data/values.html.

30. "Developers Sponsor Campaign in Pomona," *Los Angeles Times,* March 24, 1957; "Hundreds Visit New Pomona Homes Daily," *Los Angeles Times,* April 7, 1957.

31. The California legislature would first pass fair housing legislation in the Rumford Fair Housing Act (1963). The California electorate would nullify the act a year later when passing Proposition 14. See Mark Brilliant, *The Color of America Has Changed: How Racial Diversity Shaped Civil Rights Reform in California, 1941–1978* (New York: Oxford University Press, 2010); Daniel Martinez HoSang, *Racial Propositions: Ballot Initiatives and the Making of Postwar California* (Berkeley: University of California Press, 2010).

32. George J. Sánchez, "What's Good for Boyle Heights Is Good for the Jews: Creating Multiracialism on the Eastside during the 1950s," *American Quarterly* 56, no. 3 (2004); Lipsitz, *The Possessive Investment in Whiteness;* Matthew Frye Jacob-

son, *Whiteness of a Different Color: European Immigrants and the Alchemy of Race* (Cambridge, MA: Harvard University Press, 1998).

33. Deborah Dash Moore, *To the Golden Cities: Pursuing the American Jewish Dream in Miami and L.A.* (New York: Free Press, 1994), 42–44.

34. Josh Sides, *L.A. City Limits: African American Los Angeles from the Great Depression to the Present* (Berkeley: University of California Press, 2004), 107.

35. For an example of Jewish-Latina/o alliance in the fight against residential segregation, see Genevieve Carpio, "Unexpected Allies: David C. Marcus, Civil Rights, and the Mexican American Legal Landscape of Southern California," *Annual Review of the Casden Institute from the Study of the Jewish Role in American Life* 9 (2012).

36. For a ranked list of top homebuilders in the Inland Empire, see De Lara, *Inland Shift,* 143

37. Rochelle Kass, "A Family Affair," *Inland Valley Daily Bulletin,* February 15, 1999, 7.

38. "Builders will Discuss Rumford Housing Issue," *Los Angeles Times,* March 1, 1964; Tom Cameron, "Nailing it Down: Home Builder Image Changed," *Los Angeles Times,* March 15, 1964; "Fair Housing to be Topic of UL Confab," *Los Angeles Sentinel,* June 23, 1966.

39. Peyton Canary, "Commission to Be Formed to Tackle the Job of Improving Living in Pomona," *Los Angeles Times,* June 21, 1970.

40. Quoted material from "New Realty Group Backs Rumford Act," *Los Angeles Times,* December 3, 1963, 1. On the Rumford Act and Proposition 14, see Brilliant, *The Color of America Has Changed;* HoSang, *Racial Propositions.*

41. On CORE's activism, including interview excerpts with the former Pomona Valley CORE chairman, see Monica Rodriguez, "Watts Riots: Inland Valley African Americans Faced Same Problems," *Inland Valley Daily Bulletin,* August 8, 2015; on divisions among realtors, developers, and labor organizations, see Brilliant, *The Color of America Has Changed,* 197; and HoSang, *Racial Propositions,* 73. On the shifting stance of the Mexican American Chamber of Commerce, see González, *In Search of the Mexican Beverly Hills,* chapter 3.

42. Quoted material from Deirdre Pfeiffer, "Moving to Opportunity: African Americans' Safety Outcomes in the Los Angeles Exurbs," *Journal of Planning Education and Research* 33, no. 1 (2013): 51. Pfeiffer has found that 130,000 African Americans migrated to Riverside and San Bernardino Counties between 1980 and 2007. New residential development combined with color-blind sales to make the Inland Empire a new suburban frontier for African Americans. Pfeiffer, "Sprawling to Opportunity: Los Angeles African Americans on the Exurban Fringe" (PhD diss., University of California Los Angeles, 2012).

43. Garcia, *A World of Its Own,* 242–255; Judy Wright, "A Sense of History: Ruth Orday—An Intercultural Experiment," *Claremont Courier,* December 15, 2005.

44. Obituaries and career retrospectives outline the many awards received by Ralph and Goldy Lewis. Lewis Group of Companies, which grew out of Lewis

Homes, maintains a detailed website with the company's history and a list of awards. "Lewis Apartment Communities," last accessed March 30, 2013, http://www.lewisapartments.com/aboutus.aspx; the website has been updated as "Lewis Group of Companies," last accessed July 2018, https://lewisgroupofcompanies.com. Kaiser Homes provided a significant precedent to inland homebuilding: see Hise, *Magnetic Los Angeles;* and Davis, *City of Quartz,* 394.

45. On Native American settlement patterns in this period, see Gary Sandefur, "Native American Migration and Economic Opportunities," *Internal Migration Review* 20 (1986); and Gayle Wattawa, *Inlandia: A Literary Journey Through California's Inland Empire* (Santa Clara: Santa Clara University, 2006), 72; on Latina/o and Asian American suburbanization, see Cheng, *The Changs Next Door to the Diazes.*

46. On motility, see Kaufmann, *Re-Thinking Mobility.*

47. Doreen Massey, *Space, Place and Gender* (Minneapolis: University of Minnesota Press, 1994), 149.

48. For an analysis of these different models, see Jody Aguis Vallejo, *Barrios to Burbs: The Making of the Mexican-American Middle Class* (Stanford: Stanford University Press, 2012).

49. J. Eugene Grigsby III, "African American Mobility and Residential Quality in Los Angeles," in *Residential Apartheid: The American Legacy,* ed. Robert D. Bullard, J. Eugene Grigsby III, and Charles Lee (Los Angeles: CAAS Publications, University of California, 1994).

50. Ted Sell, "Pomona Gropes for Stability in Storm of Ethnic Change," *Los Angeles Times,* January 24, 1971, p. 1.

51. Interview with Albert Castro by Genevieve Carpio, 23 December 2013, Pomona.

52. Elliot frequently advertised in the *Los Angeles Sentinel:* see "Classified Ad 3," November 30, 1950; and "Classified Ad 6," October 7, 1954. Basic biographical data on Elliott can be found at U.S. Census Bureau, "Place: Jefferson City, Cole, Missouri," Roll: T627_2099, Enumeration District: 26–11 (1940), p. 22B.

53. This includes the author's father, Vince Carpio Jr.

54. Interview with Albert Castro by Genevieve Carpio, 23 December 2013, Pomona.

55. Ibid; Author's analysis of city directories held in the Pomona Public Library for 1924, 1934, and 1940 confirm that the majority of Spanish-surnamed residents lived in the 12th Street neighborhood, on the outskirts of town.

56. A regional roster of the Ku Klux Klan for 1924, a period of rapid city growth, shows that several members were employed as realtors, contributing to the stark racial lines of the city. Pomona Ku Klux Klan Roster, 10 January 1924, Pomona Valley History Collection, Pomona Public Library Special Collections.

57. There were five census tracts located predominantly in the City of Pomona, with an additional tract comprised primarily of neighboring Diamond Bar. Analysis of census tables for "country of origin and nativity" alongside "Spanish origin or descent indicator" for the five tracts comprised primarily of Pomona show that

immigrants originating from Mexico and "Other America" averaged 25 percent of the total Spanish origin population. The Cuban population is also tabulated, but included only five residents. Analysis based on population data from the 1970 Census through Social Explorer. Reports are viewable there with a subscription: Country of origin and nativity, https://www.socialexplorer.com/tables/C1970/R11874653; Spanish origin and descent indication, https://www.socialexplorer.com/tables /C1970/R11874664W; Joseph Korpsak and Carol Way, memorandum, 1 October 1974, Al Castro's Personal Collection;

58. Lipsitz, *The Possessive Investment in Whiteness.*

59. On constellations of struggle, see Gaye Theresa Johnson, *Spaces of Conflict, Sounds of Solidarity: Music, Race, and Spatial Entitlement in Los Angeles* (Berkeley: University California Press, 2013).

60. National Association of Real Estate Boards and California Real Estate Association, "Roster: The Pomona Valley Board of Realtors," 1965, Al Castro's Personal Collection.

61. Quoted material from *Los Angeles Sentinel:* "Classified Ad 4," September 21, 1961; "Classified Ad 6," March 22, 1956; "Classified Ad 4," September 21, 1961.

62. "Classified Ad 12," *Los Angeles Sentinel,* May 19, 1960; U.S. Census Bureau, "Median Home Values: Unadjusted."

63. Henri Jr. O'Bryant, "Some Observations of Little 'Tokio,'" 6 July 1943, typescript, box 1; and Letter from Katherine Kaplan of the Department of the Community Welfare Federation to Mr. Mcnutt, 30 October 1943, box 1—both in Charles Bratt Papers, Southern California Library for Social Studies and Research, Los Angeles; Sides, *L.A. City Limits;* Scott Kurashige, The Shifting Grounds of Race: Black and Japanese Americans in the Making of Multiethnic Los Angeles (Princeton: Princeton University Press, 2008).

64. "Classified Ad 7," *Los Angeles Sentinel,* July 11, 1957.

65. "Classified Ad 30," *Los Angeles Sentinel,* December 2, 1965.

66. On the pleasure of commuting and the affinities it generates, see Karen Tongson, *Relocations: Queer Suburban Imaginaries* (New York: New York University Press, 2011); on the radical affirmation of Black and Brown communities through music, see Johnson, *Spaces of Conflict, Sounds of Solidarity;* for commuting data, see Sell, "Pomona Gropes for Stability in Storm of Ethnic Change."

67. Kaufmann, Bergman, and Joye, "Motility," 753.

68. William J. Siembieda, "Suburbanization of Ethnics of Color," *Annals of the American Academy of Political and Social Science* 422 (November 1975).

69. Mike Davis, "The Suburban Nightmare: While Older Suburbs Experience Many Problems of the Inner City, 'Edge Cities' Now Offer a New Escape," *Los Angeles Times,* October 23, 1994.

70. As one example, a deed for a home in Ganesha Park states, "No part of said property shall be sold, conveyed, rented, or leased in whole or in part to any persons of African or Asiatic descent or to any person not of the white or Caucasian race," 10 February 1934, Pomona Valley History Collection, Pomona Public Library Special Collections.

71. On *Doss v. Bernal,* see Carpio, "Unexpected Allies"; Robert Chao Romero and Luis Fernando Fernandez, "Doss v. Bernal: Ending Mexican Apartheid in Orange County," *CSRC Research Note,* no. 14 (February 2012).

72. On *Shelley v. Kraemer,* see Lipsitz, *The Possessive Investment in Whiteness,* 25–33.

73. Florence Cohn, "Family Real Estate," memorandum, 26 January 1972, Al Castro's Personal Collection.

74. Interview with Albert Castro by Genevieve Carpio, 23 December 2013, Pomona. For a similar example, see Maurice Curtis, an El Monte realtor who lost his job upon selling a home to a Mexican family in a white neighborhood. González, *In Search of the Mexican Beverly Hills.*

75. Analysis based on population maps generated by the author using data from the 1970 Census through Social Explorer, a software which visualizes geospatial data. Maps are viewable here with a subscription, http://www.socialexplorer .com/40fa1e032c/view. This demographic profile matches national trends in which many urban African Americans who moved to suburbs were middle class in origin. See Andrew Wiese, *Places of Their Own: African American Suburbanization in the Twentieth Century* (Chicago: University of Chicago Press, 2004).

76. Cheng, *The Changs Next Door to the Diazes.*

77. Dick Turpin, "19 of 25 Apartment Managers Display Overt Bias: Racial Discrimination," *Los Angeles Times,* April 4, 1971.

78. These observations are confirmed by oral histories taken with area real estate agents, as well as newspaper accounts of early African American suburbanites. Interview with Bernadette Kendall by Genevieve Carpio. 22 March 2005, Claremont; interview with Albert Castro by Genevieve Carpio, 23 December 2013, Pomona; Monica Rodriguez, "Watts Riots: Inland Valley African-Americans Faced Same Problems," *Inland Valley Daily Bulletin,* August 8, 2015.

79. Despite never forming a population majority, a notable Vietnamese population resettled in Pomona; U.S. Census Bureau, "Summary of General Characteristics: 1970," Table 16 (1970); and U.S. Census Bureau, "Summary of General Characteristics: 1980," Table 14 (1980).

80. Sell, "Pomona Gropes for Stability in Storm of Ethnic Change," 4.

81. Ibid.

82. On Proposition 13 and its uneven effects in California, see Self, *American Babylon.*

83. Analysis based on population map generated by the author using data from the 1970 Census through Social Explorer. Map is viewable here with a subscription, http://www.socialexplorer.com/7c9eb98e8c/view.

84. David Harvey, *Justice, Nature and the Geography of Difference* (Oxford: Blackwell, 1996); Sell, "Pomona Gropes for Stability in Storm of Ethnic Change."

85. On the multiscalar impacts of L.A.'s policies towards the Skid Row population, see Clyde Woods, "'A Cell Is Not a Home': Asset Stripping and Trap Economics in Central City East/Skid Row, Part 2," in *Black California Dreamin': The Crises of California's African-American Communities,* ed. Ingrid Banks et al. (Santa Bar-

bara: UCSB Center for Black Studies Research, 2012); Neil Smith, "Contours of a Spatialized Politics: Homeless Vehicles and the Production of Geographic Scale," *Social Text* 33 (1992). I draw here on Massey's insightful work on the power geometry of space-time compression and mobility in *Space, Place and Gender,* 149.

86. On moral geographies, see Michael J. Shapiro, "Moral Geographies and the Ethics of Post-Sovereignty," *Public Culture* 6, no. 3 (1994); Melanie McAlister, *Epic Encounters: Culture, Media, and U.S. Interests in the Middle East, 1945–2000* (Berkeley: University of California Press, 2001).

87. Comparison of median home values by neighborhood in tables 5.8 and 5.9 in Grigsby, "African American Mobility and Residential Quality in Los Angeles," *Residential Apartheid.* This follows general trends for L.A. County property values, in which median house values of census tracts from 1940 to 1990 show declination where proportions of Hispanics and African Americans are highest. See chart 2.7 in Philip Ethington, "Segregated Diversity: Race-Ethnicity, Space, and Political Fragmentation in Los Angeles County, 1940–1994," Final Report to the John Randolph Haynes and Dora Haynes Foundation, 2000, available at http://www-bcf.usc.edu/~philipje/Segregation/Haynes_Reports/FINAL_REPORT_20000719g.pdf.

88. Bill Robertson, "Pomona Negroes Suburbia Problems," *Los Angeles Sentinel,* May 4, 1967, p. 1. For a comparative look at busing, see Matthew Delmont, *Why Busing Failed: Race, Media, and the National Resistance to School Desegregation* (Oakland: University of California Press, 2016).

89. Robert Diebold, "Pomona Schools Given Ultimatum by Chicanos," *Los Angeles Times,* April 30, 1970, p. 1.

90. Robertson, "Pomona Negroes Suburbia Problems."

91. Diebold, "Pomona Schools Given Ultimatum by Chicanos," p. 1. For more on discrimination at Pomona Schools and efforts to unravel it, see the work of Candelario Mendoza, one of the Pomona Valley's first Mexican American teachers and administrators. Candelario Mendoza interview by Genevieve Carpio, 25 April 2005, Pomona. His life's work is further documented in Garcia, *A World of Its Own.*

92. Ibid., 3.

93. Peyton Canary, "Mexican-American Students Put Off Strike Against Pomona Schools," *Los Angeles Times,* May 31, 1970. For a comparative example of the link between housing segregation and unequal schooling, as well as efforts to protest that discrimination by Black and Brown communities in California, see David G. García, *Strategies of Segregation: Race, Residence, and the Struggle for Educational Equality* (Oakland: University of California Press, 2018).

94. Vallejo, *Barrios to Burbs.*

95. Benjamin Lawing and Paul Walker, "The Public Speaks Out," *Los Angeles Times,* January 31, 1971.

96. Benjamin Lawing to Otis Chandler, correspondence, 27 January 1971, Al Castro's Personal Collection.

97. Scholars examining Mexican Americans' experiences of suburbanization have complicated the Chicago School's concentric model, which established a residential pattern in which minoritized people's upward mobility was tied to linear

assimilation and movement from the inner city to the outer suburbs. See Vallejo, *Barrios to Burbs,* 13–18.

98. Dena Rosenberry, "Prison Valley," *Pomona Progress Bulletin,* December 4, 1988, in Vertical File: Prisons, Robert E. Ellingwood Model Colony History Room, Ovitt Family Community Library, Ontario.

99. In 1970, four state-run correctional institutes and three fire camps operated within a ten-mile radius of one another. An additional fire camp operated at Crestline. For a digital map of these sites as they would have appeared in the 1970s, based on data from the Department of Corrections, see Genevieve Carpio, José Cardona, and Yazmin González, "Prison Valley, 1970" [map], https://drive.google.com/open?id=1fgQVjr6igWDkCOuZ9xpYrQGBB-Q&usp=sharing.

100. James M. Montgomery, Consulting Engineers Inc., "California Institution for Men, Chino. Draft Environmental Impact Report and Facilities Plan for Improvements to Treatment and Reclamation Facilities," November 1978; and Glenn Anderson, "Prisons have Large Impact on West End," *Ontario Daily Report,* February 6, 1968—both in Vertical File: Prisons, Robert E. Ellingwood Model Colony History Room, Ovitt Family Community Library, Ontario.

101. Dena Rosenberry, "Prison Valley," *Pomona Progress Bulletin,* December 4, 1988.

102. Michael D. Brown, *The History of Chino Prison: The First Fifty Years of the California Institute for Men, 1941–1991* (Chino: California Institute for Men, 1991).

103. As quoted in Brown, *The History of Chino Prison,* 118.

104. Kenyon J. Scudder, *Prisoners Are People* (New York: Doubleday, 1952); quoted material from Brown, *The History of Chino Prison,* 116.

105. California Institution for Men, "The California Institution for Men, Chino, California," pamphlet, n.d., in Vertical File: Prisons, Robert E. Ellingwood Model Colony History Room, Ovitt Family Community Library, Ontario.

106. Scudder, *Prisoners Are People;* Scott Harrison, "Japanese American Internment: Pomona Assembly Center," *Los Angeles Times,* March 17, 2015.

107. Phillip E. Johnson and Sheldon L. Messinger, "California's Determinate Sentencing Statute: History and Issues," *Determinate Sentencing: Reform or Regression?* (Berkeley: Berkeley Law Scholarship Repository, 1978), 13–14; emphasis in original.

108. Kara Dansky, "Understanding California Sentencing," *University of San Francisco Law Review* 43, no. 3 (Summer 2008). Micol Seigel provides an important review of recent literature in critical prison studies, in "Critical Prison Studies: Review of a Field," *American Quarterly* 70 (March 2018). Seigel's work draws connections between racialization and incarceration, the growth of neoliberalism, and continuing freedom struggles. For his focus on shifting carceral developments in the 1970s and the Los Angeles context, see Jordan T. Camp, *Incarcerating the Crisis: Freedom Struggles and the Rise of the Neoliberal State* (Oakland: University of California Press, 2016).

109. Ruth Wilson Gilmore, *Golden Gulag: Prison, Surplus, Crisis, and Opposition in Globalizing California* (Berkeley: University of California Press, 2007). On

the rise and transformations of the carceral state in the postwar period, see Heather Ann Thompson, "Why Mass Incarceration Matters: Rethinking Crisis, Decline, and Transformation in Postwar American History," *Journal of American History* 97 (December 2010).

110. A few years prior to the act's passage, official descriptions and schedules for watch positions show a shift from earlier preoccupation with rehabilitation to "discipline," "control," and "movement." See California Institution for Men, "Job Description, Third Watch—Redwood Hall—Position #123," 15 August 1972, in Philip G. Zimbardo Papers, box 54, Special Collections, Stanford University Library.

111. "CIM Inmate Beaten to Death," *Ontario Daily Report,* October 5, 1976; "Inmate Stabbed to Death at CIM," *Ontario Daily Report,* May 16, 1977; Mike Balchunas, "Court of Appeals Delays Start of Trial for Three CIM Inmates," *Ontario Daily Report,* October 8, 1977—all in Vertical File: Prisons, Robert E. Ellingwood Model Colony History Room, Ovitt Family Community Library, Ontario.

112. California Legislature, Joint Legislative Committee on Prison Construction and Operations, *California's Prisons: California Institution for Men,* Fifth series of hearings, November 28, 1985. p. 14; "Despite Empty Beds, Chino's CIM Loaded," *Ontario Daily Report,* October 25, 1978, in Vertical File: Prisons, Robert E. Ellingwood Model Colony History Room, Ovitt Family Community Library, Ontario.

113. Richard Gray, "400 CIM Prisoners Stage Work Walkout for One Day," *Ontario Daily Report,* September 17, 1982, in Vertical File: Prisons, Robert E. Ellingwood Model Colony History Room, Ovitt Family Community Library, Ontario.

114. Bruce Thornton, "CIM Among 5 Prisons Called 'Unfit for Humans,'" *Ontario Daily Report,* April 9, 1980, in Vertical File: Prisons, Robert E. Ellingwood Model Colony History Room, Ovitt Family Community Library, Ontario.

115. "Construction of El Rincon Prison South of Ontario to Give California Modern Institution," *Ontario Record,* December 8, 1937; "New Prison at Chino Seeded by State," 13 December 1939; "How New State Reformatory Will Appear When Completed," n.d.—all in Vertical File: Prisons, Robert E. Ellingwood Model Colony History Room, Ovitt Family Community Library, Ontario.

116. "Inmate Walks Away from CIM While Doing Irrigation Duty," *Ontario Daily Report,* August 10, 1977; "Inmate Four Months From Parole Escapes," *Ontario Daily Report,* October 24, 1977; Peggy Ziegler, "Ten Inmates Escape CIM; Five Captured," *Ontario Daily Report,* October 4, 1979; Sue Manning, "West Enders Will Die at Escapees' Hands,," *Ontario Daily Report,* May 14, 1972; "CIM Escapee Seizes Car, Takes 2 Hostage," *Ontario Daily Report,* September 6, 1977; "Search Intensified for CIM Escapee," *Ontario Daily Report,* September 30, 1979—all in Vertical File: Prisons, Robert E. Ellingwood Model Colony History Room, Ovitt Family Community Library, Ontario; California Department of Corrections, *California Prisoners: Summary Statistics of Prisoners and Parolees* (Sacramento: California Department of Corrections, 1972). Archived reports from 1851–2010 available in Office of Research, California Department of Corrections and Rehabilitation, https://sites.cdcr.ca.gov/research/archived-research/.

117. California Legislature, *California's Prisons.*

118. Ken Swart, "Prisoners Tell What It's Like Inside CIM," *Ontario Daily Report,* November 16, 1979, in Vertical File: Prisons, Robert E. Ellingwood Model Colony History Room, Ovitt Family Community Library, Ontario; Frank Del Olmo, "Chicano Prison Inmates Find New Purpose," *Los Angeles Times,* August 24, 1971; Brown, *The History of Chino Prison.*

119. In her important work, social scientist Joan Moore and a team of formerly incarcerated Chicano men conducted interviews with COPA members. See California Institution for Men (CIM), Chino Prison Questionnaires, 1974, box 58, folder 4, in Joan Moore Papers 1978–2004, Chicano Studies Research Center, University of California Los Angeles; Joan W. Moore with Robert Garcia, Carlos Garcia, Luis Cerda, and Frank Valencia, *Homeboys: Gangs, Drugs, and Prisons in the Barrios of Los Angeles* (Philadelphia: Temple University Press, 1978), 111.

120. Robert Abeyta, editorial, *La Raza Habla de Chino* 1, no. 1, 28 January 1970, Chicano Newspaper Collection, Chicano Studies Research Center, University of California Los Angeles; on the Mexican American Research Association and its work with the CIW through print culture, see Maylei Blackwell, *¡Chicana Power! Contested Histories of Feminism in the Chicano Movement* (Austin: University of Texas Press, 2011), 152–153.

121. Author's analysis of California Institution for Men (CIM), Chino Prison Questionnaires; see also Moore et al., *Homeboys,* esp. Appendix C: Culture Group Study; Frank Del Olmo, "Chicano Prison Inmates Find New Purpose," *Los Angeles Times,* August 24, 1971, pg. C1.

122. Rudy Alanis, "Celebracion de Lupita," *La Raza Habla de Chino* 1, no. 4. 16 May 1970, box 3, folder 33, in Enriqueta Chavez Papers, Special Collections and University Archives, San Diego State University, San Diego.

123. Rudy Alanis to Mr. Rene Nuñez, correspondence, 4 June 1970, box 3 folder 33, in Enriqueta Chavez Papers, Special Collections and University Archives, San Diego State University, San Diego; grants were announced in *La Raza Habla de Chino* newsletter.

124. Abeyta, editorial, *La Raza Habla de Chino.*

125. Quoted material from Rudy Alanis, "Cinco de Mayo," *La Raza Habla de Chino* 1, no. 4, 16 May 1970, box 3, folder 33, in Enriqueta Chavez Papers, Special Collections and University Archives, San Diego State University, San Diego.

126. Duke Gonzalez, "A Part of the Sleeping Giant," *La Raza Habla de Chino* 1, no. 4. 16 May 1970, box 3, folder 33, in Enriqueta Chavez Papers, Special Collections and University Archives, San Diego State University, San Diego.

127. Moore et al., *Homeboys.*

128. Author's analysis of California Institution for Men (CIM) Chino Prison Questionnaires.

129. Moore et al., *Homeboys;* Del Olmo, "Chicano Prison Inmates Find New Purpose"; Montgomery, "California Institution for Men, Chino. Draft Environmental Impact Report and Facilities Plan for Improvements to Treatment and Reclamation Facilities."

130. Special events are detailed in COPA's newsletter. See, for instance, Rudy Alanis, "Cinco de Mayo," *La Raza Habla de Chino* 1, no. 4, 16 May 1970, box 3, folder 33, in Enriqueta Chavez Papers, Special Collections and University Archives, San Diego State University, San Diego.

131. Karen Patterson, "Those in Need and Those Who Care," *We Guide,* January 1977, Vertical File: Prisons, in Robert E. Ellingwood Model Colony History Room, Ovitt Family Community Library, Ontario; "Friends Outside Buys Reception Trailer," *Chino Champion,* February 10, 1978. In addition to efforts by Friends Outside, MARA worked with Los Angeles-based families to secure transportation to CIW. Blackwell, *¡Chicana Power!,* 153.

132. Richard Peraza, "Chino Prison Expansion Could Hurt Police Service," *Ontario Daily Report,* n.d., Vertical File: Prisons; and Elaine Haite, "Chino Officials Say Influence of Prison Gangs Reaches Street," *Press Enterprise,* n.d.—both in Vertical File: Prisons, Robert E. Ellingwood Model Colony History Room, Ovitt Family Community Library, Ontario.

133. Brown, *The History of Chino Prison,* 181.

134. Davis, *City of Quartz,* 375.

135. Myron Orfield, "Why Are the Twin Cities so Segregated?" (Minneapolis: University of Minnesota Institute on Metropolitan Equity, February 2015); Myron Orfield and Thomas Luce, "America's Racially Diverse Suburbs: Opportunities and Challenges," *Housing Policy Debate* 23, no. 2 (2013).

136. Peter Dreier et al., *Underwater America: How the So-Called Housing Recovery Is Bypassing Many American Communities* (Berkeley: Haas Institute, University of California, 2014), 5.

137. In searching for solutions, we might look globally, to countries with a similar urban form, such as post–apartheid South Africa, where some formerly all-white suburbs are taking on new configurations that cut across class and racial lines. Daniel Schensul and Patrick Heller, "Legacies, Change and Transformation in the Post-Apartheid City: Towards an Urban Sociological Cartography," *International Journal of Urban and Regional Research* 35, no. 1 (2011).

CONCLUSION

1. After 1990, most immigrants settled in post–World War II urban developments and suburbs. Audrey Singer, Susan W. Hardwick, and Caroline B. Brettell, eds., *Twenty-First Century Gateways: Immigrant Incorporation in Suburban America* (Washington, DC: The Brookings Institution, 2008); Audrey Singer, "The Rise of New Immigrant Gateways," Washington, DC: The Brookings Institution (February 2004).

2. City of Pomona, City Council, *Council Report Number 08–140* (Pomona, April 7, 2008). Author's notes from "Talleres Informativos: Retenes, Decomisos, Derechos Humanos y Derechos Civiles," program sponsored by Alianza Nacional de Comunidades Latinoamericanas y Caribeñas, August 2010; Monica Rodriguez,

"Federal Lawsuit Filed Against Pomona Police Involving August 2008 Checkpoint Meeting," *Inland Valley Daily Bulletin,* September 8, 2009.

3. In August 2008, Pomona Habla held a community forum addressing the Cinco de Mayo checkpoint, as well as subsequent checkpoints in Pomona. Author's notes from "Pomona Checkpoints: Saving Lives or Ruining Lives," panel delivered at Cal Poly Pomona, May 26, 2009. On the rise of sobriety checkpoints and community responses in Southern California, see also Genevieve Carpio, Clara Irazábal, and Laura Pulido, "Right to the Suburb?: Rethinking Lefebvre and Immigrant Activism," *Journal of Urban Affairs* 33, no. 2 (May 2011).

4. On regional equity movements in metropolitan Los Angeles, see Manuel Pastor, Chris Benner, Martha Matsuoka, *This Could Be the Start of Something Big: How Social Movements for Regional Equity Are Reshaping Metropolitan America* (Ithaca: Cornell University Press, 2009).

5. On lowriders and cultural representation, see Brenda Jo Bright and Liza Bakewell, *Looking High and Low: Art and Cultural Identity* (Tucson: University of Arizona Press, 1995); Denise Sandoval, "Bajito y Suavecito/Low and Slow: Cruising Through Lowrider Culture" (Ph.D. diss., Claremont Graduate School, 2003). On the lowrider ban, the Salute to the Route counter-festival and its extensions, see Danny Flores interview by Joyce Hanson, 5 November 2002, transcript, San Bernardino Oral History Project, San Bernardino Public Library; and Danny Flores interviewed by Robert Gonzalez and Matt Garcia, 15 June 2004, transcript, p. 10, Inland Mexican Heritage, Redlands.

6. Philip Bump, "Rep. Steve King Wonders What 'Subgroups' Besides Whites Made Contributions to Civilization," *Washington Post,* July 18, 2016; Daniel Lombroso and Yoni Appelbaum, "'Hail Trump!': White Nationalists Salute the President Elect," *The Atlantic,* November 21, 2016.

7. Aileen Moreton-Robinson, *The White Possessive: Property, Power, and Indigenous Sovereignty* (Minneapolis: University of Minnesota Press, 2015).

8. On the "commonsense knowledge" of white possessive logics, see Aileen Moreton-Robinson, *The White Possessive: Property, Power, and Indigenous Sovereignty* (Minneapolis: University of Minnesota Press, 2015), xii.

9. George Lipsitz, *The Possessive Investment in Whiteness: How White People Profit from Identity Politics,* revised and expanded (Philadelphia: Temple University Press, 2006).

10. Scholars and public intellectuals have long critiqued the romanticized landscape of citrus country. Carey McWilliams (1939) debunked the agrarian myth when he denounced California's large-scale agricultural operations as "factories in the field," historian Douglas Sackman (2005) described the Sunkist Campaign as a systematic effort to regiment nature, and geographer Don Mitchell (1996) warned that the imaginary production of California's landscape erased contests between farmworkers and ranch owners. Carey McWilliams, *Factories in the Field: The Story of Migratory Farm Labor in California* (Boston: Little, Brown, 1939); Douglas Cazaux Sackman, *Orange Empire: California and the Fruits of Eden* (Berkeley: University of California Press, 2005); Don Mitchell, *Lie of the Land: Migrant Work-*

ers and the *California Landscape* (Minneapolis: University of Minnesota Press, 1996). On the tropes of consolidating enemy and late arrivals, see Sherene Razack, ed., *Race, Space, and the Law: Unmapping a White Settler Society* (Toronto: Between the Lines, 2002).

11. Bruce Kelley, "Eastward, Ho: Southern Californians Are Headed Inland, to the Area Around Ontario Airport—the Newest Edge City in a Region that Invented the Concept," *Los Angeles Times,* March 15, 1992, in Vertical File: Inland Empire Name, Local History Collections, Upland Public Library; Randyl Drummer, "New Owner of Ontario Center Covers its Eyesore," *The Business Press,* March 30, 1998, p. 11. On the emerging role of the Inland Empire in logistics/warehousing, see Juan D. De Lara, *Inland Shift: Race, Space, and Capital in Inland Southern California* (Oakland: University of California Press, 2018).

12. Rancho Cucamonga Redevelopment Agency, *Community and Economic Profile,* (Rancho Cucamonga, 2010), in author's possession.

13. U.S. Census Bureau, "2006–2008 American Community Survey; Community and Economic Profile" (2010).

14. U.S. Census Bureau, "Profile of General Population and Housing Characteristics," Rancho Cucamonga American Fact Finder (2010); U.S. Census Bureau, "Profile of General Demographic Characteristics," Rancho Cucamonga American Fact Finder (2000).

15. U.S. Census Bureau, "Income in the Past 12 Months in 2015 Inflation-Adjusted Dollars," American Community Survey 5-Year Estimates, American Fact Finder (2011–2015); *Next Friday* [film], New Line, 2000.

16. On distinctions between white privilege and white supremacy in urban development, see Laura Pulido, "Rethinking Environmental Racism: White Privilege and Urban Development in Southern California," *Annals of the Association of American Geographers* 90, no. 1 (2000); on moral geographies and their spatial dimensions, see George Lipsitz, *How Racism Takes Place* (Philadelphia: Temple University Press, 2011).

17. For more on rising nativist groups in Southern California, see Justin Akers Chacón and Mike Davis, *No One Is Illegal: Fighting Racism and State Violence on the U.S.-Mexico Border* (Chicago: Haymarket Books, 2006).

18. On routes and roots, I borrow from James Clifford, *Routes: Travel and Translation in the Late Twentieth Century* (Cambridge, MA: Harvard University Press, 1997). This construction has been expanded, particularly in its gendered analysis, by Elizabeth DeLoughry, *Routes and Roots: Navigating Caribbean and Pacific Island Literatures* (Honolulu: University of Hawai'i Press, 2007).

19. City of Rancho Cucamonga, Foothill Boulevard Specific Plan, September 1987, especially Section 5.0 on the community design concept and Section 8 on general design guidelines and development standards, quoted material from Section 5.5.2; see also William Lyon Company, *The Victoria Community Plan,* submitted to the City of Rancho Cucamonga, July 1980—both in Reference, Archibald Library, Rancho Cucamonga. The plans are reflexive of what Michael Sorkin terms "the new city." He describes the new city as a "city of simulations" similar to that of a theme

park. He explains, "This is the meaning of the theme park, the place that embodies it all, the ageographia, the surveillance and control, the simulations without end. The theme park presents its happy regulated vision of pleasure—all those artfully hoodwinking forms—as a substitute for the democratic political realm, and it does so appealingly by stripping troubled urbanity of its sting, of the presence of the poor, of crime, of dirt, of work." See Michael Sorkin, ed., *Variations on a Theme Park: The New American City and the End of Public Space* (New York: Hill and Wang, 1992).

20. City of Rancho Cucamonga, Foothill Boulevard Specific Plan, cover page.

21. Ibid., Section 4.2.

22. Dolores Hayden, *The Power of Place: Urban Landscapes of Public History* (Cambridge, MA: MIT Press, 1997).

23. Compare El Camino Real, in Phoebe S. Kropp, *California Vieja: Cultural Memory in a Modern American Place* (Berkeley: University of California Press, 2006).

24. William Lyon Company, *The Victoria Community Plan;* LSA Associates, Inc., *Final Environmental Impact Report: Victoria Gardens Project, City of Rancho Cucamonga,* SCH #20010301028, 19 December 2001, Reference, Archibald Library, Rancho Cucamonga.

25. City of Rancho Cucamonga, *Foothill Boulevard Specific Plan,* Sections 9.81 and 9.8.2.

26. Joseph Acenzi, "Lewis: Shift to Commercial Projects Right Move, No Regrets about Abandoning Hot Home Market," *The Business Press,* November 22, 2004; Leslie Berkman, "Lewis Family: Inland Home-Building Icons, Master Planned, After Building a Housing Empire, the Next Generation Focuses on Communities," *Riverside Press-Enterprise,* December 5, 2004. On mega homebuilders in the Inland Empire, see De Lara, *Inland Shift.*

27. "Developer Unveils Plans for Rancho Cucamonga Regional Shopping District," Rancho Cucamonga Media Packet, July 19, 2000, Archibald Library, Rancho Cucamonga; LSA Associates, Inc., *Final Environmental Impact Report: Victoria Gardens Project,* December 19, 2001, Archibald Library, Rancho Cucamonga; City of Rancho Cucamonga, *Victoria Gardens, Rancho Cucamonga, Master Plan,* January 18, 2002, available at https://www.cityofrc.us/civicax/filebank/blobdload .aspx?BlobID=12921.

28. "Forest City Honored with Two Urban Land Institute Awards for Excellence," Forest City news release, May 18, 2006.

29. Brad Berton, "Instant Roots: A Southern California City Is Seeing Development of a New Downtown Commercial District," *Urban Land* (March 2003).

30. Quoted material from Berton, "Instant Roots." See also "Developer Unveils Plans for Rancho Cucamonga Regional Shopping District"; "Forest City Honored with Two Urban Land Institute Awards for Excellence."

31. Emphasis added. Robert T. Dunphy, "TOD without Transit?: Newer Town Centers in the United States Now Have Pedestrian Appeal, But One Aspect

of Mobility that Seems to Be Missing Is Transit," *Urban Land* (August 2007), 36–37.

32. Description of the built environment based on author's field notes and photographs from March 26, 2011 and August 28, 2015. Author visited site continuously between 2011 and 2018.

33. Ibid.

34. In describing this immersive spatial experience, I draw upon the concepts of "imagineering." See John Hench, *Designing Disney: Imagineering and the Art of Show* (New York: Disney Enterprises, 2003).

35. Kropp, *California Vieja;* John Nieto-Phillips, *The Language of Blood: The Making of Spanish-American Identity in New Mexico, 1880s–1930s* (Albuquerque: University of New Mexico Press, 2004); Jill Lepore, *The Name of War: King Phillip's War and the Origins of American Identity* (New York: Vintage Books, 1998); Chris Wilson, *The Myth of Santa Fe: Creating a Modern Regional Tradition* (Albuquerque: University of New Mexico Press, 1997); Raymond Williams, *Marxism and Literature* (New York: Oxford University Press, 1977).

36. Quoted material from Frederick Jackson Turner, *The Significance of the Frontier in American History* (1893; New York: Penguin Books, 2008), 2. For a discussion of Turner's frontier thesis and its significance to the American West, see Patricia Limerick, *The Legacy of Conquest: The Unbroken Past of the American West* (New York: W. W. Norton, 1987).

37. Quoted material from Turner, *The Significance of the Frontier in American History,* 4.

38. Ibid., 30.

39. Razack, *Race, Space, and the Law.*

40. Quoted material from Turner, *The Significance of the Frontier in American History,* 14.

41. Ibid., 38.

42. Razack, *Race, Space, and the Law,* 3.

43. I draw here from Stuart Hall et al., *Policing the Crisis: Mugging, the State, and Law and Order* (New York: Holmes and Meier, 1978).

44. Geographer Tim Cresswell notes that although the legal right to mobility has been upheld consistently in the American court, the right to stay in place has not received equivalent treatment. In my use of the term "right," I'm alluding to an expanded conception of the term that does not rest on legal citizenship. See Tim Cresswell, *On the Move: Mobility in the Modern Western World* (New York: Routledge, 2006), chapter 6.

45. Riverside Latino Voter Project, "The Empire Strikes Back: Organizing Inland," press release, March 29, 2010.

46. Riverside Latino Voter Project, "The Empire Strikes Back: Organizing Inland," panel, March 29, 2010 (personal recording in author's possession).

47. Gilda Haas, "Inequality, Gentrification, and the Right to the City," paper delivered at Soja Fest, University of California, Los Angeles, 2008 (in author's possession).

BIBLIOGRAPHY

NEWSPAPERS

The Business Press (Riverside)
California Citrograph
Chino Champion
Claremont Courier
Harvard Daily Echo
Hemet News
Inland Valley Daily Bulletin
Los Angeles Herald
Los Angeles Sentinel
Los Angeles Times
New York Herald
New York Times
Ontario Daily Report

Ontario Record
Pomona Progress Bulletin
Riverside Daily Press
Riverside Enterprise. Riverside Independent, Riverside Independent Enterprise, Riverside Press Enterprise, Riverside Press-Enterprise, Riverside Press and Horticulturist
San Bernardino County Sun
San Francisco Call
Springfield Daily Republican
Washington Post

ARCHIVES AND MANUSCRIPT COLLECTIONS

Al Castro's Personal Collection
Archibald Library, Rancho Cucamonga
   Reference
Arizona Historical Society, Rio Colorado Ephemera Collection, Yuma
Boys Republic, Chino
City of Los Angeles, Office of Historic Resources
City of Riverside, Records of the City Clerk
Corona Public Library
Getty Research Institute, Los Angeles
Huntington Library, San Marino
   Cucamonga Citrus Fruit Growers' Association Records, 1896–1927
   Rare Books Collection

Inland Mexican Heritage, Redlands
  Chamber of Commerce folder
Japanese American National Museum, Los Angeles
  Iwata (Masakazu) Papers
Los Angeles Public Library
National Archives and Records Administration, Riverside
  RG 029, Records of the Bureau of the Census
  RG 11, General Records of the United States Government
  RG 21, Records of the US District Court (Southern District of California)
  RG 46, Records of the United States Senate, 1789–1990
  RG 85, Records of the Immigration and Naturalization Service
Oakland Museum of California, The Dorothea Lange Collection
Old Time Radio Researchers Group, Calling All Cars Recordings
Ovitt Family Community Library, Robert E. Ellingwood Model Colony History
Room, Ontario
  Daughters of the American Revolution Collection, 1915- 2008
  Local History: Prison Files
Pomona Public Library, Special Collections
  Citrus Label Collection
  City Directories
  Pomona Valley History Collection
Riverside Metropolitan Museum
  Harada Family Collection
  Photograph Collection
  Riverside City Collection
  Riverside County Justice Dockets
  Roy L. Haglund Collection
  Sanborn Map Collection
Riverside Public Library
  Harry W. Lawton Chinatown Papers
  Local History Collection
  Photograph Collection
  Riverside Chamber of Commerce Collection
San Bernardino County Museum, History Collection
San Bernardino Public Library, San Bernardino Oral History Project
San Diego State University, Special Collections and University Archives
  Enriqueta Chavez Papers
Sherman Indian Museum, Riverside
Southern California Library for Social Studies and Research, Los Angeles
  Charles Bratt Papers
Stanford University
  David Rumsey Historical Map Collection
  Philip G. Zimbardo Papers

University of California Berkeley, Bancroft Library
   Paul S. Taylor Papers
University of California Los Angeles, Chicano Studies Research Center
   Chicano Newspaper Collection
   Ron Lopez Papers
   Joan Moore Papers, 1978–2004
University of California Los Angeles, Young Research Library
   George Pigeon Clements Papers
University of California Riverside, Tomás Rivera Library
   Archibald D. Shamel Papers
   Avery Field Photo Collection
   San Bernardino County, California Collection Sunkist Growers Inc.
University of Pittsburgh, American Left Ephemera Collection, 1894–2008
University of Southern California, Rare Books Collection
Upland Public Library, Local History Collections
Yale University, Map Collection

SECONDARY SOURCES

Abrego, Leisy J. *Sacrificing Families: Navigating Law, Labor, and Love Across Borders*. Stanford: Stanford University Press, 2014.

Akers Chacón, Justin, and Mike Davis. *No One Is Illegal: Fighting Racism and State Violence on the U.S.-Mexico Border*. Chicago: Haymarket Books, 2006.

Alamillo, José M. *Making Lemonade Out of Lemons: Mexican American Labor and Leisure in a California Town, 1880–1960*. Chicago: University of Illinois Press, 2006.

Alamo-Pastrana, Carlos. *Seams of Empire: Race and Radicalism in Puerto Rico and the United States*. Gainesville: University Press of Florida, 2015.

Alderman, Derek H., and Joshua Inwood. "Mobility as Antiracism Work: The 'Hard Driving' of NASCAR's Wendell Scott." *Annals of the American Association of Geographers* 106, no. 3 (2016): 597–611.

Almaguer, Tomás. *Racial Fault Lines: The Historical Origins of White Supremacy in California*. Berkeley: University of California Press, 1994.

Alvarez, Luis. "From Zoot Suits to Hip Hop: Towards a Relational Chicana/o Studies." *Latino Studies* 5, no. 1 (2007): 53–75.

———. *The Power of the Zoot Suit: Youth Culture and Resistance during World War II*. Berkeley: University of California Press, 2009.

Ammon, Francesca. *Bulldozer: Demolition and Clearance of the Postwar Landscape*. New Haven: Yale University Press, 2016.

Anderson, Kay J. "The Idea of Chinatown: The Power of Place and Institutional Practice in the Making of a Racial Category." *Annals of the Association of American Geographers* 77, no. 4 (1987): 580–598.

———. *Vancouver's Chinatown: Racial Discourse in Canada, 1875–1980.* Montreal: McGill-Queen's University Press, 1991.

Andrés, Benny J. *Power and Control in the Imperial Valley: Nature, Agribusiness, and Workers on the California Borderland, 1900–1940.* College Station: Texas A&M University Press, 2015.

Aquino, Valentin R. *"The Filipino Community in Los Angeles."* Master's thesis, University of Southern California, 1952.

Avila, Eric. *Folklore of the Freeway: Race and Revolt in the Modernist City.* Minneapolis: University of Minnesota Press, 2014.

Azuma, Eiichiro. *Between Two Empires: Race, History, and Transnationalism in Japanese America.* New York: Oxford University Press, 2005.

Balderrama, Francisco E., and Raymond Rodríguez. *Decade of Betrayal: Mexican Repatriation in the 1930s.* Albuquerque: University of New Mexico Press, 1995.

Barraclough, Laura R. *Charros: How Mexican Cowboys Are Remapping Race and American Identity.* Oakland: University of California Press, forthcoming.

———. *Making the San Fernando Valley: Rural Landscapes, Urban Development, and White Privilege.* Athens: University of Georgia Press, 2011.

———. "South Central Farmers and Shadow Hills Homeowners: Land Use Policy and Relational Racialization in Los Angeles." *Professional Geographer* 61, no. 2 (2009): 164–186.

Barron, Hal. *Mixed Harvest: The Second Great Transformation in the Rural North, 1870–1930.* Chapel Hill: University of North Carolina Press, 1997.

Batschelet, Clarence E., ed. *Portfolio of United States Census Maps: 1950. A Selection of Maps Used in the Publications of the 1950 Censuses of Population and Agriculture.* Department of Commerce. Washington, DC: Government Printing Office, 1953.

Battles, Kathleen. *Calling All Cars: Radio Dragnets and the Technology of Policing.* Minneapolis: University of Minnesota Press, 2010.

Bauer, Fern Ioula. *The Historic Treasure Chest of the Madonna of the Trail Monuments.* Springfield, OH: John McEnaney Printing, 1984.

Bederman, Gail. *Manliness and Civilization: A Cultural History of Gender and Race in the United States, 1880–1917.* Chicago: University of Chicago Press, 1995.

Berton, Brad. "Instant Roots: A Southern California City Is Seeing Development of a New Downtown Commercial District." *Urban Land* (March 2003).

Blackhawk, Ned. *Violence Over the Land: Indians and Empires in the Early American West.* Cambridge, MA: Harvard University Press, 2006.

Blackwell, Maylei. *¡Chicana Power! Contested Histories of Feminism in the Chicano Movement.* Austin: University of Texas Press, 2011.

Bloch, Louie. "Facts About Mexican Immigration Before and Since the Quota Restriction Laws." *Journal of the American Statistical Association* 24, no. 165 (March 1929): 50–60.

Bloom, John. "'To Die for a Lousy Bike': Bicycles, Race, and the Regulation of Public Space on the Streets of Washington, DC, 1963–2009." *American Quarterly* 69, no. 1 (March 2017): 47–70.

Bonacich, Edna, and Jake B. Wilson. *Getting the Goods: Ports, Labor, and the Logistics Revolution*. Ithaca: Cornell University Press, 2008.

Bottles, Scott L. *Los Angeles and the Automobile: The Making of the Modern City*. Berkeley: University of California Press, 1987.

Brace, Laura. *The Politics of Property: Labour, Freedom, and Belonging*. Hampshire: Edinburgh University Press, 2004.

Briggs, Laura. *Reproducing Empire: Race, Sex, Science, and U.S. Imperialism in Puerto Rico*. Berkeley: University of California Press, 2003.

Bright, Brenda Jo, and Liza Bakewell. *Looking High and Low: Art and Cultural Identity*. Tucson: University of Arizona Press, 1995.

Brilliant, Mark. *The Color of America Has Changed: How Racial Diversity Shaped Civil Rights Reform in California, 1941–1978*. New York: Oxford University Press, 2010.

Brown, John, and James Boyd. *History of San Bernardino and Riverside Counties with Selected Biography of Actors and Witnesses of the Period of Growth and Achievement*. Chicago: The Lewis Publishing Company, 1922.

Brown, Michael D. *The History of Chino Prison: The First Fifty Years of the California Institute for Men, 1941–1991*. Chino: California Institute for Men, 1991.

Bullard, Robert D., J. Eugene Grigsby III, and Charles Lee. eds. *Residential Apartheid: The American Legacy*. Los Angeles: CAAS Publications, University of California, 1994.

Burghardt, Andrew F. "A Hypothesis About Gateway Cities." *Annals of the Association of American Geographers* 16 (June 1971): 269–285.

Burgos, Adrian. *Playing America's Game: Baseball, Latinos, and the Color Line*. Berkeley: University of California Press, 2007.

Burnight, Ralph F. "The Japanese in Rural Los Angeles County." *Studies in Sociology* 4 (June 1920): 1–16.

Cady, Daniel Jay. "'Southern' California: White Southern Migrants in Greater Los Angeles, 1920–1930." PhD diss., Claremont Graduate University, 2005.

California Department of Corrections. *California Prisoners: Summary Statistics of Prisoners and Parolees*. Sacramento: California Department of Corrections, 1972.

California Legislature, Joint Legislative Committee on Prison Construction and Operations. *California's Prisons: California Institution for Men*. Fifth series of hearings, November 28, 1985.

California Promotion Committee. *California Addresses by President Roosevelt*. San Francisco: Tomoyé Press, 1903.

California State Board of Control. *California and the Oriental: Japanese, Chinese, and Hindus*. Revised. Sacramento: California State Printing Office, 1922. First published in 1920 by California State Board of Control.

Camp, Jordan T. *Incarcerating the Crisis: Freedom Struggles and the Rise of the Neoliberal State*. Oakland: University of California Press, 2016.

Carpio, Genevieve. "Unexpected Allies: David C. Marcus, Civil Rights, and the Mexican American Legal Landscape of Southern California." *Annual Review of the Casden Institute from the Study of the Jewish Role in American Life* 9 (2012): 1–32.

Carpio, Genevieve, Clara Irazábal, and Laura Pulido. "Right to the Suburb? Rethinking Lefebvre and Immigrant Activism." *Journal of Urban Affairs* 33, no. 2 (May 2011): 185–208.

Carpio, Genevieve, and Andrzej Rutkowski. "Mapping LA-tinx Suburbs." *Boom California* (July 2017).

Castillo-Muñoz, Veronica. "Historical Roots of Rural Migration: Land Reform, Corn Credit, and the Displacement of Rural Farmers in Nayarit Mexico, 1900–1952." *Mexican Studies/ Estudios Mexicanos* 29 (Winter 2013): 36–60.

Chan, Sucheng. *The Bittersweet Soil: The Chinese in California Agriculture, 1860–1910*. Berkeley: University of California Press, 1989.

Chang, Kornel. *Pacific Connections: The Making of the U.S.-Canadian Borderlands*. Berkeley: University of California Press, 2012.

Chappel, Ben. *Lowrider Space: Aesthetics and Politics of Modern Custom Cars*. Austin: University of Texas Press, 2012.

Charr, Easurk Emsen. *The Golden Mountain: The Autobiography of a Korean Immigrant, 1895–1960*. Edited by Wayne Patterson. Urbana: University of Illinois Press, 1996.

Chávez-García, Miroslava. *Negotiating Conquest: Gender and Power in California, 1770s to 1880s*. Tucson: University of Arizona Press, 2004.

———. *States of Delinquency: Race and Science in the Making of California's Juvenile Justice System*. Berkeley: University of California Press, 2012.

Cheng, Wendy. *The Changs Next Door to the Diazes: Remapping Race in Suburban California*. Minneapolis: University of Minnesota Press, 2013.

Chiang, Connie Y. *Shaping the Shoreline: Fisheries and Tourism on the Monterey Coast*. Seattle: University of Washington Press, 2008.

Chin, Gabriel J. "'A Chinaman's Chance' in Court: Asian Pacific Americans and Racial Rules of Evidence." *UC Irvine Law Review* 3, no. 965 (December 2013): 965–990.

City of Pomona. *Council Report Number 08–140* (April 7, 2008).

City of Rancho Cucamonga. *Foothill Boulevard Specific Plan* (September 1987).

———. *Victoria Gardens, Rancho Cucamonga, Master Plan* (January 18, 2002). https://www.cityofrc.us/civicax/filebank/blobdload.aspx?BlobID=12921.

Clark, Victor. "Mexican Labor in the United States." *Bulletin of the Bureau of Labor*, no. 78 (Washington, DC: Government Printing Office, 1908): 466–522.

Clifford, James. *Routes: Travel and Translation in the Late Twentieth Century*. Cambridge, MA: Harvard University Press, 1997.

Cohen, Lizabeth. *A Consumers' Republic: The Politics of Mass Consumption in Postwar America*. New York: Alfred A. Knopf, 2003.

Collins, Patricia Hill. *Black Feminist Thought: Knowledge, Consciousness, and the Politics of Empowerment*. New York: Routledge, 2000.

Conrad, Debra, ed. *Yuma Mesa Homesteaders, 1948 and 1952*. Raleigh: Lulu Press, 2007.

Copeland, Rebecca. "Fashioning the Feminine: Images of the Modern Girl Student in Meiji Japan." *U.S.-Japan Women's Journal* 30/31 (2006): 13–35.

Crenshaw, Kimberlé. "Mapping the Margins: Intersectionality, Identity Politics, and Violence against Women of Color." *Stanford Law Review* 43, no. 6 (1991): 1241–1299.

Cresswell, Tim. *In Place/Out of Place: Geography, Ideology and Transgression.* Minneapolis: University of Minnesota Press, 1996.

———. *On the Move: Mobility in the Modern Western World.* New York: Routledge, 2006.

———. *Place: An Introduction.* 2nd ed. West Sussex: John Wiley and Sons Ltd., 2015.

———. "Race, Mobility, and the Humanities: A Geospatial Approach." In *Envisioning Landscapes, Making Worlds: Geography and the Humanities,* edited by Stephen Daniels, Dydia DeLyser, J. Nicholas Entrikin, and Doug Richardson, 74–83. New York: Routledge, 2011.

———. *The Tramp in America.* London: Reaktion Books, 2001.

Cronon, William. *Nature's Metropolis: Chicago and the Great West.* New York: W. W. Norton, 1991.

Croutch, Albert. "Housing Migratory Agricultural Workers in California, 1913–1948." Master's thesis, University of California, Berkeley, 1948.

Cruz, Alice Evans. "The Romanzas Train Señora Nurse." *The Survey* 60 (August 1928): 468–488.

Culbertson, James D. "Housing of Ranch Labor." *First Annual Report of the California Citrus Institute* (1920): 97–105.

Dansky, Kara. "Understanding California Sentencing." *University of San Francisco Law Review* 43, no. 3 (Summer 2008): 45–86.

Davis, Mike. *City of Quartz: Excavating the Future in Los Angeles.* London: Verso, 1990.

Day, Iyko. *Alien Capital: Asian Racialization and the Logic of Settler Colonial Capitalism.* Durham: Duke University Press, 2016.

de Certeau, Michel. *The Practice of Everyday Life.* Translated by Steven Rendall. Berkeley: University of California Press, 1984.

Delaney, David. *Race, Place, and the Law, 1836–1948.* Austin: University of Texas Press, 1998.

———. "The Space that Race Makes." *Professional Geographer* 54, no. 1 (2002).

DeLoughry, Elizabeth. *Routes and Roots: Navigating Caribbean and Pacific Island Literatures.* Honolulu: University of Hawai'i Press, 2007.

Denning, Michael. *The Cultural Front: The Laboring of American Culture in the Twentieth Century.* London: Verso, 1998.

Deverell, William. *Whitewashed Adobe: The Rise of Los Angeles and the Remaking of Its Mexican Past.* Berkeley: University of California Press, 2004.

Diaz, David R. *Barrio Urbanism: Chicanos, Planning, and American Cities.* New York: Routledge, 2005.

Dickenson, Samuel, A. M. Free, and Edmind Cooke. "Restriction of Immigration from Republic of Mexico." 71st Congress, 2nd Session, Report No. 1594, Part 2, May 28, 1930.

Dodge, Martin, Rob Kitchin, and Chris Perkins, eds. *The Map Reader: Theories of Mapping Practice and Cartographic Representation*. West Sussex: Wiley-Blackwell, 2011.

Douglas, Mary. *Purity and Danger: An Analysis of Concepts of Pollution and Taboo*. London: Routledge, 2002.

Dreier, Peter, Saqib Bhatti, Rob Call, Alex Schwartz, and Gregory Squires. *Underwater America: How the So-Called Housing Recovery Is Bypassing Many American Communities*. Berkeley: Haas Institute, University of California, 2014.

Dudden, Alexis. *Japan's Colonization of Korea: Discourse and Power*. Honolulu: University of Hawai'i Press, 2005.

Dunphy, Robert. "TOD without Transit?: Newer Town Centers in the United States Now Have Pedestrian Appeal, But One Aspect of Mobility That Seems to Be Missing Is Transit." *Urban Land* (August 2007): 36–39.

Dyer, Thomas G. *Theodore Roosevelt and the Idea of Race*. Baton Rouge: Louisiana State University Press, 1980.

Edmonds, Penelope. *Urbanizing Frontiers: Indigenous Peoples and Settlers in 19th-Century Pacific Rim Cities*. Vancouver: University of British Columbia Press, 2010.

Elliott, Matthew. "John Fante's *Ask the Dust* and Fictions of Whiteness." *Twentieth Century Literature* 56 (Winter 2010): 530–544.

Engstrand, Iris Wilson. *William Wolfskill 1798–1866: Frontier Trapper to California Ranchero*. Glendale: A. H. Clark, 1965.

Erman, Sam. "Meanings of Citizenship in the U.S. Empire: Puerto Rico, Isabel Gonzales, and the Supreme Court, 1898–1905." *Journal of American Ethnic History* 27, no. 4 (2008): 5–33.

Escobar, Edward J. *Race, Police, and the Making of a Political Identity: Mexican Americans and the Los Angeles Police Department, 1900–1945*. Berkeley: University of California Press, 1999.

España-Maram, Linda. *Creating Masculinity in Los Angeles's Little Manila: Working-Class Filipinos and Popular Culture, 1920s–1950s*. New York: Columbia University Press, 2006.

Espiritu, Yen Le. *Filipino American Lives*. Philadelphia: Temple University Press, 1995.

Ethington, Philip. "Segregated Diversity: Race-Ethnicity, Space, and Political Fragmentation in Los Angeles County, 1940–1994." Final Report to the John Randolph Haynes and Dora Haynes Foundation, 2000. http://www-bcf.usc.edu/~philipje/Segregation/Haynes_Reports/FINAL_REPORT_20000719g.pdf.

Fante, John. *Ask the Dust*. New York: Harper Perennial, 2006. First published in 1939 by Stackpole Sons, New York.

Ferguson, Edwin E. "The California Alien Land Law and the Fourteenth Amendment." *California Law Review* 35, no. 1 (March 1947): 61–90.

Findlay, Eileen Suárez. *Imposing Decency: The Politics of Sexuality and Race in Puerto Rico, 1870–1920*. Durham: Duke University Press, 2001.

Fingal, Sara. *Turning the Tide: The Politics of Land and Leisure During the Age of Environmentalism*. Seattle: University of Washington Press, forthcoming.

Finnegan, Cara. *Picturing Poverty: Print Culture and FSA Photographs.* Washington, DC: Smithsonian Books, 2003.

Flamming, Douglas. *Bound for Freedom: Black Los Angeles in Jim Crow America.* Berkeley: University of California Press, 2006.

Flores, Richard R. *Remembering the Alamo: Memory, Modernity, and the Master Symbol.* Austin: University of Texas Press, 2002.

Ford Motor Company. "Historia de Ford de Mexico" [The History of Ford Mexico]. http://media.ford.com/article_display.cfm?article_id=4166.

Fregoso, Rosa-Linda. *meXicana Encounters: The Making of Social Identities on the Borderlands.* Berkeley: University of California Press, 2003.

Friends for Fullerton. "Pomona PD: Officer Patrick O'Malley Freaks Out." Online video clip, August 21, 2012. http://www.youtube.com/watch?v=Dm94RiIvbiE.

Gabaccia, Donna. *Foreign Relations: American Immigration in Global Perspective.* Princeton: Princeton University Press, 2012.

Gamio, Manuel. *Mexican Immigration to the United States.* Chicago: University of Chicago Press, 1930.

García, David G. *Strategies of Segregation: Race, Residence, and the Struggle for Educational Equality.* Oakland: University of California Press, 2018.

Garcia, Matt. *A World of Its Own: Race, Labor, and Citrus in the Making of Greater Los Angeles, 1900–1970.* Chapel Hill: University of North Carolina Press, 2001.

Gardeners' Chronicle: A Weekly Illustrated Journal of Horticulture and Allied Subjects. London: Bradbury, Agnew, and Co., 1906.

Gaspar de Alba, Alicia. *[Un]Framing the "Bad Woman": Sor Juana, Malinche, Coyolxauhqui and Other Rebels with a Cause.* Austin: University of Texas Press, 2014.

Gates, Charles F. "Cycling in the Southwest." *Land of Sunshine* 5 (June to November 1896): 48.

———. "Racing and Racing Men: The Wheel in Southern California." *Overland Monthly* 28, no. 167, 2nd series, San Francisco (November 1896): 539–543.

Gilmore, Ruth. *Golden Gulag: Prison, Surplus, Crisis, and Opposition in Globalizing California.* Berkeley: University of California Press, 2007.

Glick, Clarence. *Sojourners and Settlers: Chinese Migrants in Hawaii.* Honolulu: University of Hawai'i Press, 1980.

Goff, Ron. "Reprint of a 1903 Newspaper Story: 'New Society of Historians.'" *Journal of the Riverside Historical Society* 7, no. 1 (February 2003): 8–12.

Gómez, Laura E. *Manifest Destinies: The Making of the Mexican American Race.* New York: New York University Press, 2007.

González, Gilbert G. *Labor and Community: Mexican Citrus Worker Villages in a Southern California County, 1900–1950.* Urbana: University of Illinois Press, 1994.

González, Jerry. *In Search of the Mexican Beverly Hills: Latino Suburbanization in Postwar Los Angeles.* New Brunswick, NJ: Rutgers University Press, 2018.

Goonewardena, Kanishka, Stefan Kipfer, Richard Milgrom, and Christian Schmid, eds. *Space, Difference, Everyday Life: Reading Henri Lefebvre*. New York: Routledge, 2008.

Gordon, Linda. *Dorothea Lange: A Life Beyond Limits*. New York: W. W. Norton, 2009.

———. *The Great Arizona Orphan Abduction*. Cambridge, MA: Harvard University Press, 1999.

Graves, Donna. "Japanese American Heritage and the Quest for Civil Rights in Riverside California, 1890s–1970s." *National Register of Historic Places Multiple Property Documentation Form* (May 2012).

The Great Basin Foundation, ed. *Wong Ho Leun: An American Chinatown*, vol. 1. San Diego: The Great Basin Foundation, 1987.

Greenberg, Amy. *Manifest Manhood and the Antebellum American Empire*. New York: Cambridge University Press, 2005.

Griffin, Paul F., and Ronald L. Chatham. "Population: A Challenge to California's Changing Citrus Industry." *Economic Geography* 34, no. 3 (1958): 272–276.

Griffith, R. Marie. "Apostles of Abstinence: Fasting and Masculinity during the Progressive Era." *American Quarterly* 52 (December 2000): 599–638.

Grigsby, J. Eugene, III. "African American Mobility and Residential Quality in Los Angeles." In *Residential Apartheid: The American Legacy*, edited by Robert D. Bullard, J. Eugene Grigsby III, and Charles Lee, 122–149. Los Angeles: CAAS Publications, University of California, 1994.

Gudis, Catherine. "Reconnaissance Survey and Context Statement for the Marketplace Specific Plan, City of Riverside, California." Prepared for the City of Riverside Community Development Department, July 2012.

Guerín-Gonzáles, Camille. *Mexican Workers and American Dreams: Immigration, Repatriation, and California Farm Labor, 1900–1939*. New Brunswick, NJ: Rutgers University Press, 1994.

Guevarra, Rudy, Jr. *Becoming Mexipino: Multiethnic Identities and Communities in San Diego*. New Brunswick, NJ: Rutgers University Press, 2012.

Guidotti-Hernández, Nicole M. "Affective Communities and Millennial Desires: Latinx, or Why My Computer Won't Recognize Latina/o." *Cultural Dynamics* 29, no. 3 (August 2017): 141–159.

Gutiérrez, Ramón. *When Jesus Came, the Corn Mothers Went Away*. Stanford: Stanford University Press, 1991.

Haas, Gilda. "Inequality, Gentrification, and the Right to the City." Paper delivered at Soja Fest, University of California, Los Angeles, 2008.

Haas, Lisbeth. *Conquests and Historical Identities in California, 1769–1936*. Berkeley: University of California Press, 1995.

———. *Saints and Citizens: Indigenous Histories of Colonial Missions and Mexican California*. Berkeley: University of California Press, 2014.

Hackel, Steven W. *Children of Coyote, Missionaries of Saint Francis: Indian-Spanish Relations in Colonial California, 1769–1850*. Chapel Hill: University of North Carolina Press, 2005.

Hadden, Sally E. *Slave Patrols: Law and Violence in Virginia and the Carolinas.* Cambridge, MA: Harvard University Press, 2001.

Hall, Joan. "Riverside's Historical Societies Centennial." *Journal of the Riverside Historical Society* 7 (February 2003): 1–6.

Hall, Stuart, Chas Critcher, Tony Jefferson, John Clarke, and Brian Roberts. *Policing the Crisis: Mugging, the State, and Law and Order.* New York: Holmes and Meier, 1978.

Hannam, Kevin, Mimi Sheller, and John Urry. "Mobilities, Immobilities and Moorings." *Mobilities* 1, no. 1 (2006): 1–22.

Harley, John B. "Deconstructing the Map." *Cartographica* 26, no. 2 (Spring 1989): 1–20.

Harley, R. Bruce. "Abiquiu, New Mexico: Ancestral Home of the Agua Mansa Pioneers," *San Bernardino County Museum Association Quarterly* 39 (Winter 1991).

———. "An Early Riverside Suburb at La Placita." *Journal of the Riverside Historical Society* 7 (2003): 13–24.

———. "From New Mexico to California: San Bernardino Valley's First Settlers at Agua Mansa." *San Bernardino County Museum Association Quarterly* 47, nos. 3 and 4 (2000).

———. "Reminiscences of David Santiago Garcia as Told to Helen Loehr, with Notes and Comments by R. Bruce Harley." *San Bernardino County Museum Association Quarterly* 40 (Fall 1993).

———. *The Story of Agua Mansa: Its Settlement, Churches, and People; First Community in San Bernardino Valley 1842–1893.* San Bernardino: Diocese of San Bernardino, 1995.

Harley, R. Bruce, ed. "The Agua Mansa History Trail." *San Bernardino County Museum Association Quarterly* 43 (Summer 1996).

Harootunian, Harry. *Overcome by Modernity: History, Culture, and Community in Interwar Japan.* Princeton: Princeton University Press, 2000.

Harris, Cheryl I. "Whiteness as Property." *Harvard Law Review* 106 (June 1993): 1707–1791.

Hartig, Anthea. "'In a World He Has Created': Class Collectivity and the Growers' Landscape in the Southern California Citrus Industry, 1890–1940." *California History* 74 (Spring 1995): 100–111.

Harvey, David. *A Brief History of Neoliberalism.* New York: Oxford University Press, 2005.

———. "Globalization and the 'Spatial Fix.'" *Geographische Revue* 2 (February 2001): 23–30.

———. *Justice, Nature and the Geography of Difference.* Oxford: Blackwell, 1996.

Hayden, Dolores. *The Power of Place: Urban Landscapes of Public History.* Cambridge, MA: MIT Press, 1997.

Hein, Carola, ed. *Port Cities: Dynamic Landscapes and Global Networks.* London: Routledge, 2011.

Hench, John. *Designing Disney: Imagineering and the Art of Show.* New York: Disney Enterprises, 2003.

Herlihy, David. *Bicycle: The History*. New Haven: Yale University Press, 2004.

Herod, Andrew. "Social Engineering through Spatial Engineering: Company Towns and the Geographical Imagination." In *Company Towns in the Americas: Landscape, Power, and Working-Class Communities,* edited by Oliver Dinius and Angela Vergara, 21–44. Atlanta: University of Georgia Press, 2011.

Herod, Andrew, and Melissa W. Wright. *Geographies of Power: Placing Scale.* Oxford: Wiley-Blackwell, 2002.

Hise, Greg. *Magnetic Los Angeles: Planning the Twentieth Century Metropolis.* Baltimore: Johns Hopkins University Press, 1997.

Historical Society of Southern California. "Constitution, Adopted September 4, 1897," *Publications* 4 (Los Angeles: Los Angeles County Pioneers of Southern California, 1898): 93–94.

Hoffman, Abraham. "An Unusual Monument: Paul S. Taylor's Mexican Labor in the United States Monograph Series." *Pacific Historical Review* 45 (May 1976): 255–270.

Holmes, Elmer Wallace. *History of Riverside County, California: With Biographical Sketches of Men and Women of the County Who Have Been Identified with Its Growth and Development from the Early Days to the Present.* Los Angeles: Historic Record Company, 1912.

Hondagneu-Sotelo, Pierrette. *Domestica: Immigrant Workers Cleaning and Caring in the Shadows of Affluence.* Berkeley: University of California Press, 2001.

———. *Paradise Transplanted: Migration and the Making of California Gardens.* Berkeley: University of California Press, 2014.

Horsman, Reginald. *Race and Manifest Destiny: The Origins of American Racial Anglo Saxonism.* Cambridge, MA: Harvard University Press, 1981.

HoSang, Daniel Martinez. *Racial Propositions: Ballot Initiatives and the Making of Postwar California.* Berkeley: University of California Press, 2010.

Hudson, Angela Pulley. *Creek Paths and Federal Roads: Indians, Settlers, and Slaves and the Making of the American South.* Chapel Hill: University of North Carolina Press, 2010.

Hurtado, Albert. *Intimate Encounters: Sex, Gender, and Culture in Old California.* Albuquerque: University of New Mexico Press, 1999.

Hyde, Charles. *Riding the Roller Coaster: A History of the Chrysler Corporation.* Detroit: Wayne State University Press, 2003.

Hyman, Louis. *Borrow: The American Way of Debt: How Personal Credit Created the American Middle Class and Almost Bankrupted the Nation.* New York: Vintage Books, 2012.

Ichioka, Yuji. "Japanese Immigrant Response to the 1920 California Alien Land Law." *Agricultural History* 58 (April 1984): 157–178.

Ingersoll, Luther, ed. *Ingersoll's Century Annals of San Bernardino County, 1769–1904.* Los Angeles: L. A. Ingersoll, 1904.

Jacobs, Margaret D. "Seeing Like a Settler Colonial State." *Modern American History* 1, no. 2 (2018): 257–270.

———. *White Mother to a Dark Race: Settler Colonialism, Maternalism, and the Removal of Indigenous Children in the American West and Australia, 1880–1940.* Lincoln: University of Nebraska, 2009.

Jacobson, Matthew Frye. *Whiteness of a Different Color: European Immigrants and the Alchemy of Race.* Cambridge, MA: Harvard University Press, 1998.

Jessop, Bob. "Spatial Fixes, Temporal Fixes and Spatio-Temporal Fixes." In *David Harvey: A Critical Reader,* edited by Noel Castree and Derek Gregory, 142–166. Malden: Blackwell Publishing, 2006.

Johnson, Gaye Theresa. *Spaces of Conflict, Sounds of Solidarity: Music, Race, and Spatial Entitlement in Los Angeles.* Berkeley: University California Press, 2013.

Johnson, Phillip E., and Sheldon L. Messinger. "California's Determinate Sentencing Statute: History and Issues." *Determinate Sentencing: Reform or Regression?* (Berkeley: Berkeley Law Scholarship Repository, 1978): 13–58.

Kaplan, Amy, and Donald E. Pease, eds. *Cultures of United States Imperialism.* Durham: Duke University Press, 1994.

Kaplowitz, Craig A. *LULAC: Mexican Americans and National Policy.* College Station: Texas A&M University Press, 2005.

Katz, Michael B. *The Undeserving Poor: From the War on Poverty to the War on Welfare.* New York: Pantheon Books, 1989.

Kaufmann, Vincent. *Re-Thinking Mobility Social Justice.* Burlington, VT: Ashgate, 2002.

Kaufmann, Vincent, Manfred Max Bergman, and Dominique Joye. "Motility: Mobility as Capital." *International Journal of Urban and Regional Research* 28 (December 2004): 745–756.

Kelley, Robin D. G. *Yo' Mama's Disfunktional!: Fighting the Cultural Wars in Urban America.* Boston: Beacon Press, 1997.

Kim, Claire Jean. "The Racial Triangulation of Asian Americans." *Politics and Society* 27 (March 1999): 105–138.

Kim, Jessica. *Imperial Metropolis: Los Angeles, Mexico, and the Borderlands of American Empire, 1865–1941.* Chapel Hill: University of North Carolina Press, forthcoming 2019.

Klotz, Esther H. "Eliza Tibbets and her Washington Navel Orange Trees." In *A History of Citrus in the Riverside Area,* edited by Esther H. Klotz, Harry W. Lawton, and Joan H. Hall, 13–25. Riverside: Riverside Museum Press, 1969.

———. "Griffin and Skelley, Packers and Shippers." In *A History of Citrus in the Riverside Area,* edited by Esther Klotz, Harry W. Lawton, and Joan H. Hall, 40–41. Riverside: Riverside Museum Press, 1969.

Klotz, Esther H., Harry W. Lawton, and Joan H. Hall, eds. *A History of Citrus in the Riverside Area.* Riverside: Riverside Museum Press, 1969.

Kordich, Catherine. "John Fante's *Ask the Dust:* A Border Reading." *Melus* 20 (December 1995): 17–27.

Kramer, Paul A. *The Blood of Government: Race, Empire, the United States, and the Philippines.* Chapel Hill: University of North Carolina Press, 2006.

Kropp, Phoebe S. *California Vieja: Cultural Memory in a Modern American Place.* Berkeley: University of California Press, 2006.

———. "Citizens of the Past? Olvera Street and the Construction of Race and Memory in 1930s Los Angeles." *Radical History Review* 81 (Fall 2001): 35–60.

Kurashige, Scott. "Between 'White Spot' and 'World City': Racial Integration and the Roots of Multiculturalism." In *A Companion to Los Angeles,* edited by Bill Deverell and Greg Hise, 56–71. Malden: Wiley-Blackwell, 2014.

———. *The Shifting Grounds of Race: Black and Japanese Americans in the Making of Multiethnic Los Angeles.* Princeton: Princeton University Press, 2008.

Kwan, Mei-Po, and Tim Schwanen. "Geographies of Mobility." *Annals of the American Association of Geographers* 106 (March 2016): 243–256.

Lange, Dorothea, and Paul S. Taylor. *An American Exodus: A Record of Human Erosion.* Paris: Jean Michel Place, 1999. First published in 1939 by Reynal and Hitchcock, Inc.

Lawrence, Bonita. "Rewriting Histories of the Land: Colonization and Indigenous Resistance in Eastern Canada." In *Race, Space, and the Law: Unmapping a White Settler Society,* edited by Sherene Razack, 21–46. Toronto: Between the Lines, 2002.

Lawton, Harry. "A Selected Chronological History of Chinese Pioneers in Riverside and the Southern California Citrus Belt." In *Wong Ho Leun: An American Chinatown,* edited by The Great Basin Foundation, vol. 1, 53–140. San Diego: The Great Basin Foundation, 1987.

———. "Denis Kearney among the Orange Groves: The Beginnings of the Anti-Chinese Movement in the Citrus Belt (1876–1880)." In *Wong Ho Leun: An American Chinatown,* edited by The Great Basin Foundation, vol. 1, 193–203. San Diego: The Great Basin Foundation, 1987.

———. "The Pilgrims from Gom-Benn: Migratory Origins of Chinese Pioneers in the San Bernardino Valley." In *Wong Ho Leun: An American Chinatown,* edited by The Great Basin Foundation, vol. 1, 141–166. San Diego: The Great Basin Foundation, 1987.

———. "Riverside's First Chinatown and the Boom of the Eighties." In *Wong Ho Leun: An American Chinatown,* edited by The Great Basin Foundation, vol. 1, 1–52. San Diego: The Great Basin Foundation, 1987.

———. "Two Riverside Chinatown Merchants Describe Their Operations During a Geary Act Deportation Hearing." In *Wong Ho Leun: An American Chinatown,* edited by The Great Basin Foundation, vol. 1, 287–290. San Diego: The Great Basin Foundation, 1987.

LeBlanc, Robin. *Bicycle Citizens: The Political World of the Japanese Housewife.* Berkeley: University of California Press, 1999.

Lee, Erika. *At America's Gates: Chinese Immigration During the Exclusion Era, 1882–1943.* Chapel Hill: University of North Carolina Press, 2003.

Lee, Mary Paik. *Quiet Odyssey: A Pioneer Korean Woman in America.* Seattle: University of Washington Press, 1990.

Lefebvre, Henri. *Critique of Everyday Life.* Translated by John Moore. London: Verso, 1991.

—. *The Production of Space.* Translated by Donald Nicholson-Smith. Hoboken: Wiley-Blackwell, 1991.

Leiva, Priscilla. "Stadium Struggles: The Cultural Politics of Difference and Civic Identity in Postwar Urban Imaginaries." PhD diss., University of Southern California, 2014.

Leonard, Karen. *Making Ethnic Choices: California's Punjabi Mexican Americans.* Philadelphia: Temple University Press, 1992.

Leonard, Thomas C. "Retrospectives: Eugenics and Economics in the Progressive Era." *Journal of Economic Perspectives* 19 (Fall 2005): 207–224.

Leong, Nancy. "Racial Capitalism." *Harvard Law Review* 126, no. 8 (June 2013): 2151–2226.

Lepore, Jill. *The Name of War: King Phillip's War and the Origins of American Identity.* New York: Vintage Books, 1998.

Lewis, Alfred Henry, ed. *A Compilation of the Messages and Speeches of Theodore Roosevelt, 1901–1905.* New York: Bureau of National Literature and Art, 1906.

Lewis, Ralph M. *Land Buying Checklist,* 3rd ed. Washington, DC: National Association of Home Builders, 1988.

Lightfoot, Kent G. *Indians, Missionaries, and Merchants: The Legacy of Colonial Encounters on the California Frontiers.* Berkeley: University of California Press, 2006.

Limerick, Patricia. *The Legacy of Conquest: The Unbroken Past of the American West.* New York: W.W. Norton, 1987.

Lindsay, Brendan. *Murder State: California's Native American Genocide, 1846–1873.* Lincoln: University of Nebraska Press, 2012.

Lipsitz, George. *How Racism Takes Place.* Philadelphia: Temple University Press, 2011.

—. *The Possessive Investment in Whiteness: How White People Profit from Identity Politics.* Revised and expanded. Philadelphia: Temple University Press, 2006.

López, Iris. "Borinkis and Chop Suey: Puerto Rican Identity in Hawai'i, 1900 to 2000." In *The Puerto Rican Diaspora: Historical Perspectives,* edited by Carmen Teresa Whalen and Victor Vázquez-Hernández, 43–67. Philadelphia: Temple University Press, 2005.

Lowell, Waverly B., ed. "Chinese Immigration and Chinese in the United States." Reference Information Paper 99. Records in the Regional Archives of the National Archives and Records Administration, 1996.

LSA Associates, Inc. *Final Environmental Impact Report: Victoria Gardens Project, City of Rancho Cucamonga,* SCH # 20010301028, December 19, 2001.

Lu, Sidney Xu. "Good Women for Empire: Educating Overseas Female Emigrants in Imperial Japan, 1900–45." *Journal of Global History* 8 (November 2013): 436–460.

Lui, Mary Ting Yi. *The Chinatown Trunk Mystery: Murder, Miscegenation, and Other Dangerous Encounters in Turn-of-the-Century New York City.* Princeton: Princeton University Press, 2005.

Lum, Rebecca, and Suanne Yamashita. "The Chinese Population of Riverside County in 1900: Data from the Twelfth Federal Census." In *Wong Ho Leun: An*

American Chinatown, edited by The Great Basin Foundation, vol. 1, 373–385. San Diego: The Great Basin Foundation, 1987.

Lynch, Kevin. *The Image of the City.* Cambridge, MA: MIT Press, 1960.

William Lyon Company. *The Victoria Community Plan.* Submitted to the City of Rancho Cucamonga, July 1980.

Lytle Hernández, Kelly. *City of Inmates: Conquest, Rebellion, and the Rise of Human Caging in Los Angeles, 1771–1965.* Chapel Hill: University of North Carolina Press, 2017.

———. "Hobos in Heaven: Race, Incarceration, and the Rise of Los Angeles, 1880–1910." *Pacific Historical Review* 83 (August 2014): 410–447.

———. *Migra! A History of the U.S. Border Patrol.* Berkeley: University of California Press, 2010.

———. "The Sisyphean Task: Origins of the Modern Border." In *Imaginary Lines: Border Enforcement and the Origins of Undocumented Immigration, 1882–1930,* edited by Patrick Ettinger, 145–156. Austin: University of Texas Press, 2010.

Mae, Nellie, and Sandra Ford Montgomery. "William Ford Montgomery. In *Yuma Mesa Homesteaders 1948 and 1952,* edited by Debra Conrad, 164–178. Raleigh: Lulu Press, 2007.

Maldonado, Edwin. "Contract Labor and the Origins of Puerto Rican Communities in the United States." *International Migration Review* 13, no. 1 (Spring 1979): 103–121.

Malloch, R. S. "When Asked to Put It on Paper . . ." In *Inlandia: A Literary Journey Through California's Inland Empire,* edited by Gayle Wattawa, 70–74. Santa Clara: Santa Clara University, 2006.

Margolin, Malcom, ed. *The Way We Lived: California Indian Stories, Songs, Reminiscences.* Berkeley: Heyday Books, 1993.

Márquez, Benjamin. *LULAC: The Evolution of a Mexican American Political Organization.* Austin: University of Texas Press, 1993.

Massey, Doreen. *Space, Place and Gender.* Minneapolis: University of Minnesota Press, 1994.

Mawani, Renisa. "In Between and Out of Place: Mixed-Race Identity, Liquor, and the Law in British Columbia, 1850–1913." In *Race, Space, and the Law: Unmapping a White Settler Society,* edited by Sherene Razack, 47–69. Toronto: Between the Lines, 2002.

McAlister, Melanie. *Epic Encounters: Culture, Media, and U.S. Interests in the Middle East, 1945–2000.* Berkeley: University of California Press, 2001.

McBane, Margo. "The House That Lemons Built: Race, Ethnicity, Gender, Citizenship and the Creation of a Citrus Empire, 1893–1919." PhD diss., University of California, Los Angeles, 2001.

McCann, Eugene. "Race, Protest, and Public Space: Contextualizing Lefebvre in the U.S. City." *Antipode* 31, no. 2 (2002): 163–184.

McClain, Charles J. *In Search of Equality: The Chinese Struggle against Discrimination in Nineteenth-Century America.* Berkeley: University of California Press, 1994.

McCormick, Jennifer, and Cesar J. Ayala. "Felicita 'La Prieta' Mendez (1916–1998) and the End of Latino School Segregation in California." *Centro: Journal of the Center for Puerto Rican Studies,* 19 (Fall 2007): 12–35.

McGovern, Charles. *Consumption and Citizenship, 1890–1945.* Chapel Hill: University of North Carolina Press, 2006.

McGroarty, John. *Los Angeles from the Mountain to the Seas.* Chicago and New York: American Historical Society, 1921.

McWilliams, Carey. *Factories in the Field: The Story of Migratory Farm Labor in California.* Boston: Little, Brown, 1939.

———. *Ill Fares the Land.* Boston: Little Brown, 1942.

———. *Southern California: An Island on the Land,* 9th ed. Salt Lake City: Gibbs Smith, 1980. First published in 1946 by Duell, Sloan, and Pearce.

Melamed, Jodi. "The Spirit of Neoliberalism: From Racial Liberalism to Neoliberal Multiculturalism." *Social Text* 24 (Winter 2006): 1–24.

Merlo, Catherine. *Heritage of Gold: The First 100 Years of Sunkist Growers, Inc., 1893–1993.* Van Nuys: Sunkist Growers Inc., 1994.

Mexican Fact-Finding Committee. "Mexicans in California: Report of Governor C. C. Young's Mexican Fact-Finding Committee." San Francisco: California State Printing Office, October 1930.

Mitchell, Don. *The Lie of the Land: Migrant Workers and the California Landscape.* Minneapolis: University of Minnesota Press, 1996.

Mitchell, Koritha. *Living with Lynching: African American Lynching Plays, Performance, and Citizenship, 1890–1930.* Urbana: University of Illinois Press, 2011.

Mohanram, Radhika. *Black Body: Women, Colonialism, and Space.* Minneapolis: University of Minnesota Press, 1999.

Molina, Natalia. "Examining Chicana/o History through a Relational Lens." *Pacific Historical Review* 82, no. 4 (2013): 520–541.

———. *Fit to Be Citizens?: Public Health and Race in Los Angeles, 1879–1939.* Berkeley: University of California Press, 2006.

———. *How Race Is Made in America: Immigration, Citizenship, and the Historical Power of Racial Scripts.* Berkeley: University of California Press, 2014.

———. "The Importance of Place and Place-Makers in the Life of a Los Angeles Community: What Gentrification Erases from Echo Park." *Southern California Quarterly* 97, no. 1 (2015): 69–111.

Monroy, Douglas. *Rebirth: Mexican Los Angeles from the Great Migration to the Great Depression.* Berkeley: University of California Press, 1999.

Montejano, David. *Anglos and Mexicans in the Making of Texas, 1836–1986.* Austin: University of Texas Press, 1987.

Montoya, María. *Translating Property: The Maxwell Land Grant and the Conflict over Land in the American West, 1840–1900.* Berkeley: University of California Press, 2002.

Moore, Barbara, ed. *Historic Mission Inn, Riverside, California.* Riverside: Friends of the Mission Inn, 1998.

Moore, Deborah Dash. *To the Golden Cities: Pursuing the American Jewish Dream in Miami and L.A.* New York: Free Press, 1994.

Moore, Joan W., with Robert Garcia, Carlos Garcia, Luis Cerda, and Frank Valencia. *Homeboys: Gangs, Drugs, and Prisons in the Barrios of Los Angeles.* Philadelphia: Temple University Press, 1978.

Moreton-Robinson, Aileen. *The White Possessive: Property, Power, and Indigenous Sovereignty.* Minneapolis: University of Minnesota Press, 2015.

Morokvasic, Mirjana. "Birds of Passage Are Also Women." *International Migration Review* 18, no. 4 (1984): 886–907.

Morrison, Ethel Mae. "A History of Recent Legislative Proposals Concerning Mexican Immigration." Master's thesis, University of Southern California, 1929.

Moses, Vincent H., and Celena Turney, eds. *Our Families Our Stories: From the African American Community Riverside, California 1870–1960.* Riverside: Riverside Museum Press, 1997.

Myers, Dowell, and Julie Park. "Racially Balanced Cities in Southern California, 1980–2000." Race Contours 2000 Study, Public Research Report No. 2001–05. Los Angeles: Population Dynamics Group, May 23, 2001.

Next Friday, film, New Line, 2000.

Ngai, Mae M. *Impossible Subjects: Illegal Aliens and the Making of Modern America.* Princeton: Princeton University Press, 2004.

Nicolaides, Becky. *My Blue Heaven: Life and Politics in the Working-Class Suburbs of Los Angeles, 1920–1965.* Chicago: University of Chicago Press, 2002.

Nicolaides, Becky, and Andrew Wiese, eds. *The Suburban Reader.* New York: Routledge, 2016.

Nieto-Phillips, John M. *The Language of Blood: The Making of Spanish-American Identity in New Mexico, 1880s–1930s.* Albuquerque: University of New Mexico Press, 2004.

Norris, Jim. *North for the Harvest: Mexican Workers, Growers, and the Sugar Beet Industry.* St. Paul: Minnesota Historical Society Press, 2009.

O'Brien, Jean M. *Firsting and Lasting: Writing Indians Out of Existence in New England.* Minneapolis: University of Minnesota Press, 2010.

Omi, Michael, and Howard Winant. *Racial Formation in the United States: From the 1960s to the 1990s.* 2nd ed. New York: Routledge, 1994.

Opinion of Justice Antonin Scalia. Supreme Court of the United States, No. 11–182, Arizona, et al., *Petitioners v. United States,* On Writ of Certiorari to the United States Court of Appeals for the Ninth Circuit, June 25, 2012.

Orfield, Myron. *Why Are the Twin Cities So Segregated?* Minneapolis: University of Minnesota Institute on Metropolitan Equity (February 2015).

Orfield, Myron, and Thomas Luce. "America's Racially Diverse Suburbs: Opportunities and Challenges." *Housing Policy Debate* 23, no. 2 (2013): 395–430.

Ortlieb, Patricia, and Peter Economy. *Creating an Orange Utopia: Eliza Lovell Tibbets and the Birth of California's Citrus Industry.* West Chester, PA: Swedenborg Foundation, 2011.

Paasi, Anssi. "Bounded Spaces in the Mobile World: Deconstructing 'Regional Identity.'" *Tijdschrift Voor Economische En Sociale Geografie* 93, no. 2 (2002): 137–148.

———. "Region and Place: Regional Identity in Question." *Progress in Human Geography.* 27, no. 4 (2003): 475–485.

Packer, Jeremy. *Mobility without Mayhem: Safety, Cars, and Citizenship.* Durham: Duke University Press, 2008.

Painter, Joe. "Cartographic Anxiety and the Search for Regionality." *Environment and Planning A,* 40 (2008): 342–361.

Panunzio, Constantine, and the Heller Committee for Research in Social Economics of the University of California. "Cost of Living Studies V. How Mexicans Earn and Live: A Study of the Incomes and Expenditures of One Hundred Mexican Families in San Diego, California." *University of California Publications in Economics* 13, no. 1 (1933): 1–114.

Parrenas, Rhacel Salazar. *Servants of Globalization: Migration and Domestic Work.* 2nd ed. Stanford: Stanford University Press, 2015.

Pascoe, Peggy. *What Comes Naturally: Miscegenation Law and the Making of Race in America.* New York: Oxford University Press, 2010.

Pastor, Manuel, Chris Benner, and Martha Matsuoka. *This Could Be the Start of Something Big: How Social Movements for Regional Equity Are Reshaping Metropolitan America.* Ithaca: Cornell University Press, 2009.

Patterson, Thomas C. *From Acorns to Warehouses: Historical Political Economy of Southern California's Inland Empire.* Walnut Creek: Left Coast Press, 2015.

Patterson, Tom. *A Colony for California: Riverside's First Hundred Years.* Riverside: Press-Enterprise Co., 1971.

Peffer, George Anthony. "Forbidden Families: Emigration Experiences of Chinese Women under the Page Law, 1875–1882." *Journal of American Ethnic History* 6 (Fall 1986): 28–46.

———. *If They Don't Bring Their Women Here: Chinese Female Immigration before Exclusion.* Urbana: University of Illinois Press, 1999.

Pegler-Gordon, Anna. *In Sight of America: Photography and the Development of U.S. Immigration Policy.* Berkeley: University of California Press, 2009.

Penny, H. Glenn. *Kindred by Choice: Germans and American Indians Since 1800.* Chapel Hill: University of North Carolina Press, 2015.

Pfeiffer, Deirdre. "Moving to Opportunity: African Americans' Safety Outcomes in the Los Angeles Exurbs." *Journal of Planning Education and Research* 33, no. 1 (2013): 49–65.

———. "Sprawling to Opportunity: Los Angeles African Americans on the Exurban Fringe." PhD diss., University of California Los Angeles. 2012.

Phillips, George Harwood. *Chiefs and Challengers: Indian Resistance and Cooperation in Southern California.* Berkeley: University of California Press, 1975.

Piatote, Beth. *Domestic Subjects: Gender, Citizenship, and Law in Native American Literature.* New Haven: Yale University, 2013.

Pitt, Leonard. *Decline of the Californios: A Social History of the Spanish-Speaking Californians, 1846–1890*. Berkeley: University of California Press, 1999.

Poblete, JoAnna. *Islanders in the Empire: Filipino and Puerto Rican Laborers in Hawai'i*. Urbana: University of Illinois Press, 2014.

Poli, Adon. *Japanese Farm Holdings on the Pacific Coast*. Berkeley: Bureau of Agricultural Economics, U.S. Department of Agriculture, December 1944.

"Pomona Checkpoints: Saving Lives or Ruining Lives." Panel delivered at Cal Poly Pomona, May 26, 2009.

Ponder, Stephen. "Publicity in the Interest of the People: Theodore Roosevelt's Conservation Crusade." *Presidential Studies Quarterly* 20, no. 3 (Summer 1990): 547–555.

Powell, George Harold. *Letters from the Orange Empire*. Edited by Richard Gordon Lillard and Lawrence Clark Powell. Los Angeles: Historical Society of Southern California, 2001.

Practical Common Sense Guide Book Through the World's Industrial and Cotton Centennial Exposition at New Orleans. Harrisburg, PA: L. S. Hart, 1885.

Pratt, Mary Louise. "Arts of the Contact Zone." *Profession* (1991): 33–40.

———. *Imperial Eyes: Travel Writing and Transculturation*. New York: Routledge, 1992.

Pulido, Laura. "Flint, Environmental Racism, and Racial Capitalism." *Capitalism Nature Socialism* 27, no. 3 (July 2016): 1–16. https://doi.org/10.1080/10455752.2016.1213013.

———. "Geographies of Race and Ethnicity II: Environmental Racism, Racial Capitalism, and State-Sanctioned Violence." *Progress in Human Geography* 41 (May 2016): 524–533.

———. "Rethinking Environmental Racism: White Privilege and Urban Development in Southern California." *Annals of the Association of American Geographers* 90, no. 1 (2000): 12–40.

Pulido, Laura, Laura Barraclough, and Wendy Cheng. *A People's Guide to Los Angeles*. Berkeley: University of California Press, 2012.

Rafael, Vicente L. *White Love and Other Events in Filipino History*. Durham: Duke University Press, 2000.

Ramírez, Catherine S. *The Woman in the Zoot Suit: Gender, Nationalism, and the Cultural Politics of Memory*. Durham: Duke University Press, 2009.

Rasmussen, Birgit. *Queequeg's Coffin: Indigenous Literacies and Early American Literature*. Durham: Duke University Press, 2012.

Rawls, James. "The California Mission as Symbol and Myth." *California Historical Society* 71, no. 3 (Fall 1992): 342–361.

Rawsitch, Mark. *The House on Lemon Street: Japanese Pioneers and the American Dream*. Boulder: University of Colorado Press, 2012.

Razack, Sherene, ed. *Race, Space, and the Law: Unmapping a White Settler Society*. Toronto: Between the Lines, 2002.

Reports of the Immigrant Commission. Part 25: Japanese and Other Immigrant Races in the Pacific Coast and Rocky Mountain States, U.S. Congress, Senate, 61st

Congress, 2nd Session, S. Doc. 633. Washington, DC: Government Printing Office, 1911.

Reséndez, Andrés. *Changing National Identities at the Frontier: Texas and New Mexico, 1800–1850.* New York: Cambridge University Press, 2004.

Reynolds, Nedra. *Geographies of Writing: Inhabiting Places and Encountering Difference.* Carbondale: Southern Illinois University Press, 2004.

Rinaldetti, Thierry. "Italian Migrants in the Atlantic Economies: From the Circular Migrations of the Birds of Passage to the Rise of a Dispersed Community." *Journal of American Ethnic History* 34 (Fall 2014): 5–30.

Riverside Land and Irrigating Company. *Southern California: Riverside Land and Irrigating Company of San Bernardino County, California.* San Francisco: Frank Eastman, 1877.

Riverside Latino Voter Project. "The Empire Strikes Back: Organizing Inland." Panel, March 2010.

Riverside Planning Department. *Landmarks of the City of Riverside.* Riverside: City of Riverside, 2002.

Robinson, Cedric J. *Black Marxism: The Making of the Black Radical Tradition.* Foreword by Robin D.G. Kelley, with a New Preface by the Author, 2nd ed. Chapel Hill: University of North Carolina Press, 2000. First published in 1983 by Zed Press.

Robinson, Jon G. *Classic Chevrolet Dealerships: Selling the Bowtie.* Hong Kong: Motorbooks International, 2003.

Robinson, W.W. *The Story of San Bernardino County.* San Bernardino: Pioneer Title Insurance Company, 1958.

Rocco, Raymond. "Citizenship, Culture, and Community: Restructuring in Southeast Los Angeles." In *Latino Cultural Citizenship: Claiming Identity, Space, and Rights,* edited by William V. Flores and Rena Benmayor, 97–123. Boston: Beacon Press, 1997.

Roden, Donald. "Baseball and the Quest for National Dignity in Meiji Japan." *American Historical Review* 85 (June 1980): 511–534.

Roderick, Marshall. "The 'Box Bill': Public Policy, Ethnicity, and Economic Exploitation in Texas." Master's thesis, Texas State University–San Marcos, 2011.

Roediger, David. *The Wages of Whiteness: Race and the Making of the American Working Class.* London: Verso, 1991.

Romero, Robert Chao. *The Chinese in Mexico, 1882–1940.* Tucson: University of Arizona Press, 2010.

Romero, Robert Chao, and Luis Fernando Fernandez. "Doss v. Bernal: Ending Mexican Apartheid in Orange County." *CSRC Research Note,* no. 14 (February 2012).

———. "Work and Restlessness: Occupational and Spatial Mobility among Mexicanos in Los Angeles." *Pacific Historical Review* 46 (May 1977): 157–180.

Roosevelt, Theodore. *The Winning of the West.* New York: Putnam's, 1889.

"Route 66 Special," *Access Rewind,* film, IE Media Group, 2011.

Sackman, Douglas Cazaux. *Orange Empire: California and the Fruits of Eden.* Berkeley: University of California Press, 2005.

Saito, Leland. *Race and Politics: Asian Americans, Latinos, and Whites in a Los Angeles Suburb.* Urbana: University of Illinois Press, 1998.

Saldívar, José. *Border Matters: Remapping American Cultural Studies.* Berkeley: University of California Press, 1997.

Sánchez, George J. *Becoming Mexican American: Ethnicity, Culture, and Identity in Chicano Los Angeles, 1900–1945.* New York: Oxford University Press, 1995.

———. "Face the Nation: Race, Immigration, and the Rise of Nativism in Late Twentieth Century America," *International Migration Review* 31 (Winter 1997): 1009–1030.

———. "What's Good for Boyle Heights Is Good for the Jews: Creating Multiracialism on the Eastside during the 1950s," *American Quarterly* 56, no. 3 (2004): 633–661.

Sandefur, Gary. "Native American Migration and Economic Opportunities." *Internal Migration Review* 20 (1986): 55–68.

Sandoval, Denise. "Bajito y Suavecito/Low and Slow: Cruising Through Lowrider Culture." PhD diss., Claremont Graduate School, 2003.

Sandul, Paul. *California Dreaming: Boosterism, Memory, and Rural Suburbs in the Golden State.* Morgantown: West Virginia University Press, 2014.

Santiago, Charles R. Venator. "Race, Space, and Puerto Rican Citizenship." *Denver University Law Review* 78, no. 4 (2001): 907–920.

Scharff, Virginia. *Taking the Wheel: Women and the Coming of the Motor Age.* Albuquerque: University of New Mexico, 1992.

Schensul, Daniel, and Patrick Heller. "Legacies, Change and Transformation in the Post-Apartheid City: Towards an Urban Sociological Cartography." *International Journal of Urban and Regional Research* 35, no. 1 (2011): 78–109.

Schmidt Camacho, Alicia. *Migrant Imaginaries: Latino Cultural Politics in the U.S.-Mexico Borderlands.* New York: New York University Press, 2008.

Schwartz, Stuart B. "Hurricanes and the Shaping of Circum-Caribbean Societies." Florida Historical Quarterly 83, no. 4 (2005): 381–409.

Scott, James C. *Seeing Like a State: How Certain Schemes to Improve the Human Condition Have Failed.* New Haven: Yale University Press, 1998.

Scruggs, Otey M. "The First Mexican Farm Labor Program." *Journal of the Southwest* 2 (Winter 1960): 319–326.

Scudder, Kenyon J. *Prisoners Are People.* New York: Doubleday, 1952.

Seigel, Micol. "Critical Prison Studies: Review of a Field." *American Quarterly* 70 (March 2018): 123–137.

Seiler, Cotten. *Republic of Drivers: A Cultural History of Automobility in America.* Chicago: University of Chicago Press, 2008.

———. "'So That We as a Race Might Have Something Authentic to Travel By': African American Automobility and Cold-War Liberalism." *American Quarterly* 58, no. 4 (2006): 1091–1117.

Self, Robert O. *American Babylon: Race and the Struggle for Postwar Oakland.* Princeton: Princeton University Press, 2003.

Senior, Clarence O. *Puerto Rican Emigration.* Río Pierdas: Social Science Research Center, University of Puerto Rico, 1947.

Shaffer, Marguerite S. *See America First: Tourism and National Identity, 1880–1940.* Washington, DC: Smithsonian, 2001.

Shah, Nayan. *Contagious Divides: Epidemics and Race in San Francisco's Chinatown.* Berkeley: University of California Press, 2001.

———. *Stranger Intimacy: Contesting Race, Sexuality and the Law in the North American West.* Berkeley: University of California Press, 2012.

Shapiro, Michael J. "Moral Geographies and the Ethics of Post-Sovereignty." *Public Culture* 6, no. 3 (1994): 479–502.

Sheller, Mimi. *Aluminum Dreams: The Making of Light Modernity.* Cambridge, MA: MIT Press, 2014.

———. "Mobility." *Sociopedia.isa* (2011).

Sheller, Mimi, and John Urry. "The New Mobilities Paradigm." *Environment and Planning A,* 38 (2006): 206–226.

Sides, Josh. *L.A. City Limits: African American Los Angeles from the Great Depression to the Present.* Berkeley: University of California Press, 2004.

Siembieda, William J. "Suburbanization of Ethnics of Color." *Annals of the American Academy of Political and Social Science* 422 (1975): 118–228.

Singer, Audrey. "The Rise of New Immigrant Gateways." *Living Cities Census Series.* Washington, DC: The Brookings Institution, February 2004.

Singer, Audrey, Susan W. Hardwick, and Caroline B. Brettell, eds. *Twenty-First Century Gateways: Immigrant Incorporation in Suburban America.* Washington, DC: The Brookings Institution, 2008.

Slethaug, Gordon. "Mapping the Trope: A Historical and Cultural Journey." In *Hit the Road Jack: Essays on the Culture of the American Road,* edited by Gordon E. Slethaug and Stacilee Ford, 13–38. Quebec: McGill Queens University Press, 2012.

Smethurst, Paul. *The Bicycle—Towards a Global History.* New York: Palgrave Macmillan, 2015.

Smith, Neil. "Contours of a Spatialized Politics: Homeless Vehicles and the Production of Geographic Scale." *Social Text* 33 (1992): 54–81.

———. *Uneven Development: Nature, Capital, and the Production of Space,* 3rd ed. Athens: University of Georgia Press, 2008. First published in 1984 by Blackwell.

Smith, Robert. *A Social History of the Bicycle: Its Early Life and Times in America.* New York: American Heritage Press, 1972.

Sorkin, Michael, ed. *Variations on a Theme Park: The New American City and the End of Public Space.* New York City: Hill and Wang, 1992.

Spalding, William Andrew. *The Orange: Its Culture in California: With a Brief Discussion of the Lemon, Lime, and Other Citrus Fruits.* Riverside: Press and Horticulturist Steam Print, 1885.

Steinbeck, John. *The Harvest Gypsies: On the Road to the Grapes of Wrath.* Introduction by Charles Wollenberg. Berkeley: Heyday Books, 1988. First published in 1936 by the San Francisco News.

———. *Their Blood Is Strong.* San Francisco: Simon J. Lubin Society of California, 1938.

Stern, Alexandra Minna. *Eugenic Nation: Faults and Frontiers of Better Breeding in Modern America.* Berkeley: University of California Press, 2005.

Stonehouse, Merlin. *John Wesley North and the Reform Frontier.* Minneapolis: University of Minnesota Press, 1965.

Stratton-Porter, Gene. *Her Father's Daughter.* Garden City: Doubleday, Page and Company, 1921.

Sugrue, Thomas. *The Origins of the Urban Crisis: Race and Inequality in Postwar Detroit.* Princeton: Princeton University Press, 1996.

Takaki, Ronald. *Pau Hana: Plantation Life and Labor in Hawaii, 1835–1920.* Honolulu: University of Hawaii Press, 1983.

Talbott, Mrs. William. "Annual Report of Progress in the Work of the National Old Trails Committee." Proceeding of the Continental Congress of the Daughters of the American Revolution. Washington, DC: National Society of the Daughters of the American Revolution, 1922.

"Talleres Informativos: Retenes, Decomisos, Derechos Humanos y Derechos Civiles." Program sponsored by Alianza Nacional de Comunidades Latinoamericanas y Caribeñas, Pomona, CA, August 2010.

Tatum, Beverly Daniel. *Why Are All the Black Kids Sitting Together in the Cafeteria?* New York: Basic Books, 2003.

Taylor, Paul S. "Hand Laborers in the Western Sugar Beet Industry." *Agricultural History* 41, no. 1 (January 1967): 19–26.

———. "Mexican Labor in the United States Imperial Valley." *University of California Publications in Economics* 6, no. 1 (1928): 1–94.

———. "Mexican Labor in the United States Migration Statistics. II." *University of California Publications in Economics* 12, no. 1 (1933): 1–10.

———. "Mexican Labor in the United States Migration Statistics. III." *University of California Publications in Economics* 12, no. 2 (1933): 11–22.

———. "Mexican Labor in the United States Migration Statistics. IV." *University of California Publications in Economics* 12, no. 3 (September 1934): 23–50.

———. *On the Ground in the Thirties.* Salt Lake City: Peregrine Smith Books, 1983.

Taylor, Paul S., and Dorothea Lange. "Again the Covered Wagon." *Survey Graphic* 24 (July 1935): 348–351.

Taylor, Paul S., and Tom Vasey. "Contemporary Background of California Farm Labor." *Rural Sociology* 1 (December 1936): 401–419.

Terrasa, Gabriel A. "The United States, Puerto Rico, and the Territorial Incorporation Doctrine: Reaching a Century of Constitutional Authoritarianism." *The John Marshall Law Review* 31, no. 1 (1997): 69–83.

Thompson, Carlyle Van. *The Tragic Black Buck: Racial Masquerading in the American Literary Imagination.* New York: Peter Lang Publishing, 2004.

Thompson, Heather Ann. "Why Mass Incarceration Matters: Rethinking Crisis, Decline, and Transformation in Postwar American History." *Journal of American History* 97 (December 2010): 703–734.

Tongson, Karen. *Relocations: Queer Suburban Imaginaries*. New York: New York University Press, 2011.

Torres-Rouff, David Samuel. *Before L.A.: Race, Space, and Municipal Power in Los Angeles, 1781–1894*. New Haven: Yale University Press, 2013.

Trafzer, Clifford E., Matthew Sakiestewa Gilbert, and Lorene Sisquoc, eds. *The Indian School on Magnolia Avenue: Voices and Images from Sherman Institute*. Corvallis: Oregon State University Press, 2012.

Trafzer, Clifford E., Jean A. Keller, and Lorene Sisquoc, eds. *Boarding School Blues: Revisiting American Indian Educational Experiences*. Lincoln: University of Nebraska Press, 2006.

Trouillot, Michel-Rolph. *Silencing the Past: Power and the Production of History*. Boston: Beacon Press, 1995.

Tsu, Cecilia M. *Garden of the World: Asian Immigrants and the Making of Agriculture in California's Santa Clara Valley*. New York: Oxford University Press, 2013.

Tuck, Ruth. *Not With the Fist: Mexican-Americans in a Southwest City*. New York: Harcourt, Brace, 1946.

Turner, Frederick Jackson. *The Significance of the Frontier in American History*. London: Penguin Books, 2008. First published in 1893 by the American Historical Association.

Urban Land Institute. "San Bernardino California: Crossroads of the Southwest." An Advisory Services Panel Report. Washington, DC, June 24–29, 2007.

Urquijo-Ruiz, Rita. *Wild Tongues: Transnational Mexican Popular Culture*. Austin: University of Texas Press, 2012.

Urry, John. *Mobilities*. Oxford: Polity Press, 2007.

———. *Sociology Beyond Societies: Mobilities for the Twenty-First Century*. New York: Routledge, 2000.

U.S. Congress, House of Representatives, Committee on Immigration and Naturalization. *Immigration from Mexico. Hearings Before the Committee on Immigration and Naturalization on H.R. 12382*, 71st Cong., 2nd sess. Washington, DC: Government Printing Office, May 15, 1930.

———. *Seasonal Agricultural Laborers from Mexico. Hearings January 28 and 29, February 2,9, 11, and 23, 1926 on H.R. 6741, H.R. 7559, H.R. 9036*, 69th Cong., 1st sess. Washington, DC: Government Printing Office, 1926.

———. *Western Hemisphere Immigration: Hearings Before the Committee on Immigration and Naturalization on the Bills H.R. 8523, H.R. 8530, H.R.8702 to Limit the Immigration of Aliens to the United States, and for Other Purposes*, 71st Cong., 1st sess. Washington, DC: Government Printing Office, 1930.

U.S. Congress, House of Representatives, Select Committee to Investigate the Interstate Migration of Destitute Citizens. *Interstate Migration*, 76th Cong., 3rd sess., Part 8, November 29, December 2, 3, 1940. Washington, DC: Government Printing Office, 1941.

U.S. Congress. *Investigation of Concentration of Economic Power,* 76th Cong., 3rd sess., Part 30. Washington, DC: Government Printing Office, 1940.

U.S. Immigrant Commission. *Reports of the Immigrant Commission Part 25: Japanese and Other Immigrant Races in the Pacific Coast and Rocky Mountain States,* U.S. Congress, Senate, 61st Cong, 2nd sess., S. Doc. 633. Washington, DC: Government Printing Office, 1911.

Vallejo, Jody Aguis. *Barrios to Burbs: The Making of the Mexican-American Middle Class.* Stanford: Stanford University Press, 2012.

Vargas, Zaragosa. *Proletarians of the North: A History of Mexican Industrial Workers in Detroit and the Midwest, 1917–1933.* Berkeley: University of California Press, 1999.

Varzally, Allison. *Making a Non-White America: Californians Coloring Outside Ethnic Lines, 1925–1955.* Berkeley: University of California Press, 2008.

Vasconcelos, José. *La Raza Cosmica: Mision de la Raza Iberoamericana.* Madrid: Agencia Mundial de Libreria, 1948.

Vasquez, Antonio González, and Genevieve Carpio. *Mexican Americans in Redlands.* Charleston: Arcadia Publishing, 2012.

Vickery, Joyce. *Defending Eden: New Mexican Pioneers in Southern California, 1830–1890.* Riverside: Riverside Museum Press, 1977.

Villazor, Rose Cuison. "Rediscovering Oyama v. California: At the Intersection of Property, Race, and Citizenship." *Washington University Law Review* 87 (2010): 979–1042.

Wald, Sarah. *The Nature of California: Race, Citizenship, and Farming Since the Dust Bowl.* Seattle: University of Washington Press, 2016.

Warne, Frank J. *The Tide of Immigration.* New York and London: D. Appleton and Company, 1916.

Wattawa, Gayle. *Inlandia: A Literary Journey Through California's Inland Empire.* Santa Clara: Santa Clara University, 2006.

Weber, Devra. *Dark Sweat, White Gold: California Farm Workers, Cotton, and the New Deal.* Berkeley: University of California Press, 1994.

Weiss, Thomas. "Tourism in America before World War II." *Journal of Economic History* 64, no. 2 (2004): 289–327.

Welsh, S.L. *Southern California Illustrated: Containing an Epitome of the Growth and Industry of the Three Southern Counties.* Los Angeles: Warner Brothers, 1887.

Wexler, Laura. *Tender Violence: Domestic Visions in an Age of U.S. Imperialism.* Chapel Hill: University of North Carolina Press, 2000.

Whalen, Carmen Teresa. "Colonialism, Citizenship, and the Making of the Puerto Rican Diaspora: An Introduction." In *The Puerto Rican Diaspora: Historical Perspectives,* edited by Carmen Teresa Whalen and Victor Vázquez-Hernández, 1–42. Philadelphia: Temple University Press, 2005.

———. "Labor Migrants or Submissive Wives: Competing Narratives of Puerto Rican Women in the Post-World War II Era." In *Puerto Rican Women's History:*

New Perspectives, edited by Felix V. Matos Rodriguez and Linda C. Delgado, 206–226. Armonk: M. E. Sharp, 1998.

Whalen, Carmen Teresa, and Victor Vázquez-Hernández, eds. *The Puerto Rican Diaspora: Historical Perspectives.* Philadelphia: Temple University Press, 2005.

Whalen, Kevin. "Beyond School Walls: Indigenous Mobility at Sherman Institute." *Western Historical Quarterly* 49, no. 3 (2018): 275–297.

Whelan, Harold. "Eden in Jurupa Valley: The Story of Agua Mansa." *Southern California Quarterly* 55, no. 4 (1973): 413–429.

White, Richard. *The Organic Machine: The Remaking of the Columbia River.* New York: Hill and Wang, 1996.

White, Richard, and Patricia Limerick. *The Frontier in American Culture.* Berkeley: University of California Press, 1994.

Wiese, Andrew. *Places of Their Own: African American Suburbanization in the Twentieth Century.* Chicago: University of Chicago Press, 2004.

Wild, H. Mark. "If You Ain't Got That Do-Re-Mi: The Los Angeles Border Patrol and White Migration in Depression-Era California." *Southern California Quarterly* 83 (Fall 2001): 317–334.

Williams, Raymond. *Marxism and Literature.* New York: Oxford University Press, 1977.

Wilson, Chris. *The Myth of Santa Fe: Creating a Modern Regional Tradition.* Albuquerque: University of New Mexico Press, 1997.

Wolcott, David. *Cops and Kids: Policing Juvenile Delinquency in Urban America, 1890–1940.* Columbus: Ohio State University, 2005.

Wolfe, Patrick. "Settler Colonialism and the Elimination of the Native." *Journal of Genocide Research* 8, no. 4 (2006): 387–409.

Wong, Deborah, ed. *Asian American Riverside.* University of California, Riverside, 2006. http://www.asianamericanriverside.ucr.edu/site_authors.html.

Wong, Morrison. "The Japanese in Riverside, 1890 to 1945: A Special Case in Race Relations." PhD diss., University of California, Riverside, 1977.

Wood, Denis. *Rethinking the Power of Maps.* New York: Guilford Press, 2010.

Wood, Joseph Snow. "The Mormon Settlement in San Bernardino." PhD diss., University of Utah, 1968.

Woods, Clyde. "'A Cell Is Not a Home': Asset Stripping and Trap Economics in Central City East/ Skid Row, Part 2." In *Black California Dreamin': The Crises of California's African-American Communities,* edited by Ingrid Banks, Gaye Johnson, George Lipsitz, Ula Taylor, and Daniel Widener, 191–198. Santa Barbara: UCSB Center for Black Studies Research, 2012.

———. *Development Arrested: The Blues and Plantation Power in the Mississippi Delta.* London: Verso Press, 1998.

———. "Life After Death." *Professional Geographer* 54, no. 1 (2002): 62–66.

Wormser, Paul. "Chinese Agricultural Labor in the Citrus Belt of Inland Southern California." In *Wong Ho Leun: An American Chinatown,* edited by The Great Basin Foundation, vol. 1, 173–191. San Diego: The Great Basin Foundation, 1987.

Wu, Ellen. *The Color of Success: Asian Americans and the Origins of the Model Minority*. Princeton: Princeton University Press, 2013.

Wyman, Mark. *Round-trip to America: The Immigrants Return to Europe, 1880–1930*. Ithaca: Cornell University Press, 1996.

Yoshihara, Mari. "The Flight of the Japanese Butterfly: Orientalism, Nationalism, and Performances of Japanese Womanhood." *American Quarterly* 56 (December 2004): 975–1001.

INDEX

Note: Page numbers followed by *"fig."* indicate figures; page numbers followed by *"map"* indicate maps.

Hawaii, 68, 132; Hawaiian Sugar Planters Association, 280n92; Filipino workers in, 132

Hayden, Dolores, 40

Hayward, Sam, 74

health services, 2

Heller Committee cost of living study, 145

Her Father's Daughter (Stratton-Porter), 64–65, 99–100

heritage: fictive, 230; heritage campaigns, 233; memory and, 5–6; of migration, 221; regional heritage and history, 12, 17, 31–41, 221, 231; memory and, 5–6; of migration, 221; selectively edited, 229; of travel, 221. *See also* agricultural heritage; citrus heritage; selective tradition

Hernandez, Jessie, 236

Hernandez, Joe, 148*fig.*

Hispanophilia, 39

Hispanos, 2, 23, 38; culture of, 28; emigrants, 29; recruited from New Mexico, 28. *See also* Spanish American identity

historical geography, 15, 236–37

historical recovery, work of, 15

historical societies, 33–35

historicide, 40

history: intersectional, 17, 237; vs. mythology, 230; recovery of, 14; revision of, 3. *See also* heritage; memory

Hollywood, 3

Holmes, Elmer, 34

Holt, Luther, 49–50

Home Builders Council of California, 192

home ownership, 206; African Americans and, 201 Asian and, 105–15; Japanese racial formation and, 105–15; Latinas/os and, 218; Mexican racial formation and, 105–15; nonwhite families and, 182

Homestead Act, 30

Hoover, J. Edgar, 175

Hopi nations, 37

Horabi, 80, 81*fig.*

House Committee on Immigration and Naturalization, 104, 117

"House in Mexican Village" (USDA), 111

housing: affordable, 20, 191; discrimination and, 194; housing covenants, 201; housing programs, 232; inclusive, 193; integrated, 193, 230, 234, 235; migrant, 88–99, 263n36; nonwhites and, 74–75

housing developers, 190–91

housing discrimination, 93, 184, 197; African Americans and, 191; dismantling of in Los Angeles suburbs, 194; Harada family and, 92, 101; immigrants and, 90–91; mobility and, 99; in Pomona, California, 299n70; race and, 72

"Housing the Employees of California's Citrus Ranches" (Shamel), 108

Hudson, Angela, 28, 287n36

Hudspeth, Claude, 125

humanitarianism, acts of international force cast as, 3

Hurricane San Ciriaco, 127–28

Hurricane San Felipe (Okeechobee), 126, 128, 131

hyper-mobilization, of migrant groups, 18–19, 102–40

Ice Cube, *Next Friday*, 223

"imagineering," 230

immigrant drivers, 4–5. *See also specific groups*

immigrant labor. *See specific groups*

immigrants and immigration, 2, 6, 13, 166, 236; "blackening" of, 235; into California, 6, 53; controlling mobility of, 24; eastern and southern European, 232; as economic threat, 221; erasure of, 230; federal concerns with settlement of, 18; housing discrimination and, 90–91; housing of, 263n36; immigrant settlement, 18; long-distance, 237; post-1990 settlement of, 305n1; undocumented, 2, 4–5, 219–20; to the U.S., 141; vigilante violence against, 12. *See also specific groups*

Immigration Act (1921), 116

Immigration Act (1924), 101, 104, 106, 121, 139, 235, 276n38

Immigration and Customs Enforcement (ICE), 53

Immigration and Nationality Act (1924), 9

Immigration and Naturalization Service (INS), 53, 260–61n13

immigration debates and hearings, 116–21, 230, 234

immigration enforcement, 6, 12, 234–35; *See also* border securitization

immigration policy, 13, 17, 18–19, 53, 102–40, 224, 232, 234–35, 236. *See also specific laws and policies*

immobility, 13, 18, 20; contests over, 220; debates over, 234; forced, 20; race and, 18; racialization and, 20. *See also* incarceration; prisons

imperialism, 32, 134, 261n14. *See also* expansionism

Imperial Valley, 151

incarceration, 232, 233, 302n99, 304n119. *See also* prisons

Indian Affairs, 35

Indigenous, use of the term, 240–41n10. *See also* American Indians; Indigenous people

Indigenous lands, 17; colonization of, 274n18; maps and, 16; white claims to, 236

Indigenous people, 27, 35, 44, 47, 232, 233; citrus industry and, 44; as "consolidating agent" of American colonists, 232; cultural practices, 36; dislocation of, 27; dispossession and elimination of, 9–10, 17, 23–24, 30, 37, 221, 240–41n10; erasure of, 223, 225, 230, 233; exclusion of history of, 33, 62–63; mobility and, 4, 13; non-Indigenous societies and, 11, 27; as outsiders, 17; population decline at end of nineteenth century, 247n16; property rights and, 28; settlement in California, 29, 246n6; settlement on territories of, 10, 31. *See also specific groups*

Indigenous women: land and, 27; non-Indigenous husbands of, 27

industrial agriculture: erasure of, 229; romanticization of, 306–7n10

Industrial Workers of the World, 129

inland crossroads, 6–12

Inland Empire, 6–7, 20, 122, 197, 217, 225, 235; history of, 228–29; housing boom in, 227; Latina/o population growth in, 223; as majority-minority, 231; multiracial suburbanization, 196; mythologies of, 230–31; population growth in, 8, 222; prisons and, 184; regional identity of, 227–28; suburbanization of, 222; transition from Citrus Belt, 20, 181–218; white migration in, 233; white population decline in, 223

Inland Mexican Heritage (IMH), 122, 146, 176, 231; archives, 16

Inland Southern California, 2, 6–7, 9, 30, 65, 121, 122, 143, 189, 220, 221, 222, 224, 232; agricultural economy of, 14, 24; agricultural history of, 224–25; Anglo Fantasy Past in, 22–63; bicycle racing and, 76; citrus communities, 46; cycling as a sport in, 75–76; demographics of, 28; freeways and, 190; as gateway, 222; Inland Valley, 6; memory in, 22–63; mobility in, 22–63; multiracial and global population of, 9; racial capitalism in, 222; racial hierarchies in, 23–63; significance of, 15–16; synergistic relationship with Los Angeles, 8–9; western pioneers of, 58. *See also* Inland Empire; *specific locations*

interdisciplinarity, 237–38

interethnic spaces, construction of, 9

intermodal freight transport, 8–9

interracial relationships, 134–35

intersectional histories, 17, 237

Interstate 10 freeway, 6, 222

Interstate 15 freeway, 226–27

interventionism, 16

Irish immigrants, 10, 119

Irving, John, 29

Isle, Frank, 61

Israeli checkpoints, in Palestinian West Bank, 21

Italian immigrants, 119

Jalisco, 197

Japan, 64, 72–73, 262n30

Japanese–American relations, 78–80

Japanese and Japanese Americans, 9, 64, 97, 230–31; assimilation and, 18, 64–101; housing and, 100. *See also*

postings on, 70. *See also* counter-mappings; posting
March Air Force Base, 185
marginalized people, targeting of, 219–22
Marks, Alex, 197, 198, 202
Marservey, Randolph, 61
Martin, Trayvon, 236
masculinity, 78, 82, 147. *See also* gender; manhood
Mayans, 125
McGlothin, John, 203
McKinley, William, 45
McMicken, Kenneth B., 128
McWilliams, Carey, 41, 159, 213, 306–7n10
MEChA (Movimiento Estudiantil Chicano de Aztlán), 206
mega-builders, 227
Meiji, Japan, 78; emperor, 79
melting pot, 136, 232
memory, 7, 22–63, 220; regional, 5–6 (*see also* regional heritage and history); in inland Southern California, 22–63. *See also* Anglo Fantasy Past; heritage; history; nostalgia; Spanish Fantasy Past
Messinger, Sheldon L., 210
mestizaje, racial ideology of, 125
mestizos, 124–25
Meto, S., 80
Mexican, use of the term, 239n1
Mexican agricultural workers, 155; automobiles and, 144, 146; mobility and, 151
Mexican American Research Association (MARA), 213
Mexican Americans, 9, 13, 15, 38, 117, 125, 143, 173, 180, 193–94, 200, 213, 230; automobility and, 19, 141–80, 235 (*see also* lowriders); criminalization of, 142, 174; cultural belonging and, 143; erasure of, 5; incarceration of, 184, 233; Mexican American youth, 142, 143; mobility and, 153; suburbanization and, 301–2n97; use of the term, 239n1; youth, 196, 205. *See also* Mexican American automobility
Mexican-American War, 26, 28, 42, 53, 92, 106

Mexican automobility, 19, 145, 154, 230, 235. *See also* Mexican drivers
"Mexican Browns," 153–54, 288n43
Mexican Chamber of Commerce of Los Angeles, 192
Mexican Department of Labor, 123
Mexican-descent populations, 24, 47, 62, 63, 68, 122, 151; automobile ownership and, 19, 142, 145, 157–58, 235; in California Citrus Belt, 65; California's nonwhite labor force, 142; criminalization of, 141; drivers, 141–80; internal migration of, 151; mobility and, 142–43, 145, 155–58; oral histories of, 122; as outsiders, 17; relief services and, 156; as scapegoats for worsening economic conditions, 141; suburbanization of, 202; white status and, 92. *See also* *Mexican*, use of the term; Mexican immigrants and immigration; Mexican racial formation and status
Mexican dispossession, 17, 23, 30
Mexican drivers, 141–80, 155; employment and, 144; shifting narratives of, 143. *See also* Mexican automobility
Mexican immigrants and immigration, 10, 19, 30, 33, 44, 73, 102, 230, 232, 235, 276n41; in Arizona, 121; automobiles and, 19, 141–80 (*see also* Mexican automobility; Mexican drivers); in relation to Puerto Ricans or Filipinos, 137; as "birds of passage," 104, 119, 122–23, 130, 137, 141; as both Indigenous and foreign, 125; changing meaning of, 234; children idealized as source of labor, 112; concentrated on West Coast, 138; concerns about, 141; Congressional hearings and, 18–19; criminalization of, 142, 174; denigration of, 28; deportation and, 129–30; erasure of, 3, 19, 169; immigration policy and, 102–40; Indian descent and, 124; intermarriage and, 137; long-term settlement and, 122, 137; mobility and, 19, 20, 105–6, 141–80, 234; myth of Mexican return migration, 122; national debates over, 18–19, 102–40; naturalized American

Mexican immigrants *(continued)*
citizens, 27; opponents of, 139; oral
histories of, 137; as perpetually
migrant, 235; policy concerning, 18–19,
102–40; property rights of, 27; quotas
and, 139; as racial homers, 235; racial
identity and, 153; racial profiling, 106;
racial profiling of, 153; regional industries and, 151; as reminders of a primitive past, 170; repatriation campaigns,
142; residential choices and, 72;
restricted mobility of, 20; return to
Mexico, 140; as rooted family workers,
19; as scapegoats for worsening economic conditions, 139–40; school, 112;
separation of families, 142; settlement
and, 110; Spanish descent and, 124;
stripped of African descent, 133; in
Texas, 121; unconstitutional restrictions against, 201; view of, 112; white
status of, 124. *See also* Mexican-descent
population; Mexican workers
Mexican Independence Day, 215
"Mexican Labor in the United States"
(Taylor), 151, 166–67
Mexican land grant distribution, 30
Mexican Mafia, 211
Mexican mobility, 150–51, 153, 169
Mexican racial formation and status, 124,
134, 143; debates over, 125; during the
Depression, 142; home ownership and,
105–15; mestizaje and, 125; police
surveillance on the roads, 142; popular
culture, 142
Mexican ranchers, 17, 23, 28, 42, 233
Mexican repatriates, automobiles
and, 150
Mexican Revolution, 122
Mexican rodeo (charrería), 38
Mexican settlers, 18, 102–40
Mexican workers, 11, 19, 104, 109, 129, 131,
132, 141; 1920s Immigration Hearings
and, 116–21; agriculturalists and,
234–35; automobiles and, 19, 141–80;
barracks for, 263n36; as "birds of passage," 116, 122–23, 125, 131–32, 139, 234;
as circular migrants, 104; families and,
113; housing and, 108–9, 114, 197;

immigration of, 127; as less threatening
than Puerto Ricans or Filipinos, 136;
long-term settlement and, 103–4, 106,
114; mobility and, 104–5, 107–9, 115,
130, 138, 234; as nomadic, 121; pressure
to return to Mexico, 139; racial confusion over, 121–26; racialization of, 138,
234; ranchers preference for, 113;
recruitment of, 104, 106; regulated
mobility of, 255n95; settlement of,
234–35; transportation and, 106;
during WWI, 234
Mexican youth, 174; arrests for joyriding,
174
Mexico, 127; automobiles and, 149–50;
Ford automobiles in, 286n28; secularization of mission lands, 10; U.S. invasion of, 46
Migrant Mother (Lange), 165
migrants, 6, 8; Anglo American, 23–24,
60–61, 225; "blackening" of, 235; housing and, 88–99, 263n36; hyper-mobilization of, 18–19, 102–40. immobilization of, 18; mobility and, 237; racial
hierarchies and, 237; regional attitudes
toward, 13; surveillance of, 90. *See also*
immigrants and immigration; *specific
groups*
migrant workers, 13, 159; boarding houses
and, 90; mobility of, 103; transportation of, 285n12, 289n66. *See also specific
groups*
migration, 9–10, 14; Citrus Belt and, 9–10;
Depression-era, 225; global, 66, 73, 234;
from the Midwest to Los Angeles,
19–20; migration chains, 119; racial
categories and, 160; regional, 237;
regional histories of, 221; between U.S.
and Mexico, 150; vehicle ownership
and, 153; white, 222. *See also* immigrants and immigration; *specific
groups*
migration statistics, 151–52, 153–54,
287n33, 288n43
migration studies, 13
Mile Square, 32, 48
military industry, 2, 185, 235
Miller, Frank, 39, 45

U.S. Senate, 127
U.S. Supreme Court, 4, 51, 127, 201
Ute people, 28
Uto-Aztecan language family, 246n6

vagrancy laws, 6, 27
Valentino, Rudolph, 176
Valueria, I. Ramón Rosauaro, 27
Vandegrift, Jacob, 93
vehicle ordinances, 266–67n77
Vejar family, 28
Velarde, Tomasita Edith, 137
Ventura County, 185
Verdaguer, Peter, 38
Veteran's Association, 204
Victoria Gardens, 21, 222, 223, 227–29,
   229fig., 230, 231, 307–8n19
Vietnamese population, in Pomona,
   California, 300n79
Vietnam War, 215
Vignes, Jean-Louis, 41
violence, 232

Walker, Paul, 207
Walmart, workers' health and, 12
Warehouse Workers United, 12, 237
warehousing industry, 8–9
Warne, Frank, Special Expert of the
   Foreign Population for the U.S.
   Census, 119
Washington Restaurant, 90
Watsonville Riots, 283n121
Watts Rebellion (1965), 9, 207
Weinstock, Julian, 191
Welch immigrants, 119
Wellborn, Olin, 57
West Coast, 159
Western Hemisphere, immigration from,
   104, 106, 116, 119, 121, 128, 138
western migration, 231–32
Westside community, San Bernardino,
   California, 146, 220
white allies, 221, 237
white American car culture, nostalgia
   for, 5
white flight, 200–208, 235
white male vigilantism, 135

white migrants and migration, 30, 37, 169,
   173, 233; celebration of, 25, 222, 230;
   citrus industry and, 17; commercial
   agriculture and, 17; nostalgia for,
   20–21; as pioneer settlers, 168–69;
   portrayed as western pioneers, 20. See
   also Anglo American settlers; white
   settler colonialism
whiteness, 224; construction of, 10; gradations of, 267n83; mobility and, 10;
   "moral geography" and, 11; power and,
   3; Rancho Cucamonga, California and,
   225; regional identity and, 25; regional
   ownership and, 221; white status, 10.
   See also possessive investment in
   whiteness
white population decline, 20–21, 223, 231
white possessive logics, 31, 39, 221
white privilege, 161, 200, 201, 224
white racism, 76, 98, 221, 233, 298n56
white resistance, to demographic change,
   201
whites. See Anglo Americans
white settler colonialism, 10–11, 222, 232,
   234; celebration of, 223; dispossession
   and, 26–31; narrative of, 25; racialized
   labor and, 11; tools of the state and,
   232; unsettling domination of, 11. See
   also Anglo American settlers; settler
   colonialism
white supremacy, 64, 76, 207, 221, 233,
   268n86, 298n56; ethnic supremacy, 7
white women, rationalization for racism
   and, 134, 136–37
white workers, housing and, 108
Wiley, D. B., 128
Williams, Raymond, 23
Wilson, Woodrow, 109
Winning of the West, 58
women: women's agricultural labor, 229;
   Women's Suffrage Movement, 76.
   See also specific groups
workers: freedom of mobility and, 115;
   health of, 12; marital status and, 115;
   mobility of, 9, 221. See also specific groups
World's Industrial and Cotton Centennial
   Exposition, 42–43

AMERICAN CROSSROADS

Edited by Earl Lewis, George Lipsitz, George Sánchez,
Dana Takagi, Laura Briggs, and Nikhil Pal Singh